The Writer's Voice

Murray
Write to learn

The Writer's Voice

Sandra Loy
Chemeketa Community College

Holt, Rinehart and Winston
New York Chicago San Francisco
Philadelphia Montreal Toronto London
Sydney Tokyo Mexico City
Rio de Janeiro Madrid

Library of Congress Cataloging in Publication Data
Loy, Sandra.
    The writer's voice.

    Includes index.
    1. College readers. 2. English language—Rhetoric.
I. Title.
PE1417.L7   1985   808'.0427   84-22523
ISBN 0-03-063361-3

CBS COLLEGE PUBLISHING
Holt, Rinehart and Winston
The Dryden Press
Saunders College Publishing

Credits

Credits continued on page 359.

For Rick and Shanna

Nothing is done. Everything in the world remains to be done or done over. "The greatest picture is not yet painted, the greatest play isn't written (not even by Shakespeare), the greatest poem is unsung. There isn't in all the world a perfect railroad, nor a good government, nor a sound law."
Lincoln Steffens, I Became A Student.

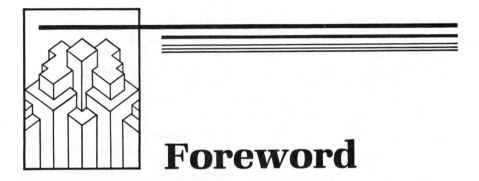

Foreword

It happened on one of those crummy, half-cloudy and half-rainy days we Oregonians so often have to suffer through. I was checking out the poetry section of my favorite bookstore when I stumbled over these two lines by Theodore Roethke:

> How he rolls the vocables,
> Brings the secret—right in Here!

Suddenly it hit me: that's it! These lines by Theodore Roethke relishing the language and celebrating the power of Wallace Stevens' poetry characterize perfectly the way I feel about Sandra's text. Her book, as I quickly reflected, does just *that*: it "rolls the vocables," helps the reader *taste* language, and reveals the power of words to bring their *secrets* (their meanings, their revelations) "right in Here"—next to the reader's heart or gut. And it came to me that above all else, *The Writer's Voice* demonstrates the magic involved in crafting words, sentences, and paragraphs for others to read, a process that makes writing an exciting, pleasurable experience.

But I want to continue with some further ideas that occurred to me after the lines from Roethke's poem and my thoughts about Sandra's book began to coalesce. An image occurred to me; if we thought of words as little constructions that carry a kind of explosive charge— like a pop-rocks candy that explodes in the mouth when we savor it— we students of language and writing might develop more of an affinity toward and appreciation for the way words can work. But stop. Imagine what I have just related to you! Words carry all kinds of *energy*. When they come into consciousness through writing and reading, thinking and hearing, they burst open and send out reverberations that jar us, sometimes imperceptibly and with tiny shock waves, sometimes with a crash and bang which makes us think our world is caving in around us, sometimes in the shape of a shadowy hand that grabs our very entrails and, squeezing and pulling, ties them up in knots. Words *are* powerful!

Think again about those almost imperceptible ways in which language works on you. "Drive the car to the store and pick up a gallon of milk," someone says to you and, chances are, you will simply grab your keys, hop into the car, and drive to the store. Perhaps going to the store causes you a minor inconvenience, but the ripples you feel within you when you hear "Drive the car to the store" are probably minimal. The words cause very tiny explosions. If, however, you are fifteen years old and have up to now spent a happy, secure childhood within a stable family environment and suddenly your mother and father tell you they are getting a DIVORCE, the word explosion is major: your world bursts apart and topples over like a building shattered by dynamite. That word carried a *charge*. But what about the gut-wrenching words "You're fired"? Those two words are terrifying, especially if you're counting on work money to pay your way through school, or to support your family, or to make monthly car payments.

I want now to turn to that other attribute of language suggested by Roethke's two lines and likewise stressed in *The Writer's Voice:* language's ability to illuminate, to reveal, to show us the *secret*. Not only do words, as tiny constructions, carry explosive charges; they also carry little beacons. Words are like little lights with rechargeable batteries that when used (strung together) create more light for us to see by. Even better, they help us to see what it is that we want to write and think about. One word leads to another, one sentence to another, one paragraph to another and, PRESTO, you have illuminated a whole new "area" of experience—perhaps about yourself, your friends, an idea, an institution. This creative stringing together of words *is* magical in that you may never have thought much about what you have just written until you discovered it while writing. You simply threw light on it with words. *They* helped you see and find a direction. Naturally, whatever light you made with your words, whatever ideas you illuminated and revealed, you passed on to your reader. Your writing has brought "the secret—right in Here!"

It is for these two basic reasons that I am enchanted by the approach *The Writer's Voice* takes to language and writing. It "rolls the vocables" and brings the power of language to *show*—right into my heart. I hope its effect on you will be the same as it has been on me. But how all this works in the book, I will leave for Sandra to explain.

Leonard Held

About This Book

Premises

The Writer's Voice is a reader about the process of finding a voice. Its premise is that with the discovery of a natural writing voice, student writing improves dramatically.

Its essays can be read not only as prose models but for their revelations of the human voice inside. Only in the tuning of a good ear for others can student writers recognize their own unique sounds, those sounds which lend life and power to their words. *The Writer's Voice* encourages students to read with an ear and an eye to words, for in the very choice of words and their arrangement is voice.

Organization

The essays, by both classic and contemporary writers, are organized around Bain's modes and a few special chapters: on the essay itself, on language, the spoken voice, the comic voice, and on consistency of voice in a mini-study of four writers. The whole book is designed to be flexible with each part accessible in any order.

Chapter 1, "The Sources of Writing," lays the foundation for the course through a unique selection of essays focusing on why essays are written, what an essay is and how it works, and the sources of the essayist's material. Chapter 2, "The Words Have to Do Everything," gives students an opportunity to start from the ground up by reading a

□

number of essays dealing with the English language and the words themselves. Chapter 3, "Description: The Language of the Senses," focuses on how writers from various cultures and periods attempt to convey the human experience. Chapter 4, "Narration: To Tell What Happened," helps students to make the connection between the spoken and the written voice, and to use their own spoken voices as a way to approach writing essays. Chapter 5, "Exposition: To Present Ideas," shows students the voice of reason and the organizational patterns called process, definition, classification, cause/effect, comparison/contrast and analysis. Chapter 6, "Argumentation: To Persuade," allows students to examine writers' appeals to emotion, to logic, and to ethics. Chapter 7, "Humor and Irony," provides a brief look at comic and ironic voices and their relationship to essay writing. Chapter 8, "A Study of Four Writers," invites students to look for the consistency of voice that identifies a writer as a thumbprint identifies each of us.

Additional Features

Each essay is followed by sections on allusions/references and vocabulary and by discussion questions—all designed to stimulate thought about matters of language, voice, and form.

Brief notes about each writer give students an impression of how writers approach writing, and biographical information.

The glossary at the back defines terms used in the book in a clear and novel manner.

The tone of the book is informal and encouraging. The voice you hear is mine. From chapter openings to discussion questions to the glossary at the back, *The Writer's Voice* is about voice. It is my hope that you will find this approach useful in improving student writing.

Sandra Loy
October, 1984

Acknowledgments

It's a big undertaking to put together a textbook. I never could have done it by myself. All along the way so many people special to me have helped. Ellie Bowen typed the manuscript; she mothered every word and comma and matter of form and spent days-off and nights at her typewriter. Of course I paid her, but she spent that inadequate gesture in one fell swoop on a motorcycle trip to Las Vegas, celebrating the twenty-fifth anniversary of her marriage. John David Nichols stood by my side through it all. He did the dirty work: the cutting and pasting, xeroxing, stapling, and sorting. He also researched and wrote the authors' biographies, but will take no credit. "It's your book," he says, "you were the creative one." Such selflessness and support is a gift of love. I have always dreamed of someone just like this. It's still hard to believe it came out right.

The others who helped become too numerous to mention, but I'm going to make an attempt anyway. Jim Lizotte, a long-time friend and field editor for Holt, Rinehart & Winston would not take no for an answer; he pursued me to an island in Puget Sound to get me to write this book. He has since taken me for a glass of wine to ask if I have forgiven him. *The Writer's Voice* would not exist had it not been for Jim, and it is infused with his optimism and enthusiasm.

I am happy also to record my debt to Richard S. Beal, Joe Cosenza, Robert Cosgrove, M. Deane White, Margaret Hyde, Robert Perrin, Ralph

□

Voss, Margaret Urie, Robert J. Pelinski, Jr., and Paul W. Ranieri who gave many hours to the reviewing of the text in its raw state. Also to Mary Stuart Garden of Holt, Rinehart who taught me many things with her sensitive copy editing of the manuscript. A special acknowledgment should be given to Charlyce Jones Owen, acquisitions editor, who saw me through this lengthy project. For the clarity and eye appeal of the book's design, I am grateful to Lou Scardino. Jeannette Ninas Johnson's careful guiding of my manuscript to this final form has made what could have been a tedious process into an enjoyable one.

Almost everything I know about writing and the teaching of writing I learned while working at Chemeketa Community College. Here is an outpost of some of the most dedicated English teachers anywhere. Tom Gill, our department head, has stood beside us through every kind of rehearsal and growing pain. Barbara Wigginton, John Mock, and Leonard Held taught me much about language, about commitment, and about faith. Barbara introduced me to Richard Hugo, who has inspired so many writers and so much of the good writing that can be found in ·the west today. In many ways I owe this book to *The Triggering Town*. "If that's what you have to say," Hugo told me once, "then bear down."

To Jack Bellamy, the best college English instructor I've ever had a hot fudge sundae with, who taught me how to sing; Brian Smith, fellow poet and permissions draftee, for his good humor in the face of a task that could make a writer cry; Paul Concepcion, Robert Bibler, Carol Hauser, Randy Maxwell, Anne Davis, Paula Paddleford, Terry Nichols, Rick Dawson, Shanna Evans, Guy Evans, the *Before The Sun* staff; all my students who have always inspired the best in me; and Mom and Dad, thank you.

Contents

To the Student

No one ever told me what essays were. I had to write them and I did well enough, but I didn't know what they were. Not really. Books didn't help much, nor did teachers with their definitions, their names for the various kinds: description, narration, exposition, and all the other "shuns" of English classrooms.

Why is it we cannot convey to you the absolute solidity of the essay? Grab a handful of essays and head for the cave, we could say, for example, and watch what you gathered. Find me two essays and an orange door. Which would be the harder?

I never knew what to write about, and I was an A student. I worried about it a good deal, before (like everyone else I knew) I finally, at the last hour, sat down and just did it. What were we supposed to do? I was no expert on anything and I was modest, too. Know that feeling?

Words are hard to talk about. They are collected together in many forms. Most of us use them and don't think twice about them, like so many pennies. You have made a great advance when you suddenly stop and look at the words. One word at a time. Whole fields of them. Essays.

This is a form with a history of satisfied users. It is smaller than a dissertation but larger than a page. In it is a long continuing dialogue of the human race, voices from the past.

Someone should have told me to *look* at essays, not merely *read* them. I never knew there were so many kinds.

Obviously, you think, somewhere along the way, I entered into a romance with the essay. I learned to respect it mostly, and only from having to teach it year after year to the nonbelievers and the bewildered.

That's when I suddenly saw how difficult it is for human beings to communicate, and how really touching were the ways we set about doing it. The next step was seeing the beauty. Marianne Moore's lines about poetry could as well apply to the essay:

> I, too, dislike it: there are things that are important beyond all this fiddle. Reading it, however, with a perfect contempt for it, one discovers in it after all, a place for the genuine.

At least let me try to convince you.

The Sources of Writing

Why is there a single word on a single page? What makes the human race record itself? We're the only ones who do this as far as I know. I hope you don't expect me to know THE answer to this. I only know we do it and with some delight and compulsion. And because we do we are always trying to answer WHY.

Why does Mark Helprin want to tell us about Johanna, a girl he once knew? Why does E. M. Forster share with us his speculations on the effects of owning property? Woody Allen seems determined we will laugh when we read his "Early Essays," actually parodies of the essay form itself, implying we care enough or know enough about the form to laugh when we see it mimicked.

I'm afraid I'm raising more questions here than I am answering and I'm supposed to be the teacher—the one who professes to know. Forster speaks of a "restlessness," of a "vague sense of a personality to express." Saroyan takes the question on directly. In "Why I Write" he

□

says he began writing to "get even on death." Then, he continued to write "for many reasons." Finally, he says, "because I want to."

Now perhaps you are thinking at this precise moment that you don't want to write. That you have been conscripted into your English class against your will. I could argue that language is the most important thing humans have ever created and that you'd better care about it, but I won't. Not everyone wants to write, or aches to express him- or herself in words. You, for the most part, only need explore this area, a visitor or tourist, so to speak. And with the same attention and courtesy you would extend as a guest.

I say "for the most part" because the essay, of all other written forms (banknotes, grocery lists, correspondence, poems, all forms inscribed on surfaces with writing implement), the essay primarily has been conscripted into service in colleges and universities as a "tool" of learning. In the essay form your history instructor discovers what you know in relation to the subject. In the essay form you discover what you know of *Billy Budd.*

Perhaps usefulness breeds contempt. I hardly think so.

I think the essay speaks for itself. If we attribute its invention to Montaigne in 1580, it is over 400 years old now. What is the essay? A literary form, a shape to pour your words into, a risky proposition to Montaigne who, in order to explain himself for writing such things, termed them "experimental." The essay is a composition of moderate length in which a human being, a writer, writes about some subject and the relationship of that subject to himself. I wish I could write "herself," but you all know of course that writers come in both genders.

This first chapter is a sampler of essayists and essays—"antique," foreign, and very contemporary. Imagine a box of chocolates. You wouldn't eat them without looking would you? Read with your eyes open to this marvelous form, the shapes and sounds of the words. Ask yourself, what is the source of writing?

Mark Helprin
(1947–   )

Mark Helprin was born June 28, 1947, in New York City. A novelist and short story writer, Helprin's background includes stints in the British Merchant Navy and both the Israeli Infantry and Air Force. A student of Middle Eastern culture, he often portrays the struggle of the modern Jew.

While some critics consider Helprin's style over-elegant or antique, he has been equally characterized as a "born teller of tales." Many of his stories have appeared in *The New Yorker.* The following selection is from his book *A Dove of the East and Other Stories.*

Willis Avenue

If, when I am drunk or sentimental or prodded by a stupid friend, I think back to the women I have really loved, most of them are covered and hidden by wishes and disappointment. But there is one of whom my memory is clear, and it is strange—she was so unimportant.

She was named Johanna, and I knew her for a summer when I worked in a typewriter-ribbon factory in the Bronx. It was very simple. She sat across from me on the production line all day long, and when either of us lifted our eyes we saw the other. Our job was to put the spools of ribbon in boxes—a very boring job, a job which left our hands automatic and faces and eyes free, so that we spent many days looking and talking. She was not such an attractive girl, and she knew it. These days, I don't like beautiful girls so much anymore. It makes them less able to cry and be sad, and I won't have a girl who cannot cry and be sad.

Now Johanna had a big wide face and big heavy limbs, although she was not fat by any means, just big. She was in fact bigger than me, but she thought like a very delicate woman, and so she moved as if she were little. Although she was not in the least self-conscious about her body, she thought that perhaps she should be, and I could always tell that she was thinking: I have to be more delicate about myself. But she could not be, and the exposure she suffered made her no less attractive to me.

I confess that at first this was not so. She was big and my image of women had been so ideal; I imagined them as princesses and perfectly clean. Then I took pity on her for her clumsiness and the way she was impressed by me. I am externally slick—rather handsome, people say. She thought I was beyond her reach; I did, too. I took her to lunch, and she blushed under the fan in the little restaurant. The heat of that summer was so intense that it made us both sweat in the shade. She was taken by me and I was therefore not very interested in her. After all, she was not very pretty. And every day we sat for eight hours sweating, our legs sometimes touching, across from one another under the inky breeze of the big fan. She looked down so much not because she needed to see to put the spool into the box but because she was shy, and, think, I had told her everything, wanting to make her a sister. She was very unhappy when I told her of the women I thought about that summer. When I first mentioned Susanna, she looked so sad that I stopped, but later I went on, and I would speak to her of my girls, and I think she cried in the women's dressing room. The other women avoided her and thought she was strange.

We had lunch together every day. All she did was keep still, and laugh with me, and smile when I spoke without thinking. She went home to her mother each afternoon; she told me about her mother. She spoke well, but she was just not pretty.

In the South Bronx one feels as though one is in the hotter part of Naples or the dull part of the Great Plains. Dirt falls from the air, and the heat makes everything, even the iron, wet. The people I don't like complain about the heat. Johanna, whom I saw, every hour of every day, sitting next to a half-painted column in the skylight light of a hot dirty workroom, did not complain about the heat but wiped her forehead with her hand now and then and seemed to me very much like myself. She seemed to be me when I was not worried about things, when I was quiet and watching, when I had fallen and could learn and feel, in the heat, the rising heat of that time. Johanna: white-faced and green-eyed, hands full of ink, wiping her brow with her wrist and getting ink on her wide white face anyway. Johanna in the South Bronx in a hot summer, when I was stronger and when I thought I would succeed, sat across from me each day. And then I left, and she had to sit there in the same place; and when January came around she was there, accepting whoever sat across from her. I don't think I would have her now, but if she could know that I loved her then, more than anything, that I would have married her, loved her, if only I had not been so young, if only I had known myself. Johanna. When she wiped her brow with her wrist she got ink on her face anyway, and she was always smiling.

Allusions/References

Naples   seaport in Southern Italy
Great Plains   sloping region of valleys and plains extending from Texas north to south Alberta, Canada, and stretching east from the base of the Rockies

Discussion

1. What is the source of Helprin's essay? What is it that spurred him to write this piece—aside from any commercial interests?
2. Memory is an eternal spring for writing. What does reading about Helprin's memory of Johanna make you remember? Write it down, just as it comes to you—in those very words that come first.
3. What do the words "she was so unimportant" mean? Obviously Helprin must intend something special by them because Johanna has been remembered where others have become "covered and hidden by wishes and disappointment." And what does that mean?
4. Notice the vocabulary level of this piece. Do you need any words defined for you? Does Helprin use primarily single syllable words or multisyllabic words? Why is it important to note this?
5. Words are to a writer what a brush stroke is to a painter. Is this a simple or complex canvas?
   Notice how many times and in what positions Helprin uses the name

Johanna. How much magic has been retained in that name for him? How effective do you feel this repetition is as a writing device?

For Further Discussion

6. Why does Helprin wish "she could know that I loved her then"? Speculate on this. Why is this important to a man who says, "I don't think I would have her now"? Do you think Helprin is expressing a universal human experience? Have you felt this way about anyone before?
7. We can only speculate, ask ourselves inside, but why do you think Helprin is sharing this memory with us? From all evidence you can glean from this piece, who do you think his audience is? For whom is he writing this piece?

E. M. Forster
(1879–1970)

Edward Morgan Forster was a British novelist and writer of nonfiction. His reputation was firmly established when, at 46, he finished his fifth and final novel, *A Passage to India*. It remains his most famous work. After that his interest turned to nonfiction.

He said of his writing: "My regret is that I haven't written a bit more . . . I think I am different from other writers; they profess much more worry (I don't know if it is genuine). I have always found writing pleasant and don't understand what people mean by 'throes of creation.'"

My Wood

A few years ago I wrote a book which dealt in part with the difficulties of the English in India. Feeling that they would have had no difficulties in India themselves, the Americans read the book freely. The more they read it the better it made them feel, and a cheque to the author was the result. I bought a wood with the cheque. It is not a large wood—it contains scarcely any trees, and it is intersected, blast it, by a public footpath. Still, it is the first property that I have owned, so it is right that other people should participate in my shame, and should ask themselves, in accents that will vary in horror, this very important question: What is the effect of property upon the character? Don't let's touch economics; the effect of private ownership upon the community as a whole as another question—a more important question, perhaps, but another one. Let's keep to psychology. If you own things, what's their effect on you? What's the effect on me of my wood?

In the first place, it makes me feel heavy. Property does have this effect. Property produces men of weight, and it was a man of weight who failed to get into the Kingdom of Heaven. He was not wicked, that unfortunate millionaire in the parable, he was only stout; he stuck out in front, not to mention behind, and as he wedged himself this way and that in the crystalline entrance and bruised his well-fed flanks, he saw beneath him a comparatively slim camel passing through the eye of a needle and being woven into the robe of God. The Gospels all through couple stoutness and slowness. They point out what is perfectly obvious, yet seldom realized: that if you have a lot of things you cannot move about a lot, that furniture requires dusting, dusters require servants, servants require insurance stamps, and the whole tangle of them makes you think twice before you accept an invitation to dinner or go for a bathe in the Jordan. Sometimes the Gospels proceed further and say with Tolstoy that property is sinful; they approach the difficult ground of asceticism here, where I cannot follow them. But as to the immediate effects of property on people, they just show straightforward logic. It produces men of weight. Men of weight cannot, by definition, move like the lightning from the East unto the West, and the ascent of a fourteen-stone bishop into a pulpit is thus the exact antithesis of the coming of the Son of Man. My wood makes me feel heavy.

In the second place, it makes me feel it ought to be larger.

The other day I heard a twig snap in it. I was annoyed at first, for I thought that someone was blackberrying, and depreciating the value of the undergrowth. On coming nearer, I saw it was not a man who had trodden on the twig and snapped it, but a bird, and I felt pleased. My bird. The bird was not equally pleased. Ignoring the relation between us, it took fright as soon as it saw the shape of my face, and flew straight over the boundary hedge into a field, the property of Mrs. Henessy, where it sat down with a loud squawk. It had become Mrs. Henessy's bird. Something seemed grossly amiss here, something that would not have occurred had the wood been larger. I could not afford to buy Mrs. Henessy out, I dared not murder her, and limitations of this sort beset me on every side. Ahab did not want that vineyard—he only needed it to round off his property, preparatory to plotting a new curve—and all the land around my wood has become necessary to me in order to round off the wood. A boundary protects. But—poor little thing—the boundary ought in its turn to be protected. Noises on the edge of it. Children throw stones. A little more, and then a little more, until we reach the sea. Happy Canute! Happier Alexander! And after all, why should even the world be the limit of possession? A rocket containing a Union Jack, will, it is hoped, be shortly fired at the moon. Mars. Sirius. Beyond which . . . But these immensities ended by saddening me. I could not suppose that my wood was the destined nucleus of universal dominion—it is so very small and contains no mineral wealth beyond the blackberries. Nor was I comforted when Mrs. Henessy's bird took alarm for the second time and flew clean away from us all, under the belief that it belonged to itself.

In the third place, property makes its owner feel that he ought to do something to it. Yet he isn't sure what. A restlessness comes over him, a vague sense that he has a personality to express—the same sense which, without any vagueness, leads the artist to an act of creation. Sometimes I think I will cut down such trees as remain in the wood, at other times I want to fill up the gaps between them with new trees. Both impulses are pretentious and empty. They are not honest movements towards money-making or beauty. They spring from a foolish desire to express myself and from an inability to enjoy what I have got. Creation, property, enjoyment form a sinister trinity in the human mind. Creation and enjoyment are both very, very good, yet they are often unattainable without a material basis, and at such moments property pushes itself in as a substitute, saying, "Accept me instead—I'm good enough for all three." It is not enough. It is, as Shakespeare said of lust, "The expense of spirit in a waste of shame"; it is "Before, a joy proposed; behind, a dream." Yet we don't know how to shun it. It is forced on us by our economic system as the alternative to starvation. It is also forced on us by an internal defect in the soul, by the feeling that in property may lie the germs of self-development and of exquisite or heroic deeds. Our life on earth is, and ought to be, material and carnal. But we have not yet learned to manage our materialism and carnality properly; they are still entangled with the desire for ownership, where (in the words of Dante) "Possession is one with loss."

And this brings us to our fourth and final point: the blackberries.

Blackberries are not plentiful in this meagre grove, but they are easily seen from the public footpath which traverses it, and all too easily gathered. Foxgloves, too—people will pull up the foxgloves, and ladies of an educational tendency even grub for toadstools to show them on the Monday in class. Other ladies, less educated, roll down the bracken in the arms of their gentlemen friends. There is paper, there are tins. Pray, does my wood belong to me or doesn't it? And, if it does, should I not own it best by allowing no one else to walk there? There is a wood near Lyme Regis, also cursed by a public footpath, where the owner has not hesitated on this point. He has built high stone walls each side of the path, and has spanned it by bridges, so that the public circulate like termites while he gorges on the blackberries unseen. He really does own his wood, this able chap. Dives in Hell did pretty well, but the gulf dividing him from Lazarus could be traversed by vision, and nothing traverses it here. And perhaps I shall come to this in time. I shall wall in and fence out until I really taste the sweets of property. Enormously stout, endlessly avaricious, pseudocreative, intensely selfish, I shall weave upon my forehead the quadruple crown of possession until those nasty Bolshies come and take it off again and thrust me aside into the outer darkness.

Vocabulary

cheque British variant of check
bracken a large, coarse fern; an area overgrown with this fern

asceticism a life of austere self-discipline, especially as an act of religious devotion

avaricious immoderately fond of accumulating wealth

fourteen-stone about 190 pounds; stone is a British unit of weight approximating 13 pounds

Allusions/References

the camel and the rich man the biblical parable from Mark 10:25

Ahab's vineyard a wicked king of Israel of the ninth century B.C., husband of Jezebel. I Kings 16:33

Canute King of England A.D. 994?–1035; called "the Great"

Alexander King of Macedonia 356–323 B.C.; conquerer of Greece, the Persian Empire, and Egypt

Dives a rich man in the parable of Lazarus; Luke 16:19–31

Lazarus the discarded beggar in the parable from Luke 16; not the Lazarus whom Jesus raised from the dead

a bathe in the Jordan the principal river of Israel and Jordan where John baptised Christ; "bathe" means to swim as well as to immerse in water as purification

Bolshies nickname for Bolshevik

Tolstoy a Russian novelist (1828–1910), author of *War and Peace*, who renounced materialism toward the end of his life

Shakespeare the English dramatist and poet (1564–1616)

Dante Italian poet, author of *Divine Comedy* (1265–1321)

Discussion

1. One glance at the vocabulary glossed above, and at the allusions Forster makes, tells you that you are now in the presence of an essay (or essayist) with some complexity. While it is always better to read each essay more than once, it is absolutely mandatory to do so in this case.

   Reread the essay, and this time with an ear to the tone of the piece, and an eye to its form. Is it primarily informative? humorous? What is its shape on the page?

2. Forster's style has been described as "precise, yet nonetheless elusive, administering a series of tiny surprises . . . a perpetual slight displacement of the expected emphasis."

   − How might the third paragraph, a sentence alone, be an example of this?

   − Were you really prepared for his "fourth and final point: the blackberries"? What other examples of Forster's "displacement," of his "tiny surprises," can you find?

3. Because of limitations on length, it is unlikely an essay will have much extraneous matter. In other words, everything "means" something or furthers the meaning of the piece. How then might Forster's first two sentences be explained?

   Find other examples of two or three sentences which at first glance appear purposeless, and then explain how they relate to the work as a whole.

4. In this essay Forster goes about answering the question: "What is the effect of property upon the character?"
   How do his answers to this question form the structure of his essay?

For Further Discussion

5. The essay was not always Forster's literary form. After finishing *A Passage to India*, he turned to writing nonfiction. We might wonder why an accomplished novelist would make this change. What is the province of the essay? What attraction might it have to a writer?
   Obviously this is a difficult question at the beginning of a text on essays, but continue to speculate on possible answers.
   What have you to say in essay form?
6. Forster says about the owner of property, "a restlessness comes over him, a vague sense that he has a personality to express—the same sense which . . . leads the artist to the act of creation."
   How is the essay then a form (like property, like canvas for the artist) in which the author can relieve a restlessness, a need to express himself?
   How is this "restlessness" a source for all writing?
7. One last comment on Forster's techniques of writing by Forster himself: "People will not realize how little conscious one is of these things . . . how one flounders about. They want us to be so much better informed than we are."
   Students, take hope.

Francis Bacon
(1561–1626)

Francis Bacon, born in 1561 in the Strand, London, was an essayist, jurist, philosopher, and statesman. Admitted to the bar in 1582, he went on to become Lord Chancellor. His career in the public arena was ruined when, in 1621, he was tried and convicted for bribery, more a victim of political enemies than of his own wrongdoing. In any case, he retired from public life to devote full time to his scientific/philosophical studies.

   Though considered to be "the father of inductive reasoning," thus a major figure in modern science, Bacon is probably most remembered for his essays. These are his philosophical treatises on humankind's social/ethical/spiritual place in the universe. Three of his essays are reprinted below (read also Woody Allen's "Early Essays" which follow). Bacon said of his life, "I found I was fitted for nothing so well as for the study of truth."

Of Suspicion

Suspicions amongst thoughts, are like bats amongst birds, they ever fly by twilight. Certainly they are to be repressed, or at least well guarded: for they cloud the mind; they leese friends; and they check with business, whereby business cannot go on currently and constantly. They dispose kings to tyranny, husbands to jealousy, wise men to irresolution and melancholy. They are defects, not in the heart, but in the brain; for they take place in the stoutest natures; as in the example of Henry the Seventh of England. There was not a more suspicious man, nor a more stout. And in such a composition they do small hurt. For commonly they are not admitted, but with examination, whether they be likely or no. But in fearful natures they gain ground too fast. There is nothing makes a man suspect much, more than to know little; and therefore men should remedy suspicion, by procuring to know more, and not to keep their suspicions in smother. What would men have? Do they think, those they employ and deal with, are saints? Do they not think, they will have their own ends, and be truer to themselves, than to them? Therefore there is no better way, to moderate suspicions, than to account upon such suspicions as true, and yet to bridle them as false. For so far a man ought to make use of suspicions, as to provide, as if that should be true, that he suspects, yet it may do him no hurt. Suspicions that the mind of itself gathers, are but buzzes; but suspicions that are artificially nourished, and put into men's heads, by the tales and whispering of others, have stings. Certainly, the best means, to clear the way in this same wood of suspicions, is frankly to communicate them with the party, that he suspects; for thereby he shall be sure to know more the truth of them, than he did before; and withal shall make that party more circumspect, not to give further cause of suspicion. But this would not be done to men of base natures; for they, if they find themselves once suspected, will never be true. The Italian says, *Sospetto licentia fede;* as if suspicion, did give a passport to faith; but it ought, rather, to kindle it to discharge itself.

Vocabulary

leese   obsolete for lose
irresolution   not determining a course of action
procuring   to bring about, effect
account upon   to consider, to reckon
bridle   a curb or check; to control or restrain as if with a harness
withal   besides, in addition
circumspect   take heed, prudent

Allusions/References

Henry the Seventh   known as Henry Tudor, 1457–1509. King of England (1485–1509); first of House of Tudor
sospetto licentia fede   licentious suspicion

Narcissus, or Self-Love

Narcissus is said to have been extremely beautiful and comely, but intolerably proud and disdainful; so that, pleased with himself, and scorning the world, he led a solitary life in the woods; hunting only with a few followers, who were his professed admirers, amongst whom the nymph Echo was his constant attendant. In this method of life, it was once his fate to approach a clear fountain, where he laid himself down to rest, in the noonday heat; when, beholding his image in the water, he fell into such a rapture and admiration of himself, that he could by no means be got away, but remained continually fixed and gazing, till at length he was turned into a flower, of his own name, which appears early in the spring, and is consecrated to the infernal deities, Pluto, Proserpine, and the Furies.

Explanation.—This fable seems to paint the behavior and fortune of those, who, for their beauty, or other endowments, wherewith nature (without any industry of their own) has graced and adorned them, are extravagantly fond of themselves; for men of such a disposition generally affect retirement, and absence from public affairs; as a life of business must necessarily subject them to many neglects and contempts, which might disturb and ruffle their minds: whence such persons commonly lead a solitary, private, and shadowy life: see little company, and those only such as highly admire and reverence them; or, like an echo, assent to all they say.

And they who are depraved, and rendered still fonder of themselves by this custom, grow strangely indolent, inactive, and perfectly stupid. The Narcissus, a spring flower, is an elegant emblem of this temper, which at first flourishes, and is talked of, but, when ripe, frustrates the expectation conceived of it.

And that this flower should be sacred to the infernal powers, carries out the allusion still further; because men of this humor are perfectly useless in all respects: for whatever yields no fruit, but passes, and is no more, like the way of a ship in the sea, was by the ancients consecrated to the infernal shades and powers.

Vocabulary

comely   attractive, handsome
disdainful   aloof, a show of scornful superiority
rapture   ecstasy, being transported by a lofty emotion
consecrated   set apart as sacred
endowment   a natural gift or quality—a beauty or talent
infernal deities   gods of the world of the dead
reverence   a feeling of profound love or respect

depraved morally corrupt
indolent disinclined to work, lazy

Allusions/References

Narcissus Greek mythological youth who spurned the love of Echo and pined
  away in love with his own image. He was transformed into a flower
Echo a nymph who pined away in love with Narcissus until only her voice
  remained
Pluto in Roman mythology the god of the dead and the underworld
Proserpine wife of Pluto, goddess of the underworld
the Furies in Greek and Roman mythology, the three terrible, winged god-
  desses with snaky hair who pursue and punish the doers of unavenged
  crimes

Tythonus, or Satiety

It is elegantly fabled by Tythonus, that being exceedingly beloved by
Aurora, she petitioned Jupiter that he might prove immortal, thereby
to secure herself the everlasting enjoyment of his company; but
through female inadvertence she forgot to add, that he might never
grow old; so that, though he proved immortal, he became miserably
worn and consumed with age, insomuch that Jupiter, out of pity, at
length transformed him to a grasshopper.

Explanation.—This fable seems to contain an ingenious description of pleasure; which at first, as it were in the morning of the day, is
so welcome, that men pray to have it everlasting, but forget that satiety
and weariness of it will, like old age, overtake them, though they think
not of it; so that at length, when their appetite for pleasurable actions
is gone, their desires and affections often continue; whence we commonly find that aged persons delight themselves with the discourse and
remembrance of the things agreeable to them in their better days. This
is very remarkable in men of a loose, and men of a military life; the
former whereof are always talking over their amours, and the latter
the exploits of their youth; like grasshoppers, that show their vigor
only by their chirping.

Vocabulary

satiety the condition of being gratified beyond the point of satisfaction; excess
inadvertence mistake, oversight
ingenious having genius, brilliant
discourse verbal exchange
amours love affairs, usually implies illicit ones

Allusions/References

Tythonus the mortal married by Aurora. Father of Memnon and Emathion, kings respectively of Ethiopia and Arabia

Aurora Roman Goddess of the Dawn who fell in love with Tythonus, a mortal. Zeus, at her request, granted him immortality but she forgot to ask for eternal youth and he eventually withered up to a mere grasshopper of himself

Jupiter in Roman mythology, the supreme god. Also called Jove

Discussion

1. To begin with, notice Bacon's ideas must be gleaned from a field of words used in antique form. It is not easy to read the voices from the past. Language is in constant change. Nevertheless, attempt to paraphrase the main points in each of these three small essays.
2. What figures of speech (metaphors, similes, images) do you find?

   "Suspicions . . . are like bats . . . "

   "Suspicions . . . are but buzzes . . . "

   " . . . same wood of suspicions . . . "

   What others? Are Bacon's metaphors effective to the modern reader?
3. Bacon's use of Greek and Roman mythology as a basis for his own personal point of view about the meaning of human actions is a common practice to the essayist. The past reinterpreted, the use of an ancient text as a basis for a continuing dialogue. Ideas all have their caretakers and their moments to be heard. How effective do you find Bacon's interpretations of the old myths to be?
4. How are voices from the past a source of ideas for writing? (See Woody Allen's "Early Essays" and the Discussion following.)
5. Francis Bacon believed in the inductive origin of ideas, the testing of ideas by controlled and scientific methods, and in the progress and improvement of ideas (and humanity) by the control of "nature" through scientific knowledge.

   This is a long way of saying he believed by looking at particular incidents, the tiny thing, we could generalize to the larger case.

   How is his looking at the myth of Narcissus or of Tythonus an example of his belief in the "inductive origin of ideas"? How does he generalize what he learns from the myths to mankind? Is his look at suspicion also inductive?
6. How might you as a student essayist, look at something particular, something even personal, and use it in writing about a larger issue?

For Further Discussion

7. The Baconian theory hypothesizes that Francis Bacon was the author of the works usually attributed to Shakespeare. Bacon's ability to write was given

that much accord. How is Bacon not only interested in his ideas (suspicions harm, too much self-love isolates and renders useless, etc.) but in the essay *form* itself?

Essays have beginnings, middles, and endings and are of a certain length. They are graced with thought transformed into words used appropriately, and with awareness of the *shape* and *form* of the words as well as with the *idea* they convey. (See the Discussion of Allen's "Early Essays" for a definition of "essay.")

Woody Allen
(1935–   )

Woody Allen (Allen Stewart Konigsberg), born in Brooklyn, December 1, 1935, began his writing career in high school by sending jokes to newspaper columnists who in turn passed them on to comedians. From this beginning he became a gag writer for celebrities such as Sid Caesar, Buddy Hackett, Carol Channing and Jack Parr. Next he began performing his own material as a stand-up comic, then as an actor, and has gone on to write, direct, and star in films that have made him not only a celebrity, but one of America's most important filmmakers.

A frequent contributor to *The New Yorker* and other magazines, Allen's work has also appeared in book form. His life's work, he says, is, "to forge in the smithy of my soul the uncreated conscience of my race. Then to see if they can be turned out in plastic." The following is from his book *Without Feathers*.

The Early Essays

Following are a few of the early essays of Woody Allen. There are no late essays, because he ran out of observations. Perhaps as Allen grows older he will understand more of life and will set it down, and then retire to his bedroom and remain there indefinitely. Like the essays of Bacon, Allen's are brief and full of practical wisdom, although space does not permit the inclusion of his most profound statement, "Looking at the Bright Side."

On Seeing a Tree in Summer

Of all the wonders of nature, a tree in summer is perhaps the most remarkable, with the possible exception of a moose singing "Embraceable You" in spats. Consider the leaves, so green and leafy (if not, something is wrong). Behold how the branches reach up to heaven as if to say, "Though I am only a branch, still I would love to collect Social Security." And the varieties! Is this tree a spruce or poplar? Or a giant redwood? No, I'm afraid it's a stately elm, and once again you've made an ass of yourself. Of course, you'd know all the trees in a minute if you were nature's creature the woodpecker, but then it would be too late and you'd never get your car started.

But why is a tree so much more delightful than, say, a babbling brook? Or anything that babbles, for that matter? Because its glorious presence is mute testimony to an intelligence far greater than any on earth, certainly in the present Administration. As the poet said, "Only God can make a tree"—probably because it's so hard to figure out how to get the bark on.

Once a lumberjack was about to chop down a tree when he noticed a heart carved on it, with two names inside. Putting away his axe, he sawed down the tree instead. The point of that story escapes me, although six months later the lumberjack was fined for teaching a dwarf Roman numerals.

On Youth and Age

The true test of maturity is not how old a person is but how he reacts to awakening in the midtown area in his shorts. What do years matter, particularly if your apartment is rent-controlled? The thing to remember is that each time of life has its appropriate rewards, whereas when you're dead it's hard to find the light switch. The chief problem about death, incidentally, is the fear that there may be no afterlife—a depressing thought, particularly for those who have bothered to shave. Also, there is the fear that there is an afterlife but no one will know where it's being held. On the plus side, death is one of the few things that can be done as easily lying down.

Consider, then: Is old age really so terrible? Not if you've brushed your teeth faithfully! And why is there no buffer to the onslaught of the years? Or a good hotel in downtown Indianapolis? Oh, well.

In short, the best thing to do is behave in a manner befitting one's age. If you are sixteen or under, try not to go bald. On the other hand, if you are over eighty, it is extremely good form to shuffle down the street clutching a brown paper bag and muttering, "The Kaiser will steal my string." Remember, everything is relative—or should be. If it's not, we must begin again.

On Frugality

As one goes through life, it is extremely important to conserve funds, and one should never spend money on anything foolish, like pear nectar or a solid-gold hat. Money is not everything, but it is better than having one's health. After all, one cannot go into a butcher shop and tell the butcher, "Look at my great suntan, and besides I never catch colds," and expect him to hand over any merchandise. (Unless, of course, the butcher is an idiot.) Money is better than poverty, if only for financial reasons. Not that it can buy happiness. Take the case of the ant and the grasshopper: The grasshopper played all summer, while the ant worked and saved. When winter came, the grasshopper had nothing, but the ant complained of chest pains. Life is hard for insects. And don't think mice are having any fun, either. The point is, we all need a nest egg to fall back on, but not while wearing a good suit.

Finally, let us bear in mind that it is easier to spend two dollars than to save one. And for God's sake don't invest money in any brokerage firm in which one of the partners is named Frenchy.

On Love

Is it better to be the lover or the loved one? Neither, if your cholesterol is over six hundred. By love, of course, I refer to romantic love—the love between man and woman, rather than between mother and child, or a boy and his dog, or two headwaiters.

The marvelous thing is that when one is in love there is an impulse to sing. This must be resisted at all costs, and care must also be taken to see that the ardent male doesn't "talk" the lyrics of songs. To be loved, certainly, is different from being admired, as one can be admired from afar but to really love someone it is essential to be in the same room with the person, crouching behind the drapes.

To be a really good lover, then, one must be strong and tender. How strong? I suppose being able to lift fifty pounds should do it. Bear in mind also that to the lover the loved one is always the most beautiful thing imaginable, even though to a stranger she may be indistinguishable from an order of smelts. Beauty is in the eye of the beholder. Should the beholder have poor eyesight, he can ask the nearest person which girls look good. (Actually, the prettiest ones are almost always the most boring, and that is why some people feel there is no God.)

"The joys of love are but a moment long," sang the troubadour, "but the pain of love endures forever." This was almost a hit song, but the melody was too close to "I'm a Yankee Doodle Dandy."

On Tripping Through a Copse and Picking Violets

This is no fun at all, and I would recommend almost any other activity. Try visiting a sick friend. If this is impossible, see a show or get into a nice warm tub and read. Anything is better than turning up in a copse with one of those vacuous smiles and accumulating flowers in a basket. Next thing you know, you'll be skipping to and fro. What are you going to do with the violets once you get them, anyhow? "Why, put them in a vase," you say. What a stupid answer. Nowadays you call the florist and order by phone. Let *him* trip through the copse, he's getting paid for it. That way, if an electrical storm comes up or a beehive is chanced upon, it will be the florist who is rushed to Mount Sinai.

Do not conclude from this, incidentally, that I am insensitive to the joys of nature, although I have come to the conclusion that for sheer fun it is hard to beat forty-eight hours at Foam Rubber City during the high holidays. But that is another story.

Vocabulary

spats a cloth or leather covering for a shoe upper and the ankle, fastening under the shoe with a strap

mute incapable of speech

frugality thrifty

brokerage acting as an agent for others in negotiating contracts, purchases, or sales

smelts any of various, small silvery fishes

copse a thicket of small trees or shrubs

vacuous devoid of meaning, empty

Allusions/References

Mount Sinai Well-known hospital in New York City; mountain on south Sinai peninsula from which, according to Exodus 19:20, God gave the Ten Commandments to the Israelites

Discussion

1. How are Allen's "Early Essays" related to your own early essays? Did you ever write the classic "What I Did on My Summer Vacation"? What shape did it have? How did it read? Does this give any hints as to one of the sources of Allen's humorous parody of early essays?

2. Notice phrases such as the following: "Behold how the branches reach up to heaven . . . ," "On tripping through a copse . . . " Aside from the models of his own early writing, how might other historically "early" essayists (such as Francis Bacon) also be sources for Allen's parody?

   What does this suggest as another possible resource for a writer?

3. *The Unabridged Webster's Third New International Dictionary* defines essay as follows:

   > An analytic, interpretative, or critical literary composition usually much shorter and less systematic and formal than a dissertation or thesis and usually dealing with its subject from a limited, often personal point of view.

   What are the limited special fields Allen purports a thorough acquaintance with?

   How is this "thorough acquaintance" shown as a pretension?

4. Much of Allen's humor arises from his tone of formality and seriousness, his language of cliché, mixed with a large dose of the mundane, everyday turn of phrase. Take any of the small essays and analyze his thought processes from one sentence to the next. Does he have anything serious to say at all? What might it be? Is Allen only poking fun at the essay form?

For Further Discussion

5. A close look at Francis Bacon's essays as the essay *form* in its historically early stages, and at Woody Allen's "Early Essays" as a parody of the essay form itself and of the human pretension of knowing, might be an informative exercise in finding a position or stance for yourself as student essayist.

   Consider throughout this collection of essays that make up *The Writer's Voice* how each essayist has used the essay as a vehicle of expression, and as a thing that needs expressing in itself ... how each essayist has been concerned with preserving, continuing, or recreating the essay form, as well as with saying what wanted to be said.

   You are not Adam or Eve to the essay. It is a long and continuing dialogue of the human race.

William Saroyan
(1908–1981)

In addition to novels and hundreds of short stories, Saroyan wrote and directed screen plays for both movies and theater. Ever the outsider of the literary establishment, he refused the Pulitzer Prize in 1940 for his play *The Time of Your Life,* saying he was opposed to wealth patronizing art.

   Saroyan wrote about life and people with simplicity, humor, and optimism. He never rewrote. Of his method he said, "I do not know a great deal about what the words come to, but the presence says, now don't get funny; just sit down and say something; it'll be all right. Say it wrong it'll be all right anyway. Half the time I do say it wrong, but somehow or other, just as the presence says, it's right anyhow." The following is his introduction to *The William Saroyan Reader.*

Why I Write

It is a quarter of a century, almost, since my first book was published, but as I began to write when I was nine, I have been writing for forty years: that is to say, I have lived in a special way for forty years—the way that takes hold of a man who is determined to understand the meaning of his own life, and to be prepared to write about it.

   But I think it goes even farther back than forty years. I think I began to live in my own special way when I became aware that I had memory. That happened before I was three. I also had a memory that went back to a time before I was *two*, but it was an isolated one. At that age I wasn't given to remembering *everything*, or rather I hadn't yet noticed that it had come to pass that I remembered.

   In the past were some of the best things I had, several of them gone: my father, for instance, who had died before I was three.

   My first memory, the one that went back to a time when I was not yet two, was of my father getting up onto a wagon, sitting beside my mother, and making a sound that told the horse to go. My two sisters and my brother and I sat in the back of the wagon as it moved slowly down a dusty road between vineyards on a hot afternoon in the summertime. I remembered sensing sorrow and feeling *with*—with mine, my people—a father, a mother, two sisters, a brother, our horse, our wagon, our pots and pans and books. The rest is lost in the sleep that soon carried me away. The next thing I knew my father was gone, which I didn't understand.

I was fascinated by having memory, and troubled by the sorrow of it. I refused to accept the theory that things end, including people, including my father. I refused to believe that my father was dead. (In the sense that every man *is* his father, I wasn't much mistaken.)

All the same, I felt impelled from the time I knew I had memory to do something about the past, about endings, about human death.

My first impulse was simple. I wanted to cause the impossible to happen, because if I was able to do that, I knew I would be able to cause *anything* to happen. Thus, death would not be death, if anybody wanted it not to be.

I found two large empty cans. One I filled with water. The empty can I placed two feet from the full can. I asked myself to cause the water in the full can to pass into the empty can, by itself, because I wanted it to.

The experiment failed. I had begun with the maximum, I had failed, and so I began to consider what might be the next best.

For a long time there didn't appear to be *any* next best at all. It was a matter of all or nothing, or at any rate the equivalent of nothing: continuous *gradual* loss, and finally total loss, or death.

What could a man do about this? Wait? That didn't seem to be enough.

Why should I be troubled by memory at all if all memory told me was that things change, fail, decline, end, and die? I didn't want good things to do that, and I didn't think they should. How could I seize a good thing when I saw it and halt its decline and death? As far as people were concerned, there just didn't seem to be *any* way.

And so I came to accept the theory that as far as I knew, as far as *anybody* knew, as far as there appeared to be any order to the action of things at all, the end of the order was invariably and inevitably decline, disappearance, and death.

And yet the world was full of people all the time. And the earth, the sea, and the sky were full of all manner of other living things: plants, animals, fish, birds.

Thus, something *did* stay, something *was* constant, or appeared to be. It was the *kind* that stayed. *One* of a kind couldn't stay, and couldn't apparently be made to. I myself was one of a kind, and everybody I knew and loved was one of a kind, and so what about us? What could I do about our impermanence?

How could I halt this action? How had other men halted it?

I learned that they never had halted it. They had only pretended to.

They had done this by means of art, or the putting of limits upon the limitless, and thereby holding something fast and making it seem constant, indestructible, unstoppable, unkillable, deathless.

A great painter painted his wife, his son, his daughter, and himself, and then one by one they all moved along and died. But the painting remained. A sculptor did the same thing with stone, a composer with musical sounds, and a writer with words.

Therefore, as the next best thing, art in one form or another would have to be the way of my life, but which form of art?

Before I was eight I didn't think it could possibly be writing, for the simple reason that I couldn't read, let alone write, and everybody else I knew could do both. At last, though, I got the hang of reading and writing, and I felt (if I didn't think), "This is for me."

It had taken me so long to learn to write that I considered being able to write the greatest thing that could happen to anybody.

If I wrote something, it *was* written, it was itself, and it might continue to be itself forever, or for what passes as forever.

Thus, I could halt the action of things, after all, and at the same time be prepared to learn new things, to achieve new forms of halting, or art.

That is roughly how and why I became a writer.

In short, I began to write in order to get even on death.

I have continued to write for many reasons.

A long time ago I said I write because it is the only way I am willing to survive.

Mainly, though, I write because I want to.

Vocabulary

continuous   without interruption or cessation, unending
impermanence   not lasting, not permanent

Discussion

1. Why does Saroyan write? Why has he written this particular piece? What is the source of his writing?
2. Let's try to answer a slightly harder set of questions. *How* does Saroyan write? Note his word choices. Difficult? How many words have been glossed for you? Note also the length of his sentences. Is there any characteristic length of sentence/rhythm Saroyan seems to be using in this piece?
   How, do you suppose, has Saroyan decided on paragraphing? Note how

many brief paragraphs are in this piece. How do they hold together one to the other?

3. Saroyan says he "never rewrote." Would this explain the form his writing takes as being "natural" rather than preplanned or worked on?

4. Consider how memory plays a part in your own life or writing. What words come to your mind when you remember something? Write a short piece from some memory of yours recording exactly the words that come to you as they come and no others. How about these words? Are they good ones, unusual and fresh? Does the shape of your piece resemble Saroyan's?

5. An essay can be seen as a vase shaped in such a way as the words might fit or as a tree with its branches asymmetrical, growing as a tree might naturally grow. Does Saroyan write a vase essay or a tree essay?

2

The Words
Have To Do
Everything

In this chapter it is my intention to slow your reading speed to a crawl. Try to remember first learning to read, the way each next word came as an obstacle and then as relief. You recognized it after all.

Words are the stuff of writing. Each word. Pebbles on a beach. The brushstrokes of a painter.

Whenever it happened, who can say when we began to care more about ideas and less about the words that made them up, but whenever it happened, in this chapter you will have to reverse the process. Newman is very concerned about cleansing the language of the tribe. That's us. And his is a noble concern, but when you read, "Is Your Team Hungry Enough, Coach?" read the words not the ideas. "Fox Trot, Yes; Cat Trot, No" should tip you off it's about words just from the looks (and sounds) of those that make up its title. Dylan Thomas says he "fell in love" with the "gusts and grunts and hiccups and heehaws of the common fun of the earth" words. Marquez, a current Latin American novelist of world reknown, summarizes how much everything depends on words in words you'll want to run your eyes across.

There are really no new thoughts, no new ideas. They're all in the void, formless and wordless and waiting for someone to give them shape. For the writer, the word is the way.

Maybe you should read these essays and essayists twice also. Good words, good ideas.

Larry McMurtry
(1936–   )

Larry McMurtry was born June 3, 1936, in Wichita Falls, Texas. A former lecturer in English at Rice University, McMurtry is author of several novels, four of which have been adapted for the movies: *Horseman Pass By (Hud)*, *Leaving Cheyenne*, *The Last Picture Show*, and more recently, *Terms of Endearment*.

McMurtry's writing is of the people of Texas and the Southwest, of "the heart faced suddenly with the loss of its country, its customary and legendary range."

Dalhart

I curved back down to Dalhart through the wind the trail herders bucked, and the last few miles, with the lights twinkling ahead of me on the plain, were among the best of the trip. It only remained to perform some *acte symbolistique* to give the drive coherence, tie the present to the past. I stopped at a cafe in Dalhart and ordered a chicken fried steak. Only a rank degenerate would drive 1,500 miles across Texas without eating a chicken fried steak. The cafe was full of boys in football jackets, and the jukebox was playing an odious number called "Billy Broke My Heart in Walgreen's and I Cried All the Way to Sears."

The waitress was a thin, sad-eyed woman with hands that looked like she had used them to twist barbed-wire all her life. She set the steak in front of me and went wearily back to the counter to get a bottle of ketchup. The meat looked like a piece of old wood that had had perhaps one coat of white paint in the thirties and then had had that sanded off by thirty years of Panhandle sandstorms.

"Here," the waitress said, setting the ketchup bottle down. "I hope that steak's done enough. There ain't nothin' like steak when you're hungry, is there, son?"

"No ma'am, there ain't," I said.

□

Vocabulary

acte symbolistique   symbolic act
odious   offensive, disgusting; deserving hatred

Allusions/References

Dalhart   a town in the Texas Panhandle

Discussion

1. *The words have to do everything.* In less than 125 words, McMurtry has provided us with a picture of himself. What do we know of him from his words? What does his use of the French phrase *acte symbolistique* tell you about him? What does "No ma'am, there ain't" add to your picture of him?
2. Of course, the purpose of this piece is not only to reveal McMurtry but to reveal human experience. What experience is McMurtry revealing here? What does he mean by "I curved *back* down to Dalhart" and by "tie the present to the past?" Have you left home? Have you come back? What is discovered?
3. Look at these words. Can you see the waitress, "a thin, sad-eyed woman with hands that looked like she had used them to twist barbed-wire all her life"? Can you hear them: "Billy broke my heart in Walgreen's and I cried all the way to Sears"? "There ain't nothin'..." "Ketchup." Why not "catsup"? How do these images and sounds (conveyed by words) allow us to experience the scene *with* McMurtry, rather than merely to hear about it? How is he *showing* rather than *telling?*
4. How is stopping at the cafe for a chicken fried steak an *acte symbolistique?* What is an *acte symbolistique* to you when you go home? What will become one?
5. The words of Dalhart: trailherders, bucked, chicken fried steak, barbed-wire—how many more? How are these words the exact right words to use? What are the authentic words of your experience? Find them as you write.
6. How do we *show* others something we've experienced alone? One way, of course, is to make a comparison to something our audience may be familiar with already. We make metaphors and similes, figures of speech implying comparisons. Take a careful look at McMurtry's figures of speech. How many can you find? How effective are they?

Bonnie Angelo

Bonnie Angelo was born in Winston-Salem, North Carolina. She is an award-winning journalist, recipient of the Paul Tobenkin National Award in 1961 for her writing on civil rights. A past president of the Women's National Press Club, she is also the first woman to head a foreign news bureau for *Time* magazine.

Good Ole Boys

It is Friday night at any of ten thousand watering holes of the small towns and crossroads hamlets of the South. The room is a cacophony of the ping-pong-dingdingding of the pinball machine, the pop-fizz of another round of Pabst, the refrain of *Red Necks, White Socks and Blue Ribbon Beer* on the juke box, the insolent roar of a souped-up engine outside and, above it all, the sound of easy laughter. The good ole boys have gathered for their fraternal ritual—the aimless diversion that they have elevated into a life-style.

Being a good ole boy is not a consequence of birth or breeding; it cuts across economic and social lines; it is a frame of mind based on the premise that life is nothing to get serious about. A glance at the brothers Carter tells a lot. There is some confusion about why Billy Carter seems in many respects the quintessential good ole boy, while Brother Jimmy couldn't even fit into the more polished subspecies of conscious good ole boys who abound in small-town country clubs. Billy, amiable, full of jokes, his REDNECK POWER T-shirt straining unsuccessfully to cover the paunch, swigs a beer, carefree on a Sunday morning, as Jimmy Carter, introspective, hard driving, teaches Sunday School. Jimmy sometimes speaks wistfully of Billy's good-ole-boy ease.

Lightheartedness permeates the good ole boy's life-style. He goes by nicknames like "Goober" or " Goat." He disdains neckties as a form of snobbery; when he dresses up, it is to wear a decorated T-shirt with newish jeans or, for state occasions, a leisure suit with a colored shirt. If discussions veer beyond football toward substance, he cuts them off with funny stories.

The core of the good ole boy's world is with his buddies, the comfortable, hyperhearty, all-male camaraderie, joshing and drinking and regaling one another with tales of assorted, exaggerated prowess. Women are outsiders; when social events are unavoidably mixed, the good ole boys cluster together at one end of the room, leaving wives at the other. The GOB'S magic doesn't work with women; he feels insecure, threatened by them. In fact, he doesn't really like women, except in bed.

What he really loves is his automobile. He overlooks his wife with her hair up in pink rollers, sagging into an upside-down question mark in her tight slacks. But he lavishes attention on his Mercury mistress, Easy Rider shocks, oversize slickers, dual exhaust. He exults in tinkering with that beautiful engine, lying cool beneath the open hood, ready to respond, quick and fiery, to his touch. The automobile is his love and his sport.

Behind his devil-may-care lightheartedness, however, runs a strain of innate wisdom, an instinct about people and an unwavering loyalty that makes him the one friend you would turn to, not just because he's a drinking buddy who'll keep you laughing, but because, well, he's a good ole boy.

Vocabulary

hamlet   a small village
cacophony   harsh, jarring sound
fraternal   a group of men drawn together by common interests
diversion   a pastime or amusement that distracts the attention
quintessential   the pure, concentrated essence of anything; the ultimate sub-
    stance of things
subspecies   belonging to the same species but showing a deviation from the
    norm
camaraderie   loyalty and warm, friendly feelings among comrades
regaling   entertaining by providing a splendid feast
prowess   bravery, valor
exults   leaps for joy, rejoices greatly
innate   inborn, so a part of one's nature as to seem born with one

Allusions/References

Pabst   a beer whose name suggests the sound of a beer can opening
Carter   Jimmy Carter, past president of the United States; Billy Carter, his
    brother
Redneck Power   from sunburned neck of laborers; a poor, white, rural resi-
    dent of the South. Often used derogatively to indicate a bigot
Goober   a peanut
GOB   good ole boy

Discussion

1. Why is Pabst a particularly good name of beer to use after "ping-pong-dingdingding of the pinball machine, the pop-fizz of another round of Pabst . . ."?
   What is the sound of the word Pabst reminiscent of? "The room is a cacophony" *tells* us of sound; the "p's" that follow let us *hear* it.
2. Notice the mixed diction in this piece. Angelo uses such latinate (formal)
   words as: cacophony, quintessential, introspective, etc., side-by-side with
   such colloquial words as: souped-up, swigs, joshing, and buddies. Why? How
   effective is this technique? (Note Larry McMurtry's similar use of mixed
   diction.)
   Which words belong to Angelo and which to the good ole boys?
3. How is Angelo's attitude toward the good ole boys revealed in her choice of
   words? What is the tone of this piece? (This is not an easy question to answer.
   Consider Angelo's last paragraph when working out your response.)
4. Look up that word "regaling." How does its full definition add another
   dimension to the good ole boy's love of camaraderie?
5. Paragraph 5 is an especially effective description of good-ole-boy love. How
   have the words, the details, contributed to our experiencing love through
   good-ole-boy eyes?
   Good ole boys aren't only Southerners. Know any yourself? What words

would come to your mind writing a description of them? What would their words be?

Jack Smith
(1916–   )

Jack Smith was born August 27, 1916, in Long Beach, California. He has worked in the newspaper industry since the late 1930s. Beginning as a sportswriter, he has also worked as a combat correspondent, reporter, and, since 1958, as a columnist for the Los Angeles *Times*. He is the author of several books.

The following is a column that appeared in the Los Angeles *Times* in 1977.

Fox Trot, Yes; Cat Trot, No

Recently I observed here, in commenting on a reader's remark about his cat trotting into the house, or perhaps out of the house, that cats don't trot.

Cats either walk, lope, run or slink, I pointed out, and are physically incapable of the gait known as trotting, which we find so charming in other animals, such as dogs, horses and pigs.

To verify this, one need only try to put a cat out on a rainy day. First, when the cat senses one's purpose, he walks in a direction away from the door, faking apathy to disguise his intention of bolting. The instant one makes a more determined move, though, the cat goes directly from a walk into a lope, skipping the trot altogether. The lope is the cat's intermediary gait, having a deceptive look of nonchalance, but covering ground a great deal faster than a walk. Also, from the lope a cat can shift in a trice to an all-out run, and anyone trying to catch him is in for a frustrating 10 minutes, I can tell you, and probably defeat. (We need not be concerned for the moment with the slink. The slink is a stalking gait, used only for hunting, and is not relied on in the cat's relations with human beings.)

But whether a cat trots or not I would have thought was not a subject of wide interest, so I was surprised and pleased to learn from a reader that the gaits of animals was the subject of an article in the December issue of *Scientific American*, by Keir Pearson.

"The content of the article suggests," writes Richard L. Pio of Hermosa Beach, "that your curt dismissal of Spike Burlingame's claim that his cat trots is at least uninformed. I take you to be an honest man and so I believe your statement that you have never seen a cat trot. Of course it does not follow that your failure to observe a trotting cat means that no cat ever trots. Observation of our long-haired calico cat Josephine leads me to agree with Burlingame that cats do in fact trot.

"In any event, we have Pearson's article which appears to be a soundly based scientific study of rhythmic movements of the leg used in walking. He identifies the four basic gaits of a cat as the walk, the trot, the pace and the gallop. The discussion appears to close the issue of the trotting cat."

Not so fast, Pio. As a layman I respect any author who can get his stuff into *Scientific American*, but I am not so intimidated that I can't point out what appears to me to be a careless choice of words if not errors of fact. What does Pearson mean, a cat has only four gaits—the walk, the trot, the pace and the gallop?

Putting aside the trot for a moment, what has become of the slink and the lope? Does Pearson confuse the gallop with the lope? This is at least an unhappy choice of words. Only hoofed animals gallop, as the onomatopoeic character of the word gallop shows. A galloping animal goes galoop galoop galoop, or sometimes galump galump galump (depending on whether it has a soft or hard shoe). It takes only a moment's thought to see that cats are quite incapable of going either galoop or galump. Pawed animals do not gallop, they lope.

In Webster's the lope is described as resembling the canter, which is defined as "a 3-beat gait resembling but smoother and slower than the gallop." The word smooth is of course the key word. A cat's lope is the very picture of fluid drive. And one can no more think of a cat's lope as a gallop than of pig's gallop as a lope.

That Pearson ignores the slink is incomprehensible. The slink is a cat's hunting gait, without which he could not stalk even the fattest and stupidest of birds, and certainly not a mouse that had any wits at all. (The slink is similar to the skulk, by the way, but the skulk is more descriptive of the stalking of other animals than cats: especially, coyotes, foxes and raccoons.)

Meanwhile, reader Pio raises yet another semantic question:

"I must add one further comment," he says. "My wife would say of a cat's locomotion that they sometimes 'tritty-trot.' This seems to me to be an example of the kind of word that you claim that women use. In my wife's defense I should point out that the Compact Edition of the Oxford English Dictionary gives: trit-trot (reduplication of trot), a word imitating the sound of trotting.

"Thus," Pio points out, "if a horse may be said to trit-trot, then it may be quite sensible to refer to the delicate and almost soundless trot of a cat as tritty-trotting. Nonetheless, I think I have never heard a man use the word."

I'm afraid that Pio is a little bit guilty of that old debating trick of altering an adversary's thesis to make it more vulnerable. What I said, of course, was that cats can't *trot*. I didn't say they can't *tritty-trot*.

Perhaps I was right in the first place, that the subject is not of wide interest. But it's the only thing I've been able to think of for the last few days except the Super Bowl, and there didn't seem to be anything left to say about that.

□

Vocabulary

lope move easily, with long, swinging stride
apathy unconcern, lack of interest
nonchalance not showing interest, casually indifferent
trice a very short time, instant
onomatopoeic formation of a word by imitating the natural sound of the object or action involved; echoism
layman a person not belonging to or skilled in a particular profession (in this case, not a scientist)
semantic meaning in language, the branch of linguistics concerned with the nature, structure, and, especially, the development and changes of the meanings of words
vulnerable open to attack or criticism

Allusions/References

Scientific American science magazine
Super Bowl yearly football championship playoff between National Football League and American Football League

Discussion

1. What is Smith writing about here, cats or words? Look up "walk," "lope," "run," "slink," "pace," "gait," etc. in your dictionary. What distinctions are suggested between these words? How do they each mean something slightly different?
2. Mark Twain once wrote: "The difference between the right word and the almost right word is the difference between lightning and the lightning bug." Does a cat "trot"? On whose side are you, Smith's, Pio's, or Pearson's?
3. Notice how Smith's delight in words is evidenced in the following: "Only hoofed animals gallop, as the onomatopoeic character of the word gallop shows. A galloping animal goes galoop galoop galoop, or sometimes galump galump galump . . ."
   Not only does Smith tell us gallop is "onomatopoeic" (see vocabulary) but he sets an animal galloping across the lines. Notice the g's repeated and the many o's and p's.
4. When we refer to the sound of a letter from the alphabet we enclose it in slashes: /g/ is the sound (jē). What sounds does Smith give us in the remainder of the article?
   Why would only a woman say "tritty-trot"? Do you feel women tend to "cutesy" up the language? Does "tritty-trot" sound like a cat's steps?
5. Words are not only sounds (and meaning) but also shapes. The reader's eyes like to be delighted by skinny shapes and fat o's, roundedness and angularity. Look at the following from Smith: " . . . cats are quite incapable of going either galoop or galump. Pawed animals do not gallop, they lope." See the way the letters' shapes repeat themselves?

☐

What do you think, is Smith deliberately playing with language? Roll his words around on your tongue. Say them aloud. Is Smith's tone in this piece only playful; is he only interested in cleaning up a matter about cats? Or can you see a more serious intent that has to do with the nature of language itself?

Edwin Newman
(1919–   )

Edwin Newman was born January 25, 1919, in New York City. He has worked in the news media, primarily broadcast journalism, since the 1940s as a reporter, writer, and commentator.

NBC'S "house grammarian," Newman has worked to make the English language clear and understandable, to make the language of government, business, and other professionals accessible to everyone. Newman says, "I believe that my books have contributed to a changing attitude to the language." The following is a selection from his book *Strictly Speaking: Will America Be the Death of English?*

Is Your Team Hungry Enough, Coach?

Meaning no disrespect, I suppose there is, if not general rejoicing, at least a sense of relief when the football season ends. It's a long season.

I have an additional reason for watching football fade out without much regret. That reason is a protective interest in the English language. The phrase "pretty good," as in "He hit him pretty good," and "We stopped them pretty good," and "He moves pretty good for a big man," gets worked out pretty good from late September to mid-January. After which it should be given a pretty good rest, or allowed to rest pretty good, or at any rate left to basketball, where they hit the backboards pretty good.

Basketball, of course, cannot be played without referees, and generally they do the officiating pretty good, but not always. Said K. C. Jones, coach of the Capital Bullets of the NBA, explaining why he would not comment on the officiating in a play-off game against New York: "No sense in risking a $2,000 fine. To hell with it. They read the papers pretty good for our remarks."

After basketball, baseball. Al Downing of the Los Angeles Dodgers, who threw home run number 715 to Henry Aaron: "I was trying to get it down to him, but I didn't and he hit it good—as he would. When he first hit it, I didn't think it might be going. But like a great hitter, when he picks his pitch, chances are he's going to hit it pretty good."

Pretty good has its final flowering in football on the Sunday of the

Superbowl, when opinion is likely to be general that one reason the winners beat the losers was that they stopped their running game pretty good. The losers might have been able to make up for this even though they were hurting pretty good, meaning that some of their players were injured, if they had got their passing game going pretty good, but they didn't, and that was that: the winners were the world champions.

When the majestic ocean liner the *QE 2* tossed gently in the balmy Atlantic, her engines dead, early in April, 1974, a number of American football players and coaches were aboard, showing films and giving chalk talks as part of the entertainment. One was Hank Stram, coach of the Kansas City Chiefs. Stram told a reporter that after emergency repairs the ship had "moved along pretty good" for thirty minutes. It is necessary to stay in shape during the off-season.

At the 1974 Superbowl, Pat Summerall, in search of a more analytical explanation, attributed the success of the Miami Dolphins' defense to their having "so many different variations," leaving us to suppose that the Minnesota Vikings' defense failed because their variations were uniform. Ray Scott, working with Summerall, told us that Larry Csonka "apparently is injured around his one eye." He may have had Csonka confused with the legendary fullback Cyclops, who helped the Giants defeat the Titans but, unlike Csonka, never played on a world championship team.

World champions—there's another point. Are they really? They are the champions of the National Football League, but they have not played any teams in other leagues. No doubt they could beat them—the others are minor leagues, after all—but that still would not make them world champions. American football is not played in other countries, and it is a little hard to be world champion in a game that is played in your country only. It is as though a Siamese claimed to be world champion in boxing Thai-style, or a Scotsman claimed to be world champion in tossing the caber. World championships require some international competition, and in American-style football there isn't any.

The same is true of the baseball World Series. It may be a series, but it is grandiose to speak of the world. Perhaps it is a harmless conceit, but the American and National leagues do not represent the world, even with two divisions each and a team in Montreal.

The teams aren't usually very good, either. In these days talent is spread so thin by expansion that some players doing regular duty swagger up to the plate with .189 batting averages and nobody thinks there is anything untoward about it. These players are often said to have a way of coming through with timely hits. When you're batting .189, any hit you get is likely to be timely.

Still, whether the World Series is played is determined not by the quality of the teams but by the annual occurrence of October, and again, whatever the quality of the teams, the series must end in seven games or less, which is the sports-page version of seven games or fewer. Equally inescapable is the pre-series analysis, in which the experts, paid and unpaid, compare the opposing sides, weigh their strengths and weaknesses, evaluate their physical condition, take note of the weather, calculate which side has more of that magical substance, momentum, and point out that the breaks can nullify any advantage, that anything can happen in a short series, and that you still have to win them one at a time.

In this arcane atmosphere you may find yourself reading an explanation of why, although Team A's first baseman hits better with men on than Team B's does, Team B's first baseman has more rbis. The explanation is that the man with more rbis (runs batted in, or ribbies to the cognoscenti) has more chances to bat in runs because he came up fourth in the order whereas the other came up sixth. However, the man who batted sixth might have done better had he been allowed to bat in the cleanup position, and indeed he wanted to but allowed himself to be placed in the sixth position for the higher good of the team and an interest-free loan from the club owner.

Even for the most knowing, comparisons are difficult in a time when a manager may platoon left field with four players of different sizes, depending on the height of the outfield grass, but once the experts' analyses are complete, they interview the managers. The answers are purely ritualistic, but nobody minds. It is part of the great fall classic. I will omit the questions and give only the answers.

"Getting runs home is the name of the game, and my boys have shown all year that they can get the runs home."

"Pitching is the name of the game, and we have the pitching."

"I think our rookies will do pretty good."

"I think our veterans will do pretty good. Their records speak for themselves."

"The double play is the name of the game, and our guys can really turn it over."

"Hustle is the name of the game, and nobody is going to outhustle us."

"Pride is the name of the game, and we didn't come this far to lose."

"Kirilenko closed with a rush this season and got his average up to .219, and I look for some real power hitting from him."

"Frelinghuysen has good speed and good power. But we think we can handle him."

"Yes, I think so." (I'd better give the question here. It was "Do you think you can put it all together?")

Putting it all together was identified as the key to success a few years ago, and it has swept all other explanations before it. When the series has ended, it accounts for one team's coming out with the right to fly the championship flag while the other does not. Many things go into putting it all together: pitchers reach back and give it everything they've got; infielders go skyward after errant throws; pivot men in twin killings elude sliding runners (nobody has come up with a synonym for slide); outfielders swing potent bats and scamper to the farthermost barrier to haul in arching blasts, while on the side that did not put it all together outfielders also scamper to the farthermost barrier to haul in arching blasts but swing once-potent bats, now shackled; bloopers barely escape desperate grasps; balls are deposited in the distant seats; heady days of glory are relived; speed on the base paths pays off; somebody trots out his assortment of breaking pitches, to his opponents' almost total frustration; and it is found once more that there is no substitute for the high hard one when the high hard one is needed. And, when starters get into trouble, relief pitchers warm up and the announcers tell us, "There is activity in the bullpen." Ogden Nash once wrote a poem about a relief pitcher named MacTivity so that he could say, "There is MacTivity in the bullpen."

The interview before the World Series closely resembles the spring training season interview. Again it is a two-character affair. The sports writer is named Buck and the manager is named Al. Buck's first question is, "Well, Al, how do you think you'll do this year?" Al is not thrown by this. He says, "Well, I think we'll do pretty good. I think we'll do all right."

Buck follows that up like a hawk. He says, a shade aggressively, "Well, are you predicting the pennant, Al?" Al replies that well, they won it last year, and the other teams are going to have to beat them. He knows one thing: they are not going to beat themselves.

The interview has been under way for about a minute at this point, and nobody has said anything about the name of the game. This is now remedied. Buck asks Al where he thinks his main strength lies, and Al replies that scoring runs is the name of the game and his boys can get the runs home. Buck then says that some people think pitching is the name of the game, and Al says it is, it is, and he thinks his pitchers will do pretty good, but he still has one outstanding need, a reliever who can go at top speed for a full inning without tiring. He has such a man on the roster, a Cuban named Felix Miguel Arbanzas Lopez y Puesto, a real flame thrower, but there is some question about Castro's letting him out and the FBI's letting him in.

Buck asks about right field, normally occupied by High Pockets Kirilenko, a somewhat moody player who (as we know) closed with a rush last season and got his average up to .219. Al says that Kirilenko has good speed and good power, but because of that big .219 average Kirilenko is holding out for a share of the concession revenue, a commitment by the club owner to cover any losses he may sustain on his investments in the stock market, and the services of a hairdresser before each game.

If High Pockets doesn't get in line, Al will try the French Canadian rookie, Willie LaBatt. LaBatt has been up before, but he really shattered the fences in the Australian Instructional League over the winter, and he may be ready. Al also has hopes for his new first baseman, Cy (The Eel) Lamprey, who should be a ballplayer because he grew up in the shadow of Ebbets Field. In fact, Lamprey was lost briefly under the debris when they tore it down, but they dug him out and he looks pretty good.

The team will, however, miss second baseman Ron Larrabee, who had so much range to his left that he crashed into the first-base stands going after a grounder and broke his shoulder at a crucial juncture of last year's pennant race. Larabee is therefore hobbled by injuries and not yet ready.

The interview is approaching its climax. Soon fielding is the name of the game, and so is base running. Buck's last question is whether pride isn't really the name of the game, and whether Al, who has pride, can communicate it to his players. Al replies that if he didn't think he could, he wouldn't be there, and while you never know in baseball, his team has a real good shot. Buck says, "You better believe it," and there, to the regret of all, the interview ends.

There is an alternative ending, more appropriate in some cases—for example, in Al's, since his team made it into the series last year. It is:

"Is your team hungry enough, Al?"

"I don't think a team can ever be hungry enough."

In the closing days of the 1973 baseball season, I watched on television a game between the Pittsburgh Pirates and the Montreal Expos that was delayed by rain several times and for a total of more than three hours. At one point the play-by-play announcer, Jim Simpson, remarked that it was "raining pretty good." He must have been embarrassed because he immediately added, "It's raining pretty hard."

There is no way to measure the destructive effect of sports broadcasting on ordinary American English, but it must be considerable. In the early days sports broadcasting was done, with occasional exceptions such as Clem McCarthy, by nonexperts, announcers. Their knowledge of the sports they described varied, but their English was generally of a high order. If they could not tell you much about the inside of the game they were covering, at any rate what they did tell you you could understand.

Then came the experts, which is to say the former athletes. They could tell you a great deal about the inside, but—again with some exceptions—not in a comprehensible way. They knew the terms the athletes themselves used, and for a while that added color to the broadcasts. But the inside terms were few, and the nonathlete announcers allowed themselves to be hemmed in by them—"He got good wood on that one," "He got the big jump," "He really challenged him on that one," "They're high on him," "They came to play," "He's really got the good hands," and "That has to be," as in "That has to be the best game Oakland ever played."

The effect is deadening on the enjoyment to be had from watching sports on television or reading about them and, since sports make up so large a part of American life and do so much to set its tone, on the language we see and hear around us.

There is one sports announcer who does not go where the former athletes lead him. That is Howard Cosell. Cosell is a phenomenon, or as some have it, phenomena. Nothing can shake him away from his own bromides, of which the supply is unquenchable. Cosell can range from a relative paucity ("Despite the relative paucity of scoring . . .") to a veritable plethora ("Let's continue on this point of this veritable plethora of field goals") without drawing a breath, and there is every reason to believe that when he says "relative paucity" and "veritable plethora" he is not kidding; he means it.

Only Cosell would have described the mood of the crowd at the Bobby Riggs–Billy Jean King match as "an admixture" or remarked that for Riggs "It has not been a comedic night." Only Cosell would speak of a football team "procuring a first down," or say that a fighter was "plagued by minutiae," or that the cards of the referee and judges, made public after each round in a fight in Quebec, "vivified" the problem facing the fighter who was behind. During a Monday night football game nobody else would say, "The Redskins have had two scoring opportunities and failed to avail themselves both times," or that "The mist is drifting over the stadium like a description in a Thomas Hardy novel." At any rate, we may hope that nobody else would say it.

I am far from arguing that the language of athletes and former athletes never adds to the gaiety of the nation. Jake LaMotta, the old middleweight, interviewed long after his fighting days were over, told his questioner that he had no fear of the future because "I got too much growing for me." Another middleweight, Rocky Graziano, during his fighting days was pleased with his reception in the Middle West. He said, "They trutt me right in Chicago." An old ballplayer, Joe Hauser, has the same sort of genius. Near the end of his career, badly slowed down, he was retired on what should have been a single to right. He said with some bitterness, "They trun me out at first."

Joe Jacobs, manager of the German heavyweight Max Schmeling in the 1930s, described his dreamlike condition when a decision unexpectedly went against his man: "I was in a transom." Before their first fight Joe Frazier said of Muhammad Ali, "He don't phrase me," and was right on both counts, and Ali spoke of not being "flustrated," which he rarely was. In one of the disputes over rules at the 1972 Olympics, a United States swimming coach spoke of signing "alphadavits." We would all be poorer without this. . . .

Vocabulary

Cyclops one-eyed mythical monster
caber a pole or beam, especially one thrown as a trial of strength
conceit a strained or bizarre figure of speech
nullify to make void, cancel out
arcane hidden or secret, understood by only a few
cognoscent experts in a field
ritualistic having the nature of, or done as a rite, as in public worship
bromide a trite saying
admixture a thing or ingredient added in mixing; a mixture

Allusions/References

Ogden Nash (1902–1971) U.S. American writer of humorous verse

Discussion

1. Why does Newman repeat "pretty good" so many times in his first six paragraphs? Is it an effective device? What does "pretty good" mean?
2. Look up these pairs of words: less, fewer; phenomenon, phenomena; relative, paucity; veritable, plethora; and different, variations. What is Newman recording these language misuses for anyway? Why is it important that distinctions between words be maintained?
3. As with McMurtry and Angelo, Newman, while recording the language of sports, is also displaying at the same time his own language choices. What does an examination of the following sentence tell you of Newman's facility with the language: the explanation is that the man with more RBIs (runs batted in, or ribbies to the cognoscenti) had more chances to bat in runs because he came up fourth in the order whereas the other came up sixth"? What does "ribbies to the cognoscenti" mean? (See vocabulary)
4. Newman says: "There is no way to measure the destructive effect of sports broadcasting on ordinary American English, but it must be considerable." From radio or television broadcasts or from the sports page of any newspaper, collect your own examples of "sportese." Do these phrases and words enliven or threaten the English language? How many times are the same words and phrases you found repeated in every sports event?
5. Examine Howard Cosell's language as recorded by Newman. What is happening to the language when words such as "procuring," "admixture," and plagued by minutiae" are used in describing a sports event?
6. Newman says at the beginning of this article that he "has a proctective interest in the English language." What does that mean? How do you reconcile his statement with his ending words: "We would all be poorer without this . . ."? Does Newman betray an interest in sports language beyond mere dismay and bordering on amusement? Support your view with Newman's own words. Find sentences, paragraphs, where the tone of this article comes clear to you.

William Saroyan
(1908–1981)

William Saroyan was born August 31, 1908, in Fresno, California, of Armenian parents. He began writing at an early age and produced an enormous amount of work in his lifetime, at times completing one short story a day.

In both his life and his art he preferred the simple and uncultured. Critics rarely accorded him much respect other than as a good storyteller, apparently not finding him "literary" enough. According to the literary critic Edmund Wilson however, Saroyan's "instinctive sense of form usually saves him." Wilson further says: "Saroyan takes you to a bar, and he creates for you there a world which is the way the world would be if it conformed to the feeling instilled by drinks. In a word he achieves the feat of making and keeping us boozy without the use of alcohol and purely by the action of art."

Saroyan apparently could not have cared less what critics thought or said. "I am so innately great that by comparison others who believe they are great or act as if they believe they are great seem to me only pathetic, although occasionally charming."

Meditations on the Letter Z

zzz in the American comic strips both ancient and modern signifies sleep: it is supposed to represent the sound of breathing, the sound of snoring. The sound might be spelled zuzz, but, zzz or zuzz, the sound does not seem to accurately or even unimportantly inaccurately represent the sound of a sleeper's breathing.

Can it be that it has always meant to represent something else? Something like unconsciousness?

If so, why should being asleep be approximated by zzz or zuzz?

Let that rest; it is important, but it is not crucial.

My summing up of zzz in American comic strips is incomplete, for zzz is also the sign of sawing, actual sawing with a saw, through a branch of a tree or through a piece of lumber, but this also connects to sleep, for the breathing of some sleepers sounds like the action of certain saws—inhale, exhale, back and forth, zzz in, zzz out, and so on. Let that also rest.

It is still not important, although sleep itself, to which we move steadily through all of our time, is as important as anything else we have, and it has engaged the thought and speculation of everybody since the beginning of dreams and the remembering of them.

We come out of sleep when we come out of the womb. The mother's mystic body is constant, and all of her tides and tie-ins with everything everywhere are constant in the womb, which is itself the equivalent of the universe and everything unknown about everything, and the first arena of human connection with private and racial sleep.

Coming out of there suggests that we go into something like it again when we stop being out, when we stop breathing, when we put it all away, or permit it all to be put away, and remember nothing, and have no way of guessing what happens after we are gone. We don't even know if the word *gone* is the proper word, for it clearly may not be at all, leaving one's private life in one's private body and one's private adjuncts of the body, mind, memory, soul, leaving the marvelous mechanics of ebb and flow, of breathing, of cellular death and birth, of intake of matter in the form of grass and its byproducts, including flesh of fish, fowl, and animal, leaving the constant chemical action of processing intake to outgo, bread and onion and wine to a light brown outgo, leaving all of it may not be leaving at all. Still, we think of death as a departure, at least from our survivors: anybody dies, he's gone from himself and from everybody else.

A man's relationship to where he has come from and to where he is going is close and intimate, although traditionally mainly ignored: everybody must sleep soon enough during the course of one turn of the apportionment of light and dark, one turn of twenty-four hours; some sleep for ten hours, some for eight, some for six, some for four, and a few for only two, and another two hours in naps.

But whatever the portion of sleep out of the full twenty-four hours may be, nobody goes for very long with his connection to sleep severed—not being able to sleep *does* seem to render the man mad, all his balances and procedures are impaired and he is literally a lunatic.

Birth is birth and death is death no matter how you look at them, most likely, but birth is also death, and consequently death may very well also be birth—the religions certainly must have picked up the hint soon after the picking up of hints became unavoidable.

Zaven Minasian was my mother Takoohi's sister Parrantzie's son, and he died in 1968 in El Paso, at the age of sixty. We were good friends from my eighth year to my twenty-eighth, when he sued *Vanity Fair* for publishing my story "Little Caruso," alleging that my comic view of his ambition to be a Metropolitan Opera star discouraged Eddie Arakelian from financing his singing lessons in New York. I told Frank Crowninshield at lunch that I would pay for any loss sustained by *Vanity Fair*, but the famous editor said such legal actions were commonplace, forget it. In the end the matter was settled out of court for something like $1,000, about half of which went to Zav's lawyer. We were friends because we were precisely the same age, had large ambitions, and shared a compulsion to take great risks and to gamble everything, without reservation—life itself.

I bet my life that if I was not a published writer by the age of thirty, I would be nothing—a full refuser, and for that reason alone likely not to be permitted to live. The story that ended my apprenticeship contains within its swift short form the title: "Application for Permission to Live."

I had good luck.

Zav had good luck, too, for he was never not his own man, at any rate. If he didn't sing in opera, he damned well did in life.

Zav and I also shared a quality of behavior which is described by the word, in the language of our families, *zavzak*. This word calls for a small portion of definition: to begin with, it is not an Armenian word, it is Turkish, but in our family it ceased being Turkish and not only became Armenian, it became Saroyan, it became Zav's word, and my word, and we used it and we knew what it meant, for it was placed *upon us* by our elders to describe the style with which we refused to take anything too seriously, all the while taking nothing at all less than totally seriously, if you can guess about that seeming contradiction.

The Turks pronounce the word nearer to *zevzek* than our *zaavzaak*, but that is also the way languages touch upon one another and stay alive and are given new vitality.

An example of *zavzak* behavior and style might be this: the son of a pompous man of wealth has come to Emerson School in neat expensive shoes while the rest of us are barefooted.

One of us says to him, "Got your shoes on?"

That's all.

That constitutes the style of being *zavzak*.

The boy with the shoes on his feet, surely innocent enough, may not even suspect that he is being ridiculed, and he may smile shyly, whereupon the barefooted boy says, "Your father's got money, has he?"

If the boy also accepts this remark, he is told, "You live in a fine house?"

And then, "Among your ancestors are kings?"

And on and on until the son of the rich man begins to suspect that he is being slowly trussed and put over a fire for roasting.

But the range of *zavzak* behavior is great, and the game has unlimited variation and subtlely. It is never so amusing as when two experts, such as Zav and myself, belittle one another politely.

It is health-giving, of course, and if nothing else causes laughter, and prevents the need of the hired help of a psychiatrist—something no Saroyan would permit because it would seem a foolish bargain to pay money to somebody just to listen to an hour of comic talk. A Saroyan would say to the psychoanalyst, "Got your notebook?" The game would be on, and the racket would be shot.

The order of the kids of Armenak Saroyan and his bride, Takoohi Saroyan, was Cosette, 1899, named after the girl in *Les Miserables*, of course, read by my father, totally unknown to my mother; Zabel, from Isabelle, most likely, but called by all of us Zabe, 1902; Henry, 1905; and myself, 1908.

Siblings fight it out, and why shouldn't they, everybody is unique, and so impossible: thus, Zabe and I got along reasonably well, and Cosette and Henry seemed to understand one another.

Zabe certainly took my side in disputes. When the going was very bad for me and I was trying to improve matters by petty gambling on Third Street in San Francisco, at Breen's Rummy Parlor, and at the Kentucky Club, and at the Barrel House, and I was sweating out not making any sense at all, or having any luck worth a damn, I walked from 348 Carl Street in San Francisco one night to Zabe's house on Fourteenth Avenue in San Francisco, walked very slowly after a full day of gambling and not winning more than a quarter now and then, only to lose it back, and finally not having a nickel for carfare, to get home for a meal of bulgur pilaf with yogurt.

Zabet had heard from the rest of the family that I was gambling, and she had probably been instructed to use her good influence, to the end that I would find a job and start making sense.

Instead of giving me a bad time, however, Zabe placed a silver dollar in my hand, and then asked me to sit down at the kitchen table with her family and have some coffee and homemade apple pie.

That was a big event in my life at that time, and ever after.

Zevart is a word as well as a girl's name: the word means blithe, sunny, wholesome, and in a sense surely it may be said that it means rosy, for the Armenian word for rose is *vart.*

Not everybody is lucky enough to have a blithe nature, but whoever has it can also have all of the black rage that the soul knows and still somehow soon enough be equal to quiet acceptance, resignation, the will, and the ability to move along—in light rather than in darkness. Finally, *zarmonk:* it means wonder.

It is an important Armenian word, both in the church and out of it. One experiences *zarmonk* by both the unaccountably good and magnificent, and the unbelievably bad and destructive: the same astonishment, the same wonder, the same disbelief applies to all opposites. I like that. If you love the sun, you know *zarmonk;* if you hate evil, you experience *zarmonk.*

The sun is wonderful, but, in another way, so is evil.

Someday perhaps I will write about *zahlah,* a very special word, even to an illiterate of Armenian, Turkish, Kurdish, Arabic, Hebrew, and all languages excepting possibly English. It has to do with the pain that comes from being nagged.

Vocabulary

mystic   one who professes to undergo mystical experiences by which he intuitively comprehends truths beyond human understanding
adjuncts   added to, but secondary or not essential

trussed   skewered or bound before cooking
blithe   showing a cheerful disposition

Discussion

1. What is the thread that binds this essay together? Is Saroyan merely rambling?
2. What do such paradoxes as these indicate about Saroyan's thesis: "leaving all of it may not be leaving at all", and "still we think of death as a departure"? "Birth is birth and death is death no matter how you look at them, most likely, but birth is also death, and consequently death may very well also be birth"? How are words important to Saroyan?
3. What are meditations? How is the form of Saroyan's essay like meditation?
4. Meditating about the letter Z takes Saroyan from wondering if the sound of the letter represents unconsciousness to speculation about sleep, to where else?
   Make an outline of the movement of this essay from subject to subject.
5. Saroyan is considered a humorist. How is the juxtaposition of the arcane, the mystical ("the sun is wonderful, but, in another way, so is evil.") with the trite ("it has to do with the pain that comes from being nagged") an illustration of Saroyan's brand of humor?

For Further Discussion

6. Why are words important? To the writer? (This is an impossible question to answer fully as are all important questions. Your speculation might include other selections from this chapter as examples of language itself being the *subject* and not just the *vehicle* for something else—thought.)
7. Note Saroyan's paragraphing. Are the frequent small paragraphs attractive or disturbing to your eye? How are his paragraphs a form for, or an outgrowth of, his meditations?

H. Allen Smith
(1907–1976)

H. Allen Smith was born in McLeansboro, Illinois, on December 19, 1907 and died February 24, 1976. After finishing the eighth grade he became a chicken plucker, then a shoeshine boy. At fifteen he got a job on a newspaper and worked in that field until 1941. He said, "In 1939 I wrote a book and in 1940 I wrote another. Their publication led me to seek employment as a crossing guard for a railroad. Luckily a third book in 1941 was a success."

Like his friends Robert Benchley and James Thurber, Smith was known as a humorist but said, "I prefer to think of myself as a reporter, a reporter with a humorous slant. I am funny only in the sense that the world is funny."

The Ugliest Word

Lullaby. Golden. Damask. Moonlight. Do these words seem aesthetically attractive to you? They have appeared with some regularity on lists of "the ten most beautiful words in our language." Along with *luminous, hush, anemone, mother,* and various others. These lists appear from time to time in the public prints, and there is almost always disagreement among the scholarly people who mine the dictionaries looking for lovely words. Sometimes these disagreements reach a point where ugly words are used. I can't recall ever having seen a list of the ten ugliest words in the language but I do remember that the late Ring Lardner, coming upon one of the beautiful word lists in a newspaper, remarked with chagrin and bitterness: "Why did they leave out *gangrene?*"

The people who assemble these lists actually can't make up their minds what they are after. Is a beautiful word beautiful because of its musical sound or because of the thing it describes? If *moonlight* was the name of the diamond-back rattlesnake, would *moonlight* be considered a romantic-sounding and pretty word? If there were no such word as *mother,* and your mother was your *sludge,* would *sludge* be poetically beautiful? You ask my opinion and I'll tell you that *gangrene* is a downright lovely word, provided you keep your mind off gangrene. You want to hear a *real* ugly word? *Ugly.*

My own choice for the most beautiful word of them all would not appeal to the generality of people; it is a word of glowing, glimmering loveliness and arouses intense feelings of well-being and even sensuality within me. The word is *End.* With a capital "E." As a professional writer of books and magazine articles, I almost swoon with gladness when, on the last page of the third draft of a long manuscript, I write: *The End.* I sit and stare at it, and the longer I do so, the more excruciatingly beautiful it becomes. *Lullaby* my ass! I have left instructions that *The End* be chiseled on my gravestone.

As for ugly words, almost every literate person has in his head an agglomeration of them—words that can cause him to wince, and even shudder, such as *agglomeration.* I lay claim to several hundred of the uglies. *Mulcted* almost nauseates me (as I've indicated in an earlier essay in this book). I cringe in the face of *albeit, and/or, yelept, obsequies, whilom,* and *tinsmith.*

My own nomination for the meanest and low-downdest and ugliest word of them all is *Oh.* Said twice, with maybe a hyphen, this way: *Oh-oh.* In its maximal ugliness, it is customarily spoken softly with inflections that would curl the toes of a South Georgia mule.

Something is wrong, let us say, with the engine of your car. You take it to the garage. The mechanic lifts the hood and pokes around a bit and then you hear him murmur: "Oh-oh." The wretched creature says it in such a restrained dramatic manner that you know instantly that your whole motor has to be derricked out and thrown away and a new one put in.

Oh-oh almost always suggests tragedy, or impending tragedy. I remember standing with another man at a cocktail party when he, glancing across the crowded room, said, "Oh-oh." I followed his gaze. A prominent actor and an equally prominent newspaperman were squaring off, and blows began raining, and a nose was bloodied, and it took some doing to pry the two gentlemen apart.

Consider again our friends the dentists. Most of them have enough gumption to conceal their opinions and judgments, but sometimes you'll run across one who forgets his chairside manner. He'll be inspecting a big molar in the back and suddenly he'll say, "Oh-oh." Or he'll come out of his darkroom carrying an X-ray taken a few minutes earlier, and he'll put it up against the light, and he'll look at it briefly, and then his head will give a jerk and he'll say, "Oh-oh." You know at once, without ESP, precisely what is meant. Out. All of them. From now on, plates. And you know what Aunt Gert says about plates. No apples. No corn on the cob. No a lot of things. You are a captive in the dentist's chair but you feel like busting out of the place and hiding in the woods.

Physicians as a general thing have schooled themselves carefully to conceal any sinister condition they may find during an examination. Yet I have run across one offender in my checkered medical career. He was giving me the annual checkup. He took my blood pressure and tapped me for knee jerks and scratched me on the bottoms of my feet for God knows what and stethoscoped me front and back and had me blow into a machine to test my "vital capacity" and then he turned the electrocardiograph loose on me. As he studied the saw-toothed dossier on my heart, his brow crinkled and I heard him say quite softly but with an undercurrent of alarm, "Oh-oh." Everything inside me suddenly bunched together in one large knot.

"What is it?" I gulped. "Whad you find there?"

"Nothing really," he said. "Nothing important."

Nothing! Cancer of the heart is *nothing?* It had to be that at the very least.

"I heard you say 'Oh-oh,'" I told him. "Come on. Give it to me. I'm a man. I can take it. Let me have it straight."

"Okay," he said, and I steeled myself manfully for seven seconds and then began to turn chicken. He resumed: "I said 'Oh-oh' because I just happened to think that I haven't made out my tax return yet, and the deadline is tomorrow."

I quit him the next day. Took my aches and agues elsewhere. I can't use a doctor who is mooning over his income tax problems while he is looking at the record of my frightful heart disorders. I don't want a doctor *ever* to say "Oh-oh" in my presence, unless perhaps he has dropped his sphygmomanometer on the floor and busted it all to hell. Even in that contingency I think he should employ a more masculine and earthy expression. I surely would.

The saying of "Oh-oh" should be forbidden by federal statute. It is the most frightening, nerve-shattering locution to come into general usage since Noah Webster quit slopping pigs on his father's farm in Connecticut. It is, in fact, so low-down mean in its usual implications that even the dictionaries won't let it in. I scorn it, and deride it, and let my mind dwell on its opposite—that most beautiful of words . . .

Vocabulary

aesthetically   from the point of view of art and beauty
chagrin   annoyance
agglomeration   a jumbled heap, mass
inflections   turns or tone of voice
derricked   moved out by use of rig
agues   chills, fit of shivering
sphygmomanometer   instrument for measuring arterial blood pressure

Allusions/References

ESP   extrasensory perception
Ring Lardner   U.S. sports reporter and American sports humorist (1885–1933)
Noah Webster   U.S. American lexicographer (1758–1843)

Discussion

1. Look up Smith's "ugly" words: mulcted, albeit, yelept, obsequies, whilom, tinsmith. Do their meanings have anything to do with their ugliness? Their shape or form? Their sounds?
   What are some of your votes for "ugly" words? Beautiful words?
2. Upon what criteria would such words as "lullaby, golden, damask, moonlight, luminous, hush, anemone, and mother" be considered beautiful?
   Words are sound. Words are form. Words are meaning. Words are surrounded by emotional response. How is it possible to create an aesthetic around them? Using your list of ugly and beautiful words, describe the rules you generated for yourself in order to select them from all others. Is it possible other words would have been selected if you had used other criteria?
   See Dylan Thomas's "Notes on the Art of Poetry" for a further discussion on the aesthetic of words.
3. What image does "the saw-toothed dossier on my heart" conjure? Find other

examples of Smith choosing words and phrases carefully for entertainment and effect, as well as to illustrate his thesis.

4. According to Smith what is the ugliest word? Is he serious or tongue-in-cheek?

Dylan Thomas
(1914–1953)

Born in Wales in 1914, Thomas was recognized primarily as a poet though his life-style gained him as much fame as his writing. He was known as a rowdy, hard-drinking Irishman. Alcohol, in fact, contributed to his early death in 1953 at age 39.

His writing has been called romantic, sensual, and emotional, and criticized as clumsy, sentimental , and obscure. Many consider him the greatest lyric poet of his generation. Certainly he was a lover of words, of their sounds and rhythms, and used them with rarely equalled passion and grace. (See also ''Reminiscences of Childhood'' Chapter Four, for more biographical information.)

Notes on the Art of Poetry

You want to know why and how I first began to write poetry, and which poets or kind of poetry I was first moved and influenced by.

To answer the first part of this question, I should say I wanted to write poetry in the beginning because I had fallen in love with words. The first poems I knew were nursery rhymes, and before I could read them for myself I had come to love just the words of them, the words alone. What the words stood for, symbolised, or meant, was of very secondary importance; what mattered was the *sound* of them as I heard them for the first time on the lips of the remote and incomprehensible grown-ups who seemed, for some reason, to be living in my world. And these words were, to me, as the notes of bells, the sounds of musical instruments, the noises of wind, sea, and rain, the rattle of milkcarts, the clopping of hooves on cobbles, the fingering of branches on a window pane, might be to someone, deaf from birth, who has miraculously found his hearing. I did not care what the words said, overmuch, nor what happened to Jack & Jill & the Mother Goose rest of them; I cared for the shapes of sound that their names, and the words describing their actions, made in my ears: I cared for the colours the words cast on my eyes. I realise that I may be, as I think back all that way, romanticising my reactions to the simple and beautiful words of those pure poems; but that is all I can honestly remember, however much time might have falsified my memory. I fell in love—that is the only expression I can think of—at once, and am still at the mercy of words, though sometimes now, knowing a little of their behaviour very

well, I think I can influence them slightly and have even learned to beat
them now and then, which they appear to enjoy. I tumbled for words
at once. And, when I began to read the nursery rhymes for myself, and,
later, to read other verses and ballads, I knew that I had discovered the
most important things, to me, that could be ever. There they were,
seemingly lifeless, made only of black and white, but out of them, out
of their own being, came love and terror and pity and pain and wonder
and all the other vague abstractions that make our ephemeral lives dangerous, great, and bearable. Out of them came the gusts and grunts and
hiccups and heehaws of the common fun of the earth; and though
what the words meant was, in its own way, often deliciously funny
enough, so much funnier seemed to me, at that almost forgotten time,
the shape and shade and size and noise of the words as they hummed,
strummed, jigged and galloped along. That was the time of innocence;
words burst upon me, unencumbered by trivial or portentous association; words were their spring-like selves, fresh with Eden's dew, as
they flew out of the air. They made their own original associations as
they sprang and shone. The words, "Ride a cock-horse to Banbury
Cross," were as haunting to me, who did not know then what a cock-
horse was nor cared a damn where Banbury Cross might be, as, much
later, were such lines as John Donne's, "Go and catch a falling star, Get
with child a mandrake root," which also I could not understand when
I first read them. And as I read more and more, and it was not all verse,
by any means, my love for the real life of words increased until I knew
that I must live *with* them and *in* them, always. I knew, in fact, that I
must be a writer of words, and nothing else. The first thing was to feel
and know their sound and substance; what I was going to do with those
words, what use I was going to make of them, what I was going to *say*
through them, would come later. I knew I had to know them most inti-
mately in all their forms and moods, their ups and downs, their chops
and changes, their needs and demands (Here, I am afraid, I am beginning to talk too vaguely. I do not like writing *about* words, because then
I often use bad and wrong and stale and woolly words. What I like to
do is to treat words as a craftsman does his wood or stone or what-have-
you, to hew, carve, mould, coil, polish and plane them into patterns,
sequences, sculptures, fugues of sound expressing some lyrical
impulse, some spiritual doubt or conviction, some dimly-realised truth
I must try to reach and realise.) It was when I was very young, and just
at school, that, in my father's study, before homework that was never
done, I began to know one kind of writing from another, one kind of
goodness, one kind of badness. My first, and greatest, liberty was that
of being able to read everything and anything I cared to. I read indis-
criminately, and with my eyes hanging out. I could never have dreamt
that there were such goings-on in the world between the covers of
books, such sand-storms and ice-blasts of words, such slashing of humbug, and humbug too, such staggering peace, such enormous laughter,

such and so many blinding bright lights breaking across the just-awaking wits and splashing all over the pages in a million bits and pieces all of which were words, words, words, and each of which was alive forever in its own delight and glory and oddity and light.

Vocabulary

abstractions thought, apart from any concrete object (beauty is an abstract word)
ephemeral short-lived, transitory
unencumbered not burdened or hindered
portentous arousing awe or amazement
fugues a flight, a musical form in which a subject is introduced in one voice and developed by counterpoint by each of the other voices

Allusions/References

Eden's dew dew of the garden of Eden, suggests morning, youth, the first blush of paradise itself

Discussion

1. How does Thomas *show* us he loves words and not just *tell* us he does?
2. Examine the following lines: "And these words were, to me, as the notes of bells, the sounds of musical instruments, the noises of wind, sea, and rain, the rattle of milkcarts, the clopping of hooves on cobbles, the fingering of branches on a window pane, might be to someone, deaf from birth, who has miraculously found his hearing." How are the very words onomatopoetic that Thomas uses to talk about sound?
3. Gusts, grunts, hiccups, heehaws. List words that stand out to your eye and ear from Thomas's cobbled prose. (To understand what is meant by "cobbled," imagine each word as a rock on a pebbly beach. How many would "stand out" from grayness, and be collectible?)
4. What does Thomas mean by "That was the time of innocence; words burst upon me, unencumbered by trivial or portentous association ..."? What do you love best, words or ideas?
   When you write, are you trying to get your thoughts into words? Any words? Or are you also, like Thomas in his youth, entranced primarily by the words themselves?
5. What does Thomas mean by his statement he must be "a writer of words and nothing else," that what he was "going to *say* through them—would come later"?
6. Why is writing *about* words so difficult?

Gabriel Marquez
(1928–   )

Gabriel Garcia Marquez was born March 6, 1928, in Aracataca, an isolated area of Colombia. He began writing as a child, inspired by the fabulous stories his grandparents told of the family's history. Through much of his writing career he worked as a journalist, writing and publishing novels and short stories, the value of which even he felt unsure.

With publication of *One Hundred Years of Solitude* in 1967 he has been recognized as among the finest writers in literature. It is "the first piece of literature since the Book of Genesis that should be required reading for the entire human race," wrote William Kennedy in the *National Observer*.

Garcia Marquez has been published in more than twenty languages. Gregory Rabassa, who has translated much of Garcia Marquez's work into English, (including this selection from *One Hundred Years of Solitude*) is said by *The New York Times* to be " . . . one of the best translators who ever drew breath."

The Insomnia Plague

In the meantime, through an oversight that José Arcadio Buendía never forgave himelf for, the candy animals made in the house were still being sold in the town. Children and adults sucked with delight on the delicious little green roosters of insomnia, the exquisite pink fish of insomnia, and the tender yellow ponies of insomnia, so that dawn on Monday found the whole town awake. No one was alarmed at first. On the contrary, they were happy at not sleeping because there was so much to do in Macondo in those days that there was barely enough time. They worked so hard that soon they had nothing else to do and they could be found at three o'clock in the morning with their arms crossed, counting the notes in the waltz of the clock. Those who wanted to sleep, not from fatigue but because of the nostalgia for dreams, tried all kinds of methods of exhausting themselves. They would gather together to converse endlessly, to tell over and over for hours on end the same jokes, to complicate to the limits of exasperation the story about the capon, which was an endless game in which the narrator asked if they wanted him to tell them the story about the capon, and when they answered yes, the narrator would say that he had not asked them to say yes, but whether they wanted him to tell them the story about the capon, and when they answered no, the narrator told them that he had not asked them to say no, but whether they wanted him to tell them the story about the capon, and when they remained silent the narrator told them that he had not asked them to remain silent but whether they wanted him to tell them the story about the capon, and no one could leave because the narrator would say that he had not asked them to leave but whether they wanted him to tell them the story about the capon, and so on and on in a vicious circle that lasted entire nights.

When José Arcadio Buendía realized that the plague had invaded the town, he gathered together the heads of families to explain to them what he knew about the sickness of insomnia, and they agreed on methods to prevent the scourge from spreading to other towns in the swamp. That was why they took the bells off the goats, bells that the Arabs had swapped them for macaws, and put them at the entrance to town at the disposal of those who would not listen to the advice and entreaties of the sentinels and insisted on visiting the town. All strangers who passed through the streets of Macondo at that time had to ring their bells so that the sick people would know that they were healthy. They were not allowed to eat or drink anything during their stay, for there was no doubt but that the illness was transmitted by mouth, and all food and drink had been contaminated by insomnia. In that way they kept the plague restricted to the perimeter of the town. So effective was the quarantine that the day came when the emergency situation was accepted as a natural thing and life was organized in such a way that work picked up its rhythm again and no one worried any more about the useless habit of sleeping.

It was Aureliano who conceived the formula that was to protect them against loss of memory for several months. He discovered it by chance. An expert insomniac, having been one of the first, he had learned the art of silverwork to perfection. One day he was looking for the small anvil that he used for laminating metals and he could not remember its name. His father told him: "Stake." Aureliano wrote the name on a piece of paper that he pasted to the base of the small anvil: *stake*. In that way he was sure of not forgetting it in the future. It did not occur to him that this was the first manifestation of a loss of memory, because the object had a difficult name to remember. But a few days later he discovered that he had trouble remembering almost every object in the laboratory. Then he marked them with their respective names so that all he had to do was read the inscription in order to identify them. When his father told him about his alarm at having forgotten even the most impressive happenings of his childhood, Aureliano explained his method to him, and José Arcadio Buendía put it into practice all through the house and later on imposed it on the whole village. With an inked brush he marked everything with its name: *table, chair, clock, door, wall, bed, pan.* He went to the corral and marked the animals and plants: *cow, goat, pig, hen, cassava, caladium, banana.* Little by little, studying the infinite possibilites of a loss of memory, he realized that the day might come when things would be recognized by their inscriptions but that no one would remember their use. Then he was more explicit. The sign that he hung on the neck of the cow was an exemplary proof of the way in which the inhabitants of Macondo were prepared to fight against loss of memory: *This is the cow. She must be milked every morning so that she will produce milk, and the milk must be boiled in order to be mixed with coffee to make coffee and milk.* Thus they went on living in a reality that was slipping away, momentarily captured by words, but which would escape irremediably when they forgot the values of the written letters.

Vocabulary

capon   a castrated rooster
scourge   affliction (from insomnia, in this instance)
macaws   any of various tropical American parrots
cassava   tropical plant with large starchy root
caladium   tropical plant with showy, variegated foliage

Discussion

1. How are "the delicious little green roosters of insomnia, the exquisite pink fish of insomnia, and the tender yellow ponies of insomnia" better than merely saying "candy animals" (of insomnia)? Notice how the details not only add to your interest and understanding but stimulate your eye and ear. Why does the ear like to hear "of insomnia" repeated? Why does the eye like to see "green roosters," "pink fish," and "yellow ponies?"

2. Count the words that make up the game about the capon. How many sentences? How has Marquez given the reader a labyrinth of words not unlike the capon game itself?

3. How has Marquez not only *told* us about José Arcadio Buendía's "inked brush," but *shown* us his brushstrokes?

For Further Discussion

4. *The words have to do everything.* Aureliano's "formula" demonstrates a critical function of language—as memory of the race. Further in *One Hundred Years of Solitude* the cards are read not to discover the future but to read the past. Examine the last sentence above. What does "a reality . . . momentarily captured by words" mean?
   What implications does it have for the importance of language to humans?

Description:
The Language
of the Senses

"Description" is a kind of writing that attempts in words to convey a picture or experience.

> The incident of the quiche. I took it bubbling from the oven and put it on a burner to cool. Do you want a cup of tea? he asked me. Yes, I said. The next thing I knew I heard glass shatter and he was standing against a wall in the hall. I never knew a pie plate to fly apart like that. I felt bad too seeing all that good food oozing into the coils and rising a column of burnt smoke.

The words of description come from the language of the senses, words that symbolize or stand for what we hear, see, smell, touch, and taste. Our sensual language is particular, rather than abstract. Its words name things we *see*, pie plates, eggs—*hear*, rattle, shatter—*taste*, soot—*smell*, smoke—and *touch*, rubber.

Description is a verbal snapshot. It is an impression in words of scene, sensation, character, and room; of whatever exists in space.

51

Description is rarely found in its pure form since writing, a fluid thing, also takes place in time ("and then what happened?"). Nevertheless, let's look at some snapshots snipped from the pieces that follow in this chapter. Keep your eyes to the words and your ears ready to hear anything. Even Bogie.

"old women with jet-black faces and braided hair"

"old men with work-gnarled hands"

"knickerbockered legs"

"a seat with a chalk circle drawn around it"

"a brown and orange and white plaid mackinaw"

"the groan of a picture on the wall"

"little possumlike looks"

"a tug at an earlobe, a slight squinting of the eyes"

"I don't want 'im bleeding all over my cushions."

In this chapter you get to see with eyes other than your own and hear with other ears. A wondrous privilege of being human, locked in our skins as we are, to experience through words what others have experienced. Dick Gregory and Langston Hughes show us their feeling of shame by taking us into their experience. "He looked right holding a gun," Bogdanovich says of Bogie. Obviously it is a generous act to share experience, the feel of things to us, even though the people of Thomas Wolfe's hometown in North Carolina felt otherwise when they saw themselves thinly veiled in *You Can't Go Home Again*, the novel from which "Tim Wagner" is extracted.

Description has as one of its tenets that: *it is not the fact of the thing that is important but the feel of it.* Remember this when the "two women balloon to the floor" in Fitzgerald's "Tom Buchanan." Remember also, it is all a matter of language. The first stroke of description is a word. You have the words.

Thomas Wolfe
(1900–1938)

Thomas Wolfe was born in Asheville, North Carolina, in 1900. His work was largely autobiographical. He felt all good literature came from the writer's own experience even if facts were altered.

Wolfe's writing was "a torrential and ungovernable flood" focusing on America and the American experience. Editing and condensing his voluminous writing into manageable books was a major task. Wolfe died at age 38 leaving an eight-foot pile of manuscript that his editors turned into two novels, including *You Can't Go Home Again* from which the following is taken.

Tim Wagner

J. Timothy Wagner—the "J" was a recent and completely arbitrary addition of his own, appropriated, no doubt, to fit his ideas of personal grandeur, and to match the eminent position in the town's affairs to which he had belatedly risen—was the black sheep of one of the old, established families in the community. At the time George Webber was a boy, Tim Wagner had been for so long the product of complete disillusion that there was no longer any vestige of respect attached to him.

He had been preëminently the town sot. His title to this office was unquestioned. In this capacity he was even held in a kind of affection. His exploits were notorious, the subjects of a hundred stories. One night, for example, the loafers in McCormack's pharmacy had seen Tim swallow something and then shudder convulsively. This process was repeated several times, until the curiosity of the loafers was aroused. They began to observe him furtively but closely, and in a few minutes Tim thrust out his hand slyly, fumbled around in the gold fish bowl, and withdrew his hand with a wriggling little shape between his fingers. Then the quick swallow and the convulsive shudder were repeated.

He had inherited two fortunes before his twenty-fifth year and had run through them both. Hilarious stories were told of Tim's celebrated pleasure tour upon the inheritance of the second fortune. He had chartered a private car, stocked it plentifully with liquor, and selected as his traveling companions the most notorious sots, vagabonds, and tramps the community could furnish. The debauch had lasted eight months. This party of itinerant bacchuses had made a tour of the entire country. They had exploded their empty flasks against the ramparts of the Rocky Mountains, tossed their empty kegs into San Francisco Bay, strewn the plains with their beer bottles. At last the party had achieved a condition of exhausted satiety in the nation's capital, where Tim, with what was left of his inheritance, had engaged an entire floor at one of the leading hotels. Then, one by one, the exhausted wanderers had drifted back to town, bringing tales of bacchanalian orgies that had not been equaled since the days of the Roman emperors, and leaving Tim finally in solitary possession of the wreckage of empty suites.

From that time on he had slipped rapidly into a state of perpetual sottishness. Even then, however, he had retained the traces of an attractive and engaging personality. Everyone had had a tolerant and unspoken affection for him. Save for the harm he did himself, Tim was an inoffensive and good-natured creature.

His figure on the streets of the town at night had been a familiar one. From sunset on, he might be found almost anywhere. It was easy to tell what progressive state of intoxication he had reached simply by observing his method of locomotion. No one ever saw him stagger. He did not weave drunkenly along the pavement. Rather, when he approached the saturation point, he walked very straight, very rapidly, but with funny little short steps. As he walked he kept his face partly lowered, glancing quickly and comically from side to side, with little possumlike looks. If he approached complete paralysis, he just stood quietly and leaned against something—a lamp post or a doorway or the side of a building or the front of the drug store. Here he would remain for hours in a state of solemn immobility, broken only by an occasional belch. His face, already grown thin and flabby-jowled, with its flaming beacon of a nose, would at these times be composed in an expression of drunken gravity, and his whole condition would be characterized by a remarkable alertness, perceptiveness, and control. He rarely degenerated into complete collapse. Almost always he could respond instantly and briskly to a word of greeting.

Even the police had had a benevolent regard for him, and they had exercised a friendly guardianship over him. Through long experience and observation, every policeman on the force was thoroughly acquainted with Tim's symptoms. They could tell at a glance just what degree of intoxication he had reached, and if they thought he had crossed the final border line and that his collapse in doorway or gutter was imminent, they would take charge of him, speaking to him kindly, but with a stern warning:

"Tim, if you're on the streets again tonight, we're going to lock you up. Now you go on home and go to bed."

To this Tim would nod briskly, with instant and amiable agreement: "Yes, sir, yes, sir. Just what I was going to do, Captain Crane, when you spoke to me. Going home right this minute. Yes, sir."

With these words he would start off briskly across the street, his legs making their little fast, short steps and his eyes darting comically from side to side, until he had vanished around the corner. Within ten or fifteen minutes, however, he might be seen again, easing his way along cautiously in the dark shadow of a building, creeping up to the corner, and peeking around with a sly look on his face to see if any of the watchdogs of the law were in sight.

As time went on and his life lapsed more and more into total vagabondage, one of his wealthy aunts, in the hope that some employment might partially retrieve him, had given him the use of a vacant lot behind some buildings in the business section of the town, a short half block from Main Street. The automobile had now come in sufficient numbers to make parking laws important, and Tim was allowed by his aunt to use this lot as parking space for cars and to keep the money thus obtained. In this employment he succeeded far better than anyone expected. He had little to do except stay on the premises, and this was not difficult for him so long as he was plentifully supplied with corn whiskey.

During this period of his life some canvassers at a local election had looked for Tim to enroll him in the interest of their candidate, but they had been unable to find out where he lived. He had not lived, of course, with any member of his family for years, and investigation failed to disclose that he had a room anywhere. The question then began to go around: "Where does Tim Wagner live? Where does he sleep?" No one could find out. And Tim's own answers, when pressed for information, were slyly evasive.

One day, however, the answer came to light. The automobile had come, and come so thoroughly that people were even getting buried by motor car. The day of the horse-drawn hearse had passed forever. Accordingly, one of the local undertaking firms had told Tim he could have their old horse-drawn hearse if he would only take it off their premises. Tim had accepted the macabre gift and had parked the hearse in his lot. One day when Tim was absent the canvassers came back again, still persistent in their efforts to learn his address so they could enroll him. They noticed the old hearse, and, seeing that its raven curtains were so closely drawn that the interior was hidden from view, they decided to investigate. Cautiously they opened the doors of the hearse. A cot was inside. There was even a chair. It was completely furnished as a small but adequate bedroom.

So at last his secret had been found out. Henceforth all the town knew where he lived.

Vocabulary

sot   a chronic drunkard
debauch   period of dissipation (indulgence in sensual pleasures)
itinerant   traveling from place to place
bacchuses   riotous, drunken friends (from Roman god Bacchus, god of wine)
satiety   full beyond the point of satisfaction
imminent   about to occur, impending
macabre   gruesome, ghastly

Discussion

1. Description has as its intent *to show* the reader something in such a way as to cause the reader to *experience it* (vicariously, of course—and isn't this why film is fun, and safe?). In this wedge of description (out of an eight-foot pile), how is J. Timothy Wagner brought to life for us? Find words and phrases that allow you to "see" him. Find words and phrases that allow you to "hear" him.
2. Figures of speech (metaphors, similes) are often used in good descriptive writing to make comparisons that will recreate for the reader the experi-

ence. Find as many as you can and comment on their effectiveness. For example:

> "Flaming beacon of a nose"—can you *see* it? how would it look? a good metaphor?

> "Party of itinerant bacchuses"—once you have unraveled any difficulty with the vocabulary or the allusion, can you see them? how would they look? an effective comparison?

Get your instructor to help you with this. Perhaps the entire class ought to go on the "hunt." Wolfe's prose is jungley with words (See For Further Discussion), and metaphors, similes, and illusions are concepts not always easily understood at first.

For Further Discussion

3. You might wish to look at sentence length in this piece. Thomas Wolfe wrote in the 1930s when prose had a richer, thicker texture than the lean prose of today. Jack Kerouac, highly influenced by Wolfe, has often been compared to him. Take a long paragraph from each writer to compare and contrast rhythms, word choices, sentence length, attitude toward their material, etc. The paragraph beginning, "His figure on the streets of town . . ." would be an excellent one for Wolfe. Kerouac can be found in Chapter Eight. A selective paragraph from "The Flop Hotel" would afford a good comparison.
4. Another good comparison of "style" might be with F. Scott Fitzgerald following this piece. Fitzgerald, a contemporary of Wolfe's, was not likely to create an eight-foot pile of manuscript. Why not? Compare and contrast Tim Wagner descriptions with Tom Buchanan descriptions. Which author is more interesting to you? Which comes closer to your own way of stringing words on a line?

F. Scott Fitzgerald
(1886–1940)

F. Scott Fitzgerald was born September 24, 1896, and died December 21, 1940. He was raised among the wealthy in St. Paul, Minnesota, and except for fifteen months in the army and four months in an advertising firm, writing was his only occupation.

"You've got to sell your heart," he told a young writer less than three years before his death. And during his lifetime most critics felt he sold his soul as well, wasting his talents writing "pap" for magazines and movies to support a life of high living. At the time of his death at 44 from alcohol and shattered dreams, he left an unfinished novel, *The Last Tycoon,* that was to begin the recognition of Fitzgerald as one of the finest novelists and short story writers in literature.

His novel *The Great Gatsby,* from which the following is taken, is perhaps his best writing, and is considered by some to be the best American novel ever written.

The Buchanan Mansion

And so it happened that on a warm windy evening I drove over to East Egg to see two old friends whom I scarcely knew at all. Their house was even more elaborate than I expected, a cheerful red-and-white Georgian Colonial mansion, overlooking the bay. The lawn started at the beach and ran toward the front door for a quarter of a mile, jumping over sun-dials and brick walks and burning gardens—finally when it reached the house drifting up the side in bright vines as though from the momentum of its run. The front was broken by a line of French windows, glowing now with reflected gold and wide open to the warm windy evening, and Tom Buchanan in riding clothes was standing with his legs apart on the front porch.

He had changed since his New Haven years. Now he was a sturdy straw-haired man of thirty with a rather hard mouth and a supercilious manner. Two shining arrogant eyes had established dominance over his face and gave him the appearance of always leaning aggressively forward. Not even the effeminate swank of his riding clothes could hide the enormous power of that body—he seemed to fill those glistening boots until he strained the top lacing, and you coud see a great pack of muscle shifting when his shoulder moved under his thin coat. It was a body capable of enormous leverage—a cruel body.

His speaking voice, a gruff husky tenor, added to the impression of fractiousness he conveyed. There was a touch of paternal contempt in it, even toward people he liked—and there were men at New Haven who had hated his guts.

"Now, don't think my opinion on these matters is final," he seemed to say, "just because I'm stronger and more of a man than you are." We were in the same senior society, and while we were never intimate I always had the impression that he approved of me and wanted me to like him with some harsh, defiant wistfulness of his own.

We talked for a few minutes on the sunny porch.

"I've got a nice place here," he said, his eyes flashing about restlessly.

Turning me around by one arm, he moved a broad flat hand along the front vista, including in its sweep a sunken Italian garden, a half acre of deep, pungent roses, and a snub-nosed motor-boat that bumped the tide offshore.

"It belonged to Demaine, the oil man." He turned me around again, politely and abruptly. "We'll go inside."

We walked through a high hallway into a bright rosy-colored space, fragilely bound into the house by French windows at either end. The windows were ajar and gleaming white against the fresh grass outside that seemed to grow a little way into the house. A breeze blew through the room, blew curtains in at one end and out the other like pale flags, twisting them up toward the frosted wedding-cake of the ceiling, and then rippled over the wine-colored rug, making a shadow on it as wind does on the sea.

The only completely stationary object in the room was an enormous couch on which two young women were buoyed up as though upon an anchored balloon. They were both in white, and their dresses were rippling and fluttering as if they had just been blown back in after a short flight around the house. I must have stood for a few moments listening to the whip and snap of the curtains and the groan of a picture on the wall. Then there was a boom as Tom Buchanan shut the rear windows and the caught wind died out about the room, and the curtains and the rugs and the two young women ballooned slowly to the floor.

Vocabulary

supercilious   haughty, disdainful
fractiousness   irritable, inclined to make trouble
pungent   penetrating, biting (odor)
buoyed   kept afloat

Allusions/References

Georgian   in a style imitative of the period (1714–1830) of the first four Georges of England

Discussion

1. This piece from *The Great Gatsby* could be seen as two separate but related descriptions: the mansion, and its owner, Tom Buchanan. How do the two compare? How is Buchanan an unlikely owner of the Georgian mansion? (When you go about answering a question of this nature, collect the descriptive words that lend support to your answer. How is Buchanan described? The mansion?)
2. Examine closely the last two paragraphs in the piece for tactile imagery and for sound and motion. How do words such as "rippling and fluttering" and "whip and snap" not only *show* you but let you *hear* the action? What other indications of onomatopoetic words can you find in this piece?
3. Note even more closely the last two sentences. What is the effect on the eye and ear of the words: "groan," "boom," "room," "ballooned," and "floor?" Do you feel a writer is aware of the effects of words beyond their mere meaning, including even their sound and shape printed on the page?

☐

For Further Discussion

4. Notice the rhythmical effects of nouns strung on a line of repeated adjectives and conjunctions: "and the caught wind died out about the room, and the curtains and the rugs and the two young women . . ." Such a construction of parallelism in language could be displayed as follows:

> and the caught wind died out about the room,
>
> and the curtains
>
> and the rugs
>
> and the two young women

What other indications of Fitzgerald's awareness of parallelism, of repetition in words and structure and sounds, can you find in this piece? How effective is it?

5. Fitzgerald once wrote, "All fine prose is based upon the verbs carrying the sentence." What about Fitzgerald's verbs in this brief piece? Analyze any two paragraphs for strong verbs. Does he practice what he preaches?

Peter Bogdanovich
(1939–   )

Peter Bogdanovich has worked as an actor, director, and producer in addition to writing essays and criticism primarily in the area of film. Since age 12 he has collected his opinions of movies he has seen. He is best known for such films as "Paper Moon" and "The Last Picture Show," a film he both wrote and directed. He is quoted as saying "I was born and then I liked movies."

Bogie in Excelsis

Usually he wore the trench coat unbuttoned, just tied with the belt, and a slouch hat, rarely tilted. Sometimes it was a captain's cap and a yachting jacket. Almost always his trousers were held up by a cowboy belt. You know the kind: one an Easterner waiting for a plane out of Phoenix buys just as a joke and then takes a liking to. Occasionally, he'd hitch up his slacks with it, and he often jabbed his thumbs behind it, his hands ready for a fight or a dame.

Whether it was Sirocco or Casablanca, Martinique or Sahara, he was the only American around (except maybe for the girl) and you didn't ask him how he got there, and he always worked alone—except for the fellow who thought he took care of him, the rummy, the piano player, the one *he* took care of, the one you didn't mess with. There was very little he couldn't do, and in a jam he could do anything: remove a slug from a guy's arm, fix a truck that wouldn't start. He was an excellent driver, knowing precisely how to take those curves or how to lose a guy that was tailing him. He could smell a piece of a broken glass and tell you right away if there'd been poison in it, or he could walk into a room and know just where the button was that opened the secret door. At the wheel of a boat, he was beautiful.

His expression was usually sour and when he smiled only the lower lip moved. There was a scar on his upper lip—maybe that's what gave him the faint lisp. He would tug meditatively at his earlobe when he was trying to figure something out and every so often he had a strange little twitch—a kind of backward jerk of the sides of his mouth coupled with a slight squinting of the eyes. He held his cigarette (a Chesterfield) cupped in his hand. He looked right holding a gun.

Unsentimental was a good word for him. "Leave 'im where he is," he might say to a woman whose husband has just been wounded, "I don't want 'im bleeding all over my cushions." And blunt: "I don't like you. I don't like your friends and I don't like the idea of her bein' married to you." And straight: "When a man's partner is killed he's supposed to do something about it. It doesn't make any difference what you thought of him. He was your partner and you're supposed to do something about it."

He was tough; he could stop you with a look or a line. "Go ahead, slap *me*," he'd say, or, "That's right, *go* for it," and there was in the way he said it just the right blend of malice, gleeful anticipation and the promise of certain doom. He didn't like taking orders. Or favors. It was smart not to fool around with him too much.

As far as the ladies were concerned, he didn't have too much trouble with them, except maybe keeping them away. It was the girl who said if he needed anything, all he had to do was whistle; he never said that to the girl. Most of the time he'd call her "angel," and if he liked her he'd tell her she was "good, awful good."

Whatever he was engaged in, whether it was being a reporter, a saloon-keeper, a gangster, a detective, a fishing-boat owner, a D.A. or a lawyer, he was impeccably, if casually, a complete professional. "You take chances," someone would say. "I get paid to," was his answer. But he never took himself too seriously. What was his job, a girl would ask. Conspiratorially, he'd lean in and say with the slightest flicker of a grin, "I'm a private dick on a case." He wasn't going to be taken in by Art either; he'd been to college, but he was a bit suspicious of the intellectuals. If someone mentioned Proust, he'd ask, "Who's he?" even though he knew.

Finally, he was wary of Causes. He liked to get paid for taking chances. He was a man who tried very hard to be Bad because he knew it was easier to get along in the world that way. He always failed because of an innate goodness which surely nauseated him. Almost always he went from belligerent neutrality to reluctant commitment. From: "I stick my neck out for nobody." To: "I'm no good at being noble, but it doesn't take much to see that the problems of three little people don't amount to a hill o'beans in this crazy world." At the start, if the question was, "What are your sympathies?", the answer was invariably, "Minding my own business." But by the end, if asked why he was helping, risking his life, he might say, "Maybe 'cause I like you. Maybe 'cause I don't like them." Of course it was always "maybe" because he wasn't going to be that much of a sap, wasn't making any speeches, wasn't going to be a Good guy. Probably he rationalized it: "I'm just doing my job." But we felt good inside. We knew better.

Discussion

1. Description is a language of the senses. Which of the senses are primarily evoked in Bogdanovich's description of Bogie? Find examples of each.
2. Explore more fully the sense of sound. What do you *hear* in this piece? "Hill o' beans," "private dick," "sap," are words that add authenticity to Bogdanovich's portrait of Bogie's character (or characterizations). What others like this can you find in the piece?
3. Read Bogie's dialogue separate from Bogdanovich's descriptions of him. Can you describe the difference in Bogdanovich's voice, diction, from that of Bogie's? What does this indicate about a writer's (Bogdanovich's) "ear"?
4. Better to show than to tell is a rule writers follow. How does Bogdanovich bring Bogie alive for us, *show* us Bogie, rather than merely *tell* us about him?
5. Bogdanovich's original title for this piece was "An Authentic American Hero." Why do you suppose he changed it to "Bogie in Excelsis"? What does the current title mean?

For Further Discussion

6. Although this is an excerpt from a longer piece, you may wish to attempt an analysis of structure. What is the unifying principle in this piece? How does Bogdanovich progress from his first stroke of description to his last paragraph about Bogie? (Count out the number of paragraphs and in a sentence or two indicate the focus of each.)

Langston Hughes
(1902–1967)

Langston Hughes was born in Joplin, Missouri. Though known primarily as a poet, he also wrote novels, short stories, plays, operas, song lyrics, translations, and children's books. He came to prominence in the 1920s during the "Harlem Renaissance," and was known (and often criticized) for his simple, humorous approach which made use of black dialects and the sounds and rhythms of blues and jazz.

Hughes said he wrote about "workers, roustabouts, and singers and job hunters . . . people up today and down tomorrow, working this week and fired the next, beaten and baffled, but determined not to be wholly beaten . . ."

Salvation

I was saved from sin when I was going on thirteen. But not really saved. It happened like this. There was a big revival at my Auntie Reed's church. Every night for weeks there had been much preaching, singing, praying, and shouting, and some very hardened sinners had been brought to Christ, and the membership of the church had grown by leaps and bounds. Then just before the revival ended, they held a special meeting for children, "to bring the young lambs to the fold." My aunt spoke of it for days ahead. That night I was escorted to the front row and placed on the mourner's bench with all the other young sinners, who had not yet been brought to Jesus.

My aunt told me that when you were saved you saw a light, and something happened to you inside! And Jesus came into your life! And God was with you from then on! She said you could see and hear and feel Jesus in your soul. I believed her. I have heard a great many old people say the same thing and it seemed to me they ought to know. So I sat there calmly in the hot, crowded church, waiting for Jesus to come to me.

The preacher preached a wonderful rhythmical sermon, all moans and shouts and lonely cries and dire pictures of hell, and then he sang a song about the ninety and nine safe in the fold, but one little lamb was left out in the cold. Then he said: "Won't you come?" And he held out his arms to all us young sinners there on the mourners' bench. And the little girls cried. And some of them jumped up and went to Jesus right away. But most of us just sat there.

A great many old people came and knelt around us and prayed, old women with jet-black faces and braided hair, old men with work-gnarled hands. And the church sang a song about the lower lights are burning, some poor sinners to be saved. And the whole building rocked with prayer and song.

Still I kept waiting to *see* Jesus.

Finally all the young people had gone to the altar and were saved, but one boy and me. He was a rounder's son named Westley. Westley and I were surrounded by sisters and deacons praying. It was very hot in the church, and getting late now. Finally Westley said to me in a whisper: "God damn! I'm tired o' sitting here. Let's get up and be saved." So he got up and was saved.

Then I was left all alone on the mourners' bench. My aunt came and knelt at my knees and cried, while prayers and songs swirled all around me in the little church. The whole congregation prayed for me alone, in a mighty wail of moans and voices. And I kept waiting serenely for Jesus, waiting, waiting—but he didn't come. I wanted to see him, but nothing happened to me. Nothing! I wanted something to happen to me, but nothing happened.

I heard the songs and the minister saying: " Why don't you come? My dear child, why don't you come to Jesus? Jesus is waiting for you. He wants you. Why don't you come? Sister Reed, what is this child's name?"

"Langston," my aunt sobbed.

"Langston, why don't you come? Why don't you come and be saved? Oh, Lamb of God! Why don't you come?"

Now it was really getting late. I began to be ashamed of myself, holding everything up so long. I began to wonder what God thought about Westley, who certainly hadn't seen Jesus either, but who was now sitting proudly on the platform, swinging his knickerbockered legs and grinning down at me, surrounded by deacons and old women on their knees praying. God had not struck Westley dead for taking his name in vain or for lying in the temple. So I decided that maybe to save further trouble, I'd better lie, too and say that Jesus had come, and get up and be saved.

So I got up.

Suddenly the whole room broke into a sea of shouting, as they saw me rise. Waves of rejoicing swept the place. Women leaped in the air. My aunt threw her arms around me. The minister took me by the hand and led me to the platform.

When things quieted down, in a hushed silence, punctuated by a few ecstatic "Amens," all the new young lambs were blessed in the name of God. Then joyous singing filled the room.

That night, for the last time in my life but one—for I was a big boy twelve years old—I cried. I cried, in bed alone, and couldn't stop. I buried my head under the quilts, but my aunt heard me. She woke up and told my uncle I was crying because the Holy Ghost had come into my life, and because I had seen Jesus. But I was really crying because I couldn't bear to tell her that I had lied, that I had deceived everybody in the church, that I hadn't seen Jesus, and that now I didn't believe there was a Jesus any more, since he didn't come to help me.

Vocabulary

rounder a Methodist preacher who travels a circuit among his congregations

Discussion

1. How is Hughes's writing very like the "wonderful rhythmical sermon" of the preacher? What elements of repetition and sentence length contribute

toward the rhythm of this piece? (Examine the repetition of the phrase "won't you come", for starters.)

2. A pivotal moment in the piece is the paragraph containing the single sentence "So I got up." Why one sentence? How effective is this? How is the paragraph that follows a counterpoint to this one?

3. Examine the "little lamb" metaphor throughout the piece. How is the boy, Langston, identified as that lamb "left out in the cold"? (Other traditional altar call hymns are included in this piece. Can you identify them? How effective is it to *hear* these pieces rather than merely to be *told* hymns were sung?

For Further Discussion

4. Hughes is not the only writer to use the sounds and rhythms of blues and jazz in his writing. Read Kerouac's "Frisco Jazz" for another expression of writing as sound experience related to music.

   What music do you listen to? Can you write a description paper, not about music, but with the rhythms of your heard music infusing the piece? You will want to consider the length of an "idea," the words as notes/sounds to repeat and vary, the silences, or spaces on the page. This is not easy. Good luck.

Dick Gregory
(1932–   )

Raised in poverty, Gregory was able to attend college on a track scholarship. After two years in the army he began a career as a comedian, supporting himself largely by odd jobs. In the early 1960s his career took off and he became known for his humor which focused on social/political issues like segregation and poverty. As his fame grew, so did his involvement in social and political activism, to the point he no longer works as an entertainer.

He has written several books, mostly autobiographical. This piece was taken from his second book, *Nigger,* an autobiography.

Shame

I never learned hate at home, or shame. I had to go to school for that. I was about seven years old when I got my first big lesson. I was in love with a little girl named Helene Tucker, a light-complected little girl with pigtails and nice manners. She was always clean and she was smart in school. I think I went to school then mostly to look at her. I brushed my hair and even got me a little old handkerchief. It was a lady's handkerchief, but I didn't want Helene to see me wipe my nose on my hand. The pipes were frozen again, there was no water in the house, but I washed my socks and shirt every night. I'd get a pot, and go over to Mister Ben's grocery store, and stick my pot down into his soda machine. Scoop out some chopped ice. By evening the ice melted to water for washing. I got sick a lot that winter because the fire would go out at night before the clothes were dry. In the morning I'd put them on, wet or dry, because they were the only clothes I had.

Everybody's got a Helene Tucker, a symbol of everything you want. I loved her for her goodness, her cleanness, her popularity. She'd walk down my street and my brothers and sister would yell, "Here comes Helene," and I'd rub my tennis sneakers on the back of my pants and wish my hair wasn't so nappy and the white folks' shirt fit me better. I'd run out on the street. If I knew my place and didn't come too close, she'd wink at me and say hello. That was a good feeling. Sometimes I'd follow her all the way home, and shovel the snow off her walk and try to make friends with her Momma and her aunts. I'd drop money on her stoop late at night on my way back from shining shoes in the taverns. And she had a Daddy, and he had a good job. He was a paper hanger.

I guess I would have gotten over Helene by summertime, but something happened in that classroom that made her face hang in front of me for the next twenty-two years. When I played the drums in high school it was for Helene and when I broke track records in college it was for Helene and when I started standing behind microphones and heard applause I wished Helene could hear it, too. It wasn't until I was twenty-nine years old and married and making money that I finally got her out of my system. Helene was sitting in that classroom when I learned to be ashamed of myself.

It was on a Thursday. I was sitting in the back of the room, in a seat with a chalk circle drawn around it. The idiot's seat, the trouble-maker's seat.

The teacher thought I was stupid. Couldn't spell, couldn't read, couldn't do arithmetic. Just stupid. Teachers were never interested in finding out that you couldn't concentrate because you were so hungry, because you hadn't had any breakfast. All you could think about was noontime, would it ever come? Maybe you could sneak into the cloak-room and steal a bite of some kid's lunch out of a coat pocket. A bite of something. Paste. You can't really make a meal of paste, or put it on bread for a sandwich, but sometimes I'd scoop a few spoonfuls out of the big paste jar in the back of the room. Pregnant people get strange tastes. I was pregnant with poverty. Pregnant with dirt and pregnant with smells that made people turn away, pregnant with cold and pregnant with shoes that were never bought for me, pregnant with five other people in my bed and no Daddy in the next room and pregnant with hunger. Paste doesn't taste too bad when you're hungry.

The teacher thought I was a troublemaker. All she saw from the front of the room was a little black boy who squirmed in his idiot's seat and made noises and poked the kids around him. I guess she couldn't see a kid who made noises because he wanted someone to know he was there.

It was on a Thursday, the day before the Negro payday. The eagle always flew on Friday. The teacher was asking each student how much his father would give to the Community Chest. On Friday night, each kid would get the money from his father, and on Monday he would bring it to the school. I decided I was going to buy me a Daddy right then. I had money in my pocket from shining shoes and selling papers, and whatever Helene Tucker pledged for her Daddy I was going to top it. And I'd hand the money right in. I wasn't going to wait until Monday to buy me a Daddy.

I was shaking, scared to death. The teacher opened her book and started calling out names alphabetically.

"Helene Tucker?"

"My Daddy said he'd give two dollars and fifty cents."

"That's very nice, Helene. Very, very nice indeed."

That made me feel pretty good. It wouldn't take too much to top that. I had almost three dollars in dimes and quarters in my pocket. I stuck my hand in my pocket and held onto the money, waiting for her to call my name. But the teacher closed her book after she called everybody else in the class.

I stood up and raised my hand.

"What is it now?"

"You forgot me."

She turned toward the blackboard. "I don't have time to be playing with you, Richard."

"My Daddy said he'd . . ."

"Sit down, Richard, you're disturbing the class."

"My Daddy said he'd give . . . fifteen dollars."

She turned around and looked mad. "We are collecting this money for you and your kind, Richard Gregory. If your Daddy can give fifteen dollars you have no business being on relief."

"I got it right now, I got it right now, my Daddy gave it to me to turn in today, my Daddy said . . ."

"And furthermore," she said, looking right at me, her nostrils getting big and her lips getting thin and her eyes opening wide. "We know you don't have a Daddy."

Helene Tucker turned around, her eyes full of tears. She felt sorry for me. Then I couldn't see her too well because I was crying, too.

"Sit down, Richard."

And I always thought the teacher kind of liked me. She always picked me to wash the blackboard on Friday, after school. That was a big thrill, it made me feel important. If I didn't wash it, come Monday the school might not function right.

"Where are you going, Richard?"

□

I walked out of school that day, and for a long time I didn't go back very often. There was shame there.

Now there was shame everywhere. It seemed like the whole world had been inside that classroom, everyone had heard what the teacher had said, everyone had turned around and felt sorry for me. There was shame in going to the Worthy Boys Annual Christmas Dinner for you and your kind, because everybody knew what a worthy boy was. Why couldn't they just call it the Boys Annual Dinner, why'd they have to give it a name? There was shame in wearing the brown and orange and white plaid mackinaw the welfare gave to 3,000 boys. Why'd it have to be the same for everybody so when you walked down the street the people could see you were on relief? It was a nice warm mackinaw and it had a hood, and my Momma beat me and called me a little rat when she found out I stuffed it in the bottom of a pail full of garbage way over on Cottage Street. There was shame in running over to Mister Ben's at the end of the day and asking for his rotten peaches, there was shame in asking Mrs. Simmons for a spoonful of sugar, there was shame in running out to meet the relief truck. I hated that truck, full of food for you and your kind. I ran into the house and hid when it came. And then I started to sneak through alleys, to take the long way home so the people going into White's Eat Shop wouldn't see me. Yeah, the whole world heard the teacher that day, we all know you don't have a Daddy.

It lasted for a while, this kind of numbness. I spent a lot of time feeling worry for myself. And then one day I met this wino in a restaurant. I'd been out hustling all day, shining shoes, selling newspapers, and I had googobs of money in my pocket. Bought me a bowl of chili for fifteen cents, and a cheeseburger for fifteen cents, and a Pepsi for five cents, and a piece of chocolate cake for ten cents. That was a good meal. I was eating when this old wino came in. I love winos because they never hurt anyone but themselves.

The old wino sat down at the counter and ordered twenty-six cents worth of food. He ate it like he really enjoyed it. When the owner, Mister Williams, asked him to pay the check, the old wino didn't lie or go through his pocket like he suddenly found a hole.

He just said: "Don't have no money."

The owner yelled: "Why in hell you come in here and eat my food if you don't have no money? That food cost me money."

Mister Williams jumped over the counter and knocked the wino off his stool and beat him over the head with a pop bottle. Then he stepped back and watched the wino bleed. Then he kicked him. And he kicked him again.

I looked at the wino with blood all over his face and I went over. "Leave him alone, Mister Williams. I'll pay the twenty-six cents."

The wino got up, slowly, pulling himself up to the stool, then up to the counter, holding on for a minute until his legs stopped shaking so bad. He looked at me with pure hate. "Keep your twenty-six cents. You don't have to pay, not now. I just finished paying for it."

He started to walk out, and as he passed me, he reached down and touched my shoulder. "Thanks, sonny, but it's too late now. Why didn't you pay it before?"

I was pretty sick about that. I waited too long to help another man.

Vocabulary

nappy   curly, fuzzy
mackinaw   a wool jacket, usually plaid

Discussion

1. Gregory does not merely *tell* us what happened in the classroom to make him experience shame, he *shows* us, by recreating the experience. Examine how the sensory detail (what was seen, heard, tasted, touched, or smelled) contributes toward giving the reader the sensation of having shared in Gregory's experience.
2. Good descriptive writing does not only want the reader to *know* what happened, but to *feel* it too. Which details contribute to giving you the sensation of "feeling" Gregory's shame?
3. What is the function of the first three paragraphs?
4. Why does Gregory include the story of the wino at the end? How is this incident related to the Helene story? Would it have been better to leave the wino story out?
5. While dialogue, "my daddy said . . . ," and word choice, "googobs," give the reader the sensation of sound, the rhythm of a piece also contributes to its overall sound and sense. Examine the rhythm of the third paragraph beginning "I guess I would have gotten over Helene . . ." How does sentence length contribute to rhythm? How effective is the repetition of "Helene"?
6. Examine also the rhythm of the fifth paragraph beginning: "The teacher thought I was stupid." Why are "A bite of something" and "Paste" punctuated as sentences? (How is rhythm affected by these staccato notes?)
7. How effective is Gregory's metaphorical use of the word "pregnant"? How does the word *sound* repeated as it is eight times? (Notice the juxtaposition of similar words/sounds in "people," "poverty," "paste," and even "dirt.")

Narration: To Tell What Happened

☐ The Spoken Voice

Phemius sang such fine tales that Odysseus spared the storyteller when he killed Penelope's suitors in the Great Hall. A good narrator is hard to find.

We think little of the words we use and hear each day. We get the message we hang up the phone. Yet in earlier times, before the masses could read and write, the spoken language was everything, to some even an art. Today descriptive linguists tell us the spoken language is *the* language. Change in language, which the linguists further tell us is constant and normal, comes from usage. Think of how language is used. Do you think enough about it? Imagine practicing how to talk, rolling l's off your tongue in a mirror. Not such an absurd idea when you really consider how important and how beautiful are the sounds and performance of language.

69

In the following selections you will read recorded spoken words. Black Elk speaks from a great oral tradition. Vanzetti's "Apology," recorded by the court, retains the sounds of his cracked English and the intimacy of a voice in the ear. Maxine Hong Kingston, a writer, captures in the written form the exact sound of her "immigrant" voice.

In each case the written word has preserved these voices for us in their inflection, emotionalism and pitch—as closely as words on a page can approximate such things. Tune your ear to what you are hearing here and all around you. All writing is improved by the heartblood of speech. And all speech is improved by a mouth with an ear in it.

Black Elk
(1863–1950)

Black Elk was born in December 1863 alongside the Little Powder River in Dakota territory. He died in 1950, having lived through the destruction of the Indian Nations in the late 1800s and the intervening years of fading dreams. Black Elk was an Oglala Sioux holy man. His visions and accounts of the Oglala Sioux have been recorded in two books: *Black Elk Speaks,* with John G. Neihardt and *The Sacred Pipe,* with Joseph Epes Brown.

In *Black Elk Speaks* (excerpted below) John G. Neihardt, poet and Indian scholar, records Black Elk's words to "save his great vision for men." "It was my function to translate the old man's story," wrote Neihardt, "not only in the factual sense—for it was not the facts that mattered most—but rather to recreate in English the mood and manner of the old man's narrative."

"This they tell," Black Elk says at the end of one of his stories, "and whether it happened so or not I do not know; but if you think about it, you can see that it is true."

High Horse's Courting

You know, in the old days, it was not so very easy to get a girl when you wanted to be married. Sometimes it was hard work for a young man and he had to stand a great deal. Say I am a young man and I have seen a young girl who looks so beautiful to me that I feel all sick when I think about her. I can not just go and tell her about it and then get married if she is willing. I have to be a very sneaky fellow to talk to her at all, and after I have managed to talk to her, that is only the beginning.

Probably for a long time I have been feeling sick about a certain girl because I love her so much, but she will not even look at me, and her parents keep a good watch over her. But I keep feeling worse and worse all the time; so maybe I sneak up to her tepee in the dark and wait until she comes out. Maybe I just wait there all night and don't get any sleep at all and she does not come out. Then I feel sicker than ever about her.

Maybe I hide in the brush by a spring where she sometimes goes to get water, and when she comes by, if nobody is looking, then I jump out and hold her and just make her listen to me. If she likes me too, I can tell that from the way she acts, for she is very bashful and maybe will not say a word or even look at me the first time. So I let her go, and then maybe I sneak around until I can see her father alone, and I tell him how many horses I can give him for his beautiful girl, and by now I am feeling so sick that maybe I would give him all the horses in the world if I had them.

Well, this young man I am telling about was called High Horse, and there was a girl in the village who looked so beautiful to him that he was just sick all over from thinking about her so much and he was getting sicker all the time. The girl was very shy, and her parents thought a great deal of her because they were not young anymore and this was the only child they had. So they watched her all day long, and they fixed it so that she would be safe at night too when they were asleep. They thought so much of her that they had made a rawhide bed for her to sleep in, and after they knew that High Horse was sneaking around after her, they took rawhide thongs and tied the girl in bed at night so that nobody could steal her when they were asleep, for they were not sure but that their girl might really want to be stolen.

Well, after High Horse had been sneaking around a good while and hiding and waiting for the girl and getting sicker all the time, he finally caught her alone and made her talk to him. Then he found out that she liked him maybe a little. Of course this did not make him feel well. It made him sicker than ever, but now he felt as brave as a bison bull, and so he went right to her father and said he loved the girl so much that he would give two good horses for her—one of them young and the other not so very old.

But the old man just waved his hand, meaning for High Horse to go away and quit talking foolishness like that.

High Horse was feeling sicker than ever about it; but there was another young fellow who said he would loan High Horse two ponies and when he got some more horses, why, he could just give them back for the ones he had borrowed.

Then High Horse went back to the old man and said he would give four horses for the girl—two of them young and the other two not hardly old at all. But the old man just waved his hand and would not say anything.

So High Horse sneaked around until he could talk to the girl again, and he asked her to run away with him. He told her he thought he would just fall over and die if she did not. But she said she would not do that; she wanted to be bought like a fine woman. You see she thought a great deal of herself too.

That made High Horse feel so very sick that he could not eat a bite, and he went around with his head hanging down as though he might just fall down and die any time.

Red Deer was another young fellow, and he and High Horse were great comrades, always doing things together. Red Deer saw how High Horse was acting, and he said: "Cousin, what is the matter? Are you sick in the belly? You look as though you were going to die."

Then High Horse told Red Deer how it was, and said he thought he could not stay alive much longer if he could not marry the girl pretty quick.

Red Deer thought awhile about it, and then he said: "Cousin, I have a plan, and if you are man enough to do as I tell you, then everything will be all right. She will not run away with you; her old man will not take four horses; and four horses are all you can get. You must steal her and run away with her. Then afterwhile you can come back and the old man cannot do anything because she will be your woman. Probably she wants you to steal her anyway."

So, they planned what High Horse had to do, and he said he loved the girl so much that he was man enough to do anything Red Deer or anybody else could think up.

So this is what they did.

That night late they sneaked up to the girl's tepee and waited until it sounded inside as though the old man and the old woman and the girl were sound asleep. Then High Horse crawled under the tepee with a knife. He had to cut the rawhide thongs first, and then Red Deer, who was pulling up the stakes around that side of the tepee, was going to help drag the girl outside and gag her. After that, High Horse could put her across his pony in front of him and hurry out of there and be happy all the rest of his life.

When High Horse had crawled inside, he felt so nervous that he could hear his heart drumming, and it seemed so loud he felt sure it would waken the old folks. But it did not, and afterwhile he began cutting the thongs. Every time he cut one it made a pop and nearly scared him to death. But he was getting along all right and all the thongs were cut down as far as the girl's thighs, when he became so nervous that his knife slipped and stuck the girl. She gave a big, loud yell. Then the old folks jumped up and yelled too. By this time High Horse was outside, and he and Red Deer were running away like antelope. The old man and some other people chased the young men but they got away in the dark and nobody knew who it was.

Well, if you ever wanted a beautiful girl you will know how sick High Horse was now. It was very bad the way he felt, and it looked as though he would starve even if he did not drop over dead sometime.

Red Deer kept thinking about this, and after a few days he went to High Horse and said: "Cousin, take courage! I have another plan, and I am sure, if you are man enough, we can steal her this time." And High

Horse said: "I am man enough to do anything anybody can think up, if I can only get that girl."

So this is what they did.

They went away from the village alone, and Red Deer made High Horse strip naked. Then he painted High Horse solid white all over, and after that he painted black stripes all over the white and put black rings around High Horse's eyes. High Horse looked terrible. He looked so terrible that when Red Deer was through painting and took a good look at what he had done, he said it scared even him a little.

"Now," Red Deer said, "if you get caught again, everybody will be so scared they will think you are a bad spirit and will be afraid to chase you."

So when the night was getting old and everybody was sound asleep, they sneaked back to the girl's tepee. High Horse crawled in with his knife, as before, and Red Deer waited outside, ready to drag the girl out and gag her when High Horse had all the thongs cut.

High Horse crept up by the girl's bed and began cutting at the thongs. But he kept thinking, "If they see me they will shoot me because I look so terrible." The girl was restless and kept squirming around in bed, and when a thong was cut, it popped. So High Horse worked very slowly and carefully.

But he must have made some noise, for suddenly the old woman awoke and said to her old man: "Old Man, wake up! There is somebody in this tepee!" But the old man was sleepy and didn't want to be bothered. He said: "Of course there is somebody in this tepee. Go to sleep and don't bother me." Then he snored some more.

But High Horse was so scared by now that he lay very still and as flat to the ground as he could. Now, you see, he had not been sleeping very well for a long time because he was so sick about the girl. And while he was lying there waiting for the old woman to snore, he just forgot everything, even how beautiful the girl was. Red Deer who was lying outside ready to do his part, wondered and wondered what had happened in there, but he did not dare call out to High Horse.

Afterwhile the day began to break and Red Deer had to leave with the two ponies he had staked for his comrade and girl, or somebody would see him.

So he left.

Now when it was getting light in the tepee, the girl awoke and the first thing she saw was a terrible animal, all white with black stripes on it, lying asleep beside her bed. So she screamed, and then the old woman screamed and the old man yelled. High Horse jumped up, scared almost to death, and he nearly knocked the tepee down getting out of there.

People were coming running from all over the village with guns and bows and axes, and everybody was yelling.

By now High Horse was running so fast that he hardly touched the ground at all, and he looked so terrible that the people fled from him and let him run. Some braves wanted to shoot at him, but the others said he might be some sacred being and it would bring bad trouble to kill him.

High Horse made for the river that was near, and in among the brush he found a hollow tree and dived into it. Afterwhile some braves came there and he could hear them saying that it was some bad spirit that had come out of the water and gone back in again.

That morning the people were ordered to break camp and move away from there. So they did, while High Horse was hiding in his hollow tree.

Now Red Deer had been watching all this from his own tepee and trying to look as though he were as much surprised and scared as all the others. So when the camp moved, he sneaked back to where he had seen his comrade disappear. When he was down there in the brush, he called, and High Horse answered, because he knew his friend's voice. They washed off the paint from High Horse and sat down on the river bank to talk about their troubles.

High Horse said he never would go back to the village as long as he lived and he did not care what happened to him now. He said he was going to go on the war-path all by himself. Red Deer said: "No, cousin, you are not going on the war-path alone, because I am going with you."

So Red Deer got everything ready, and at night they started out on the war-path all alone. After several days they came to a Crow camp just about sundown, and when it was dark they sneaked up to where the Crow horses were grazing, killed the horse guard, who was not thinking about enemies because he thought all the Lakotas were far away, and drove off about a hundred horses.

They got a big start because all the Crow horses stampeded and it was probably morning before the Crow warriors could catch any horses to ride. Red Deer and High Horse fled with their herd three days and nights before they reached the village of their people. Then they drove the whole herd right into the village and up in front of the girl's tepee. The old man was there, and High Horse called out to him and asked if he thought maybe that would be enough horses for his girl. The old man did not wave him away that time. It was not the horses that he wanted. What he wanted was a son who was a real man and good for something.

So High Horse got his girl after all, and I think he deserved her.

Vocabulary

bison bull   buffalo

Discussion

1. Black Elk was not a writer per se, but a storyteller and spiritual leader. While "High Horse's Courting" is Black Elk's story, it is John G. Neihardt who is responsible for recording it in written form. How is the oral voice still conveyed in this piece much more strongly than in primarily *written* pieces? Notice even the opening phrase, "You know . . ." Might that have been edited out of a written piece?
2. What is the function of Black Elk's opening to his tale? (The first three paragraphs?)
3. Notice transitions from one part of Black Elk's story to another part. How are there indications in these transitions of his need to keep his listeners involved? Notice particularly transitions such as, "So this is what they did." Or, "Well if you ever wanted a beautiful girl you will know how sick High Horse was now." How might this story have looked (and sounded) if it had been meant to be read rather than listened to?
   What are some differences between the written and the spoken word?
4. How would you characterize Black Elk's voice? What attributes make it distinct? What is "the mood and manner of the old man's narrative"? What evidence is there in it of the high regard people had for Black Elk as a spiritual leader?

For Further Discussion

5. Tell a story into a tape recorder and then transcribe it word for word onto the page. How is your spoken voice different from your written voice? How is the written voice more economical? Which "voice" do you prefer?
   Students, don't be afraid of your own voice—on a page or on a recorder. This is no time to be shy or embarrassed or reticent. Your voice is your voice—the only one you have.

Maxine Hong Kingston
(1940–   )

Maxine Kingston was born in 1940 in Stockton, California, of Chinese immigrant parents. In *The Woman Warrior: Memoirs of a Girlhood among Ghosts* (from which this excerpt was taken) and its later companion book, *China Men,* she uses myth, legend, history, and memory to confront her Chinese/American heritage.

She says, "I have no idea how people who don't write endure their lives."

The Woman Warrior

When we Chinese girls listened to the adults talking-story, we learned that we failed if we grew up to be but wives or slaves. We could be heroines, swordswomen. Even if she had to rage across all China, a swordswoman got even with anybody who hurt her family. Perhaps women were once so dangerous that they had to have their feet bound. It was a woman who invented white crane boxing only two hundred years ago. She was already an expert pole fighter, daughter of a teacher trained at the Shao-lin temple, where there lived an order of fighting monks. She was combing her hair one morning when a white crane alighted outside her window. She teased it with her pole, which it pushed aside with a soft brush of its wing. Amazed, she dashed outside and tried to knock the crane off its perch. It snapped her pole in two. Recognizing the presence of great power, she asked the spirit of the white crane if it would teach her to fight. It answered with a cry that white crane boxers imitate today. Later the bird returned as an old man, and he guided her boxing for many years. Thus she gave the world a new martial art.

This was one of the tamer, more modern stories, mere introduction. My mother told others that followed swordswomen through woods and palaces for years. Night after night my mother would talk-story until we fell asleep. I couldn't tell where the stories left off and the dreams began, her voice the voice of the heroines in my sleep. And on Sundays, from noon to midnight, we went to the movies at the Confucius Church. We saw swordswomen jump over houses from a standstill; they didn't even need a running start.

At last I saw that I too had been in the presence of great power, my mother talking-story. After I grew up, I heard the chant of Fa Mu Lan, the girl who took her father's place in battle. Instantly I remembered that as a child I had followed my mother about the house, the two of us singing about how Fa Mu Lan fought gloriously and returned alive from war to settle in the village. I had forgotten this chant that was once mine, given me by my mother, who may not have known its power to remind. She said I would grow up a wife and a slave, but she taught me the song of the warrior woman, Fa Mu Lan. I would have to grow up a warrior woman. . . .

My American life has been such a disappointment.

"I got straight A's, Mama."

"Let me tell you a true story about a girl who saved her village."

I could not figure out what was my village. And it was important that I do something big and fine, or else my parents would sell me when we made our way back to China. In China there were solutions for what to do with little girls who ate up food and threw tantrums. You can't eat straight A's.

When one of my parents or the emigrant villagers said, "Feeding girls is feeding cowbirds," I would thrash on the floor and scream so hard I couldn't talk. I couldn't stop.

"What's the matter with her?"

"I don't know. Bad, I guess. You know how girls are. 'There's no profit in raising girls. Better to raise geese than girls.'"

"I would hit her if she were mine. But then there's no use wasting all the discipline on a girl. 'When you raise girls, you're raising children for strangers.'"

"Stop that crying!" my mother would yell. "I'm going to hit you if you don't stop. Bad girl! Stop!" I'm going to remember never to hit or to scold my children for crying, I thought, because then they will only cry more.

"I'm not a bad girl," I would scream. "I'm not a bad girl. I'm not a bad girl." I might as well have said, "I'm not a girl."

"When you were little, all you had to say was 'I'm not a bad girl,' and you could make yourself cry," my mother says, talking-story about my childhood.

I minded that the emigrant villagers shook their heads at my sister and me. "One girl—and another girl," they said, and made our parents ashamed to take us out together. The good part about my brothers being born was that people stopped saying, "All girls," but I learned new grievances. "Did you roll an egg on *my* face like that when *I* was born?" "Did you have a full-month party for *me?*" "Did you turn on all the lights?" "Did you send *my* picture to Grandmother?" "Why not? Because I'm a girl? Is that why not?" "Why didn't you teach me English?" "You like having me beaten up at school, don't you?"

"She is very mean, isn't she?" the emigrant villagers would say.

"Come, children. Hurry. Hurry. Who wants to go out with Great-Uncle?" On Saturday mornings my great-uncle, the ex-river pirate, did the shopping. "Get your coats, whoever's coming."

"I'm coming. I'm coming. Wait for me."

When he heard girls' voices, he turned on us and roared, "No girls!" and left my sisters and me hanging our coats back up, not looking at one another. The boys came back with candy and new toys. When they walked through Chinatown, the people must have said, "A boy—and another boy—and another boy!" At my great-uncle's funeral I secretly tested out feeling glad that he was dead—the six-foot bearish masculinity of him.

I went away to college—Berkeley in the sixties—and I studied, and I marched to change the world, but I did not turn into a boy. I would have liked to bring myself back as a boy for my parents to welcome with chickens and pigs. That was for my brother, who returned alive from Vietnam.

If I went to Vietnam, I would not come back; females desert families. It was said, "There is an outward tendency in females," which meant that I was getting straight A's for the good of my future husband's family, not my own. I did not plan ever to have a husband. I would show my mother and father and the nosey emigrant villagers that girls have no outward tendency. I stopped getting straight A's.

And all the time I was having to turn myself American-feminine, or no dates.

There is a Chinese word for the female *I*—which is "slave." Break the women with their own tongues!

I refused to cook. When I had to wash dishes, I would crack one or two. "Bad girl," my mother yelled, and sometimes that made me gloat rather than cry. Isn't a bad girl almost a boy?

"What do you want to be when you grow up, little girl?"

"A lumberjack in Oregon."

Even now, unless I'm happy, I burn the food when I cook. I do not feed people. I let dirty dishes rot. I eat at other people's tables but won't invite them to mine, where the dishes are rotting.

If I could not eat, perhaps I could make myself a warrior like the swordswoman who drives me. I will—I must—rise and plow the fields as soon as the baby comes out.

Vocabulary

martial art   a system of self-defense practiced as an art form
emigrant   one who left his homeland
cowbirds   any of various blackbirds that lay eggs in nests of other birds
gloat   to regard with malicious pleasure or satisfaction

Discussion

1. How is Kingston's "voice" more like "talking-story" than it is like a written voice? (See others in this chapter for comparison.)
   Do you find it effective or bothersome that Kingston's syntax is "nonstandard"? Find phrases you particularly like or dislike and say why. How is her syntax uniquely her own, a contributor to her "voice"?
2. What does Kingston mean when she says, "Break the women with their own tongues"?
   How have words affected her life? (All of our lives?)
3. Speculate on what Kingston's writing must mean that makes her say, "I have no idea how people who don't write endure their lives."

Bartolomeo Vanzetti
(1888–1927)

Vanzetti was born June 11, 1888, in Villafalletto, Italy. In spite of the young boy's obvious intelligence his father scorned education and apprenticed him to a baker at thirteen. In later years Vanzetti would read history, science, philosophy, literature, and political treatises.

Emigrating to the United States at twenty he found work in restaurants, on farms, as a fish peddler, and in other such occupations. He and a friend, Nicola Sacco, both considered political radicals, were found guilty of murder in 1921 and electrocuted in August 1927. The following excerpt is from Vanzetti's address to the court during his trial.

Apology

What I say is that I am innocent, not only of the Braintree crime, but also of the Bridgewater crime. That I am not only innocent of these two crimes, but in all my life I have never stole and I have never killed and I have never spilled blood. That is what I want to say. And it is not all. Not only am I innocent of these two crimes, not only in all my life I have never stole, never killed, never spilled blood, but I have struggled all my life, since I began to reason, to eliminate crime from the earth.

Everybody that knows these two arms knows very well that I did not need to go in between the street and kill a man to take the money. I can live with my two arms and live well. But besides that, I can live even without work with my arm for other people. I have had plenty of chance to live independently and to live what the world conceives to be a higher life than not to gain our bread with the sweat of our brow.

My father in Italy is in a good condition. I could have come back in Italy and he would have welcomed me every time with open arms. Even if I come back there with not a cent in my pocket, my father could have give me a possession, not to work but to make business, or to oversee upon the land that he owns. He has wrote me many letters in that sense, and other well to do relatives have wrote me many letters in that sense that I can produce.

Well, I want to reach a little point farther, and it is this,—that not only have I not been trying to steal in Bridgewater, not only have I not been in Braintree to steal and kill and have never steal or kill or spilt blood in all my life, not only have I struggled hard against crimes, but I have refused myself the commodity or glory of life, the pride of life of a good position, because in my consideration it is not right to exploit man. I have refused to go in business because I understand that business is a speculation of profit upon certain people that must depend upon the business man, and I do not consider that that is right and therefore I refuse to do that.

Now, I should say that I am not only innocent of all these things, not only have I never committed a real crime in my life—though some sins but not crimes—not only have I struggled all my life to eliminate crimes, the crimes that the official law and the official moral condemns, but also the crime that the official moral and the official law sanctions and sanctifies,—the exploitation and the oppression of the man by the man, and if there is a reason why I am here as a guilty man, if there is a reason why you in a few minutes can doom me, it is this reason and none else.

You see it is seven years that we are in jail. What we have suffered during these seven years no human tongue can say, and yet you see me before you, not trembling, you see me looking you in your eyes straight, not blushing, nor changing color, not ashamed or in fear.

Eugene Debs say that not even a dog—something like that—not even a dog that kill the chickens would have been found guilty by American jury with the evidence that the Commonwealth have produced against us. I say that not even a leprous dog would have his appeal refused two times by the Supreme Court of Massachusetts—not even a leprous dog.

They have given a new trial to Madeiros for the reason that the Judge had either forgot or omitted to tell the jury that they should consider the man innocent until found guilty in the court, or something of that sort. That man has confessed, and the court give him another trial. We have proved that there could not have been another Judge on the face of the earth more prejudiced and more cruel than you have been against us. We have proven that. Still they refuse the new trial. We know, and you know in your heart, that you have been against us from the very beginning, before you see us. Before you see us you already know that we were radicals, that we were underdogs, that we were the enemy of the institution that you can believe in good faith in their goodness—I don't want to condemn that—and that it was easy on the time of the first trial to get a verdict of guiltiness.

We know that you have spoke yourself and have spoke your hostility against us, and your despisement against us with friends of yours on the train, at the University Club of Boston, on the Golf Club of Worcester, Massachusetts. I am sure that if the people who know all what you say against us would have the civil courage to take the stand, maybe your Honor—I am sorry to say this because you are an old man, and I have an old father—but maybe you would be beside us in good justice at this time.

This is what I say: I would not wish to a dog or to a snake, to the most low and misfortunate creature of the earth—I would not wish to any of them what I have had to suffer for things that I am not guilty of. But my conviction is that I have suffered for things that I am guilty of. I am suffering because I am a radical and indeed I am a radical; I have suffered because I was an Italian, and indeed I am an Italian; I have suffered more for my family and for my beloved than for myself; but I am so convinced to be right that if you could execute me two times, and if I could be reborn two other times, I would live again to do what I have done already.

I have finished. Thank you.

The Court. Under the law of Massachusetts the jury says whether a defendant is guilty or innocent. The Court has absolutely nothing to do with that question. The law of Massachusetts provides that a Judge cannot deal in any way with the facts. As far as he can go under our law is to state the evidence.

During the trial many exceptions were taken. Those exceptions were taken to the Supreme Judicial Court. That Court, after examining the entire record, after examining all the exceptions,—that Court in its final words said, "The verdicts of the jury should stand; exceptions overruled." That being true, there is only one thing that this Court can do. It is not a matter of discretion. It is a matter of statutory requirement, and that being true there is only one duty that now devolves upon this Court, and that is to pronounce the sentences.

First, the Court pronounces sentence upon Nicola Sacco. It is considered and ordered by the Court that you, Nicola Sacco, suffer the punishment of death by the passage of a current of electricity through your body within the week beginning on Sunday, the tenth day of July, in the year of our Lord, one thousand, nine hundred and twenty-seven. This the sentence of the law.

It is considered and ordered by the Court that you, Bartolomeo Vanzetti——

Mr. Vanzetti. Wait a minute, please, your Honor. May I speak for a minute with my lawyer, Mr. Thompson?

Mr. Thompson. I do not know what he wants to say.

The Court. I think I should pronounce the sentence.—Bartolomeo Vanzetti, suffer the punishment of death——

Mr. Sacco. You know I am innocent. That is the same words I pronounced seven years ago. You condemn two innocent men.

The Court. ——by the passage of a current of electricity through your body within the week beginning on Sunday, the tenth day of July, in the year of our Lord, one thousand nine hundred and twenty-seven. This is the sentence of the law.

We will now take a recess.

[*At 11:00* A.M., *the Court adjourned without delay.*]

Post Script

"If it had not been for these things," says Vanzetti, "I might have live out my life, talking at street corners to scorning men. I might have die, unmarked, unknown, a failure. Now we are not a failure. This is our career and our triumph. Never in our full life can we hope to do such work for tolerance, for joostice, for man's onderstanding of man, as now we do by an accident.

"Our words—our lives—our pains—nothing! The taking of our lives—lives of a good shoemaker and a poor fish peddler—all! That last moment belong to us—that agony is our triumph!"

□
Allusions/References

Braintree crime   the attempted robbery on December 24, 1919, of a truck carrying the payroll of the L. Q. White Shoe Company by four men also thought to be "reds" or "anarchists"
Bridgewater crime   the April 15, 1920, robbery of the payroll for the Slater & Morill Shoe Company during which the paymaster and a guard were killed; the crime for which Sacco and Vanzetti were tried and executed
Madeiros's motion   the sixth supplementary motion for a new trial
Eugene Debs   leader of the Socialist party, tried and convicted under the Espionage Act

Discussion

1. Vanzetti's "voice" in this address to the court has been troublesome to many people. What quality in his voice arouses suspicions as to his guilt or innocence? (We are not here to retry Vanzetti, but to learn more about voice and its effect on an audience. Find specific words and phrasing that define his voice [to you]. Is it a voice you would trust?)
2. What evidence is there of this being an oral form rather than a written form?
3. The juxtaposition of simple language and broken diction with elevated thought is quite evident in Vanzetti's "Address." Find specific examples of this. What is its effect on you, the reader?

□ The Written Voice

His mattress was on top of upended milk crates. "You know," he said, coming out of his bedroom shirtless and rumpled, "sleeping so high in the air makes me feel closer to God. Or, at least further away from the fleas," he added.

I call this the story of Rick. There are a lot of details you don't know, how his words indicated thought, and wit. Just weeks before Ralph had told him why he preferred to sleep on the floor. "To be closer to earth," he had said. And not once since Ralph left had Rick given any indication of having thought about those words until now, and they were coming out in parody. We laughed at his lines because they meant all this to us. And more. What can I say—Rick is a slob. But he has afforded me a narrative to illustrate a chapter on narration, and also the opportunity to show you something about our words, how they can live on in someone's mind's ear.

A narration is a written or spoken story. Like description, on which so much good narration relies, it presents a picture. The difference between narration and description is the difference between the movies and a book of snapshots. Narration is concerned with the movement, the sounds, tastes, smells, looks, and feel of something, through both space and time. It is a story with plot, character, and action. For the sake of a class on essay writing, it is a true story, something that comes from your own experience, perhaps, and is written with attention to all the details.

I often tell a beginning student to look around. Stories are happening right now. Your narrative doesn't have to be about a big event, a bout with life or death. It can be the story of your day, how you got to be here in this moment.

I also find it helpful to mention how one might begin a narrative. Remember "Once upon a time . . ."? Dylan Thomas begins his "Reminiscences" with: "I like very much people telling me about their childhood, but they'll have to be quick or else I'll be telling them about mine." For centuries stories began by invocation to the Muse of Poetry, asking the goddess for her assistance. Not many modern narratives begin in this manner; however, more of you may resort to the invocation, waiting for the words to come, than I know about.

It *is* difficult to begin. So I suggest you jump right in. Start anywhere. Don't explain a thing. When you get to the point where you really ought to begin, the words will declare themselves on the page. How, you might ask me, will these words make themselves manifest? Simple, I say, they will be the most exciting. Your reader will be unable to resist. Start right in the middle of the best part. All the ambling you did before this point you can throw away later when you edit.

Description and narration are not only the province of the fiction writer. All essays are enhanced by the use of these two modes. Above all others, they appeal to the total human—the emotions and senses as well as to the intellect. Everyone has a story. Tell it any way you like: from the beginning, first things first, flashback, flashforward, or lateral hold (meanwhile back at the ranch). It's your story. Most student-writers find narration fun.

In the following selections Collin Turnbull tells with gentle humor how differing cultural mores brought him to a difficult moment. Anaïs Nin lets you into her *Diary* on the occasion of a visit to Mexico. And Michael Herr, a volunteer correspondent of the Vietnam war, introduces us to the Lurps.

Colin Turnbull

(1924–   )

Colin Turnbull was born in 1924 in England and is now a naturalized American. He is a noted educator and writer in the area of social anthropology. He has

□

authored several books, mostly on the people of Africa. The intimate, personal approach he brings to his studies of these people has occasionally brought criticism from fellow anthropologists who feel "scientific method" demands strict objectivity. But as Turnbull has pointed out in the preface to *The Mountain People,* a book about the Ik tribe: "In living the experience . . . , and perhaps in reading it, one finds it is oneself one is looking at and questioning."

In fact it has been said that implicit in Turnbull's writing is "the concept of anthropology as an art as well as a science. . . ." Truly the people he writes about could be our neighbors in the global village. The following excerpt is from *The Forest People,* about the Ituri pygmies.

The Village Wife

The forest is the world of the Pygmy, and he is not bashful about telling a villager who outstays his welcome just what he thinks of him.

I stayed in one camp which was only a few hours from the village and on the way to a Negro fishing ground. We were constantly beset by villagers passing through, and after a while the Pygmies got tired of feeding them, tired of being used as a convenient stopping place. So when they were asked for food, the Pygmies would agree on condition that the villagers join them in a game of *panda.* This is a gambling game in which beans are thrown on a mat, or on a flat piece of ground. Some of them are quickly scooped up by one of the two players. The other, looking to see how many are left, has to estimate at a glance how many his opponent has taken. He then tells his opponent to throw down one, two, or three beans, or to stay as he is. The count is then made—also at a glance—and if the player has an exact multiple of four he wins. But against villagers Pygmies always win. For one thing they have an uncanny sense of form that enables them in a moment to know the exact number thrown down. And for another the villagers are not so nimble as the Pygmies. When a Pygmy sees that he is going to lose by a couple of beans, he quickly drops them from the store he has concealed between his fingers, or even in his hair, thus by a triumphant jerk of his hands or his head throwing in the winning beans.

The villagers left that camp stripped of their fish, their tobacco, and whatever else they had to gamble away, and they soon came to prefer an alternative route that by-passed our camp.

There are a few villagers that are welcome in a Pygmy camp, but they are rare. Others can come with sackloads of food and still get a cold reception. I have seen this happen; as soon as the Pygmies have divided up the food they send the villagers on their way. But others can come empty-handed and be received gladly, because they understand the Pygmies and the forest. For the Pygmies this is the criterion of a "real person," as opposed to the animal-humans who live in permanent villages out in the open, away from the shelter and affection of the trees.

Any visitations by villagers are temporary, and they usually have some political significance. A Negro chief who wants to win more Pygmies to his village may send out a son with gifts to stay in a Pygmy camp. Every day more gifts and food are sent out so that he can distribute these. It is a risky business because, as the villagers say, "The BaMbuti eat us up until we have nothing left for ourselves!" But if a chief's son wins the affection of the Pygmies, his father will have won a steady supply of meat—for a time, anyway.

One afternoon I saw two village girls arrive, followed by two servants who threw down loads of plantains and sweet bananas, and a sack of manioc flour. The servants left and the girls came over and sat down unconcernedly at Masamba's fire. Masamba came out of her hut and greeted them with warmth, and soon a number of women gathered around, chattering away gaily and asking for news of the village.

The girls were Amina, daughter of an important BaBira subchief, and her cousin. Her father was hoping, she said, that she might be allowed to stay for a few days and bring him back some meat. She obviously knew the Pygmies well, because without waiting to be asked she distributed the plantains. She said she would keep the manioc flour until the meat began to come in. Apparently she was well liked, because as soon as people heard of her presence they came over to shake her hand, in the manner of villagers, grasping each other's wrists. Kenge told me all about her, and said that her father was one of the least animal-like villagers. He asked me which of the two girls I thought looked the more attractive. I said Amina, without a doubt. She was the most beautiful girl I had seen in a long time; the BaBira are by no means noted for their good looks. Amina was tall and a warm brown in color. She carried herself with the inborn grace of Bantu women; her eyes were deep and thoughtful; her expression was kind and gentle. Yes, she was certainly the more beautiful of the two. Kenge nodded thoughtfully and changed the conversation.

That night I sat up late with the men, and when I went back to my hut I was surprised not to see any bachelors sleeping on the floor as they usually did. But three logs were placed beside the bed and were glowing cheerfully. I sat down on the edge of the bed and found, as I had expected, that Kenge had curled up in my blanket. He was considerate enough, on such occasions, not to take my blanket onto the floor, but rather to take half of the bed. So I crawled in beside him and was about to say something when I realized that the body beside me was considerably taller than Kenge, and very differently shaped. It was Amina.

It was a difficult moment, but I could see the whole situation at once. I had become the center of a nice political maneuver. The chief had sent his daughter to win the Pygmies, not by her gifts of plantains and manioc flour, but by winning me. The Pygmies, anxious to get what they could out of the situation, liking Amina anyway, but having some consideration for me, got Kenge to find out which of the two girls I preferred. That, evidently, was to be the limit of my choice in the matter. I confess I was glad I had chosen Amina, but I could see all sorts of difficulties arising if I were to take advantage of the situation. No doubt the chief had in mind the considerable bride-wealth he could demand should, by any chance, his daughter bear a mulatto child. Still, it was good of him to send his prettiest daughter.

I considered for a minute or two and then said, "Amina," very quietly. It had begun to rain, and I half hoped she would not hear me. It would be a terrible disgrace to her—and to me—if I turned her out, but I wanted no part of a lengthy and costly dispute over bride-wealth. But Amina was by no means asleep. She laughed lightly and made fun of my KiNgwana name, which means "the long one." So I said, "Amina!" once more, a little more sharply, still trying to think what a supposed gentleman and scholar should do in such circumstances. But Amina was not helping. She just snuggled closer and said. "Yes, tall one?" Then in a moment of inspiration I simply said, "Amina the roof is leaking." And with masculine authority I added, "Get up and fix it."

Without a word she got up and started searching for the leak, pulling at the leaves until a steady trickle of water came down, splashing on the floor beside the bed. By the time she had repaired the damage and checked the whole roof with womanly efficiency I was asleep—at least so I pretended. With a sigh she pulled the blanket from me and also went to sleep—or perhaps she too was pretending. But it was a solution, if a chilly one. My last thoughts that night were that Kenge would at least have left me some of the blanket, no matter how annoyed with me he was. These villagers—they were just animals.

When I awoke in the morning I hardly dared open my eyes, but a tentative exploration proved that the other half of the bed was empty. I thought all was well after all. Amina had cut her losses and left at dawn. But when I had put my trousers on and stooped through the low entrance of the hut into the camp, there she was. She was sitting on a log beside the hut, quietly fanning the fire and cooking my breakfast, just as every other wife was doing for her husband. Kenge was making it very obvious to everyone that he was eating with the bachelors, who were making it obvious that they had not slept in my hut that night. Everyone else studiously ignored my appearance, except old Moke, who was walking past on his way to the stream to bathe. He looked at me sideways, shook his head and gave a little knowing old laugh. And as he walked on he shook his head all the more vigorously and laughed all the louder.

I was about to go after him, thinking that at least I could ask his advice, but Amina caught hold of my trouser leg and said, "There is no need for you to go to the stream to bathe. I have brought you water— behind the hut." So I went behind the hut and washed, and then sat down and had breakfast, while Amina went to join the other women and chat with them. While she was gone Kenge strolled by and elaborately asked me if the food was all right. He also asked me, rather loudly, if I had slept well. Amina answered from across the camp, "Yes, he told me to mend the leak in the roof!" This proof of domestic bliss brought howls of mirth from all around, the more infuriating because I could not see what was funny about it. Then Kenge told me that this was what men always said to their wives when they wanted to be allowed to sleep in peace.

That night, Amina and I came to an agreement. She was to stay with me and cook my food—and mend leaks in the roof every night. This way she would preserve her reputation and I mine, and there would be no complications. And so it was.

I grew very fond of Amina, and some time later, when I was in a village and became very ill, she walked ten miles every day to see me, and ten miles back. She brought me refreshing fruits and sweet-smelling plants and flowers, and sat beside my bed without saying a word. Only once, I woke up and found she was sitting on the edge of the bed and holding my hand in hers.

When the Pygmies moved camp, Amina took the opportunity to go back to her father's village. I was never sure whether I was glad, or more than just a little sorry, to see her go. But when I thought about it, I realized that apart from all the other reasons, Amina could never have stayed. No matter how well she was liked by the Pygmies, she was still a villager. She had not been brought up to do the hundred and one little things that a Pygmy woman has to know how to do. She did not even know how to beat on the hunt, let alone which vines to follow to find the delicacies hidden in the ground by their roots. She belonged to another world.

Discussion

1. What is the Pygmy definition of a "real person"? What do you think of this definition?
2. How do the details leading up to the Amina story add to this narrative about the village girl?
3. Why do the Pygmies shake hands with Amina and her cousin "in the manner of villagers"?
4. Turnbull is a skillful storyteller. How long are you kept in suspense about the real "action" in this narrative? Locate the exact line where you can say you "caught on."
   Beginnings of sentences and beginnings of paragraphs are very important positions, structurally. As in a relay the first runner sets the course for what will happen to the team in competition, the first positions are important for the writer to command. Why does Turnbull wait until the end of a paragraph to say, "It was Amina."?

5. What do we learn about Turnbull by his admission, "I considered for a minute or two. . . ."? Is a minute or two a long consideration?
How does Turnbull define himself as a man when he writes "a supposed
gentleman and scholar. . . ."?
6. How is this narrative about the human belief in custom and ritual, as much
as it is about Turnbull and the village girl? How important is ritual in sepa-
rating the human being from the mere animal? According to the Pygmies?
According to Turnbull?

Anaïs Nin
(1903–1977)

Anaïs Nin was born in 1903 in Paris and, though an American citizen since
1914, considered herself an "international writer." She worked as a model,
dancer, teacher, lecturer, and psychoanalyst.

Her writing has been called "literary surrealism" and "autobiographical
fantasy." She said, "I have wanted my writing to unmask the deeper self that
has hidden behind the self we present to the world." A writer since age eleven,
she attempted to find, "the uninhibited inner monologue."

A House in Acapulco

One day we decided to visit the jungle *ranchita* of Hatcher, an American
engineer who had married a local Mexican woman and was attempting
to achieve the American dream of "going native." His place was near
San Luis, north of Acapulco, on the road to Zihuatanejo. The road was
dusty and difficult, but we had the feeling of penetrating into a wilder,
less explored part of Mexico. Villages were few and far between; we
met rancheros on horseback, in their white suits and ponchos and
enormous hats, carrying their machetes rigidly. We saw women washing clothes by the river. Some huts were without walls, just a web of
branches supported by four slender tree trunks. Babies lay in
hammocks.

The river beyond San Luis was wide, and cars had to be ferried.
We waited for the ferry, a flat raft made of logs tied together. The men
pushed it along with long bamboo poles.

When we left the raft we started a journey into the jungle. A dust
road with just enough room for the car. Cactus and banana leaves
scraped our faces. When we were deep in the forest and seemingly far
from any village, we saw a young man waiting for a ride. He carried a
heavy, small doctor's bag.

"I'm Dr. Palas," he said, "Will you give me a ride?"

When he was settled he explained: "I have just delivered a child.
I'm stationed at Zihuatanejo."

He was carrying a French novel like the ones Dr. Hernandez must have carried at his age, for they all studied medicine in France. Was he devoted to his patients? The Mexican medical plan rules that interns must work a year in a village where there is no doctor. This was the way Dr. Hernandez first came to Acapulco when it was a fishing village.

When we reached his village, where we were to spend the night, we had rooms across from his bungalow. A workman came in the middle of the night and called out to him, pleading and begging: "I have a splinter in my eye." But Dr. Palas did not come out. The poor workman stayed until dawn, and then the doctor deigned to come out and attend to him. I was shocked by his callousness. We went off without saying goodbye to him. I remembered his cynical words: "I have a year of this to endure."

Hatcher's place was deep in the jungle on a hill overlooking the sea. On a small open space he had built a roof on posts, with only one wall in the back. The cooking was done out of doors. A Mexican woman was bending over her washing. She only came to greet us when Hatcher called her. She was small and heavy, and sad-faced, but she gave Hatcher a caressing look and a brilliant smile. She showed only a conscious politeness to us.

"You must excuse us, the place is not finished yet. My husband works alone and he has a lot to do."

"Bring the coffee, Maria." She left us sitting around a table on the terrace, staring at an unbelievable stretch of white sand, dazzling white foam spraying a gigantic, sprawling vegetation which grew to the very edge of the sand. Birds sang deliriously, and monkeys clowned in the trees. The colors seemed purer and clearer, like those of a fresh place never inhabited before.

Maria came with coffee in a Thermos.

Hatcher said: "She is a most marvelous wife."

"And he is a wonderful husband," said Maria. "Mexican husbands never go around telling everyone they are married. He goes about buying presents for his wife, talking about his wife."

Turning to me she said in a low voice: "I don't know why he loves me. I am so short and squatty. He was once married to a tall, slim American woman like you. He never talks about her. I worked for him at first. I was his secretary. We are going to build a beautiful place here. This is only the beginning."

They had their bedroom in the back, protected by curtains. Visitors slept in hammocks on the terrace.

We took a walk to the beach. The flowers which opened their velvety faces toward us were so eloquent they seemed about to speak. The sand did not seem like sand, but like powdered glass which reflected the light.

The sea folded its layers around me, touching my legs, my hips, my breasts like a liquid sculptor with warm hands.

When I came out of the sea, I felt reborn. I longed for this simplified life. Cooking over a wood fire, sleeping out of doors in a hammock, with only a Mexican blanket. I longed for naked feet in sandals, the freedom of the body in summer clothes, hair washed by the sea.

When we returned Maria had set the table. The lights were weak bulbs hanging from wires. The generator made a loud throbbing. But the trees were full of fireflies, crickets, and pungent odors. There was a natural pool fed by mountain water where we could wash off the salt from the sea.

After a dinner of fish and black beans, Hatcher offered to show us the rest of his house. Behind the wall there was a storage room of which he was immensely proud. It was enormous, as large as the house itself, with shelves reaching to the ceiling. There was in it every brand of canned food, medicines, tools, hunting guns, fishing equipment, garden tools, vitamins, seeds. He reveled in the completeness of it. "What would you like? Cling peaches? Asparagus? Quinine? Magazines? Newspapers? I even have a pair of crutches in case of need. I have ether, and instruments for surgery."

I felt immensely tired and depressed. I lay in my hammock pondering why I was so disappointed. I had imagined Hatcher free. I admired him as a man who had won independence from our culture and could live like a native, a simplified existence with few needs. And here he demonstrated complete dependence on complex and artificial products. America the mother and father had been transported into a supply shed, bottled and canned. He was not able to live here without possessions, with fresh fish and fruit and vegetables in abundance, with cow's milk and the products of hunting.

His fears made me question: was there no open road, simple, clear, unique? Could I live a new life here in Mexico, free of all that had wounded me in the past, and free of dependency? Hatcher was not free of his bitterness about his first marriage, nor free of America. He was not free of the past.

My lacquered nails reminded him of his first wife. He was hostile to me because of his first wife.

I wanted to stay in Mexico, I wanted to have a little house in Acapulco, overlooking the sea, where I could watch the dawns like oriental spectacles, watch the whales at play, without need of books, concerts, plays, provisions of any kind.

When I awakened I first saw a coral tree with orange flowers that seemed like tongues of flames. Between its branches rose thin wisps of smoke from Maria's *brasero*. Maria was patting tortillas between her hands in an even rhythm.

I did not want to stay and Hatcher was offended. He thought our battery was too low and that we should get a new one. He tinkered with the car. I felt that now he represented slavery to an inescapable past and not the freedom of a natural, native life. He loved all this only

□

because he had been hurt by the other. He loved Maria because she was not the American woman with painted nails who had hurt him. It would take days to get a new battery and I refused to stay.

When the car was repaired we left. Driving back in the violent sun we did not talk. The light filled the eyes, the mind, the nerves, the bones, and it was only when we drove through the shade that we came out of this anaesthesia of sunlight.

A truck full of Mexican workmen with guns was driving a short distance behind us. Our car stalled. They caught up with us. They offered to tow us to the nearest town for a new battery.

But they did not know I understood Spanish, and among themselves they discussed how easy it would be to get both our money and the car. I had to think quickly.

We explained that Mr. Hatcher was following close behind us and would soon be here with a new battery.

It was, as I knew, a lie. But I thought it would drive them away. They all knew Mr. Hatcher, and he had guns. They hesitated. And then Hatcher arrived! He had been uneasy about us and had decided to follow. The men filed quietly into the truck. Hatcher said they would have taken our money and the car and left us there. He towed us to San Luis and left us in the hands of a very dubious Mexican garage to wait for a new battery.

It was New Year's Eve. We had reached San Luis in time for fireworks and dancing in the street. At seven o'clock, when we arrived, the streets were silent and it began to grow dark. The owner of the café was a pale-faced Spaniard with the manners of a courtier. He fixed us a dinner. Then he told us we could not go out that night.

"San Luis looks quiet now, but it is only because they are dressing for New Year's Eve. Pretty soon they will all be out in the streets. There will be dancing. But the men will drink heavily. The women know when it is time to leave. I advise you not to mix with them. The women go home with the children. The men continue to drink. Soon they begin to shoot at mirrors, glasses, bottles, at anything. Sometimes they shoot at each other. I entreat you, I beg you to stay right here. I have clean rooms I can let you have for the night. Stay in your rooms, I advise you strongly."

At ten o'clock music, fireworks, shouts and shooting began.

I lay on my plain white cot, in a whitewashed room, bare and simple, shivering with cold, imprisoned by mosquito netting, listening to the noise, and feeling lonely and lost.

In the morning the streets were littered with confetti. The street vendors' baskets were empty and they were asleep beside them rolled in their ponchos. The scent of malabar was in the air and that of burnt firecrackers. There were three men dead and a little boy injured by the fireworks.

In Acapulco I looked for a house I could afford. Even if I had to

□

return to the United States, this would remain the place of joy and health.

I found the smallest house in Acapulco at the very tip of the rock I loved, the highest one above Caleta Beach, looking out to sea and to the island where the beacon light stood.

It was built of stucco, all open on the sea side, and the walls on the side of the street were latticed to let the breeze through. I was euphoric. The people who sold it lived below me. I startled everyone who had heard me say I never wanted to be tied down anywhere by announcing that I had chosen a place to live.

I bought simple native things at the market, pottery, serapes, straw mats, baskets. There was a bed there already. I was deliriously happy. A walk down the hill and I was at Caleta, the Mexican beach. The tourists swam at other beaches.

The beach is lined with thatched roof shanties where one can eat fresh clams and shrimp. The guitar players clustered around the shanties. They were treated to beer and sang all day.

The glass-bottomed boat was tied there, and the trips on it were full of marvels; coral, sea plants, and colorful fishes. The American who ran it was also collecting animals for his zoo. They could be seen at his house—monkeys, kinkajous, birds of all kinds, parrots, iguanas, snakes. He paid the native boys to hunt for him.

But several things happened in the little house. The tank on the roof which supplied water for the bath and for cooking would either run dry or overflow during the night. The insects I pursued with Flytox turned out to be scorpions, who liked to nest behind the straw mats. Rats came at night, ate the food, ran over my body and frightened me to death.

When I asked advice from the Mexicans, they counseled resignation. I bought rat poison and began to fight them, but a new batch came every night through the terrace.

The young men of the town found out I was living alone and came to call me, or serenade me behind the latticed walls. I would put out the lights and lie in the dark.

I had to walk up the steep hill with food and ice.

I invited Alice Rahon to stay with me. She brought her long beautiful black hair, her radiant smile, her superb swimming. Her talk was full of fascination. She was a painter and also known for her surrealist poems. We talked endlessly and formed a deep friendship.

I had finally frightened away the scorpions and the rats. But now I had a new enemy. It was the neighbor's rooster. He was not only the most arrogant rooster I ever met but he crowed ahead of time. He did not wait for the dawn, he wanted to show that he could bring it on, cause it to happen by his sonorous announcements and prophecies.

So at four in the morning I was awakened by the rooster, who did not surrender until the dawn gave in and appeared.

When the rooster crowed that was a signal for the old man next door to start his asthmatic cough, a long, continuous, raucous cough which seemed to strangle him.

I was told about the early Acapulco. There were no hotels, only Mexican boardinghouses. You arrived on a donkey because the train did not go that far. You ate purée of black beans and fish for breakfast, lunch, and dinner, for a dollar a day.

Painters had discovered it. It must have seemed like Tahiti. The women did not wear bathing suits, just a piece of cloth resembling the Tahitian *pareu*. The children went about naked. There was an abundance of fish. The people were poor but lived with a certain kind of beauty. Always a palm-leaf hut with a garden filled with flowers.

Their boats were painted in soft colors. The fishermen repaired their nets on the beach. The pottery people used, the baskets, the water jugs were all beautiful and handmade. It was only later that they built tin shacks, without gardens, like the ones behind the bullring, shacks crowded together with no room at all so that they hung their laundry in the narrow alleys. Animals and children slept together.

The beauty of Acapulco was unspoiled.

I took delight in the market. The mere arrangement of ribbons women wore in their hair, the decorative way fruit was laid out in huge round baskets, the birdcages, the smell of melons and oranges, the playfulness of the children. I took delight in the animated and crowded square, in the jetty where the fishing boats returned with their colored pennants flying. I loved to watch the fishermen pulling in their nets at sundown.

Every scene in Mexico is so natural that it alters the color of violence itself, of death. A stabbed Mexican staggered across the night club, his shirt all bloody, but the fatalism of the Mexicans subdued the horror, the shock. It was all made to seem a part of nature, natural, inevitable. Violence and innocence, the two natural aspects of man.

Everything was natural, the dirt floors in the huts, the babies in hammocks, the minimum of possessions: one shawl, one fan, one necklace, one trunk of clothes, no sheets.

I made friends with Pablo at the post office because he was interested in my stamps from foreign countries. He collected post cards from America.

It was he who took me dancing to the places where the people of the town went, the poor. I had to leap over an open sewer. These cafés were antechambers to the whorehouses. A young man with absolutely no hair was singing. ("Complete baldness results from a tropical disease," Dr. Hernandez solemnly informed me.) The prostitutes were modest, not arrogant or overdressed as in America, gentle and courteous.

The music was marvelous, native dance music far better than at the hotel night clubs. People danced in bare feet. My friends were shocked when I threw off my sandals. I loved the texture of the earth, and the touch of other feet.

Everyone knew each other. The town policeman was there, enjoying himself. He had discarded his belt and gun to dance with the prostitutes.

A widower asked me: "If I rent a motorboat for tomorrow will you come and see the sunrise with me at La Roqueta?"

His offer was known to the whole town. He was always looking for women who would be willing to see the sunrise with him on a desert island.

Allusions/References

kinkajous a brownish-furred mammal of tropical America that lives in trees and has a long prehensile tail; also called honey bear

Discussion

1. This piece is taken from a six-volume diary Anaïs Nin kept that spanned sixty years of her life. Is there any indication in its "voice" that the diary was meant to remain private?
   How would you describe Nin's voice from what you have read here?
2. What do you hear, feel, see, taste, and smell in her writing? What descriptive elements stand out in your mind?
3. How is Nin's use of language also detailed and descriptive? Note the following:

   "cactus and banana leaves scraped our faces"

   "dazzling white foam spraying a gigantic, sprawling vegetation"

   "Birds sang deliriously, and monkeys clowned in the trees"

   "the sand did not seem like sand, but like powdered glass"

   "The sea folded its layers around me, touching my legs, my lips, my breasts like a liquid sculptor with warm hands"

   "anaesthesia of sunlight"

   "his asthmatic cough, a long, continuous, raucous cough"

   What can you find in the text that you can add to this list? Remember to look at the words themselves, at how "asthmatic cough," "continuous," and "raucous cough" not only convey a picture but imitate, in sound, the sound of the cough itself.
4. "When I don't write I feel my world shrinking, I feel I am in a prison," Anaïs Nin once wrote. What does she mean by this?
   How is this piece an example of Nin's world expanding?
5. What are the troubles she finds in paradise? Would a man find this primitive "paradise" less troublesome than it appears to a woman?

For Further Discussion

6. "The role of the writer is not to say what we can all say but what we are unable to say," Nin once said. What indications are there in this narrative of "what we are unable to say"? What does Nin mean by this?
7. You might wish to write your own narrative with Nin's dictum of the role of the writer in mind—saying things "we are unable to say." (This is difficult. Have you never heard anyone else say or write what you're thinking?)

Michael Herr
(1940–   )

Besides *Dispatches,* the account of his time as a war correspondent covering the Vietnam war, Herr has written articles for various magazines and journals and collaborated with Francis Ford Coppola and John Milius on the screenplay for "Apocalypse Now."

Of his time in Vietnam he said, "I went to cover the war, and the war covered me." He found the experience so intense, "it was almost marvelous." Critics have said *Dispatches,* from which this excerpt is taken, is reporting "achieving literature."

Breathing In

Going out at night the medics gave you pills, Dexedrine breath like dead snakes kept too long in a jar. I never saw the need for them myself, a little contact or anything that even sounded like contact would give me more speed than I could bear. Whenever I heard something outside of our clenched little circle I'd practically flip, hoping to God that I wasn't the only one who'd noticed it. A couple of rounds fired off in the dark a kilometer away and the Elephant would be there kneeling on my chest, sending me down into my boots for a breath. Once I thought I saw a light moving in the jungle and I caught myself just under a whisper saying, "I'm not ready for this, I'm not ready for this." That's when I decided to drop it and do something else with my nights. And I wasn't going out like the night ambushers did, or the Lurps, long-range recon patrollers who did it night after night for weeks and months, creeping up on VC base camps or around moving columns of North Vietnamese. I was living too close to my bones as it was; all I had to do was accept it. Anyway, I'd save the pills for later, for Saigon and the awful depressions I always had there.

I knew one 4th Division Lurp who took his pills by the fistful, downs from the left pocket of his tiger suit and ups from the right, one to cut the trail for him and the other to send him down it. He told me that they cooled things out just right for him, that he could see that old jungle at night like he was looking at it through a starlight scope. "They sure give you the range," he said.

This was his third tour. In 1965 he'd been the only survivor in a platoon of the Cav wiped out going into the Ia Drang Valley. In '66 he'd come back with the Special Forces and one morning after an ambush he'd hidden under the bodies of his team while the VC walked all around them with knives, making sure. They stripped the bodies of their gear, the berets too, and finally went away, laughing. After that, there was nothing left for him in the war except the Lurps.

"I just can't hack it back in the World," he said. He told me that after he'd come back home the last time he would sit in his room all day, and sometimes he'd stick a hunting rifle out the window, leading people and cars as they passed his house until the only feeling he was aware of was all up in the tip of that one finger. "It used to put my folks real uptight," he said. But he put people uptight here too, even here.

"No man, I'm sorry, he's just too crazy for me," one of the men in his team said. "All's you got to do is look in his eyes, that's the whole . . . story right there."

"Yeah, but you better do it quick," someone else said. "I mean, you don't want to let him catch you at it."

But he always seemed to be watching for it, I think he slept with his eyes open, and I was afraid of him anyway. All I ever managed was one quick look in, and that was like looking at the floor of an ocean. He wore a gold earring and a headband torn from a piece of camouflage parachute material, and since nobody was about to tell him to get his hair cut it fell below his shoulders, covering a thick purple scar. Even at division he never went anywhere without at least a .45 and a knife, and he thought I was a freak because I wouldn't carry a weapon.

"Didn't you ever meet a reporter before?" I asked him.

"Tits on a bull," he said. "Nothing personal."

But what a story he told me, as one-pointed and resonant as any war story I ever heard, it took me a year to understand it:

"Patrol went up the mountain. One man came back. He died before he could tell us what happened."

I waited for the rest, but it seemed not to be that kind of story; when I asked him what had happened he just looked like he felt sorry for me. . . .

His face was all painted up for night walking now like a bad hallucination, not like the painted faces I'd seen in San Francisco only a few weeks before, the other extreme of the same theater. In the coming hours he'd stand as faceless and quiet in the jungle as a fallen tree, and God help his opposite numbers unless they had at least half a squad along, he was a good killer, one of our best. The rest of his team were gathered outside the tent, set a little apart from the other division units, with its own Lurp-designated latrine and its own exclusive freeze-dry rations, three-star war food, the same chop they sold at Abercrombie &

Fitch. The regular division troops would almost shy off the path when they passed the area on their way to and from the mess tent. No matter how toughened up they became in the war, they still looked innocent compared to the Lurps. When the team had grouped they walked in a file down the hill to the lz across the strip to the perimeter and into the treeline.

I never spoke to him again, but I saw him. When they came back in the next morning he had a prisoner with him, blindfolded and with his elbows bound sharply behind him. The Lurp area would definitely be off limits during the interrogation, and anyway, I was already down at the strip waiting for a helicopter to come and take me out of there.

Vocabulary

Dexedrine   an amphetamine known on the streets as "speed"
Lurps   long-range reconnaissance patrollers
VC   Viet Cong
Cav   cavalry
resonant   continuing to sound, to be intensified and enriched
lz   landing zone
kilometer   0.62 mile

Discussion

1. What accounts for the intensity of Herr's voice? Examine the first paragraph closely. How does he string words like beads on the line of a sentence, on the line of a printed line? (Copy a sentence or two from any other writer and compare it with one or two of Herr's.)

   How does sentence length contribute to this intensity? Is it only the subject matter that makes us feel a heightened sense of interest in Herr's every word, or is it the look and sound of the words themselves? Or both?

2. This piece also contains the voices of American soldiers in Vietnam. How are their "voices" similar or dissimilar from Herr's? Do you feel his voice was influenced by theirs? (See Bogdanovich's, "Bogie in Excelsis" for a similar paradigm. Are Bogie's and Bogdanovich's voices more distinct from each other than Herr's and the men he records?)

3. Inside this narrative is a very brief narrative related to Herr by the "Lurp" he is writing about. It goes like this:

   > "Patrol went up the mountain. One man came back. He died before he could tell us what happened."

   Why does it take Herr a year to understand it?

4. What does it mean to say Herr's writing is "reporting achieving literature"? Certainly Herr is not being accused of imaginative or creative plot or theme. How is his language like the language of literature? (Look especially at Chapter Two—on "Words"—for some indication of how many layers of possibil-

☐

ity lie in a writer's use of language. What special ways are words thought
about ordinarily in literature that they might not be thought about in correspondence or journalism?)
5. Compare Herr to Fitzgerald (in chapter Three) for a closer analysis of how
Herr's words approach literature. How are these two writers similar? How
are they different? (Remember, you are looking at only a small sample of
both as you make your judgments.)

Exposition: To Present Ideas

☐ By Process

How did humans start language? How did they agree that *this* sound would mean *that*? How did they discover fire, poetry? How did they learn to fly? Isn't it all amazing, and isn't it all endlessly interesting to speculate about? This inherent curiosity about life, about ways people have found to do things, how we solve the mysteries of day-to-day existence, lies behind the college essay called "process."

In this kind of essay you will demonstrate that you can organize your thoughts about *how something is done* (give directions), or about *how something has come to be* (give information). The first kind of organization details an event, step-by-step, in such a way that the reader could possibly perform it after studying the steps. The second asks that you recount how something came to be, in such a way that the reader has information about it. The difference, of course, is subtle

□

but important. An essay on how heart surgery is performed does not enable its readers to attempt such surgeries.

In either case process essays are rarely pure instruction. Like any other essay, the process essay has something to say in *language* that is interesting in itself, in language that says it with truth and clarity.

Oliver Lafarge details how one rows in "The Eight-Oared Shell," but in doing so conveys something deeper than the mere physical process. He is telling you about this sport's worthiness, about why he participates in it. Why else would he take so much delight in *putting into words* the subtlety of movement involved in cutting water with oar blade? In rowing, Lafarge says he has found a separate and parallel stream to the mainstream of his life. The movements and rituals of this canoeing world are a source of wonder, and he delights in the performance and mastery. In the art of rowing he finds meaning and purpose for the larger sphere of his life.

It is in this blend of meaning and the mechanical that a good process essay is born. No one wants to read how to do something, or wants information about how anything was done, if there is no good reason. Your reasons for writing about the particular process you choose should infuse your essay.

In "To Bid the World Farewell" Jessica Mitford, describing the process of embalming, builds a striking case against the American system of death. Her process is no idle listing of how something is done, but a piece of considerable persuasion. Yasunari Kawabata uses the weaving and bleaching of the rare Japanese Chijimi linen as a metaphor for all things made of the human heart, and as a way of revealing certain qualities of his characters. Ernest Hemingway describes a bullfight from picador to the kill, not for the mere listing of the events, but to demonstrate its larger meaning, something about humans and their rituals, man against beast, and the human drama.

Of course, none of the authors in this section on process set out to write a college process essay, on request, as you must do. This makes your task a little different from theirs, and also perilous. It is important to put your mind to the analysis of an action in such a way that you can communicate it to others, in an order that is both clear and involving. To do this you must first discover something you know how to do well, or something you know enough about that you could convey information about it. This may seem impossible at first, but you need only to think more of what you know how to do.

How do you win high scores on an arcade game step by step? How do you watch a good film? How do you apply makeup in the morning? How do you lift weights for toning and shaping muscles? How do you make a good pie crust? How do you listen to the Rolling Stones? How do you prepare yourself for an exam? How do you read science fiction? How do you make a poem?

Why do you do these things?

Put the how together with a strong sense of why and you will have the makings of a college process essay. You've got good reasons for enjoying the things you enjoy in life. Organize your thoughts about one of them in such a way that you can convey the how and why.

When you read the process essays in this chapter, read them to answer the following questions:

1. How, from the first sentence, is the reader's interest enlisted?
2. Why has the author written about this process?
3. Is the process clear?
4. What are the time cues (transitional words), that indicate when one part of the process ends and another begins?
5. And lastly, how has the author written this in such a way that it might inform you about the writing of your own essay?

Oliver Lafarge
(1901–1963)

Oliver Lafarge was born in New York City, December 12, 1901, and died in 1963. A descendant of Benjamin Franklin and Commodore Oliver Hazard Perry, Lafarge was educated as an anthropologist. Although he taught and did field studies as an archeologist, his abiding interest was the American Indian.

Lafarge's writing, which included novels, short stories, an autobiography, and newspaper columns, most often dealt with the Indians. His first book, *Laughing Boy*, won the Pulitzer Prize for fiction.

The following selection was published in *Harper's* in 1942.

The Eight-Oared Shell

For most of us who have rowed in an eight-oared shell there is no hope whatever of continuing after we have left college, but the love of it remains. . . . No writer has told the nature of rowing in an eight-oared shell to landsmen; none who haven't rowed understand what it is we remember—the crash of the oars in the locks, the shell leaping at the catch, the unity and rhythm and the desperate effort. . . .

What is the nature of it? To begin with the setting—the green-banked river or the Charles Basin ringed by the city, both are beautiful. The shell swinging through open country on a fine spring day is hard to beat. . . . There is the slight excitement and the echoing change of sound in shooting under a bridge, there is the fresh day on the river as you carry your shell down to the float. Rural or urban water, rowing is set in beauty to begin with.

There is the nature of the stroke itself, the most perfect combination I have ever known of skill and the full release of one's power. It takes more than a dumb ox to make a fine oarsman, the traditional "weak brain and strong back" won't serve. To my mind it begins with the "recovery," the forward reach to get ready for a stroke. You are sitting on a slide, a seat on rollers, which runs on a track about two feet long, set variously according to the type of stroke your coach favors. Your two hands are on the loom of your twelve-foot oar, balancing it neatly. If you lower them too far you sky the blade of your oar, and the shift of the center of gravity will make the boat rock and cost you precious headway; if you raise them too high your oar will touch the waves and you may cause a jolt that will throw the whole boat out of time. So your hands are balancing delicately—next time you see a good crew rowing watch the oars moving together clear of the water on the recovery; see how narrow that long shell is and realize the miracle of balance that keeps it steady while those big men swing aft and the long sweeps reach forward. Or watch a green crew, see the oars at eight different levels and the shell wallowing from side to side.

You are moving your hands, your shoulders, and your tail aft (you are facing aft) at three different speeds, to bring each to its stopping point at the same time. If you rush your slide to the end of its run, that sharp motion and possibly the abrupt stopping at the end will check the motion of the shell, you can see it happen, and you yourself will fall into the position of your maximum effort with a jerk which will put you out of balance. Hands, shoulders, slide, must move *in related time* one to another, and in perfect time with the other seven men, so that at the right moment you are leaning forward just far enough for reach and not too far for power, your slide is all the way aft, your legs and knees are ready, your back is arched, not slumped, and your balancing hands are holding firmly to the oar. In the very last part of your swing your outside hand, the one toward the blade, makes a half turn so that the blade, which was parallel to the water, is perpendicular to it.

Catch! A slight raising of your hands and arms has dropped your blade into the water, and instantaneously your shoulders take hold. That simple action is not quite so simple. If you have not done it minutely right your oar may skitter out above the water, slice too deeply into the water to help the boat, or you may catch a crab—entangle your oar in water so that you can't get it out. That last is virtual shipwreck, it may knock you out of the boat, and it will almost certainly lose a race. Once you and seven other men are driving with all your forces it is too late to attempt to turn or guide your oar. You must have dropped it into the water so accurately that it will stay with the blade just submerged all the way through your pull and come out willingly. That is part of the turn of your outside hand and the act of slightly raising your arms.

An immeasurably short time after your shoulders, your legs start to drive. Now your arms are merely straps attaching your hands to your body; legs and shoulders and back are pulling on the oar for all they are worth; everything you've got is going into it, but you have taken care that your tail, driven by your legs, will not shoot on the slide ahead of your shoulders.

You have driven through almost to the end of your catch, your slide is almost home, your shoulders are back. Now your arms come in, and just as your knees come downlocked, your hands touch your stomach. Here is the prettiest part of the stroke, the shoot of the hands to start the recovery. Remember, your oar is still deep in the water rushing past your boat; if it is caught in that it turns to a wild machine. As your hands touch your belly they drop, shoot out, in a motion "as fast and smooth as a billiard ball caroming," at the same time your inside wrist turns and the blade is once more parallel to the water— feathered. The shoot of your hands and arms brings your shoulders forward and you begin your recovery once more.

All this that I have described happens in a single stroke by a good oarsman. This stroke, its predecessors and successors, is performed in a unison with seven other men which is more perfect than merely being in time, with the balance of the body maintained also in relation to the keel so that the boat shall not roll. At a moderate racing rate it is performed thirty-two to thirty-six times to the minute—all of this, nothing omitted—and in a rhythm which keeps the time of the recovery not less than double that of the catch.

This is not the whole of rowing, but it is the basic part of the individual's job in it. Unite it to another fundamental and you can have a crew.

The other fundamental is unison. I have said that a crew does not merely keep time; it does something subtler than that, it becomes one. This it cannot do if there is bad feeling among the men in the boat; a single antagonistic personality can keep eight oarsmen from becoming a crew rowing together even though they are accurately following the stroke's oar and the coxswain's counting. Crews are not made up on a basis of personalities, but according to the coaches' estimate of individual capacities; it is after they are rowing together that they become friends. . . .

I find in writing about rowing that I tend to concentrate rather technically upon the sport itself, with the attendant danger of losing that very background of its relation to a boy's life which would give it validity. This is partly because the average man who reads this has played football, and many women have at least had the game explained to them and have learned how to watch it, while the essentials of rowing are widely unknown. The sport became for me something complete in itself, into which I entered and from which I returned to ordinary life; it maintained its own, unbroken stream winding through the other currents of my existence. I believe you will find this true of anyone who is really devoted to any game. But it had to relate to all the rest.

□
Vocabulary

aft   behind, the stern of a ship
keel   a ridge on the bottom of a hull that provides strength to resist sagging
coxswain   a steersman of a racing shell who directs the crew

Discussion

1. What is the nature of the first two paragraphs? Why has Lafarge included these in his description of the process of rowing?
2. Notice how the language works to recreate for the reader the sensual experience of rowing:

   "the crash of the oars in the locks"

   "the shell leaping at the touch"

   "the echoing change of sound in shooting under a bridge"

   What other words or phrases in this process essay appeal directly to the reader's senses?
3. Telling how to do something step-by-step and still making what you write interesting, is a difficult task. Examine closely the paragraphs that deal directly with the process of rowing (paragraphs three through nine). Has Lafarge succeeded in describing the procedure? (What are the "recovery," "the loom of your twelve-foot oar," "a green crew," and "feathered"?)
4. Has Lafarge maintained your interest? If so, how has he done so?
5. How has Lafarge's description imitated the effects of a slow-motion camera? ("All this that I have described happens in a single stroke by a good oarsman.")
6. How is the "camera" put back to normal speed? Do you find this writing technique effective? Why or why not?
7. Why does Lafarge feel he must "concentrate rather technically on the sport itself"?

For Further Discussion

8. What does Lafarge mean when he writes: "The sport became for me something complete in itself, into which I entered and from which I returned to ordinary life. . . ."?
   How does this statement relate back to the first three paragraphs in the piece?

Jessica Mitford
(1917–   )

Jessica Mitford was born September 11, 1917, in Batsford, Gloucestershire, England. She now lives in the United States. Her work history has included stints as a market researcher, bartender, salesperson, and executive secretary. Mitford began writing at age 38. Her first book, *The American Way of Death* (from which the following piece is excerpted), is about the funeral industry. It helped earn her the distinction of "Queen of the Muckrakers."

In the introduction to *Poison Penmanship: The Gentle Art of Muckraking* she describes her techniques, which include:

> Choice of Subject— . . . one does by far one's best work when besotted by and absorbed in the matter at hand.

> Gathering Background Information—the goal is to know, if possible, *more* about your subject than the target of the investigation does.

> Picking Other People's Brains— . . . find (an expert) who is sufficiently interested in you or your subject to give advice gratis.

> Interviewing— . . . where the fun begins, and where you may uncover information that is accessible no other way.

Other subjects of exposé by Mitford have included the famous Writer's School, "fat farms" for the well-to-do, prisons, and television executives. In addition, she has written a book about the Mitford family, *Daughters and Rebels*.

To Bid the World Farewell

Embalming is indeed a most extraordinary procedure, and one must wonder at the docility of Americans who each year pay hundreds of millions of dollars for its perpetuation, blissfully ignorant of what it is all about, what is done, how it is done. Not one in ten thousand has any idea of what actually takes place. Books on the subject are extremely hard to come by. They are not to be found in most libraries or bookshops.

In an era when huge television audiences watch surgical operations in the comfort of their living rooms, when, thanks to the animated cartoon, the geography of the digestive system has become familiar territory even to the nursery school set, in a land where the satisfaction of curiosity about almost all matters is a national pastime, the secrecy surrounding embalming can, surely, hardly be attributed to the inherent gruesomeness of the subject. Custom in this regard has within this century suffered a complete reversal. In the early days of American embalming, when it was performed in the home of the deceased, it was almost mandatory for some relative to stay by the embalmer's side and witness the procedure. Today, family members who might wish to be in attendance would certainly be dissuaded by the funeral director. All others, except apprentices, are excluded by law from the preparation room.

A close look at what does actually take place may explain in large measure the undertaker's intractable reticence concerning a procedure that has become his major *raison d'être*. Is it possible he fears that public information about embalming might lead patrons to wonder if they

□

really want this service? If the funeral men are loath to discuss the subject outside the trade, the reader may, understandably, be equally loath to go on reading at this point. For those who have the stomach for it, let us part the formaldehyde curtain. . . .

The body is first laid out in the undertaker's morgue—or rather, Mr. Jones is reposing in the preparation room—to be readied to bid the world farewell.

The preparation room in any of the better funeral establishments has the tiled and sterile look of a surgery, and indeed the embalmer-restorative artist who does his chores there is beginning to adopt the term "dermasurgeon" (appropriately corrupted by some mortician-writers as "demisurgeon") to describe his calling. His equipment, consisting of scalpels, scissors, augers, forceps, clamps, needles, pumps, tubes, bowls and basins, is crudely imitative of the surgeon's as is his technique, acquired in a nine- or twelve-month post-high-school course in an embalming school. He is supplied by an advanced chemical industry with a bewildering array of fluids, sprays, pastes, oils, powders, creams, to fix or soften tissue, shrink or distend it as needed, dry it here, restore the moisture there. There are cosmetics, waxes and paints to fill and cover features, even plaster of Paris to replace entire limbs. There are ingenious aids to prop and stabilize the cadaver: a Vari-Pose Head Rest, the Edwards Arm and Hand Positioner, the Repose Block (to support the shoulders during the embalming), and the Throop Foot Positioner, which resembles an old-fashioned stocks.

Mr. John H. Eckels, president of the Eckels College of Mortuary Science, thus describes the first part of the embalming procedure: "In the hands of a skilled practitioner, this work may be done in a comparatively short time and without mutilating the body other than by slight incision—so slight that it scarcely would cause serious inconvenience if made upon a living person. It is necessary to remove the blood, and doing this not only helps in the disinfecting, but removes the principal cause of disfigurements due to discoloration."

Another textbook discusses the all-important time element: "The earlier this is done, the better, for every hour that elapses between death and embalming will add to the problems and complications encountered. . . . " Just how soon should one get going on the embalming? The author tells us, "On the basis of such scanty information made available to this profession through its rudimentary and haphazard system of technical research, we must conclude that the best results are to be obtained if the subject is embalmed before life is completely extinct—that is, before cellular death has occurred. In the average case, this would mean within an hour after somatic death." For those who feel that there is something a little rudimentary, not to say haphazard, about this advice, a comforting thought is offered by another writer. Speaking of fears entertained in early days of premature burial, he points out, "One of the effects of embalming by chemical injection, however, has been to dispel fears of live burial." How true; once the blood is removed, chances of live burial are indeed remote.

To return to Mr. Jones, the blood is drained out through the veins and replaced by embalming fluid pumped in through the arteries. As noted in *The Principles and Practices of Embalming*, "every operator has a favorite injection and drainage point—a fact which becomes a handicap only if he fails or refuses to forsake his favorites when conditions demand it." Typical favorites are the carotid artery, femoral artery, jugular vein, subclavian vein. There are various choices of embalming fluid. If Flextone is used, it will produce a "mild, flexible rigidity. The skin retains a velvety softness, the tissues are rubbery and pliable. Ideal for women and children." It may be blended with B. and G. Products Company's Lyf-Lyk tint, which is guaranteed to reproduce "nature's own skin texture . . . the velvety appearance of living tissue." Suntone comes in three separate tints: Suntan; Special Cosmetic Tint, a pink shade "especially indicated for young female subjects"; and Regular Cosmetic Tint, moderately pink.

About three to six gallons of a dyed and perfumed solution of formaldehyde, glycerin, borax, phenol, alcohol and water is soon circulating through Mr. Jones, whose mouth has been sewn together with a "needle directed upward between the upper lip and gum and brought out through the left nostril," with the corners raised slightly "for a more pleasant expression." If he should be bucktoothed, his teeth are cleaned with Bon Ami and coated with colorless nail polish. His eyes, meanwhile, are closed with flesh-tinted eye caps and eye cement.

The next step is to have at Mr. Jones with a thing called a trocar. This is a long, hollow needle attached to a tube. It is jabbed into the abdomen, poked around the entrails and chest cavity, the contents of which are pumped out and replaced with "cavity fluid." This done, and the hole in the abdomen sewed up, Mr. Jones's face is heavily creamed (to protect the skin from burns which may be caused by leakage of the chemicals), and he is covered with a sheet and left unmolested for a while. But not for long—there is more, much more, in store for him. He has been embalmed, but not yet restored, and the best time to start the restorative work is eight to ten hours after embalming, when the tissues have become firm and dry.

The object of all this attention to the corpse, it must be remembered, is to make it presentable for viewing in an attitude of healthy repose. "Our customs require the presentation of our dead in the semblance of normality . . . unmarred by the ravages of illness, disease or mutilation," says Mr. J. Sheridan Mayer in his *Restorative Art*. This is rather a large order since few people die in the full bloom of health, unravaged by illness and unmarked by some disfigurement. The funeral industry is equal to the challenge: "In some cases the gruesome appearance of a mutilated or disease-ridden subject may be quite discouraging. The task of restoration may seem impossible and shake the

□

confidence of the embalmer. This is the time for intestinal fortitude and determination. Once the formative work is begun and affected tissues are cleaned or removed, all doubts of success vanish. It is surprising and gratifying to discover the results which may be obtained."

The embalmer, having allowed an appropriate interval to elapse, returns to the attack, but now he brings into play the skill and equipment of sculptor and cosmetician. Is a hand missing? Casting one in plaster of Paris is a simple matter. "For replacement purposes, only a cast of the back of the hand is necessary; this is within the ability of the average operator and is quite adequate." If a lip or two, a nose or an ear should be missing, the embalmer has at hand a variety of restorative waxes with which to model replacements. Pores and skin texture are simulated by stippling with a little brush, and over this cosmetics are laid on. Head off? Decapitation cases are rather routinely handled. Ragged edges are trimmed, and head joined to torso with a series of splints, wires and sutures. It is a good idea to have a little something at the neck—a scarf or high collar—when time for viewing comes. Swollen mouth? Cut out tissue as needed from inside the lips. If too much is removed, the surface contour can easily be restored by padding with cotton. Swollen necks and cheeks are reduced by removing tissue through vertical incisions made down each side of the neck. "When the deceased is casketed, the pillow will hide the suture incisions . . . as an extra precaution against leakage, the suture may be painted with liquid sealer."

The opposite condition is more likely to present itself—that of emaciation. His hypodermic syringe now loaded with massage cream, the embalmer seeks out and fills the hollowed and sunken areas by injection. In this procedure the backs of the hands and fingers and the under-chin area should not be neglected.

Positioning the lips is a problem that recurrently challenges the ingenuity of the embalmer. Closed too tightly, they tend to give a stern, even disapproving expression. Ideally, embalmers feel, the lips should give the impression of being ever so slightly parted, the upper lip protruding slightly for a more youthful appearance. This takes some engineering, however, as the lips tend to drift apart. Lip drift can sometimes be remedied by pushing one or two straight pins through the inner margin of the lower lip and then inserting them between the two front upper teeth. If Mr. Jones happens to have no teeth, the pins can just as easily be anchored in his Armstrong Face Former and Denture Replacer. Another method to maintain lip closure is to dislocate the lower jaw, which is then held in its new position by a wire run through holes which have been drilled through the upper and lower jaws at the midline. As the French are fond of saying, *il faut souffrir pour être belle.*

If Mr. Jones has died of jaundice, the embalming fluid will very likely turn him green. Does this deter the embalmer? Not if he has intestinal fortitude. Masking pastes and cosmetics are heavily laid on, burial garments and casket interiors are color-correlated with particular care, and Jones is displayed beneath rose-colored lights. Friends will say, "How *well* he looks." Death by carbon monoxide, on the other hand, can be rather a good thing from the embalmer's viewpoint: "One advantage is the fact that this type of discoloration is an exaggerated form of a natural pink coloration." This is nice because the healthy glow is already present and needs but little attention.

The patching and filling completed, Mr. Jones is now shaved, washed and dressed. Cream-based cosmetic, available in pink, flesh, suntan, brunette and blond, is applied to his hands and face, his hair is shampooed and combed (and, in the case of Mrs. Jones, set), his hands manicured. For the horny-handed son of toil special care must be taken; cream should be applied to remove ingrained grime, and the nails cleaned. "If he were not in the habit of having them manicured in life, trimming and shaping is advised for better appearance—never questioned by kin."

Jones is now ready for casketing (this is the present participle of the verb "to casket"). In this operation his right shoulder should be depressed slightly "to turn the body a bit to the right and soften the appearance of lying flat on the back." Positioning the hands is a matter of importance, and special rubber positioning blocks may be used. The hands should be cupped slightly for a more lifelike, relaxed appearance. Proper placement of the body requires a delicate sense of balance. It should lie as high as possible in the casket, yet not so high that the lid, when lowered, will hit the nose. On the other hand, we are cautioned, placing the body too low "creates the impression that the body is in a box."

Jones is next wheeled into the appointed slumber room where a few last touches may be added—his favorite pipe placed in his hand or, if he was a great reader, a book propped into position. (In the case of little Master Jones a Teddy bear may be clutched.) Here he will hold open house for a few days, visiting hours 10 A.M. to 9 P.M.

Vocabulary

intractable reticence   stubborn
raison d'étre   reason for being
dermasurgeon   specializes in surgery on the skin
auger   a tool for boring
somatic   pertaining to the cellular body
sutures   joining of a wound or the like by stitching
il faut souffrir pour étre belle   French for "one must suffer to be beautiful"

□
Discussion

1. How do the first three paragraphs work to introduce the embalming process? How does Mitford gain your interest?
2. Paragraph four introduces a mythical cadaver, Mr. Jones. What is the effect of "personalizing" this process?
3. Follow the references to Jones throughout the essay. How effective a writing device is this?
4. Briefly describe the process involved in each of the following: embalming, restoration, and casketing.
5. How have Mitford's details (names of "tools" of the trade, product names, quotes from "authorities") added to the realism of her account?
6. Examine the tone of this piece. "For those who feel that there is something a little rudimentary, not to say haphazard, about this advice. . . ." Or, "The next step is to have at Mr. Jones with a thing called a trocar." What is Mitford's attitude toward the subject?
7. Is her essay merely analyzing a process, step by step, or is it also, and primarily, persuasive?
   Does she succeed in persuading you? To do what?
8. In the first paragraph Mitford states her thesis: "One must wonder at the docility of Americans who each year pay hundreds of millions of dollars for its perpetuation blissfully ignorant. . . ." How does she develop her thesis in the paragraphs that follow?

For Further Discussion

9. Process analysis, like any kind of analysis, divides the subject into parts. How do the parts Mitford has divided her subject into serve as the structure for her essay? (Paragraph by paragraph, reconstruct Mitford's "outline" or plan for the paper.)
10. Process essays often include cues for when one part of the procedure ends and another begins. Ordinarily such cues in writing are termed transitions, words that take the reader from one idea to the next, one paragraph to the next. In process, such transitions might be termed *time cues*. Common time cues include *first, second, next,* and *finally.*
    Explore Mitford's use of time cues. List the cues you find, paragraph by paragraph.
11. How has Mitford kept her time cues from being merely mechanical, predictable? (First, second, third, etc.)
    Does she begin every sentence or paragraph with a time cue?

Yasunari Kawabata
(1899–1972)

Yasunari Kawabata was born June 11, 1899, near Osaka, Japan. Though he came to be known as one of Japan's finest traditional stylists in the 1920s, he and others founded *Bungei Jidai,* an avant-garde literary journal. Known as the "neo-sensualists," they experimented in cubism, dadaism, futurism, and surrealism. Kawabata, however, soon reverted to a style critics most often trace to the seventeenth-century haiku form. The Eastern classics were his favorite literature. He said, "I value the Buddhist scriptures in particular, not so much as religious teachings, but as literary visions, fantasies."

Kawabata wrote novels, short stories, plays, criticism, and translation. In 1968 he won the Nobel Prize in literature, the first Japanese to do so. Originally he intended to be a painter, and this probably is responsible for the visual quality of his writing. The following selection from his novel *Snow Country* is an example.

Kawabata committed suicide in 1972 without explanation, though he had been greatly saddened by the ritual suicide of his protegé, Yukio Mishima, in 1970.

Chijimi Linen

The thread was spun in the snow, and the cloth woven in the snow, washed in the snow, and bleached in the snow. Everything, from the first spinning of the thread to the last finishing touches, was done in the snow. "There is Chijimi linen because there is snow," someone wrote long ago. "Snow is the mother of Chijimi."

The Chijimi grass-linen of this snow country was the handwork of the mountain maiden through the long, snowbound winters. Shimamura searched for the cloth in old-clothes shops to use for summer Kimonos. Through acquaintances in the dance world he had found a shop that specialized in old Nō robes, and he had a standing order that when a good piece of Chijimi came in he was to see it.

In the old days, it is said, the early Chijimi fair was held in the spring, when the snow had melted and the snow blinds were taken down from the houses. People came from far and near to buy Chijimi, even wholesalers from the great commercial cities, Edo, Nagoya, and Osaka; and the inns at which they stayed were fixed by tradition. Since the labors of half a year were on display, youths and maidens gathered from all the mountain villages. Sellers' booths and buyers' booths were lined up side by side, and the market took on the air of a festival. With prizes awarded for the best pieces of weaving, it came also to be sort of competition for husbands. The girls learned to weave as children, and they turned out their best work between the ages of perhaps fourteen and twenty-four. As they grew older they lost the touch that gave tone to the finest Chijimi. In their desire to be numbered among the few outstanding weavers, they put their whole labor and love into this product of the long snowbound months—the months of seclusion and boredom, between October, under the old lunar calendar, when the spinning began, and mid-February of the following year, when the last bleaching was finished.

There may have been among Shimamura's kimonos one or more

woven by these mountain maidens toward the middle of the last century.

He still sent his kimonos back for "snow-bleaching." It was a great deal of trouble to return old kimonos—that had touched the skin of he could not know whom—for rebleaching each year to the country that had produced them; but when he considered the labors of those mountain maidens, he wanted the bleaching to be done properly in the country where the maidens had lived. The thought of the white linen, spread out on the deep snow, the cloth and the snow glowing scarlet in the rising sun, was enough to make him feel that the dirt of the summer had been washed away, even that he himself had been bleached clean. It must be added, however, that a Tokyo shop took care of the details for him, and he had no way of knowing that the bleaching had really been done in the old manner.

From ancient times there were houses that specialized in bleaching. The weavers for the most part did not do their own. White Chijimi was spread out on the snow after it was woven, colored Chijimi bleached on frames while still in thread. The bleaching season came in January and February under the lunar calendar, and snow-covered fields and gardens were the bleaching grounds.

The cloth or thread was soaked overnight in ash water. The next morning it was washed over and over again, wrung, and put out to bleach. The process was repeated day after day, and the sight when, as the bleaching came to an end, the rays of the rising sun turned the white Chijimi blood-red was quite beyond description, Shimamura had read in an old book. It was something to be shown to natives of warmer provinces. And the end of the bleaching was a sign that spring was coming to the snow country.

The land of the Chijimi was very near this hot spring, just down the river, where the valley began to widen out. Indeed it must almost have been visible from Shimamura's window. All of the Chijimi market towns now had railway stations, and the region was still a well-known weaving center.

Since Shimamura had never come to the snow country in midsummer, when he wore Chijimi, or in the snowy season, when it was woven, he had never had occasion to talk of it to Komako; and she hardly seemed the person to ask about the fate of an old folk art.

When he heard the song Yoko sang in the bath, it had come to him that, had she been born long ago, she might have sung thus as she worked over her spools and looms, so exactly suited to the fancy was her voice.

The thread of the grass-linen, finer than animal hair, is difficult to work except in the humidity of the snow, it is said, and the dark, cold season is therefore ideal for weaving. The ancients used to add that the way this product of the cold has of feeling cool to the skin in the hottest weather is a play of the principles of light and darkness. This Komako too, who had so fastened herself to him, seemed at center cool, and the remarkable, concentrated warmth was for that fact all the more touching.

But this love would leave behind it nothing so definite as a piece of Chijimi. Though cloth to be worn is among the most short-lived of craftworks, a good piece of Chijimi, if it has been taken care of, can be worn quite unfaded a half-century and more after weaving. As Shima-mura thought absently how human intimacies have not even so long a life, the image of Komako as the mother of another man's children suddenly floated into his mind. He looked around, startled. Possibly he was tired.

He had stayed so long that one might wonder whether he had forgotten his wife and children. He stayed not because he could not leave Komako nor because he did not want to. He had simply fallen into the habit of waiting for those frequent visits. And the more continuous the assault became, the more he began to wonder what was lacking in him, what kept him from living as completely. He stood gazing at his own coldness, so to speak. He could not understand how she had so lost herself. All of Komako came to him, but it seemed that nothing went out from him to her. He heard in his chest, like snow piling up, the sound of Komako, an echo beating against empty walls. And he knew that he could not go on pampering himself forever.

He leaned against the brazier, provided against the coming of the snowy season, and thought how unlikely it was that he would come again once he had left. The innkeeper had lent him an old Kyoto tea-kettle, skillfully inlaid in silver with flowers and birds, and from it came the sound of wind in the pines. He could make out two pine breezes, as a matter of fact, a near one and a far one. Just beyond the far breeze he heard faintly the tinkling of a bell. He put his ear to the kettle and listened. Far away, where the bell tinkled on, he suddenly saw Komako's feet, tripping in time with the bell. He drew back. The time had come to leave.

He thought of going to see the Chijimi country. That excursion might set him on his way toward breaking away from this hot spring.

He did not know at which of the towns downstream he should get off the train. Not interested in modern weaving centers, he chose a station that looked suitably lonesome and backward. After walking for a time he came out on what seemed to be the main street of an old post town.

The eaves pushing out far beyond the houses were supported by pillars along both sides of the street, and in their shade were passages for communication when the snow was deep, rather like the open lean-to the old Edo shopkeeper used for displaying his wares. With deep eaves on one side of each house, the passages stretched on down the street.

Since the houses were joined in a solid block, the snow from the roofs could only be thrown down into the street. One might more accurately say that at its deepest the snow was thrown not down but up, to a high bank of snow in the middle of the street. Tunnels were cut through for passage from one side to the other.

The houses in Komako's hot-spring village, for all of its being a part of this same snow country, were separated by open spaces, and this was therefore the first time Shimamura had seen the snow passages. He tried walking in one of them. The shade under the old eaves was dark, and the leaning pillars were beginning to rot at their bases. He walked along looking into the houses as into the gloom where generation after generation of his ancestors had endured the long snows.

He saw that the weaver maidens, giving themselves up to their work here under the snow, had lived lives far from as bright and fresh as the Chijimi they made. With an allusion to a Chinese poem, Shimamura's old book had pointed out that in harsh economic terms the making of Chijimi was quite impractical, so great was the expenditure of effort that went into even one piece. It followed that none of the Chijimi houses had been able to hire weavers from outside.

The nameless workers, so diligent while they lived, had presently died, and only the Chijimi remained, the plaything of men like Shimamura, cool and fresh against the skin in the summer. This rather unremarkable thought struck him as most remarkable. The labor into which a heart has poured its whole love—where will it have its say, to excite and inspire, and when?

Allusions/References

Nō robes   robes used in classical drama of Japan with stylized manner of music and dance

Discussion

1. Examine the structure of the first paragraph of this piece. How does it serve as an introduction to everything that follows?
   Words and phrases repeated deliberately, and in the same positions in sentences, make up what is termed *parallel structure*. Notice how the word "snow" is repeated in a final position in the sentences and phrases: "spun in the *snow*, washed in the *snow*, and bleached in the *snow*."
   How does this positioning enhance the effect of its appearance as first word in the last sentence?
   How does the structure of the last sentence enhance its meaning?
2. Two processes are described in this passage. What are they?
3. How is information about the weaving of Chijimi revealed little by little as the reader proceeds with the story?
   What can you say about the weaving process by the end of the passage?
4. Describe the process of bleaching.
   Why is snow "the mother of Chijimi"?

□

For Further Discussion

5. Kawabata weaves his story as carefully as the weavers weave their cloth. The Chijimi emerges as a remarkable linen, a real fabric, but it also begins to take on symbolic value.

 What does Shimamura learn about himself through his excursion into the Chijimi snow country?

 What does he learn about Komako?

6. Examine the last paragraph. How might the geisha, Komako, be compared to the Chijimi?

 How is anything made beautifully, heart filled, and enduring (music, art, poetry), like the Chijimi?

7. How do you answer Shimamura's final question?

8. What qualities of Kawabata's writing remind you of haiku?

 (A simple definition of haiku—there are many forms—is a Japanese lyric form of 17 syllables that points to a thing or a pairing of things in nature that has moved the poet.)

Ernest Hemingway
(1899–1961)

Ernest Hemingway was born July 21, 1899, in Oak Park, Illinois. In high school he wrote for the school newspaper and its literary magazine. After graduation he worked briefly as a newspaper reporter, before enlisting as a Red Cross ambulance driver and going to Europe and to war for the first time. Both would continue to be major influences in his life and writing.

His second trip to Europe, or more specifically, Paris, was in 1921 at age 22. This time he went to be a writer. While working primarily as a journalist, he made the acquaintance of Gertrude Stein, Ezra Pound, James Joyce, and other literary figures of the era who were to be known as "The Lost Generation." Stein, in particular, befriended Hemingway and encouraged him with his maturing style. Though Hemingway continued writing as a journalist and war correspondent for many years, he began in Paris to write the short stories that were the first works of a major literary stylist. His writing would eventually earn both Nobel and Pulitzer prizes.

"The writer's job is to tell the truth," Hemingway said. In his early days in Paris, when he would have trouble writing, he would tell himself: "All you have to do is write one true sentence. Write the finest sentence that you know. So finally I would write one true sentence, and then go on from there. It was easy then because there was always one true sentence that I knew or had seen or had heard someone say."

Killing a Bull

Bull fighting is not a sport. It is a tragedy, and it symbolizes the struggle between man and the beasts. There are usually six bulls to a fight. A fight is called a corrida de toros. Fighting bulls are bred like race horses, some of the oldest breeding establishments being several hundred years

☐

old. A good bull is worth about $2,000. They are bred for speed, strength and viciousness. In other words, a good fighting bull is an absolutely incorrigible bad bull.

Bull fighting is an exceedingly dangerous occupation. In sixteen fights I saw there were only two in which there was no one badly hurt. On the other hand it is very remunerative. A popular espada gets $5,000 for his afternoon's work. An unpopular espada though may not get $500. Both run the same risks. It is a good deal like Grand Opera for the really great matadors except they run the chance of being killed every time they cannot hit high C.

No one at any time in the fight can approach the bull at any time except directly from the front. That is where the danger comes. There are also all sorts of complicated passes that must be done with the cape, each requiring as much technique as a champion billiard player. And underneath it all is the necessity for playing the old tragedy in the absolutely custom bound, law-laid-down way. It must all be done gracefully, seemingly effortlessly and always with dignity. The worst criticism the Spaniards ever make of a bull fighter is that his work is "vulgar."

The three absolute acts of the tragedy are first the entry of the bull when the picadors receive the shock of his attacks and attempt to protect their horses with their lances. Then the horses go out and the second act is the planting of the banderillos. This is one of the most interesting and difficult parts but among the easiest for a new bull fight fan to appreciate in technique. The banderillos are three-foot, gaily colored darts with a small fish hook prong in the end. The man who is going to plant them walks out into the arena alone with the bull. He lifts the banderillos at arm's length and points them toward the bull. Then he calls "Toro! Toro!" The bull charges and the banderillero rises to his toes, bends in a curve forward and just as the bull is about to hit him drops the darts into the bull's hump just back of his horns.

They must go in evenly, one on each side. They must not be shoved, or thrown or stuck in from the side. This is the first time the bull has been completely baffled, there is the prick of the darts that he cannot escape and there are no horses for him to charge into. But he charges the man again and again and each time he gets a pair of the long banderillos that hang from his hump by their tiny barbs and flop like porcupine quills.

Last is the death of the bull, which is in the hands of the matador who has had charge of the bull since his first attack. Each matador has two bulls in the afternoon. The death of the bull is most formal and can only be brought about in one way, directly from the front by the matador who must receive the bull in full charge and kill him with a sword thrust between the shoulders just back of the neck and between the horns. Before killing the bull he must first do a series of passes with the muleta, a piece of red cloth he carries about the size of a large napkin. With the muleta the torero must show his complete mastery of the bull, must make the bull miss him again and again by inches, before he is allowed to kill him. It is in this phase that most of the fatal accidents occur.

The word "toreador" is obsolete Spanish and is never used. The torero is usually called an espada or swordsman. He must be proficient in all three acts of the fight. In the first he uses the cape and does veronicas and protects the picadors by taking the bull out and away from them when they are spilled to the ground. In the second act he plants the banderillos. In the third act he masters the bull with the muleta and kills him.

Few toreros excel in all three departments. Some, like young Chicuelo, are unapproachable in their cape work. Others like the late Joselito are wonderful banderilleros. Only a few are great killers. Most of the greatest killers are gypsies.

Vocabulary

remunerative   payment for services rendered
espada   torero, swordsman, the matador (bull fighter)
veronica   a maneuver in which the matador stands immobile and passes the cape slowly before the charging bull
muleta   a short red cape attached to a staff and used by the matador to maneuver the bull

Discussion

1. Hemingway's first two sentences in this piece challenge the reader to think about the process of bullfighting in a special light. What does he mean by the word "tragedy"?
   (Look up the word "tragedy" in a dictionary. The importance of Hemingway's statement cannot be understood without a full definition of the word.) What then, does he mean by "it symbolizes the struggle between man and the beasts"?
2. How does the comparison of the bullfights with the Grand Opera reinforce Hemingway's underlying ideas about bullfighting?
   What are Hemingway's underlying ideas about bullfighting? (Compare Kerouac's description of the same events in Chapter Eight, "The Bullfight." This would make an excellent comparison-contrast paper. See For Further Discussion under Kerouac.)
3. How is a process essay more than merely instructions on how to do something, or how something is done?
   (Note that an essay is a forum for ideas. It is *not* primarily a listing, even when it is analyzing a process.)
4. How does Hemingway carry out his metaphor of bullfighting as tragedy? What are "the three absolute acts of the tragedy"?

☐

5. What time cues (transitional words used in process essays) does Hemingway employ to give order to the process he is describing?
(Look at the essay paragraph by paragraph to find the word cues.)

For Further Discussion

6. Hemingway writes: "Underneath it all is the necessity for playing the old tragedy in the absolutely custom bound, law-laid-down way."
Oliver Lafarge, in "The Eight-Oared Shell," writes that canoeing for him is, "something complete in itself, into which I entered and from which I returned to ordinary life; it maintained its own, unbroken stream winding through the other currents of my existence."
How are all sports, or games, mini universes of their own?
7. Do we admire those who can master the rituals surrounding some human activity? (Consider not only sports, but haiku, opera, fine holiday dinners, the writing of process essays.)
8. What language in Hemingway's "Killing a Bull" indicates his admiration, or lack of admiration, for the ritual of bullfighting?
Is Hemingway being only objective?
9. Write a process essay about a ritualistic act you engage in (getting up in the morning, preparation for writing, concert going, applying makeup, registering for classes, brushing your teeth, etc.). In this essay, not only tell your reader about *how* you go about your activity, but *why*, what it means to you. This is the true essence of a good essay on process, the exploration of the rituals of human life.

☐ By Definition

We have a good deal of foggy thinking around the ideas that direct our actions. As long as it is not necessary for us to communicate them, the fog may not seem to hinder us too much. At least we like to think we're not hindered by the fuzzy areas of our thoughts; we function don't we? But none of us lives in isolation from one another, and it is in the necessity for ideas to be shared, clearly and distinctly, that the college definition essay finds its importance.

The meaning or significance of an idea cannot be understood until its outline, its shape and extent and limits, can be found and agreed upon. Essentially this is what the organizational pattern known as definition sets out to do. In it:

1. a context is found for an idea as it is used in its current sense;
2. the idea is assigned to its general class, to other ideas similar to it;

□

3. it is then distinguished from all other things in that same class; it is separated out from all ideas with which it might be confused;
4. examples and illustrations are given so that it can be shown in specific terms.

Obviously, defining a single word or term would seem to you difficult enough, but the task of the definition essay is a much greater thing. You must not only define a subject of your own choosing, but must do so in writing that engages your reader's interest. Huston Smith, by use of legend, attempts to define the nature of Lao Tzu, father of one of mankind's great spiritual philosophies.

Rachael Carson defines the wind wave by distinguishing it from other kinds, and by following it from its formation far out at sea to its dissolution as a "seething confusion of foam."

Jack Kerouac, in a spill and tumble of words, defines the beat generation, the popular culture out of which it arose, and the beatific nature of its vision. Dennis Farney defines the aesthetic of the Venturis, a husband and wife architectural team, whose ideas are termed "ugly" and "banal."

In these essays the authors are writing about subjects close to the heart, not about organizational patterns of rhetoric, like definition. Writers rarely write from the trigger of a form. Instead they allow their ideas to take shape in the ways natural to them. As a student you must walk a tightrope. The most difficult part of writing a college definition essay is in finding a subject you care about and can organize in this manner. Search out the most commonplace, everyday events for clues, the things you know about and enjoy. What is rock 'n roll? What is new wave? What is science-fiction writing, and how is it distinct from fantasy? What is the liberated woman? What is fashion? What is the computer? What is MTV? What is matedness? What is a college education? What is the future?

And then ask yourself why you want to share your ideas about the topic you finally choose. As in all essays, the definition essay is only as good as it is imbued with its reason for being.

Kerouac wanted to clarify what he considered to be a gross misunderstanding about the "beats"—that they were not merely wild livers, seekers of pleasure and abandonment—for the sake of keeping alive their vision. Smith wished to demonstrate the selflessness of a man who would originate a vision of existence, and then not claim it as his own.

What do you want to define or redefine in such a way as to open up its meaning or significance to the reader?

Read the following essays with an eye to the language, and the use of illustrations, as well as to the organizational pattern of definition. Ask yourself how these essays inform you about the writing of your own definition essay.

Huston Smith

(1919–   )

Huston Smith was born May 31, 1919, in Soochow, China. He has taught philosophy at several institutions including MIT and Washington University, and is currently professor of religion at Syracuse University in New York.

In his book *The Purposes of Higher Education* Smith writes: "The aim of all writing is the transfer of some thought or feeling from one's own mind to that of someone else. Effective communication needs two things: clarity in the ideas to be conveyed, and words that serve as good conductors. Whether these two—the ideas and the words that express them—are really separable is a moot point.... The point is only that in writing the sole object is communication."

Smith is the author of several books of philosophy. The following is excerpted from his *The Religions of Man.*

The Story of Lao Tzu

According to tradition, Taoism (pronounced Dowism) originated with a man named Lao Tzu, said to have been born about 604 B.C. Some scholars date his life as much as three centuries later than this; some doubt that he ever lived. If he did we know almost nothing about him. We don't even know his name, Lao Tzu—which can be translated "the Old Boy," "the Old Fellow," or "the Grand Old Master"—being obviously a title of endearment and respect. All we really have is a mosaic of legends. Some of these are fantastic: that he was immaculately conceived by a shooting star; carried in his mother's womb for eighty-two years; and born already a wise old man with white hair. Other parts of the story have the ring of authenticity: that his occupation was that of keeper of the archives in his native western state; and that around this occupation he lived a simple and undemanding life. Estimates of his personality have been based almost entirely on one slim volume attributed to him. From this it has been surmised by some that he must have been a solitary recluse wound up in his personal occult meditations; others picture him as "the everlasting neighbor," as natural, genial, and homely as Lincoln with Lincoln's sense of humor and proportion as well. The one purportedly contemporary portrait speaks only of the enigmatic impression he left—the sense that here were depths that defied ready comprehension. Confucius, intrigued by what he had heard of Lao Tzu, once visited him. His description suggests that he was baffled by the strange man yet came away respecting him. "Of birds," he told his disciples, "I know that they have wings to fly with, of fish that they have fins to swim with, of wild beasts that they have feet to run with. For feet there are traps, for fins nets, for wings arrows. But who knows how dragons surmount wind and cloud into heaven. This day I have seen Lao Tzu. Today I have seen a dragon."

Saddened by men's disinclination to cultivate the natural goodness he advocated, and seeking greater personal solitude for his closing years, Lao Tzu is said at length to have climbed on a water buffalo and ridden westward toward what is now Tibet. At the Hankao Pass a gatekeeper sensing the unusual character of the truant tried to persuade him to turn back. Failing this, he asked the "Old Boy" if he would not at least leave a record of his beliefs to the civilization he was deserting. This Lao Tzu consented to do. He retired for three days and returned with a slim volume of 5000 characters titled *Tao Te Ching*, or "The Way and Its Power." A testament to man's at-home-ness in the universe, it can be read, as one chooses, in half an hour or a lifetime and remains to this day the basic text of all Taoist thought.

What a curious life this was for the supposed founder of a religion. He didn't preach; he didn't organize a church. He wrote a few pages, rode off on a water buffalo, and that (as far as he was concerned) was the end of the matter. How unlike Buddha who trudged the dusty roads of India for forty-five years to make his point. How unlike Confucius who hit the capitols for thirteen years trying to gain an administrative foothold for his philosophy. Here was a man so little concerned with the success of his own ideas, to say nothing of fame and fortune, that he didn't even stay around to answer questions. And yet, whether the story of this life be fact or fiction, it is so true to Taoist values that it will remain a part of the religion forever.

Vocabulary

occult   beyond common understanding, secret knowledge

Allusions/References

Taoism   A philosophy and a religious system of China based on the teachings of Lao Tzu; Tao means "the Way."
Confucius   Chinese philosopher, 551–479 B.C.
Buddha   Title of Gautama Siddhartha, an Indian philosopher, founder of Buddhism; Buddha means "awakened."

Discussion

1. Explain the image, "a mosaic of legends." How does this image work?
2. What does the word "fantastic" actually mean? How is what follows "fantastical"?
3. How does Smith's use of "a mosaic of legends" and "fantastic" begin to define Lao Tzu? How does the name "Lao Tzu" further define the man?
4. Look up the word "enigmatic." How is Smith's portrait of Lao Tzu also enig-

matic? Why does he choose the word "truant" to describe Lao Tzu's leaving on a water buffalo? Why the word "deserting"? (Writers' word choices are clues to point-of-view, to their own definition of the subject.)

5. What is Smith's point-of-view regarding Lao Tzu? List words and phrases that he uses to define Lao Tzu to you.

Rachel Carson
(1907–1964)

Rachel Carson was born in Springfield, Pennsylvania, May 27, 1907. Though she grew up inland early in life, she had "a feeling of absolute fascination for everything relating to the ocean, and a determination that I would some day be a writer."

In 1936 she went to work as an aquatic biologist for what is now the U.S. Fish and Wildlife Service. In 1952 she resigned to devote full time to writing. Her second book, *The Sea Around Us,* was published in 1951 while she was still working for the government. Writing it was a grueling affair: "I write slowly, often in longhand, with frequent revision." All in all, the book took nearly three years to write. As she was nearing its finish she wrote, "I have done the chapter on waves, but it is over long and very unevenly written, requiring a lot of work before it will do." The result is excerpted below.

Carson's most well-known and influential book, *Silent Spring,* was instrumental in alerting the public to the dangers of chemical fertilizers and insecticides. She died of cancer in 1964.

Waves

As long as there has been an earth, the moving masses of air that we call winds have swept back and forth across its surface. And as long as there has been an ocean, its waters have stirred to the passage of the winds. Most waves are the result of the action of wind on water. There are exceptions, such as the tidal waves sometimes produced by earthquakes under the sea. But the waves most of us know best are wind waves.

It is a confused pattern that the waves make in the open sea—a mixture of countless different wave trains, intermingling, overtaking, passing, or sometimes engulfing one another; each group differing from the others in the place and manner of its origin, in its speed, its direction of movement; some doomed never to reach any shore, others destined to roll across half an ocean before they dissolve in thunder on a distant beach.

Out of such seemingly hopeless confusion the patient study of many men over many years has brought a surprising amount of order. While there is still much to be learned about waves, and much to be done to apply what is known to man's advantage, there is a solid basis of fact on which to reconstruct the life history of a wave, predict its behavior under all the changing circumstances of its life, and foretell its effect on human affairs.

Before constructing an imaginary life history of a typical wave, we need to become familiar with some of its physical characteristics. A wave has height, from trough to crest. It has length, the distance from its crest to that of the following wave. The period of the wave refers to the time required for succeeding crests to pass a fixed point. None of these dimensions is static; all change, but bear definite relations to the wind, the depth of the water, and many other matters. Furthermore, the water that composes a wave does not advance with it across the sea; each water particle describes a circular or elliptical orbit with the passage of the wave form, but returns very nearly to its original position. And it is fortunate that this is so, for if the huge masses of water that comprise a wave actually moved across the sea, navigation would be impossible. Those who deal professionally in the lore of waves make frequent use of a picturesque expression—the "length of fetch." The "fetch" is the distance that the waves have run, under the drive of a wind blowing in a constant direction, without obstruction. The greater the fetch, the higher the waves. Really large waves cannot be generated within the confined space of a bay or a small sea. A fetch of perhaps 600 to 800 miles, with winds of gale velocity, is required to get up the largest ocean waves.

Now let us suppose that, after a period of calm, a storm develops far out in the Atlantic, perhaps a thousand miles from the New Jersey coast where we are spending a summer holiday. Its winds blow irregularly, with sudden gusts, shifting direction but in general blowing shoreward. The sheet of water under the wind responds to the changing pressures. It is no longer a level surface; it becomes furrowed with alternating troughs and ridges. The waves move toward the coast, and the wind that created them controls their destiny. As the storm continues and the waves move shoreward, they receive energy from the wind and increase in height. Up to a point they will continue to take to themselves the fierce energy of the wind, growing in height as the strength of the gale is absorbed, but when a wave becomes about a seventh as high from trough to crest as the distance to the next crest, it will begin to topple in foaming whitecaps. Winds of hurricane force often blow the tops off the waves by their sheer violence; in such a storm the highest waves may develop after the wind has begun to subside.

But to return to our typical wave, born of wind and water far out in the Atlantic, grown to its full height on the energy of the winds, with its fellow waves forming a confused, irregular pattern known as a "sea." As the waves gradually pass out of the storm area their height diminishes, the distance between successive crests increases, and the "sea" becomes a "swell," moving at an average speed of about 15 miles an hour. Near the coast a pattern of long, regular swells is substituted for the turbulence of open ocean. But as the swell enters shallow water a startling transformation takes place. For the first time in its existence, the wave feels the drag of shoaling bottom. Its speed slackens, crests of following waves crowd in toward it, abruptly its height increases and the wave form steepens. Then with a spilling, tumbling rush of water falling down into its trough, it dissolves in a seething confusion of foam.

An observer sitting on a beach can make at least an intelligent guess whether the surf spilling out onto the sand before him has been produced by a gale close offshore or by a distant storm. Young waves, only recently shaped by the wind, have a steep, peaked shape even well out at sea. From far out on the horizon you can see them forming whitecaps as they come in; bits of foam are spilling down their fronts and boiling and bubbling over the advancing face, and the final breaking of the wave is a prolonged and deliberate process. But if a wave, on coming into the surf zone, rears high as though gathering all its strength for the final act of its life, if the crest forms all along its advancing front and then begins to curl forward, if the whole mass of water plunges suddenly with a booming roar into its trough—then you may take it that these waves are visitors from some very distant part of the ocean, that they have traveled long and far before their final dissolution at your feet.

What is true of the Atlantic wave we have followed is true, in general, of wind waves the world over. The incidents in the life of a wave are many. How long it will live, how far it will travel, to what manner of end it will come are all determined, in large measure, by the conditions it meets in its progression across the face of the sea. For the one essential quality of a wave is that it moves; anything that retards or stops its motion dooms it to dissolution and death.

Vocabulary

shoaling bottom   the elevation of land coming close to, but not above the surface of the water

dissolution   extinction by dispersing, to dissolve

Discussion

1. How do Carson's first two sentences enlist your interest in the subject of waves?
2. How does she define a wave?
   Which kind of wave is she most concerned with here?
3. How can you tell a young wave from an old wave?
4. How does the narrative of the hypothetical "storm far out in the Atlantic" add to your understanding of waves?
   How does this "for example" writing technique, the describing of an illustrative situation, add to the reader's knowledge and enjoyment of a subject?

5. Carson was a careful writer, caring about the evenness of her writing. What examples of careful crafting can you find in this piece?
Consider the shapes and sounds of words (descriptive elements), and the telling of an event (narrative elements).

For Further Discussion

6. As with all essays, more underlies the subject than a first reading will indicate. If you can get the message, you can hang up the phone. But an essay is designed so that the words cannot be killed by extracting the information from them.
Consider the following:

> Then with a spilling, tumbling rush of water falling down into its trough, it dissolves in a seething confusion of foam.

How is "seething confusion of foam" nearly echoic of what is being described? How does the uniting of sound and sense add another dimension to Carson's writing—a dimension beyond merely conveying information? Examine Carson's other language choices in this manner.
7. How has Carson nearly personified (made almost humanlike) waves?
How does defining in human terms add to the reader's interest in the subject? Definition essays should never be attempted in a simply mechanical way. You must have a reason for defining something in an essay form, and the reason should always involve the reader and be subtly evident.

Dennis Farney

Dennis Farney was born on a wheat farm in central Kansas. He has appeared in various magazines including *Harper's, American Home, Atlantic,* and *National Geographic.*

In the following essay he writes about Robert Venturi and his wife Denise Scott Brown, who with John Rauch are the architectural firm of Venturi and Rauch. It is a look at the development of their school of the "banal" and of the Venturis themselves. Farney writes: "The Venturis take ordinary things and build on them." And in doing so they challenge us to see the world around us differently. Farney further says, "What they mean by 'ugly' buildings are buildings that don't look like a lot of modern architects think buildings ought to look."

The School of 'Messy Vitality'

Sometimes, by working very hard, architect Robert Venturi succeeds in designing a truly "dumb" building. This pleases him. What pleases his tongue-in-cheek nature even more, though, is a building that also looks "ugly," "expedient" and "banal."

The rest of the time he and his wife, Denise, an architect and urban planner, seem to work at enraging people. They're succeeding. Other architects, in particular, grow livid when the Venturis explain how "ugly" architecture can be beautiful and "banal" architecture interesting. Or how a billboard can be more beautiful than a tree. Or how a commercial strip, with its neon signs, utility poles and filling stations, looks "almost all right."

The Venturis really do believe all these things, which makes them about as welcome in most architectural circles as a drive-in carwash in the gardens of Versailles. Critics often pan them, and potential clients mostly ignore them. And yet their philosophy and their architecture— architecture they perversely label "ugly and ordinary" although admirers find it neither—have made them among the most influential of U.S. architects today.

For they have emerged as the most articulate champions of an architectural counterrevolution of sorts. It puts the changing tastes of a "third generation" of younger architects against the stern dictates and gee-whiz geometries of the "first generation" of Frank Lloyd Wright and his contemporaries.

The first generation, considered revolutionary in the 1920s, established the styles and the values that dominate architecture today. Now the counterrevolutionaries are railing against both. If they succeed, architects will have to stop hating, and start learning from, the existing environment of ordinary things made by ordinary people—things like McDonald's hamburger stands and A&P parking lots, Levittown and great big billboards. Indeed, the Venturi school might be called the school of "messy vitality."

The Venturis drew inspiration from one messy element of the ordinary environment, the billboard, when they recently designed a theater for the Hartford Stage Company. As the theater's front facade curves around a corner of the site, the wall peels away and veers off to become a kind of billboard without a message. The Venturis say Las Vegas inspired this feature. The building's exterior is straightforwardly decorated with a checkerboard of gray and reddish panels of porcelain enamel—except for the color, the same kind as used on White Tower hamburger stands, the Venturis point out.

But despite an occasional commission like the one in Hartford, the Venturis and their counterrevolutionary crowd may fail in their aims of changing architectural values. For arrayed against them are phalanxes of architects and architecture critics who believe the counterrevolutionaries advocate nothing less than a surrender to everything that is tasteless and vulgar in contemporary American society.

"No matter how long the article or clever the words," an infuriated architect wrote after reading about the mathematics building the Venturis have designed for Yale University, "the building is still a piece of junk." (The Venturis say they made the building determinedly "ordinary" by employing conventional windows and brick curtain-wall construction. To admirers, it defers to its surroundings and therefore helps tie the area together. But to critics, it's so modest that it looks no better than the kind of ordinary office buildings they can see anywhere.)

If the Venturis are avant-garde, another critic said, this is the first time the avant-garde is leading from the rear.

The objects of all this vitriol are a deceptively mild-mannered couple whose idea of a good time runs toward quiet evenings at home with their 2½-year-old son, Jimmy. Robert Venturi, who is 48 but looks a decade younger, is a scholarly man with an ironic sense of humor. Denise, 42, red-haired and pale complexioned, could strike an observer as almost frail. The observer would be making a big mistake.

For when attacked, both Venturis fight back with a fierceness that belies their gentle exteriors. Some years ago, the Washington, D.C. Fine Arts Commission rather curtly vetoed their firm's design for a major office complex as "ugly and ordinary." "The Venturis came in with a building that would have been, shall we say, unnoticed," recalls the commission's most outspoken member at the time, architect Gordon Bunshaft of Skidmore, Owings & Merrill. The Venturis have neither forgotten nor forgiven.

"When you create a fine arts commission," Denise observed recently in her correct British accent, "it's like creating an SS. All the thugs in the world are drawn to it." As for Mr. Bunshaft, her verdict was unequivocal: "a thug," she said.

Denise, a South African who had recently earned degrees in architecture at London's Architectural Association, met Bob when she came to the University of Pennsylvania to study city planning. Bob was teaching architecture there, while working in the office of Philadelphia architect Louis Kahn. Married in 1967, the Venturis collaborate on both architecture and essays. "When our work was first called 'ugly and ordinary' it was very hurting," Denise admits. But then, in a kind of verbal jujitsu, they defiantly appropriated the terms for their own rallying cry.

When they champion "ugly and ordinary" architecture, though, they're deliberately exaggerating to emphasize how their architecture differs from orthodox modern architecture. What they really mean by "ordinary," "dumb," "banal" and "expedient" buildings are relatively modest-looking buildings built by conventional methods, as opposed to spectacular-looking buildings built by revolutionary methods. What they mean by "ugly" buildings are buildings that don't look like a lot of modern architects think buildings ought to look.

The "first generation" believed the architect should try to transform the existing environment and uplift mankind through buildings that awed and inspired. It held that an "honest" building didn't rely on surface decoration for effect. Instead, it expressed itself through such purely architectural elements as its form. First-generation architect

Mies van der Rohe, principal designer of New York's steel-and-glass Seagram buildng, was observing this code when he refined each design down to a kind of irreducible essence—spare, abstract and elegant. As he put it: "less is more."

The "second generation," which currently dominates the profession, has largely devoted itself to adapting the ideas of the first. Enter the third, and the Venturis, who say: "Less is a bore."

Mr. Venturi threw down the gauntlet in a 1966 book, *Complexity and Contradiction in Architecture.* In a sweeping historical analysis that ranged from Michelangelo to Wright, he argued that great architecture has often not been pure and simple like a modern glass skyscraper, but rather impure, complex and even ambiguous. "I am for messy vitality over obvious unity," he declared.

The Venturis argue that in casting out superficial ornamentation, architects have often been tempted to show off their talents by distorting whole buildings into giant ornaments. Not only are these "monuments" expensive, they argue, but rather sterile, too. "Decoration is cheaper" and more interesting. As connoisseurs of "messy vitality," the Venturis found inspiration for their latest book in the glitter and the honky tonk of the Las Vegas Strip.

Learning from Las Vegas argues that urban sprawl is here to stay and that architects might as well learn how to work with it. Pop artist Andy Warhol pointed the way when he painted a giant portrait of a Campbell's soup can, the Venturis suggest. He took a banal object and transformed it into art. The book argues that there is beauty, even a hidden kind of order, in Las Vegas' mélange of casinos, drive-in marriage chapels and utility poles—and a direct and valid kind of communication in neon signs that say things like "Free Aspirin Ask Us Anything."

This is more than many architects can take. "Las Vegas," says New York architect James Stewart Polshek, "is nothing more than a lesion, a sore on the landscape. As far as I'm concerned, the only thing to be learned from the ordinary environment is how to level it. This is beyond me."

Nor has the book done much for the Venturi firm. The firm, headquartered in a rather threadbare old townhouse here [Philadelphia], expects to gross little more than $275,000 this year. As partners, the Venturis and John Rauch pay themselves base annual salaries of $25,000 apiece, less than they could make working anonymously for someone else.

"Don't feel too bad," Mr. Rauch consoled Mr. Venturi on a particularly dark day. "You're only a failure. I'm an assistant failure."

But failure is emphatically not the verdict of a small but forceful band of Venturi admirers. "The Venturis have the profession on the run," flatly declares Robert Stern, a New York architect and writer on architecture. "They're the most influential architects practicing in the

U.S. What they've done is to free architects to solve each problem as it comes along, rather than to fit it obsessively into some preconceived style."

Another champion is Vincent Scully, the Yale architectural historian and author. He served on a jury that unanimously selected the Venturi and Rauch design for the contemplated Yale mathematics building over 478 other entries. Most other architects, Mr. Scully commented, seemed to be "knocking themselves out with great heroic gestures." In contrast, he called the winning design "absolutely straightforward and pleasingly understated."

Like Dave Brubeck, the Venturis "take ordinary things and build on them," explains architect Charles Moore, whose own work often follows the same approach. Were the Venturis to design, say, a Holiday Inn, "their design would look enough like a Holiday Inn so that whatever emotions Holiday Inns are supposed to stir would be stirred. But it would look enough unlike it so that the building would be making a commentary. Elements would be turned upside down or sideways, or they'd be surprisingly large, so that for the first time you'd notice them."

This illustration is a good deal easier to understand than the Venturis themselves when they plunge into the subtleties of how ugly can be beautiful. Which they did a few years ago when they designed a beach house in New Jersey.

The site was a drab world of sand, houses and utility poles. A pretty house would merely emphasize the drabness, the Venturis reasoned. So they designed a "kind of bold little ugly banal box." In a paradoxical kind of way, an ugly house in an ugly landscape made the ugly landscape look less ugly, and the ugly house came out looking, well, almost pretty—or so the Venturis reasoned.

Put it another way, one of them explained to an interviewer. The house is "ordinary and extraordinary at the same time. It is like the landscape and not like the landscape, ugly and beautiful. It is the tension between these opposites. We are saying it is like everything else; yet it isn't like everything else, we admit that. It is like everything else in the way that the pop artists make something like a Campbell's soup can. It is like, but it isn't like. See what I mean?"

In a word, no. At least, this is the reaction of some critics, who wonder: Are the Venturis putting us on? Architecture critic Peter Blake, for one, has conceded that Mr. Venturi can be "a very talented architect." But he suspected a big put-on in the Venturis' solemn justifications for things that, in his view, are just plain dumb. Among them is a feature of the house Mr. Venturi designed for his mother—a "nowhere stair" that, predictably enough, goes nowhere.

The stairway goes from the floor to the ceiling of an upstairs room—a "whimsical" touch, Mr. Venturi thinks. Actually, it does serve a purpose when it's time to wash a big clerestory window or paint the wall. And in any event it is a minor feature of a house that is perhaps the most explicitly "complex and contradictory" of any Mr. Venturi has designed.

The outside facade of the Venturi house is a symmetrical rectangle that has been distorted—pushed and pulled out of shape—by the asymmetrical rooms and features inside. Similarly, the fireplace distorts the main stairway that runs behind it at one point, while the stairway distorts the fireplace at another.

Some of the Venturi buildings don't look as bad as the Venturis make them sound, critics concede, and partner John Rauch admits that "we turn a lot of people off with our rhetoric." He goes on: "Ugly and ordinary—that's another academic conceit that has been a mistake."

"Bob and Denise both have academic backgrounds, and they both have a tendency to want to record their innovations for posterity," he says. "But I don't want posterity to remember our innovations. I want posterity to remember us as a large and successful and prosperous firm."

And will this happen? "We ran out in front of the ranks and planted a flag," Mr. Rauch says. "Now we'll have to wait for the ranks to catch up."

Vocabulary

banal commonplace
phalanxes a close-knit body of people (intimating an army)
defers yields to the surroundings
avant-garde artists, writers, ahead of the times
vitriol harsh criticism
verbal jujitsu as in the Japanese art of self-defense, the opponent's strength (words) is used against himself
mélange a mixture
academic conceit intellectual "vanity," exaggeration of judgment

Discussion

1. Notice the first paragraph of this essay. How is the reader's interest immediately whetted?
   (Read the first sentences, and even the first paragraphs, of random essays in this book. How are they often immediate attention-grabbers? What does this suggest about your own first sentences and paragraphs?)
2. A paradox is obvious in Farney's description (or treatment) of the Venturis from the first sentence. What is Farney's attitude toward his subject? Show the language that would indicate this to you. (See also question #7.)
3. What is the paradox inherent in the Venturis' attitude toward aesthetics, and in the words they use to describe what they do? What do *they* mean by "ugly ," "expedient," "banal"?

What standards are being used to declare the Venturis' work as ugly? The "first generation's"?
What was the aesthetic of "the first generation"?
Should this be the final aesthetic?

4. What did the critic mean who said: "If the Venturis are avante-garde . . . this is the first time the avante-garde is leading from the rear."?
What is the rear? What is the front? Do you agree?

5. How do the many testimonials and examples in this piece add to the humor and complexity of the Venturi definition of ugly and banal?

6. How do these same testimonials and examples add to Farney's definition of the Venturi school?

For Further Discussion

7. What is the *tone* of the Venturis' description of the New Jersey beach house:

> . . . ordinary and extraordinary at the same time. It is like the land-scape and not like the landscape, ugly and beautiful. It is the tension between these opposites. We are saying it is like everything else; yet it isn't like everything else, we admit that. It is like everything else in the way that the pop artists make something like a Campbell's soup can. It is like, but it isn't like. See what I mean?

What is the *tone* of Farney's lines that follow: "In a word, no. At least this is the reaction of some critics, who wonder: Are the Venturis putting us on?"
(Tone is the writer's attitude toward himself, his subject, or his audience. It can be humorous, serious, distant, immediate, ironic, sincere, etc.)

8. Does this essay merely define "the school of 'messy vitality'," or does it also sway us to recognition of its value?
What is "messy vitality"?
What is good about it? Or bad?

9. How might Farney's own writing be like the Venturis' architecture? What is it most like? Magazine articles or essays, popular fiction or art?
Notice Farney's use of fragments. See especially paragraph two, the "or how" fragments.
How might Farney himself be considered an "avante-garde essayist, leading from the rear"?

10. How should the *way* an essay is written (its form) complement its *meaning?*
How should form complement meaning?

Jack Kerouac
(1922–1969)

Kerouac published his first novel *The Town and the City* in 1950. From then until 1957 he wrote twelve more books and published none. In that year *On the Road* was printed and a legend was begun.

What allowed Kerouac to write twelve books and made him unpublishable for that long was a writing "technique" he called "spontaneous bop prosody." Kerouac describes the process in a *Paris Review* interview: "You think out what actually happened, you tell friends long stories about it, you mull it over in your mind, you connect it together at leisure, then when the time comes to pay the rent again you force yourself to sit at the typewriter, or at the writing notebook and get it over as fast as you can. . . ." The published version of *On the Road* was written in three weeks; *The Subterraneans* in three nights and three days. Kerouac called himself "a great rememberer redeeming life from darkness."

Writing in *Evergreen Review* his "Essentials of Spontaneous Prose," Kerouac described the ideal mental state for his writing: "If possible write 'without consciousness' in semi-trance . . . allowing subconscious to admit in own uninhibited interesting necessary and so 'modern' language what conscious art would censor."

The Origins of the Beat Generation

This necessarily'll have to be about myself. I'm going all out.

That nutty picture of me on the cover of *On the Road* results from the fact that I had just gotten down from a high mountain where I'd been for two months completely alone and usually I was in the habit of combing my hair of course because you have to get rides on the highway and all that and you usually want girls to look at you as though you were a man and not a wild beast but my poet friend Gregory Corso opened his shirt and took out a silver crucifix that was hanging from a chain and said "Wear this and wear it outside your shirt and don't comb your hair!" so I spent several days around San Francisco going around with him and others like that, to parties, arties, parts, jam sessions, bars, poetry readings, churches, walking talking poetry in the streets, walking talking God in the streets (and at one point a strange gang of hoodlums got mad and said "What right does he got to wear that?" and my own gang of musicians and poets told them to cool it) and finally on the third day *Mademoiselle* magazine wanted to take pictures of us all so I posed just like that, wild hair, crucifix, and all, with Gregory Corso, Allen Ginsberg and Phil Whalen, and the only publication which later did not erase the crucifix from my breast (from that plaid sleeveless cotton shirt-front) was *The New York Times*, therefore *The New York Times* is as beat as I am, and I'm glad I've got a friend. I mean it sincerely, God bless *The New York Times* for not erasing the crucifix from my picture as though it was something distasteful. As a matter of fact, who's *really* beat around here, I mean if you wanta talk of Beat as "beat down" the people who erased the cruicifix are really the "beat down" ones and not *The New York Times*, myself, and Gregory Corso the poet. I am not ashamed to wear the crucifix of my Lord. It is because I am Beat, that is, I believe in beatitude and that God so loved the world that he gave his only begotten son to it. I am sure no priest would've condemned me for wearing the crucifix outside my shirt everywhere and *no matter where* I went, even to have my picture taken by *Mademoiselle*. So you people don't believe in God. So you're all big smart know-it-all Marxists and Freudians, hey? Why don't you come back in a million years and tell me all about it, angels?

Recently Ben Hecht said to me on TV "Why are you afraid to speak out your mind, what's wrong with this country, what is everybody afraid of?" Was he talking to me? And all he wanted me to do was speak out my mind *against* people, he sneeringly brought up Dulles, Eisenhower, the Pope, all kinds of people like that habitually he would sneer at with Drew Pearson, *against* the world he wanted, this is his idea of freedom, he calls it freedom. Who knows, my God, but that the universe is not one vast sea of compassion actually, the veritable holy honey, beneath all this show of personality and cruelty. In fact who knows but that it isn't the solitude of the oneness of the essence of everything, the solitude of the actual oneness of the unbornness of the unborn essence of everything, nay the true pure foreverhood, that big blank potential that can ray forth anything it wants from its pure store, that blazing bliss, *Mattivajrakaruna* the Transcendental Diamond Compassion! No, I want to speak *for* things, for the crucifix I speak out, for the Star of Israel I speak out, for the divinest man who ever lived who was a German (Bach) I speak out, for sweet Mohammed I speak out, for Buddha I speak out, for Lao-tse and Chuang-tse I speak out, for D. T. Suzuki I speak out ... why should I attack what I love out of life. This is Beat. Live your lives out? Naw, *love* your lives out. When they come and stone you at least you won't have a glass house, just your glassy flesh.

That wild eager picture of me on the cover of *On the Road* where I look so Beat goes back much further than 1948 when John Clellon Holmes (author of *Go* and *The Horn*) and I were sitting around trying to think up the meaning of the Lost Generation and the subsequent existentialism and I said "You know, this is really a beat generation" and he leapt up and said "That's it, that's right!" It goes back to the 1880s when my grandfather Jean-Baptiste Kerouac used to go out on the porch in big thunderstorms and swing his kerosene lamp at the lightning and yell "Go ahead, go, if you're more powerful than I am strike me and put the light out!" while the mother and the children cowered in the kitchen. And the light never went out. Maybe since I'm supposed to be the spokesman of the Beat Generation (I *am* the originator of the term, and around it the term and the generation have taken shape) it should be pointed out that all this "Beat" guts therefore goes back to my ancestors who were Bretons who were the most independent group of nobles in all old Europe and kept fighting Latin France to the last wall (although a big blond bosun on a merchant ship snorted when I told him my ancestors were Bretons in Cornwall, Brittany, "Why, we Wikings used to swoop down and steal your nets!"). Breton, Wiking, Irishman, Indian, madboy, it doesn't make any difference, there is no doubt about the Beat Generation, at least the core of it, being a swinging group of new American men intent on joy. . . . Irresponsibility? Who wouldn't help a dying man on an empty road? No and the Beat Generation goes back to the wild parties my father used to have at home in the 1920s and 1930s in New England that were so fantastically loud nobody could sleep for blocks around and when the cops came they always had a drink. It goes back to the wild and raving childhood of playing the Shadow under windswept trees of New England's gleeful autumn, and the howl of the Moon Man on the sandbank until we caught him in a tree (he was an "older" guy of fifteen), the maniacal laugh of certain neighborhood madboys, the furious humor of whole gangs playing basketball till long after dark in the park, it goes back to those crazy days before World War II when teenagers drank beer on Friday nights at Lake ballrooms and worked off their hangovers playing baseball on Saturday afternoon followed by a dive in the brook—and our fathers wore straw hats like W. C. Fields. It goes back to the completely senseless babble of the Three Stooges, the ravings of the Marx Brothers (the tenderness of Angel Harpo at harp, too).

It goes back to the inky ditties of old cartoons (Krazy Kat with the irrational brick)—to Laurel and Hardy in the Foreign Legion—to Count Dracula and his *smile* to Count Dracula shivering and hissing back before the Cross—to the Golem horrifying the persecutors of the Ghetto—to the quiet sage in a movie about India, unconcerned about the plot—to the giggling old Tao Chinaman trotting down the sidewalk of old Clark Gable Shanghai—to the holy old Arab warning the hotbloods that Ramadan is near. To the Werewolf of London a distinguished doctor in his velour smoking jacket smoking his pipe over a lamplit tome on botany and suddenly hairs grow on his hands, his cat hisses, and he slips out into the night with a cape and a slanty cap like the caps of people in breadlines—to Lamont Cranston so cool and sure suddenly becoming the frantic Shadow going mwee hee hee ha ha in the alleys of New York imagination. To Popeye the sailor and the Sea Hag and the meaty gunwales of boats, to Cap'n Easy and Wash Tubbs screaming with ecstasy over canned peaches on a cannibal isle, to Wimpy looking X-eyed for a juicy hamburger such as they make no more. To Jiggs ducking before a household of furniture flying through the air, to Jiggs and the boys at the bar and the corned beef and cabbage of old woodfence noons—to King Kong his eyes looking into the hotel window with tender huge love for Fay Wray—nay, to Bruce Cabot in mate's cap leaning over the rail to a fogbound ship saying "Come aboard." It goes back to when grapefruits were thrown at crooners and harvest-workers at bar-rails slapped burlesque queens on the rump. To when fathers took their sons to the Twin League game. To the days of Babe Callahan on the waterfront, Dick Barthelmess camping under a London streetlamp. To dear old Basil Rathbone looking for the Hound

of the Baskervilles (a dog big as the Gray Wolf who will destroy Odin)—
to dear old bleary Doctor Watson with a brandy in his hand. To Joan
Crawford her raw shanks in the fog, in striped blouse smoking a cigarette at sticky lips in the door of the waterfront dive. To train whistles
of steam engines out above the moony pines. To Maw and Paw in the
Model A clanking on to get a job in California selling used cars making
a whole lotta money. To the glee of America, the honesty of America,
the honesty of oldtime grafters in straw hats as well as the honesty of
oldtime waiters in line at the Brooklyn Bridge in *Winterset*, the funny
spitelessness of old big-fisted America like Big Boy Williams saying
"Hoo? Hee? Huh?" in a movie about Mack Trucks and sliding-door
lunchcarts. To Clark Cable, his certain smile, his confident leer. Like my
grandfather this America was invested with wild self-believing individ-
uality and this had begun to disappear around the end of World War II
with so many great guys dead (I can think of half a dozen from my own
boyhood groups) when suddenly it began to emerge again, the hipsters
began to appear gliding around saying "Crazy, man."

When I first saw the hipsters creeping around Times Square in
1944 I didn't like them either. One of them, Huncke of Chicago, came
up to me and said "Man, I'm beat." I knew right away what he meant
somehow. At that time I still didn't like bop which was then being
introduced by Bird Parker and Dizzy Gillespie and Bags Jackson (on
vibes), the last of the great swing musicians was Don Byas who went to
Spain right after, but then I began . . . but earlier I'd dug all my jazz in
the old Minton Playhouse (Lester Young, Ben Webster, Joey Guy, Charlie Christian, others) and when I first heard Bird and Diz in the Three
Deuces I knew they were serious musicians playing a goofy new sound
and didn't care what I thought, or what my friend Seymour thought.
In fact I was leaning against the bar with a beer when Dizzy came over
for a glass of water from the bartender, put himself right against me
and reached both arms around both sides of my head to get the glass
and danced away, as though knowing I'd be singing about him someday, or that one of his arrangements would be named after me someday by some goofy circumstance. Charlie Parker was spoken of in Harlem as the greatest new musician since Chu Berry and Louis
Armstrong.

Anyway, the hipsters, whose music was bop, they looked like
criminals but they kept talking about the same things I liked, long out-
lines of personal experience and vision, night-long confessions full of
hope that had become illicit and repressed by War, stirrings, rumblings
of a new soul (that same old human soul). And so Huncke appeared to
us and said "I'm beat" with radiant light shining out of his despairing
eyes . . . a word perhaps brought from some midwest carnival or junk
cafeteria. It was a new language, actually spade (Negro) jargon but you
soon learned it, like "hung up" couldn't be a more economical term to
mean so many things. Some of these hipsters were raving mad and

talked continually. It was jazzy. Symphony Sid's all-night modern jazz and bop show was always on. By 1948 it began to take shape. That was a wild vibrating year when a group of us would walk down the street and yell hello and even stop and talk to anybody that gave us a friendly look. The hipsters had eyes. That was the year I saw Montgomery Clift, unshaven, wearing a sloppy jacket, slouching down Madison Avenue with a companion. It was the year I saw Charlie Bird Parker strolling down Eighth Avenue in a black turtleneck sweater with Babs Gonzales and a beautiful girl.

By 1948 the hipsters, or beatsters, were divided into cool and hot. Much of the misunderstanding about hipsters and the Beat Generation in general today derives from the fact that there are two distinct styles of hipsterism: the "cool" today is your bearded laconic sage, or schlerm, before a hardly touched beer in a beatnik dive, whose speech is low and unfriendly, whose girls say nothing and wear black: the "hot" today is the crazy talkative shining-eyed (often innocent and open-hearted) nut who runs from bar to bar, pad to pad looking for everybody, shouting, restless, lushy, trying to "make it" with the subterranean beatniks who ignore him. Most Beat Generation artists belong to the hot school, naturally since that hard gemlike flame needs a little heat. In many cases the mixture is fifty-fifty. It was a hot hipster like myself who finally cooled it in Buddhist meditation, though when I go in a jazz joint I still feel like yelling "Blow baby blow!" to the musicians though nowadays I'd get eighty-sixed for this. In 1948 the "hot hipsters" were racing around in cars like in *On the Road* looking for wild bawling jazz like Willis Jackson or Lucky Thompson (the early) or Chubby Jackson's big band while the "cool hipsters" cooled it in dead silence before formal and excellent musical groups like Lennie Tristanó or Miles Davis. It's still just about the same, except that it has begun to grow into a national generation and the name "Beat" has stuck (though all hipsters hate the word).

The word "beat" originally meant poor, down and out, deadbeat, on the bum, sad, sleeping in subways. Now that the word is belonging officially it is being made to stretch to include people who do not sleep in subways but have a certain new gesture, or attitude, which I can only describe as a new *more*. "Beat Generation" has simply become the slogan or label for a revolution in manners in America. Marlon Brando was not really first to portray it on the screen. Dane Clark with his pinched Dostoyevskyan face and Brooklyn accent, and of course Garfield, were first. The private eyes were Beat, if you will recall. Bogart. Lorre was Beat. In *M*, Peter Lorre started a whole revival, I mean the slouchy street walk.

I wrote *On the Road* in three weeks in the beautiful month of May 1951 while living in the Chelsea district of lower West Side Manhattan, on a 100-foot roll and put the Beat Generation in words in there, saying at the point where I am taking part in a wild kind of collegiate party with a bunch of kids in an abandoned miner's shack "These kids are great but where are Dean Moriarty and Carlo Marx? Oh well I guess they wouldn't belong in this gang, they're too *dark*, too strange, too subterranean and I am slowly beginning to join a new kind of *beat* generation." The manuscript of *Road* was turned down on the grounds that it would displease the sales manager of my publisher at that time, though the editor, a very intelligent man, said "Jack this is just like Dostoyevsky, but what can I do at this time?" It was too early. So for the next six years I was a bum, a breakman, a seaman, a panhandler, a pseudo-Indian in Mexico, anything and everything, and went on writing because my hero was Goethe and I believed in art and hoped some day to write the third part of *Faust*, which I have done in *Doctor Sax*. Then in 1952 an article was published in *The New York Times* Sunday magazine saying, the headline, "'This is a Beat Generation'" (in quotes like that) and in the article it said that I had come up with the term first "when the face was harder to recognize," the face of the generation. After that there was some talk of the Beat Generation but in 1955 I published an excerpt from *Road* (melding it with parts of *Visions of Neal*) under the pseudonym "Jean-Louis," it was entitled *Jazz of the Beat Generation* and was copyrighted as being an excerpt from a novel-in-progress entitled *Beat Generation* (which I later changed to *On the Road* at the insistence of my new editor) and so then the term moved a little faster. The term and the cats. Everywhere began to appear strange hepcats and even college kids went around hep and cool and using the terms I'd heard on Time Square in the early forties, it was growing somehow. But when the publishers finally took a dare and published *On the Road* in 1957 it burst open, it mushroomed, everybody began yelling about a Beat Generation. I was being interviewed everywhere I went for "what I meant" by such a thing. People began to call themselves beatniks, beats, jazzniks, bopniks, bugniks and finally I was called the "avatar" of all this.

Yet it was as a Catholic, it was not at the insistence of any of these "niks" and certainly not with their approval either, that I went one afternoon to the church of my childhood (one of them), Ste. Jeanne d'Arc in Lowell, Mass., and suddenly with tears in my eyes and had a vision of what I must have really meant with "Beat" anyhow when I heard the holy silence in the church (I was the only one in there, it was five P.M., dogs were barking outside, children yelling, the fall leaves, the candles were flickering alone just for me), the vision of the word Beat as being to mean beatific. . . . There's the priest preaching on Sunday morning, all of a sudden through a side door of the church comes a group of Beat Generation characters in strapped raincoats like the I.R.A. coming in silently to "dig" the religion . . . I knew it then.

But this was 1954, so then what horror I felt in 1957 and later 1958 naturally to suddenly see "Beat" being taken up by everybody, press and TV and Hollywood borscht circuit to include the "juvenile delinquency" shot and the horrors of a mad teeming billyclub New York and L.A. and they began to call *that* Beat, *that* beatific. . . . Bunch of fools marching against the San Francisco Giants protesting baseball, as if (now) in my name and I, my childhood ambition to be a big league base-ball star hitter like Ted Williams so that when Bobby Thomson hit that homerun in 1951 I trembled with joy and couldn't get over it for days and wrote poems about how it is possible for the human spirit to win after all! Or, when a murder, a routine murder took place in North Beach, they labeled it a Beat Generation slaying although in my child-hood I'd been famous as an eccentric in my block for stopping the younger kids from throwing rocks at the squirrels, for stopping them from frying snakes in cans or trying to blow up frogs with straws. Because my brother had died at the age of nine, his name was Gerard Kerouac, and he'd told me "Ti Jean never hurt any living being, all liv-ing beings whether it's just a little cat or squirrel or whatever, all, are going to heaven straight into God's snowy arms so never hurt anything and if you see anybody hurt anything stop them as best you can" and when he died a file of gloomy nuns in black from St. Louis de France parish had filed (1926) to his deathbed to hear his last words about Heaven. And my father too, Leo, had never lifted a hand to punish me, or to punish the little pets in our house, and this teaching was delivered to me by the men in my house and I have never had anything to do with violence, hatred, cruelty, and all that horrible nonsense which, nevertheless, because God is gracious beyond all human imagining, he will forgive in the long end . . . that million years I'm asking about you, America.

And so now they have beatnik routines on TV, starting with satires about girls in black and fellows in jeans with snapknives and sweat-shirts and swastikas tattooed under their armpits, it will come to respectable MCs of spectaculars coming out nattily attired in Brooks Brothers jean-type tailoring and sweater-type pull-ons, in other words, it's a simple change in fashion and manners, just a history crust—like from the Age of Reason, from old Voltaire in a chair to romantic Chat-terton in the moonlight—from Teddy Roosevelt to Scott Fitzgerald. . . . So there's nothing to get excited about. Beat comes out, actually, of old American whoopee and it will only change a few dresses and pants and make chairs useless in the living room and pretty soon we'll have Beat Secretaries of State and there will be instituted new tinsels, in fact new reasons for malice and new reasons for virtue and new reasons for forgiveness. . . .

But yet, but yet, woe, woe unto those who think that the Beat Gen-eration means crime, deliquency, immorality, amorality . . . woe unto those who attack it on the grounds that they simply don't understand history and the yearnings of human souls . . . woe unto those who don't realize that America must, will, is, changing now, for the better I say. Woe unto those who believe in the atom bomb, who believe in hating mothers and fathers, who deny the most important of the Ten Commandments, woe unto those (though) who don't believe in the unbelievable sweetness of sex love, woe unto those who are the standard bearers of death, woe unto those who believe in conflict and horror and violence and fill our books and screens and living rooms with all that crap, woe in fact unto those who make evil movies about the Beat Generation where innocent housewives are raped by beatniks! Woe unto those who are the real dreary sinners that even God finds room to forgive. . . .

Woe unto those who spit on the Beat Generation, the wind'll blow it back.

Vocabulary

tome   a large or scholarly book
hipster   a slang word for a "hip" person, "cool" because enlightened
avatar   a noble manifestation, archetype
borscht   A Russian beet soup

Allusions/References

Gregory Corso, Allen Ginsberg, Phil Whalen   beat poets, friends of Kerouac
W. C. Fields, Marx Brothers, Clark Gable, Shanghai, Popeye the Sailor, Jiggs, etc.   Kerouac's essay is filled with references to "gleeful America," the popular shared consciousness
On the Road   Kerouac's autobiographical second novel, an American odyssey
Dean Moriarty   fictional name for Neal Cassady, a main character in *On the Road* and other of Kerouac's novels
Carlo Marx   Allen Ginsberg's name in *On the Road* and other novels by Kerouac

Discussion

1. Why does Kerouac begin his treatise on the beat generation with that first sentence? Aside from the fact that he is considered the Father of the Beat Generation, what other reasons can he have for saying, "this necessarily'll have to be about myself."? What do you think of seeing that word "necessarily'll" in an essay?
2. Define the word "beat" as it begins to emerge from the end of paragraph one. How many meanings does it have?
   How does a further meaning (or meanings) appear by the end of paragraph two?
3. Writers can follow a form (a vase essay, a shaped essay), or they can let form follow content (a tree essay, an organic form). Obviously Kerouac is letting

what he has to say follow its own form. What special things are let into an organic essay such as this? What do you miss in it?

4. Trace the tumble of words Kerouac uses to describe the roots of beat beginning with the third paragraph: "That wild eager picture of me on the cover . . ." to the paragraph beginning, "When I first saw the hipsters . . ." and ending with "the greatest new musician since Chu Berry and Louis Armstrong." Can you follow this seemingly wild ranting? How would you paraphrase what Kerouac is saying here?

5. Kerouac further defines hipsterism as cool or hot. What are the distinctions he makes? How has "beat" supplanted the word "hipster?"

6. Can you define "beat" after finishing this essay? Is Kerouac's intent to define the term or to show you what he means? How is his own writing "beat"?

For Further Discussion

7. Chapter Eight, "A Study of Four Writers," includes Jack Kerouac. From his description of the Beat Generation, you might wish to read at least one other piece of his looking for evidence of what he says here.

8. Note particularly Kerouac's use of words: "the veritable holy honey," "glassy flesh," "shining eyed." What does he mean by these?

What does the ending sentence in paragraph one mean: "Why don't you come back in a million years and tell me all about it, angels?"

□ By Classification

Ellie is the kind of secretary who could run the world. The phone rang. I answered. It was Ellie. "What's the worst thing that could happen?" she asked. My heart fell. I'd been fired; no, that wasn't bad enough. Something awful had happened to someone I cared about. "My typewriter's broken," she said. I could hardly believe my ears. In the background, TAP TAP TAP, Ellie was playing her typewriter. I felt like a kid who had been let out of school because of snow. I wouldn't have to meet my deadline because of natural disaster. "You seem happy," she said, "you don't understand. I like my typewriter." I tried to reassure her everything was fine, though I heard tapping even as we hung up.

It wasn't fifteen minutes before the phone rang again. It was Ellie. "Nobody ever said I wasn't ingenious." I imagined a hairpin holding her typewriter in repair. No, she had found another machine exactly like her own and had already requisitioned it from its owner. It was sitting on a cart with wheels beside her desk. Classification asks the question, what kind is it? Ellie is the best kind.

□

If you asked me how I would classify the essays that follow in this section I would respond something like this. Two of the essayists are scientists. Alex Petrunkevitch, in "The Spider and the Wasp," tells how the tarantula is overcome by its natural enemy the wasp, in a classic play of intelligence against instinct. He reveals in his curiosity and interest for the spider a kind of sympathy. Lewis Thomas, in "Death in the Open," classifies death as "a natural marvel." A biologist, he watches "the constant renewal and replacement" of the billions of life forms on the earth with wonder. He says we're going to have "to give up the notion that death is catastrophe. . . ."

Simone de Beauvoir's "The Discovery and Assumption of Old Age" and Robert Sherrill's "The Saturday Night Special" are a look at human problems and sorrows. De Beauvoir writes about old age as "an abnormal condition," a condition "halfway between illness and health." Sherrill uncovers America's romance with guns and outlaws.

Common to all four of the essays anthologized here is an uncommon love of language and of subject. They could finally be classified as informative essays and as good reading. I hope you will enjoy them and that they inform you about how to classify your own subject as a part of a larger group with shared features. Remember, as with definition and all the other expository modes, classification is an underlying pattern of thought, a way of thinking about the things of our existence.

Alex Petrunkevitch
(1875–1964)

Petrunkevitch was born December 22, 1875, in Pliski, Russia. A zoologist, or more correctly an arachnologist, he was called by *Time* magazine at the time of his death in 1964, "the 20th Century's greatest authority on spiders." His own collection of spiders included 180 live tarantulas. He wrote more than 100 books and monographs in his field.

Petrunkevitch taught at Yale University from 1910 to 1944. He knew so many of the more than 75,000 spider species, he once grabbed a spider from the shoulder of a woman passerby. In response to her surprise and fright he said, "It is only an *Epeira marmorea* female, madam."

The Spider and the Wasp

In the feeding and safeguarding of their progeny insects and spiders exhibit some interesting analogies to reasoning and some crass examples of blind instinct. The case I propose to describe here is that of the tarantula spiders and their archenemy, the digger wasps of the genus Pepsis. It is a classic example of what looks like intelligence pitted against instinct—a strange situation in which the victim, though fully able to defend itself, submits unwittingly to its destruction.

Most tarantulas live in the tropics, but several species occur in the temperate zone and a few are common in the southern U.S. Some varieties are large and have powerful fangs with which they can inflict a deep wound. These formidable looking spiders do not, however, attack man; you can hold one in your hand, if you are gentle, without being bitten. Their bite is dangerous only to insects and small mammals such as mice; for man it is no worse than a hornet's sting.

Tarantulas customarily live in deep cylindrical burrows, from which they emerge at dusk and into which they retire at dawn. Mature males wander about after dark in search of females and occasionally stray into houses. After mating, the male dies in a few weeks, but a female lives much longer and can mate several years in succession. In a Paris museum is a tropical specimen which is said to have been living in captivity for 25 years.

A fertilized female tarantula lays from 200 to 400 eggs at a time; thus it is possible for a single tarantula to produce several thousand young. She takes no care of them beyond weaving a cocoon of silk to enclose the eggs. After they hatch, the young walk away, find convenient places in which to dig their burrows and spend the rest of their lives in solitude. The eyesight of tarantulas is poor, being limited to a sensing of change in the intensity of light and to the perception of moving objects. They apparently have little or no sense of hearing, for a hungry tarantula will pay no attention to a loudly chirping cricket placed in its cage unless the insect happens to touch one of its legs.

But all spiders, and especially hairy ones, have an extremely delicate sense of touch. Laboratory experiments prove that tarantulas can distinguish three types of touch: pressure against the body wall, stroking of the body hair, and riffling of certain very fine hairs on the legs called trichobothria. Pressure against the body, by the finger or the end of a pencil, causes the tarantula to move off slowly for a short distance. The touch excites no defensive response unless the approach is from above where the spider can see the motion, in which case it rises on its hind legs, lifts its front legs, opens its fangs and holds this threatening posture as long as the object continues to move.

The entire body of a tarantula, especially its legs, is thickly clothed with hair. Some of it is short and wooly, some long and stiff. Touching this body hair produces one of two distinct reactions. When the spider is hungry, it responds with an immediate and swift attack. At the touch of a cricket's antennae the tarantula seizes the insect so swiftly that a motion picture taken at the rate of 64 frames per second shows only the result and not the process of capture. But when the spider is not hungry, the stimulation of its hairs merely causes it to shake the touched limb. An insect can walk under its hairy belly unharmed.

The trichobothria, very fine hairs growing from dislike membranes on the legs, are sensitive only to air movement. A light breeze makes them vibrate slowly, without disturbing the common hair. When one blows gently on the trichobothria, the tarantula reacts with a quick jerk of its four front legs. If the front and hind legs are stimulated at the same time, the spider makes a sudden jump. This reaction is quite independent of the state of its appetite.

These three tactile responses—to pressure on the body wall, to moving of the common hair, and to flexing of the trichobothria—are so different from one another that there is no possibility of confusing them. They serve the tarantula adequately for most of its needs and enable it to avoid most annoyances and dangers. But they fail the spider completely when it meets its deadly enemy, the digger wasp Pepsis.

These solitary wasps are beautiful and formidable creatures. Most species are either a deep shiny blue all over, or deep blue with rusty wings. The largest have a wing span of about four inches. They live on nectar. When excited, they give off a pungent odor—a warning that they are ready to attack. The sting is much worse than that of a bee or common wasp, and the pain and swelling last longer. In the adult stage the wasp lives only a few months. The female produces but a few eggs, one at a time at intervals of two or three days. For each egg the mother must provide one adult tarantula, alive but paralyzed. The mother wasp attaches the egg to the paralyzed spider's abdomen. Upon hatching from the egg, the larva is many hundreds of times smaller than its living but helpless victim. It eats no other food and drinks no water. By the time it has finished its single Gargantuan meal and become ready for wasphood, nothing remains of the tarantula but its indigestible chitinous skeleton.

The mother wasp goes tarantula-hunting when the egg in her ovary is almost ready to be laid. Flying low over the ground late on a sunny afternoon, the wasp looks for its victim or for the mouth of a tarantula burrow, a round hole edged by a bit of silk. The sex of the spider makes no difference, but the mother is highly discriminating as to species. Each species of Pepsis requires a certain species of tarantula, and the wasp will not attack the wrong species. In a cage with a tarantula which is not its normal prey, the wasp avoids the spider and is usually killed by it in the night.

Yet when a wasp finds the correct species, it is the other way about. To identify the species the wasp apparently must explore the spider with her antennae. The tarantula shows an amazing tolerance to this exploration. The wasp crawls under it and walks over it without evoking any hostile response. The molestation is so great and so persistent that the tarantula often rises on all eight legs, as if it were on stilts. It may stand this way for several minutes. Meanwhile the wasp, having satisfied itself that the victim is of the right species, moves off a few inches to dig the spider's grave. Working vigorously with legs and jaws, it excavates a hole 8 to 10 inches deep with a diameter slightly larger than the spider's girth. Now and again the wasp pops out of the hole to make sure that the spider is still there.

When the grave is finished, the wasp returns to the tarantula to complete her ghastly enterprise. First she feels it all over once more with her antennae. Then her behavior becomes more aggressive. She bends her abdomen, protruding her sting, and searches for the soft membrane at the point where the spider's legs join its body—the only spot where she can penetrate the horny skeleton. From time to time, as the exasperated spider slowly shifts ground, the wasp turns on her back and slides along with the aid of her wings, trying to get under the tarantula for a shot at the vital spot. During all this maneuvering, which can last for several minutes, the tarantula makes no move to save itself. Finally the wasp corners it against some obstruction and grasps one of its legs in her powerful jaws. Now at last the harassed spider tries a desperate but vain defense. The two contestants roll over and over on the ground. It is a terrifying sight and the outcome is always the same. The wasp finally manages to thrust her sting into the soft spot and holds it there for a few seconds while she pumps in the poison. Almost immediately the tarantula falls paralyzed on its back. Its legs stop twitching; its heart stops beating. Yet it is not dead, as is shown by the fact that if taken from the wasp it can be restored to some sensitivity by being kept in a moist chamber for several months.

After paralyzing the tarantula, the wasp cleans herself by dragging her body along the ground and rubbing her feet, sucks the drop of blood oozing from the wound in the spider's abdomen, then grabs a leg of the flabby, helpless animal in her jaws and drags it down to the bottom of the grave. She stays there for many minutes, sometimes for several hours, and what she does all that time in the dark we do not know. Eventually she lays her egg and attaches it to the side of the spider's abdomen with a sticky secretion. Then she emerges, fills the grave with soil carried bit by bit in her jaws, and finally tramples the ground all around to hide any trace of the grave from prowlers. Then she flies away, leaving her descendant safely started in life.

In all this the behavior of the wasp evidently is qualitatively different from that of the spider. The wasp acts like an intelligent animal. This is not to say that instinct plays no part or that she reasons as man does. But her actions are to the point; they are not automatic and can be modified to fit the situation. We do not know for certain how she identifies the tarantula—probably it is by some olfactory or chemo-tactile sense—but she does it purposefully and does not blindly tackle a wrong species.

On the other hand, the tarantula's behavior shows only confusion. Evidently the wasp's pawing gives it no pleasure, for it tries to move away. That the wasp is not simulating sexual stimulation is certain because male and female tarantulas react in the same way to its advances. That the spider is not anesthetized by some odorless secretion is easily shown by blowing lightly at the tarantula and making it jump suddenly. What, then, makes the tarantula behave as stupidly as it does?

No clear, simple answer is available. Possibly the stimulation by the wasp's antennae is masked by a heavier pressure on the spider's body, so that it reacts as when prodded by a pencil. But the explanation may be much more complex. Initiative in attack is not in the nature of tarantulas; most species fight only when cornered so that escape is impossible. Their inherited patterns of behavior apparently prompt them to avoid problems rather than attack them. For example, spiders always weave their webs in three dimensions, and when a spider finds that there is insufficient space to attach certain threads in the third dimension, it leaves the place and seeks another, instead of finishing the web in a single plane. This urge to escape seems to arise under all circumstances, in all phases of life, and to take the place of reasoning. For a spider to change the pattern of its web is as impossible as for an inexperienced man to build a bridge across a chasm obstructing his way.

In a way the instinctive urge to escape is not only easier but often more efficient than reasoning. The tarantula does exactly what is most efficient in all cases except in an encounter with a ruthless and determined attacker dependent for the existence of her own species on killing as many tarantulas as she can lay eggs. Perhaps in this case the spider follows its usual pattern of trying to escape, instead of seizing and killing the wasp, because it is not aware of its danger. In any case, the survival of the tarantula species as a whole is protected by the fact that the spider is much more fertile than the wasp.

Vocabulary

progeny   offspring
chitinous   a semitransparent horny substance that forms insect exoskeletons

Discussion

1. How is Petrunkevitch's first paragraph the thesis for this essay?
2. Which insect does Petrunkevitch classify as showing "intelligence," and which does he see as behaving by "blind instinct"?
3. List the qualities of the tarantula that Petrunkevitch uses to further describe the insect.
   How do these qualities, these facts, contribute to the structure of this essay?
4. What purpose does the section concerning the tarantula's sense of touch have in the larger scope of the essay?
5. Why does Petrunkevitch reconstruct the struggle between the spider and the wasp, and not merely *tell* you of its outcome?

6. What does Petrunkevitch mean in the last paragraph when he says: "In a way the instinctive urge to escape is not only easier but often more efficient than reasoning"?

For Further Discussion

7. Petrunkevitch has had a lifelong interest in spiders. What qualities of word choice and of example demonstrate his fascination and knowledge concerning these insects?
   Does he favor the spider over the wasp? Prove your answer with lines from the text that would support your assumption.
8. How are the spider's qualities more clearly seen by its comparison with the wasp?
   How might one thing serve as a foil to the classification of another?

Simone de Beauvoir
(1908–   )

Simone de Beauvoir was born January 9, 1908, in Paris, France. While earning a degree in philosophy at the Sorbonne, she met Jean-Paul Sartre. The two became central figures in the French existential movement. Together they worked on *Les Temps Modernes,* an existentialist magazine. They remained close until his death in 1980.

De Beauvoir taught philosophy for many years before giving it up, in 1943, to devote herself full-time to writing. One of her most widely read and acclaimed books is *The Second Sex,* a study of woman's secondary status in society. It was also controversial. Karl Menninger called it "a pretentious and inflated tract on feminism"; Philip Wylie, "one of the few great books of our era."

Old age and death are also common themes in de Beauvoir's writing. "I've always been haunted by the passing of time and by the fact that death keeps closing in on us." She called old-age societies "secret shame," and said: "We need a revolution, but I don't think it will be tomorrow. Still if one can dream of certain things, one can dream of society really existing for man, a society where perhaps an old man can be a man and not a ruin." The following is from her book *The Coming of Age.*

The Discovery and Assumption of Old Age

Die early or grow old: there is no other alternative. And yet, as Goethe said, "Age takes hold of us by surprise." For himself each man is the sole, unique subject, and we are often astonished when the common fate becomes our own—when we are struck by sickness, a shattered relationship, or bereavement. I remember my own stupefaction when I was seriously ill for the first time in my life and I said to myself, "This woman they are carrying on a stretcher is me." Nevertheless, we accept fortuitous accidents readily enough, making them part of our history, because they affect us as unique beings: but old age is the general fate, and when it seizes upon our own personal life we are dumbfounded. "Why, what has happened?" writes Aragon. "It is life that has happened; and I am old." The fact that the passage of universal time should have brought about a private, personal metamorphosis is something that takes us completely aback. When I was only forty I still could not believe it when I stood there in front of the looking-glass and said to myself, "I am forty." Children and adolescents are of some particular age. The mass of prohibitions and duties to which they are subjected and the behaviour of others towards them do not allow them to forget it. When we are grown up we hardly think about our age any more: we feel that the notion does not apply to us; for it is one which assumes that we look back towards the past and draw a line under the total, whereas in fact we are reaching out towards the future, gliding on imperceptibly from day to day, from year to year. Old age is particularly difficult to assume because we have always regarded it as something alien, a foreign species: "Can I have become a different being while I still remain myself?"

"False dilemma," people have said to me. "So long as you feel young, you are young." This shows a complete misunderstanding of the complex truth of old age: for the outsider it is a dialectic relationship between my being as he defines it objectively and the awareness of myself that I acquire by means of him. Within me it is the Other—that is to say the person I am for the outsider—who is old: and that Other is myself. In most cases, for the rest of the world our being is as many-sided as the rest of the world itself. Any observation made about us may be challenged on the basis of some differing opinion. But in this particular instance no challenge is permissible: the words "a sixty-year-old" interpret the same fact for everybody. They correspond to biological phenomena that may be detected by examination. Yet our private, inward experience does not tell us the number of our years; no fresh perception comes into being to show us the decline of age. This is one of the characteristics that distinguish growing old from disease. Illness warns us of its presence and the organism defends itself, sometimes in a way that is more harmful than the initial stimulus: the existence of the disease is more evident to the subject who undergoes it than to those around him, who often do not appreciate its importance. Old age is more apparent to others than to the subject himself: it is a new state of biological equilibrium, and if the aging individual adapts himself to it smoothly he does not notice the change. Habit and compensatory attitudes mean that psychomotor shortcomings can be alleviated for a long while.

Even if the body does send us signals, they are ambiguous. There is a temptation to confuse some curable disease with irreversible old age. Trotsky lived only for working and fighting, and he dreaded growing old: he was filled with anxiety when he remembered Turgenev's remark, one that Lenin often quoted—"Do you know the worst of all vices? It is being over fifty-five." And in 1933, when he was exactly fifty-five himself, he wrote a letter to his wife, complaining of tiredness, lack of sleep, a failing memory; it seemed to him that his strength was going, and it worried him. "Can this be age that has come for good, or is it no more than a temporary, though sudden, decline that I shall recover from? We shall see." Sadly he called the past to mind: "I have a painful longing for your old photograph, the picture that shows us both when we were so young." He did get better and he took up all his activities again.

The reverse applies: the discomforts caused by age may sometimes be scarcely noticed or mentioned. They are taken for superficial and curable disorders. One must already be fully aware of one's age before it can be detected in one's body. And even then, the body does not always help us to a full inward realization of our condition. We know that this rheumatism, for example, or that arthritis, are caused by old age; yet we fail to see that they represent a new status. We remain what we were, with the rheumatism as something additional. . . .

All in all, there is truth in the idea of Galen, who placed old age half-way between illness and health. What is so disconcerting about old age is that normally it is an abnormal condition. As Canghilem says, "It is normal, that is to say it is in accordance with the biological laws of aging, that the progressive diminution of the margins of safety should bring about a lowering of the threshold of resistance to attack from the environment. What is normal for an old man would be reckoned deficient in the same person in his middle years." When elderly people say that they are ill—even when they are not—they are emphasizing this anomaly: they are adopting the point of view of a man who is still young, and who would be worried by being rather deaf and dim-sighted, by feeling poorly from time to time and by tiring easily. When they say that they are satisfied with their health and when they will not look after themselves, then they are settling down into old age—they realize what is the matter. Their attitude depends upon how they choose to regard age in general. They know that elderly people are looked upon as an inferior species. So many of them take any allusion to their age as an insult: they want to regard themselves as young come what may, and they would rather think of themselves as unwell than old. Others find it convenient to speak of themselves as elderly, even before the time has really come—age provides alibis; it allows them to lower their standards; and it is less tiring to let oneself go than to fight.

Vocabulary

fortuitous unplanned, happening by accident or chance
anomaly deviation from the normal (or common) order

Allusions/References

Goethe German poet and dramatist (1749–1832)
Trotsky, Lenin Russian revolutionists and Soviet statesmen; Lenin was the first premier of the U.S.S.R.; Trotsky (1877–1940), Lenin (1870–1924)
Turgenev Russian novelist (1818–1903)
Galen Greek anatomist, physiologist, and physician (A.D. 130?–201?)

Discussion

1. What does de Beauvoir mean when she writes: "For himself each man is the sole, unique subject, and we are often astonished when the common fate becomes our own . . ."?
   How is this statement important to de Beauvoir's ideas about old age?
2. How does the use of allusions fortify her thesis about old age?
   Who, by the way, are Aragon and Canghilem?
   (What do de Beauvoir's references indicate about her reading at the time?)
3. According to de Beauvoir, what are the characteristics of old age?
   Why are we "dumbfounded" when old age "seizes upon our own personal life"?
4. What is de Beauvoir's attitude about her subject?
   (What is her reason for writing about "the common fate"? Can you find in her language her attitude or reason for writing this piece?)

Robert Sherrill
(1925–   )

Robert Sherrill was born Christmas Eve, 1925, in Frogtown, Georgia. The son of a reporter, he has held various newspaper jobs and has been Washington editor for *The Nation* since 1965. His books include a biography of Lyndon Johnson, *The Accidental President,* and *Military Justice Is to Justice What Military Music Is to Music.*

In the prefatory note to *The Saturday Night Special* from which the following selection is taken, Sherrill writes: "Thumbing through a Library of Congress bibliography on gun controls recently, I was flabbergasted to find that, because of assignments from *The Nation* and *The New York Times Magazine,* I had written nearly as much on the subject as anybody around."

The Saturday Night Special

In the City of New York a handgun of any price and any description is simply a "piece." Whether it shows a democratic spirit or lack of imagination, to a New Yorker all guns are called by the same nickname, used by cops and hoodlums alike.

But in some other parts of the country where the little issues of life and death inspire more jocularity, a cheerful special name has been reserved for the low-class gun that draws heavily on the emotions but lightly on the purse. The discrimination is quite deserved; guns are as identifiable by caste and class and even ethnic features as people are. The design of the Luger, for example, could have come only from the national mentality that gave birth to Nazism. The design of the Berreta looks like something out of Leonardo's notebooks. Where else but in America could the Colt Peacemaker have been conceived, where else but in Britain the Webley? You look at such guns, and you know.

The low-caste gun is the "Saturday Night Special." It is the nigger, the white trash, the untouchable of gundom; and like its human counterpart, nothing can stamp it out. It is especially impervious to salvation.

Though it has something of a Gay Nineties ring to it, the term Saturday Night Special has actually been around for only a few years. Fittingly, its place of birth was Detroit. Something is always happening there in the way of firearms. When Sidney Hillman, the labor leader, visited Detroit in the mid-1930s to help settle a strike, a group of union men met with him in his hotel room. He noted the bulges under their coats. "Guns! Always guns!" he cried despairingly. "Why is it there are always guns in Detroit?"

Not that Detroit is the easiest place to buy a gun; it's just that a determined Detroiter won't be stopped when he wants one. So it was that in the late 1950s and early 1960s, when mischievous residents of Detroit could not get their hands on guns in their hometown, they would simply hop in their cars and tool down to Toledo, Ohio, less than an hour away, where guns were sold in candy stores, flower shops, filling stations, shoeshine stands, anywhere at all. Since a great many of these purchases were made to satisfy the passions of Saturday Night, Detroit lawmen began to refer to the weapons as Saturday Night Specials. And thus the language of Americana was enriched.

Like many folk terms, it does not have a fixed meaning. Like most targets of snobbery, its definition depends largely on who is talking. To the major American gun manufacturers, who naturally don't like competition, any cheap import is a Saturday Night Special, as is any cheap American-manufactured gun not a product of their assembly line. To the cops and to some members of Congress, just about any gun that causes trouble is a Saturday Night Special. They were even using that designation on the gun Arthur Bremer bought at the Casanova Gun

Shop in Milwaukee for his assassination attempt on George Wallace. It was an $85 Charter Arms "Undercover-2," a steel pistol with a barrel only 1⅞ inches long; the gun weighs 16 ounces and measures 6¼ inches overall—one of the smallest, lightest .38 special steel-frame revolvers made. If that's a Saturday Night Special, then the police of America are loaded down with them, for Bremer's gun was very similar to the style and quality gun preferred by many cops.

The caliber doesn't disqualify it: .38s can be Saturday Night Specials if they're junky enough. But most Saturday Night Specials are .22s and .25s, or at most .32s. Nowadays the cruddy assembly line just seems to gravitate in that direction.

For about the last fifty years the small, inexpensive, easily concealed handgun has been getting an increasingly bad reputation, subjected to such denigrating nicknames as "murder special," "suicide special," "7-11," etc. The genre wasn't always judged that way. The Saturday Night Special's proud predecessors, considered highly practical articles of personal equipment, almost as necessary as garters and belts at every level of society, included the little pearl-handled whatsis that ladies of the evening carried in their handbags to ward off non-paying drunks; the derringer that the professional gambler whipped from his sleeve to defend, or protest, a deal; the tiny gun concealed in the sheriff/outlaw's boot which he drew after he had been otherwise disarmed; the vest-pocket pistol the judge carried to reduce the possibility of unorthodox appeals. They are as commonplace on the late, late movie today as they were once in reality. And they were not scorned.

Congressmen and men of business were as grateful to Henry Deringer, Jr., for producing his handy little pocket pistols as were the thieves and gamblers and whores of the pre-Civil War period. So popular was the Deringer, some of which were only 3¾ inches long, that very soon dozens of manufacturers were copying it (Deringer had forgotten to take out a patent). Some were two-shot guns, the barrels over and under; but the one-shot pistol was the most popular. Eventually all small single-shots came to be referred to as "derringers," to disguise slightly the theft of the design. One bullet from it was big enough to stop an opponent permanently—.33 to .51 caliber, but usually around .41. Because of their short barrels, derringers were not accurate, but the kind of quarrel that they figured in was usually the short-range kind, over a card table or a saloon table or a bed, and at that distance aiming by gesture was quite adequate.

Equally popular in its day was the pepperbox pistol, such as the four-barrel sweetie, smaller than a woman's hand, that Christian Sharps began manufacturing in 1859. Though Sharps has a far more impressive place in gun history for the big-bore buffalo rifle he produced, his pepperbox pistol, which came in .22, .30, and .32 calibers, was the most popular handgun of its type: Americans bought 150,000 of them over a twenty-year period. In the 1870s the price for the .32-

caliber was $5.75—very much in the Saturday Night Special price range. (Until they were embargoed by the 1968 Gun Control Act, a Japanese copy of the Sharps four-barrel using .22 long ammunition could be imported for $27.50, which put it at the upper range of SNS prices.)

Perhaps the most remarkable feature of the Saturday Night Special's bad reputation is that the major U.S. gun manufacturers have managed to channel most of the odium onto their less ritzy competitors while engaging in exactly the same commerce, appealing to the same market.

If you thump the piety of such outfits as Colt and Smith & Wesson, you'll find it is pretty hollow. All their talk about wanting to get rid of the Saturday Night Special because cheap guns entice the uninitiated and the violence-prone sounds good until you look back at some of the cheap little guns they were only too proud to push before the Pentagon came along with its unending contracts and made gentlemen out of these companies.

Many of the old-line respectable companies got into the equivalent of the Saturday Night Special market as early as possible. (I don't know why I use "respectable"; they didn't really become respectable until they became rich, and the big manufacturers are neither more nor less "respectable" than the "cottage industry" gunmakers who employ Social Security retirees on their assembly line.) Indeed, if it wishes the credit, Smith & Wesson could claim to have invented the first real Saturday Night Special, for when Horace Smith and Daniel B. Wesson took out a patent for their metallic cartridge in 1854 and began to produce pistols with a patented bored-through cylinder to go with their ammunition in 1857, they specialized in .22-caliber revolvers—producing 126,000 during the next dozen years in which their patent held. Although many other companies cribbed from their cylinder design, it was during this period that the small S & W seven-shot pistol became enormously popular, preferred over the derringer by many ladies and gents of beleaguered occupations. In the 1870s and 1880s small cheap revolvers were turned out by at least fifty companies—many of them peddling their wares by mail order; many of them producing such shoddy pistols, albeit at bargain prices (some went for as little as sixty cents, new), that they were ashamed to put their own company's name on the gun but instead would stamp some catchy, frivolous name on the barrel, like Protector, Little All Right, Little Giant, Tramps Terror, and Banker's Pal.

Marlin is best known these days for its quality rifles and shotguns, but one of the company's earliest production firearms a hundred years ago was a .22 single-shot pistol about as long as a king-size cigaret—a perfect Saturday Night Special. Its first model was called Little Joker. Remington came out in the late 1870s with a runt .22 revolver easily hidden in the palm of the hand.

To understand the sermons against the Saturday Night Special being delivered today from the executive boardrooms in the major gun companies, one must ask for definitions. Would Colt have put into that category the seven-dollar derringer it was turning out in the 1870s and 1880s—the derringer that was constructed in such a way that it could also be used as a knuckleduster? Today one gathers from the remarks made by the officials of such outfits as Colt and S & W that while they consider cheapness and shoddiness great evils, they do not see anything wrong about some other characteristics of the Saturday Night Special, such as ease of concealment; perhaps that is because they have been making easily concealed guns for so many years.

Here's an ad in the Colt catalog of 1909, for example, pushing a six-shot .25-caliber hammerless automatic pistol with a two-inch barrel: "Being flat and compact (only 13 ounces in weight and four and one-half inches long) this arm can be conveniently carried in a vest pocket (or other easily accessible place), ready for instant use, with perfect safety, and has no equal in its size for Power, Accuracy, and Effectiveness." Here's an ad that Colt carried in its catalog from 1933 to 1940, for the Bankers' Special: "This powerful, compact pocket revolver has a dozen important uses—ranging all the way from personal protection to service as a snug little all around arm for camping and outdoors. It handles . . . the .22 High Speed Hollow Point for those who want knock down and stopping power . . . can be easily tucked away in the pocket—ready for service at an instant's notice. $28.50 walnut stock."

Just so there won't be any illusions about the manufacturer's suggestion, remember that the hollow-point bullet mentioned above is the dumdum, which spreads on impact and carries a fist of flesh with it; it's the kind of bullet that blew open the back of Robert Kennedy's head.

Colt also had the Pocket Positive Revolver, six shots, with a 2½ inch barrel, "small enough to be almost concealed in the palm of the hand. . . . It is an ideal lady's revolver . . . for the Home, Office, Store or Pocket—wherever concentrated energy is desirable. . . . A favorite with travelers as it may be packed in small space and is safe under the pillow or in the pocket as in the dresser drawer"; and a .25-caliber automatic pistol, overall length only 4½ inches, six-shot, "conveniently carried in vest pocket or a lady's hand bag . . . fits the feminine hand. . . . May be safely carried in any convenient pocket or easily concealed in the hand."

Today Colt is said to be among the world's leading suppliers of .25-caliber pocket automatics, one of the most popular being its six-shot automatic that weighs only 12½ ounces and measures 4⅞ inches overall. You could keep that one hidden in the palm of your hand until you get right up next to the banker, and even then he probably wouldn't see it until you nudged him in the ribs. Colt looks down its nose at the small-caliber cheap foreign import, but until the 1968 Gun Control Act inter-

☐

rupted the flow, it was only too happy to make use of the cheap labor of Spain to have the weapons manufactured there and then shipped to America. Since then, Colt has been making them in this country.

When gun buffs talk to each other and don't feel the outside, critical world is listening, they sometimes are quite candid. Thus, in the September 1972 *Gunsport & Gun Collector* magazine, Harvey Hurwitz wrote of the Saturday Night Special market competition:

> The year 1968 will always be remembered by those who follow and engage in shooting sports but anyone with a little foresight could read the handwriting on the wall in 1967. Apparently the design and marketing group at Smith and Wesson foresaw the changing times and forecast the rules that would be promulgated by the Internal Revenue Service, whereby tons of small foreign automatic pistols that were literally inundating these shores would be turned back. Based on these facts, the greater truth that a huge market existed for handguns of this nature, a concentrated effort was made [by S&W] to create a new gun that would plug the coming gap.

Among the items offered by Smith & Wesson to supply the enormous market for small handguns is a $46.50 five-shot .22-caliber automatic called the Escort, 5¼ inches long and weighing 14 ounces. S & W advertises it in the usual derring-do tones as "small enough to fit in a uniform pocket, yet packs enough fire power (.22 Long Rifle) to pull you through when the going gets rough." That is, if it goes off. A *Gunsport & Gun Collector* expert tested the gun and found "it jammed up solidly on the first shot."

Which is rather funny, for the old-line gunmakers in this country have a long solemn catechism they run through at the slightest opportunity to persuade you what a perfectly efficient product they turn out. I asked an official at Smith & Wesson what differentiated his company's products from the typical Saturday Night Special. Drawing in an executive breath, he replied without pause:

> Item one. We drop-forge all the major parts of the revolver. In this way we control the granular structure of the steel and compress this granular structure for very fine grain and great strength.

> Item two. Where the cheap guns, especially the cheap imports, are made of whatever metal is handy, the guns of our manufacture are made of aircraft-quality steel. We use the very finest ordnance steel available to us for the purpose. We spare no horses there.

> Number three. We heat-treat all of the major parts to give them great strength and keep a very close check on this, because hardness is a very important factor.

> Number four. I'll give you a specific. One form of heat-treating is case-hardening. We case-harden all hammers and triggers in our revolvers. In fact, this is so important to us that it is a copyrighted procedure. It is

sometimes called pack-hardening. It is a surface-hardening process that gives a mottled blue-gray finish to the exterior. Its value to us is that we can get a glass-hard exterior, so hard that it will cut a piece of glass, yet beneath this—about a ten-thousandth of an inch beneath this—is a steel that is more resilient. In hammers and triggers, where there is a considerable amount of vibration and impact from firing and continuous snapping, this is exclusive with us. The resilience absorbs the jarring.

Number five. In the manufacture of the ordinary standard revolver of our production, there are approximately eleven hundred inspection operations on each gun. There are ninety inspection operations on the hammer alone. These are not productive operations. They don't make any money for you. They just make sure your production is up to standard.

Number six. Every gun that we manufacture is tested in three different ways. It is function-tested with standard commercial ammunition to make sure it is a working machine. It is tested by an inspector who is also a shooter. Next, we spot-check with definitive proof loads to make sure the gun will handle everything it is supposed to handle in the line of ammunition, everything in its caliber. The proof loads will be 50 to 55 percent over normal working pressures. Not *every* gun. Where we have been making a gun for forty years without trouble, we do this test on a spot-check basis. If it is a newer gun, we'll check each individual gun until we are satisfied that everything is running fine. We also target every gun. And the guns are fired by qualified men with normal eyesight, who use a forearm rest to prevent fatigue, and they fire every gun on a target at a prescribed distance. Every gun that leaves our plant has been targeted and it shoots where it is supposed to shoot.

From the world of the acknowledged Saturday Night Special, one hears much more modest claims. In this realm one finds executives praising their product because it does *not* shoot where it is supposed to shoot. Harry Friedman, President of Arms Corporation of America in Nashville, a modest little company that puts together about thirty-five thousand .22-caliber MARK-059 revolvers every year, speaks of his $16.96 product as though it were no more deadly than a scarecrow:

No, we don't test-fire our guns. Our pistols aren't for heavy-duty use. But the American people are entitled to this market. If you are a dollar-sixty-an-hour workingman and your wife is scared and you can't afford a $95 Colt, you may want ours for $16.95. Your wife will never use it. How many women get raped, percentagewise? How many houses get broken into?

I find that most people buy guns for their wives, for the table beside their beds. Not to shoot. Just to make their wives feel good, to feel like they've got protection. I had a gentleman call me yesterday who said, "I want one of those inexpensive guns to give to my wife *to make some noise*, to make her feel like she's got protection." She doesn't know how to shoot it. She takes it out once and shoots it to see if she can do it, and that's the last time the gun is fired.

□

Anybody who wants to take up crime seriously would be stupid to buy a Saturday Night Special, said Friedman. "These guns are not accurate. A holdup man would have to be right next to a man to hit him. Criminals aren't going to buy our guns, but if they did we'd be lots safer than if they carried .38 Colts. If you want a gun to give to your wife to make a noise, or a gun to stick in your tackle box for killing snakes on fishing trips, okay, this one is okay."

Though he didn't go into other "safety" features of the Saturday Night Special, Friedman could also have pointed out that the little gun is notoriously erratic. This can be both bad and good. Sometimes, though rarely, the cylinders have been placed so close together that when one bullet is fired, it accidentally sets off the adjacent bullet as well, a potentially dangerous situation; sometimes, though again rarely, the bullet will stick, exploding the cylinder, a piece of which will go whizzing off like shrapnel. On those occasions, admittedly, the marksman is in more danger than the target. But the erratic nature of the Saturday Night Special also has an accidentally benign side: more common, much more common, than two bullets firing or one bullet firing and getting stuck is *no* bullet firing; the hammer and firing pin are often so far out of alignment because of faulty craftsmanship that they don't discharge the bullet—and of course when that happens, the Saturday Night Special is the safest gun on the market.

Vocabulary

odium   state of contempt
knuckleduster   slang for brass knuckles

Allusions/References

Leonardo's notebooks   Leonardo da Vinci (1452–1519), whose notebooks were filled with his own inventions

Discussion

1. Classification answers the question, what kind is it? What kind of a gun is the Saturday Night Special?
   List the various ways, paragraph by paragraph, the Saturday Night Special is classified.
2. What is Sherrill's attitude toward his subject? Examine closely such word choices as the following, and others you find:

   . . . to a New Yorker all guns are called by the same nickname, *used by cops and hoodlums alike.*

   . . . they would simply *hop in their cars* and *tool down* to Toledo. . . .

Is Sherrill interested in what he is writing about? What evidence supports
your view?

3. What would you say is behind Sherrill's classification of the Saturday Night
    Special? Is he advocating anything?
4. How effective are the quotes Sherrill uses to support his own ideas?
    Look at each of the longer pieces of quoted material. How does inclusion of
    such information add to the authority of the author?

Lewis Thomas
(1913–   )

Lewis Thomas was born November 25, 1913, in Flushing, New York. The son of
a surgeon, he is a medical researcher and educator whose specialty is pathol-
ogy. He has been president and chief executive officer of Memorial Sloan-Ket-
tering Cancer Center, and is now its chancellor. For Thomas, scientific
research is much more than a job. "Others play golf or bridge. I go to the lab."

In 1971 he started a column in the *New England Journal of Medicine,*
installments of which were collected in 1974 as *The Lives of a Cell: Notes of a
Biology Watcher.* The following essay is from this book.

Some reviewers have spoken of Thomas's writing as the language of
poetry. He has been called evolution's "most accomplished prose stylist."
Thomas himself says, "I mean it's not really fair to have a book with a cover
and everything when you never wrote a book, except in such little tiny bits."

A second book, *The Medusa and the Snail: More Notes of a Biology
Watcher,* was published in 1979.

Death in the Open

Most of the dead animals you see on highways near the cities are dogs,
a few cats. Out in the countryside, the forms and coloring of the dead
are strange; these are the wild creatures. Seen from a car window they
appear as fragments, evoking memories of woodchucks, badgers,
skunks, voles, snakes, sometimes the mysterious wreckage of a deer.

It is always a queer shock, part a sudden upwelling of grief, part
unaccountable amazement. It is simply astounding to see an animal
dead on a highway. The outrage is more than just the location; it is the
impropriety of such visible death, anywhere. You do not expect to see
dead animals in the open. It is the nature of animals to die alone, off
somewhere, hidden. It is wrong to see them lying out on the highway;
it is wrong to see them anywhere.

Everything in the world dies, but we only know about it as a kind
of abstraction. If you stand in a meadow, at the end of a hillside, and
look around carefully, almost everything you can catch sight of is in
the process of dying, and most things will be dead long before you are.
If it were not for the constant renewal and replacement going on before
your eyes, the whole place would turn to stone and sand under your
feet.

There are some creatures that do not seem to die at all; they simply vanish totally into their own progeny. Single cells do this. The cell becomes two, then four, and so on, and after a while the last trace is gone. It cannot be seen as death; barring mutation, the descendants are simply the first cell, living all over again. The cycles of the slime mold have episodes that seem as conclusive as death, but the withered slug, with its stalk and fruiting body, is plainly the transient tissue of a developing animal; the free-swimming amebocytes use this organ collectively in order to produce more of themselves.

There are said to be a billion billion insects on the earth at any moment, most of them with very short life expectancies by our standards. Someone has estimated that there are 25 million assorted insects hanging in the air over every temperate square mile, in a column extending upward for thousands of feet, drifting through the layers of the atmosphere like plankton. They are dying steadily, some by being eaten, some just dropping in their tracks, tons of them around the earth, disintegrating as they die, invisibly.

Who ever sees dead birds, in anything like the huge numbers stipulated by the certainty of the death of all birds? A dead bird is an incongruity, more startling than an unexpected live bird, sure evidence to the human mind that something has gone wrong. Birds do their dying off somewhere, behind things, under things, never on the wing.

Animals seem to have an instinct for performing death alone, hidden. Even the largest, most conspicuous ones find ways to conceal themselves in time. If an elephant missteps and dies in an open place, the herd will not leave him there; the others will pick him up and carry the body from place to place, finally putting it down in some inexplicably suitable location. When elephants encounter the skeleton of an elephant out in the open, they methodically take up each of the bones and distribute them, in a ponderous ceremony, over neighboring acres.

It is a natural marvel. All of the life of the earth dies, all of the time, in the same volume as the new life that dazzles us each morning, each spring. All we see of this is the odd stump, the fly struggling on the porch floor of the summer house in October, the fragment on the highway. I have lived all my life with an embarrassment of squirrels in my backyard, they are all over the place, all year long, and I have never seen, anywhere, a dead squirrel.

I suppose it is just as well. If the earth were otherwise, and all the dying were done in the open, with the dead there to be looked at, we would never have it out of our minds. We can forget about it much of the time, or think of it as an accident to be avoided, somehow. But it does make the process of dying seem more exceptional than it really is, and harder to engage in at the times when we must ourselves engage.

In our way, we conform as best we can to the rest of nature. The obituary pages tell us of the news that we are dying away, while the birth announcements in finer print, off at the side of the page, inform us of our replacements, but we get no grasp from this of the enormity of scale. There are 3 billion of us on the earth, and all 3 billion must be dead, on a schedule, within this lifetime. The vast mortality, involving something over 50 million of us each year, takes place in relative secrecy. We can only really know of the deaths in our households, or among our friends. These, detached in our minds from all the rest, we take to be unnatural events, anomalies, outrages. We speak of our own dead in low voices; struck down, we say, as though visible death can only occur for cause, by disease or violence, avoidably. We send off for flowers, grieve, make ceremonies, scatter bones, unaware of the rest of the 3 billion on the same schedule. All of that immense mass of flesh and bone and consciousness will disappear by absorption into the earth, without recognition by the transient survivors.

Less than a half century from now, our replacements will have more than doubled the numbers. It is hard to see how we can continue to keep the secret, with such multitudes doing the dying. We will have to give up the notion that death is catastrophe, or detestable, or avoidable, or even strange. We will need to learn more about the cycling of life in the rest of the system, and about our connection to the process. Everything that comes alive seems to be in trade for something that dies, cell for cell. There might be some comfort in the recognition of synchrony, in the information that we all go down together, in the best of company.

Vocabulary

progeny offspring
amebocytes any cell having an amoebic form
anomalies unnatural events, abnormal
transient decaying with time
synchrony occurring at the same time

Discussion

1. What does Thomas mean by his statement: "Everything in the world dies, but we only know about it as a kind of abstraction"?
2. How does Thomas illustrate this thesis above? Cite examples from the essay.
3. Thomas's language choice is remarkably clear and imagistic. (An image, in this sense, is a picture formed in your mind by words.) How do Thomas's images of death contribute to his classification of it? Note such images as: "the odd stump," "the fly struggling on the porch floor of the summer house in October," "the fragment on the highway."
   What other especially imagistic language can you find in this piece?
4. While seemingly a discussion about death, a classification of death as a natural phenomenon, Lewis Thomas is obviously building a case for something at the same time.

☐

What is his reason for writing this piece? What evidence (from the words themselves) do you have to support your idea?

For Further Discussion

5. "Language is what human beings talk with," writes L. M. Myers in *The Roots of Modern English*. "Writing is not language, but merely a way of recording language by means of visible marks."
   How would you classify the language of the physician, Lewis Thomas, as reflected in the "visible marks" of his essay?
   What can you say about his word choices, sentence and paragraph lengths, punctuation?
6. What does the evolution of language suggest to you about your own language use and writing style?

☐ By Cause/Effect

Here is a cause/effect. Language can't stay in one place. It follows the same natural imperatives as everything else. This means that your use of words is going to influence and in turn be influenced by change. When you read fine essayists, such as E. M. Forster or William Saroyan or James Thurber, you read another generation of language users from yourself. You might ask yourself, what does my generation have to say, and in what words?

Lincoln Steffens, in "I Became a Student," tells how he discovered a reason to believe in himself; how finding that everything is not yet perfect, or done, allowed him to see that what he had to offer was vital. The "cause" was a discovery, a change in awareness. The effect was sight—seeing everything with new eyes—insight.

Cause/effect essays are not easy. There is never only *one* cause for any given effect. The discovery Steffens writes about is *one* natural outcome of education: the more you learn, the more you know how much is yet unknown. Everything is interconnected when you tune in to the chain of cause/effect.

Virginia Woolf, in "The Death of a Moth," traces death to a "force," the true nature of life which is the energy encapsulated in every living thing. She finds in the moth a metaphor for the eternal tension of life against death, and the perpetual repetition of the drama, seeing life and death as equally "strange"—or marvelous, mysterious.

Modesty in your cause/effect paper is a good thing; so also, is keeping your subject close to home, to those things you actually know about. Sir James Jeans, an astronomer, relates how it is that the eye sees the sky as blue, and Sylvia Plath, in an excerpt from *The Bell Jar*, shows how her eyes see absurdity in the human condition, and how helpless Esther, her persona, is against this vision. I hope these essays give you some idea of how you might approach your own cause/ effect essay, and that you enjoy the kind of mental activity that examines phenomena for whys.

Sir James Jeans
(1877–1946)

Sir James Jeans was born September 11, 1877, in London. An astronomer and mathematical physicist, Jeans was both an important theoretician and a writer who applied scientific inquiry toward a philosophic understanding of our place in the cosmos. He saw mathematics as an elementary tool for explaining objective reality.

Though Jeans felt even modern man is "still too engulfed in the greyness of the morning mists" to see his place in the universe, science could help find an answer. He believed astronomy "may have something to say on the enthralling question of the relation of human life to the universe in which it is placed, and on the beginnings, meaning, and destiny of the human race."

Why the Sky Looks Blue

Imagine that we stand on an ordinary seaside pier, and watch the waves rolling in and striking against the iron columns of the pier. Large waves pay very little attention to the columns—they divide right and left and reunite after passing each column, much as a regiment of soldiers would if a tree stood in their road; it is almost as though the columns had not been there. But the short waves and ripples find the columns of the pier a much more formidable obstacle. When the short waves impinge on the columns, they are reflected back and spread as new ripples in all directions. To use the technical term, they are "scattered." The obstacle provided by the iron columns hardly affects the long waves at all, but scatters the short ripples.

We have been watching a sort of working model of the way in which sunlight struggles through the earth's atmosphere. Between us on earth and outer space the atmosphere interposes innumerable obstacles in the form of molecules of air, tiny droplets of water, and small particles of dust. These are represented by the columns of the pier.

The waves of the sea represent the sunlight. We know that sunlight is a blend of many colors—as we can prove for ourselves by passing it through a prism, or even through a jug of water, or as nature demonstrates to us when she passes it through the raindrops of a summer shower and produces a rainbow. We also know that light consists of waves, and that the different colors of light are produced by waves of different lengths, red light by long waves and blue light by short waves. The mixture of waves which constitutes sunlight has to struggle past the columns of the pier. And these obstacles treat the light waves much as the columns of the pier treat the sea-waves. The long waves which constitute red light are hardly affected but the short waves which constitute blue light are scattered in all directions.

Thus the different constituents of sunlight are treated in different ways as they struggle through the earth's atmosphere. A wave of blue light may be scattered by a dust particle, and turned out of its course. After a time a second dust particle again turns it out of its course, and so on, until finally it enters our eyes by a path as zigzag as that of a flash of lightning. Consequently the blue waves of the sunlight enter our eyes from all directions. And that is why the sky looks blue.

Discussion

1. Here is a delightfully clear explanation of why the sky looks blue. Remember asking that question as a child? What was the response you got?
2. What is the effect of the first paragraph?
   How does making an analogy to the sea, to waves striking a pier, help you *see* the "unseeable" light waves?
3. How is each paragraph a working out of Jeans's analogy?
4. The dust, water, and air molecules that become obstacles for light waves also comprise earth's atmosphere. What is the effect of these obstacles on our sensory impression of color?
   How does Jeans's analogy further contribute to your thinking about "atmosphere" and "sky" in a less abstract, more concrete way?

Virginia Woolf
(1882–1941)

Virginia Woolf was born January 25, 1882, in London. She was raised in a cultured home, and at an early age exposed to talented and educated people. She became a central figure in the Bloomsbury Group, made up of several important literary and artistic personages, including her sister Vanessa Bell and E. M. Forster. The group rebelled against the Victorian mores of the day. With her husband, writer and political thinker Leonard Woolf, she set up the Hogarth Press in 1917.

Woolf began her writing career as a critic for *The Times Literary Supplement* and continued to write criticism, as well as novels and essays, all her life. While her first two novels were in fairly traditional form, she soon became known for her stream-of-consciousness technique. Her impressionistic, experimental style was in response to writing which "ceases to resemble the vision in our minds." She felt the writing of her time failed to convey "life or spirit, truth or reality, the essential thing." In a lecture at Cambridge she defined reality as "something very erratic, very undependable—now to be found in a dusty road, now as a scrap of newspaper in the street, now a daffodil in the sun." She went on to say the novelist "has the chance to live more than other people in the presence of this reality."

Woolf had a history of mental illness. In 1941, depressed over an apparent relapse and the ongoing Second World War, she committed suicide by drowning in the River Ouse.

The Death of a Moth

Moths that fly by day are not properly to be called moths; they do not excite that pleasant sense of dark autumn nights and ivyblossom which the commonest yellow underwing asleep in the shadow of the curtain never fails to rouse in us. They are hybrid creatures, neither gay like butterflies nor sombre like their own species. Nevertheless, the present specimen, with his narrow hay-coloured wings, fringed with a tassel of the same colour, seemed to be content with life. It was a pleasant morning, mid-September, mild, benignant, yet with a keener breath than that of the summer months. The plough was already scoring the field opposite the window, and where the share had been, the earth was pressed flat and gleamed with moisture. Such vigour came rolling in from the fields and down beyond that it was difficult to keep the eyes strictly turned upon the book. The rooks too were keeping one of their annual festivities; soaring round the tree-tops until it looked as if a vast net with thousands of black knots in it has been cast up into the air; which, after a few moments sank slowly down upon the trees until every twig seemed to have a knot at the end of it. Then, suddenly, the net would be thrown into the air again in a wider circle this time, with the utmost clamour and vociferation, as though to be thrown into the air and settle slowly down upon the tree-tops were a tremendously exciting experience.

The same energy which inspired the rooks, the ploughmen, the horses, and even, it seemed, the lean bare-backed downs, sent the moth fluttering from side to side of his square of the window-pane. One could not help watching him. One was, indeed, conscious of a queer feeling of pity for him. The possibilities of pleasure seemed that morning so enormous and so various that to have only a moth's part in life, and a day moth's at that, appeared a hard fate, and his zest in enjoying his meagre opportunities to the full, pathetic. He flew vigorously to one corner of his compartment, and, after waiting there a second, flew across to the other. What remained for him but to fly to a third corner and then to a fourth? That was all he could do, in spite of the size of the downs, the width of the sky, the far-off smoke of houses, and the romantic voice, now and then, of a steamer out at sea. What he could do he did. Watching him, it seemed as if a fibre, very thin but pure, of the enormous energy of the world had been thrust into his frail and diminutive body. As often as he crossed the pane, I could fancy that a thread of vital light became visible. He was little or nothing but life.

Yet, because he was so small, and so simple a form of the energy that was rolling in at the open window and driving its way through so many narrow and intricate corridors in my own brain and in those of other human beings, there was something marvelous as well as pathetic about him. It was as if someone had taken a tiny bead of pure life and decking it as lightly as possible with down and feathers, had set it dancing and zigzagging to show us the true nature of life. Thus displayed one could not get over the strangeness of it. One is apt to forget all about life, seeing it humped and bossed and garnished and cumbered so that it has to move with the greatest circumspection and dignity. Again, the thought of all that life might have been had he been born in any other shape caused one to view his simple activities with a kind of pity.

After a time, tired by his dancing apparently, he settled on the window ledge in the sun, and the queer spectacle being at an end, I forgot about him. Then, looking up, my eye was caught by him. He was trying to resume his dancing, but seemed either so stiff or so awkward that he could only flutter to the bottom of the window-pane; and when he tried to fly across it he failed. Being intent on other matters I watched these futile attempts for a time without thinking, unconsciously waiting for him to resume his flight, as one waits for a machine, that has stopped momentarily, to start again without considering the reason for its failure. After perhaps a seventh attempt he slipped from the wooden ledge and fell, fluttering his wings, on to his back on the windowsill. The helplessness of his attitude roused me. It flashed upon me that he was in difficulties; he could no longer raise himself; his legs struggled vainly. But, as I stretched out a pencil, meaning to help him to right himself, it came over me that the failure and awkwardness were the approach of death. I laid the pencil down again.

The legs agitated themselves once more. I looked as if for the enemy against which he struggled. I looked out of doors. What had happened there? Presumably it was midday, and work in the fields had stopped. Stillness and quiet had replaced the previous animation. The birds had taken themselves off to feed in the brooks. The horses stood still. Yet the power was there all the same, massed outside indifferent, impersonal, not attending to anything in particular. Somehow it was opposed to the little hay-coloured moth. It was useless to try to do anything. One could only watch the extraordinary efforts made by those tiny legs against an oncoming doom which could, had it chosen, have submerged an entire city, not merely a city, but masses of human beings; nothing, I knew, had any chance against death. Nevertheless after a pause of exhaustion the legs fluttered again. It was superb this last protest and so frantic that he succeeded at last in righting himself.

One's sympathies, of course, were all on the side of life. Also, when there was nobody to care or to know, this gigantic effort on the part of an insignificant little moth, against a power of such magnitude, to retain what no one else valued or desired to keep, moved one strangely. Again, somehow, one saw life, a pure bead. I lifted the pencil again, useless though I knew it to be. But even as I did so, the unmistakable tokens of death showed themselves. The body relaxed, and instantly grew stiff. The struggle was over. The insignificant little creature now knew death. As I looked at the dead moth, this minute wayside triumph of so great a force over so mean an antagonist filled me with wonder. Just as life had been strange a few minutes before, so death was now as strange. The moth having righted himself now lay most decently and uncomplainingly composed. O yes, he seemed to say, death is stronger than I am.

Vocabulary

benignant   favorable, gracious
rooks   a crowlike old-world bird
vociferation   loud clamor
mean   humble origin

Discussion

1. What does Woolf mean by the following: "The same energy which inspired the rooks, the ploughmen, the horses, and even, it seemed, the lean bare-backed downs, sent the moth fluttering. . . ."?
   What is this "same energy"?
2. What does Woolf mean by: "Yet the power was there all the same, massed outside indifferent, impersonal, not attending to anything in particular."?
   What is the counterpoint to this "power" or "energy" Woolf writes of?
3. Describe the simple cause/effect of the moth's behavior. (Cause/effect answers the question, why did it happen? Why did it happen?)
4. What is the meaning behind Woolf's concern with the moth? Why did she want to put it in words? What did the story of the moth illustrate to her? What is the larger cause/effect, the answer to the question why does it happen?

For Further Discussion

5. Virginia Woolf, being removed from your own language use by time and custom, is a good author to study for evidence of the evolution of language. Collect words, phrases, sentence structures, that seem foreign to your own. How would you describe (objectively now, no judgments of good or bad) the conventions of your language use as compared to hers, in this sample?

Speculate on the causes and effects of this discernible change in language habits.

Lincoln Steffens
(1866–1936)

Lincoln Steffens was born April 6, 1866, in San Francisco. His early record as a student was dismal: because of his poor academic performance his father sent him to military school where he ended up in the guardhouse for "drunkenness" and failed to pass his entrance exams for college. Eventually, though, he graduated from the University of California and went to Europe to study an additional three years.

Upon returning to the United States, Steffens went to work for the *New York Evening Post* as a reporter. He worked as a journalist for the rest of his life. Along with associates Ida M. Tarbell and Ray Baker, he became known for his articles on corruption in business and government. Theodore Roosevelt coined the word "muckrakers" in reference to their investigative reporting.

Considered a "reformer," Steffens's success was in part due to his belief that he was no better than those he investigated. His openness toward those he interviewed gained him information no other reporter could get. "I never tell all of the truth," he once remarked. "I don't have to—one-tenth is sufficient to make any decent man rise feeling outraged." But Steffens's strength as a writer is typified in his belief in "the true ideal for an artist and for a newspaper: to get the news so completely and report it so humanly that the reader will see himself in the other fellow's place."

The following selection is from Steffens's autobiography.

I Became a Student

It is possible to get an education at a university. It has been done; not often, but the fact that a proportion, however small, of college students do get a start in interested, methodical study, proves my thesis, and the two personal experiences I have to offer illustrate it and show how to circumvent the faculty, the other students, and the whole college system of mind-fixing. My method might lose a boy his degree, but a degree is not worth so much as the capacity and the drive to learn, and the undergraduate desire for any empty baccalaureate is one of the holds the educational system has on students. Wise students some day will refuse to take degrees, as the best men (in England, for instance) give, but do not themselves accept, titles.

My method was hit on by accident and some instinct. I specialized. With several courses prescribed, I concentrated on the one or two that interested me most, and letting the others go, I worked intensively on my favorites. In my first two years, for example, I worked at English and political economy and read philosophy. At the beginning of my junior year I had several cinches in history. Now I like history; I had neglected it partly because I rebelled at the way it was taught, as positive knowledge unrelated to politics, art, life, or anything else. The professors gave us chapters out of a few books to read, con, and be quizzed on. Blessed as I was with a "bad memory," I could not commit to it anything that I did not understand and intellectually need. The bare record of the story of man, with names, dates, and irrelative events, bored me. But I had discovered in my readings of literature, philosophy, and political economy that history had light to throw upon unhistorical questions. So I proposed in my junior and senior year to specialize in history, taking all the courses required and those also that I had flunked in. With this in mind I listened attentively to the first introductory talk of Professor William Cary Jones on American constitutional history. He was a dull lecturer, but I noticed that, after telling us what pages of what books we must be prepared in, he mumbled off some other references "for those that may care to dig deeper."

When the rest of the class rushed out into the sunshine, I went up to the professor and, to his surprise, asked for this memorandum. He gave it to me. Up in the library I ran through the required chapters in the two different books, and they differed on several points. Turning to the other authorities, I saw that they disagreed on the same facts and also on others. The librarian, appealed to, helped me search the bookshelves till the library closed, and then I called on Professor Jones for more references. He was astonished, invited me in, and began to approve my industry, which astonished me. I was not trying to be a good boy; I was better than that: I was a curious boy. He lent me a couple of his books, and I went off to my club to read them. They only deepened the mystery, clearing up the historical question, but leaving the answer to be dug for and written.

The historians did not know! History was not a science, but a field for research, a field for me, for any young man, to explore, to make discoveries in and write a scientific report about. I was fascinated. As I went on from chapter to chapter, day after day, finding frequently essential differences of opinion and of fact, I saw more and more work to do. In this course, American constitutional history, I hunted far enough to suspect that the fathers of the Republic who wrote our sacred Constitution of the United States not only did not, but did not want to, establish a democratic government, and I dreamed for awhile—as I used as a child to play I was Napoleon or a trapper—I promised myself to write a true history of the making of the American Constitution. I did not do it; that chapter has been done or well begun since by two men: Smith of the University of Washington and Beard (then) of Columbia (afterward forced out, perhaps for this very work). I found other events, men, and epochs waiting for students. In all my other courses, in ancient, in European, and in modern history, the disagreeing authorities carried me back to the need for a fresh search for (or of) the original documents or other clinching testimony. Of course I did well in my classes. The history professors soon knew me as a student and seldom put a question to me except when the class had flunked it. Then Professor Jones would say, "Well, Steffens, tell them about it."

Fine. But vanity wasn't my ruling passion then. What I had was a quickening sense that I was learning a method for studying history and that every chapter of it, from the beginning of the world to the end, is crying out to be rewritten. There was something for Youth to do; these superior old men had not done anything, finally.

Years afterward I came out of the graft prosecution office in San Francisco with Rudolph Spreckels, the banker and backer of the investigation. We were to go somewhere, quick, in his car, and we couldn't. The chauffeur was trying to repair something wrong. Mr. Spreckels smiled; he looked closely at the defective part, and to my silent, wondering inquiry he answered: "Always, when I see something badly done or not done at all, I see an opportunity to make a fortune. I never kick at bad work by my class: there's lots of it and we suffer from it. But our failures and neglects are chances for the young fellows coming along and looking for work."

Nothing is done. Everything in the world remains to be done or done over. "The greatest picture is not yet painted, the greatest play isn't written (not even by Shakespeare), the greatest poem is unsung. There isn't in all the world a perfect railroad, nor a good government, nor a sound law." Physics, mathematics, and especially the most advanced and exact of the sciences, are being fundamentally revised. Chemistry is just becoming a science; psychology, economics, and sociology are awaiting a Darwin, whose work in turn is awaiting an Einstein. If the rah-rah boys in our colleges could be told this, they might not all be such specialists in football, petting parties, and unearned degrees. They are not told it, however; they are told to learn what is known. This is nothing, philosophically speaking.

Somehow or other in my later years at Berkeley, two professors, Moses and Howison, representing opposite schools of thought, got into a controversy, probably about their classes. They brought together in the house of one of them a few of their picked students, with the evident intention of letting us show in conversation how much or how little we had understood of their respective teachings. I don't remember just what the subject was that they threw into the ring, but we wrestled with it till the professors could stand it no longer. Then they broke in, and while we sat silent and highly entertained, they went at each other hard and fast and long. It was after midnight when, the debate over, we went home. I asked the other fellows what they had got out of it, and their answers showed that they had seen nothing but a fine, fair fight. When I laughed, they asked me what I, the D.S.,[1] had seen that was so much more profound.

[1] Damn Stinker.

☐

I said that I had seen two highly trained, well-educated Masters of Arts and Doctors of Philosophy disagreeing upon every essential point of thought and knowledge. They had all there was of the sciences; and yet they could not find any knowledge upon which they could base an acceptable conclusion. They had no test of knowledge; they didn't know what is and what is not. And they have no test of right and wrong; they have no basis for even an ethics.

Well, and what of it? They asked me that, and that I did not answer. I was stunned by the discovery that it was philosophically true, in a most literal sense, that nothing is known; that it is precisely the foundation that is lacking for science; that all we call knowledge rested upon assumptions which the scientists did not all accept; and that, likewise, there is no scientific reason for saying, for example, that stealing is wrong. In brief: there was no scientific basis for an ethics. No wonder men said one thing and did another; no wonder they could settle nothing either in life or in the academies.

I could hardly believe this. Maybe these professors, whom I greatly respected, did not know it all. I read the books over again with a fresh eye, with a real interest, and I could see that, as in history, so in other branches of knowledge, everything was in the air. And I was glad of it. Rebel though I was, I had got the religion of scholarship and science; I was in awe of the authorities in the academic world. It was a release to feel my worship cool and pass. But I could not be sure. I must go elsewhere, see and hear other professors, men these California professors quoted and looked up to as their high priests. I decided to go as a student to Europe when I was through Berkeley, and I would start with the German universities.

My father listened to my plan, and he was disappointed. He had hoped I would succeed him in his business; it was for that that he was staying in it. When I said that, whatever I might do, I would never go into business, he said rather sadly, that he would sell out his interest and retire. And he did soon after our talk. But he wanted me to stay home and, to keep me, offered to buy an interest in a certain San Francisco daily paper. He had evidently had this in mind for some time. I had always done some writing, verse at the poetical age of puberty, then a novel which my mother alone treasured. Journalism was the business for a boy who liked to write, he thought, and he said I had often spoken of a newspaper as my ambition. No doubt I had in the intervals between my campaigns as Napoleon. But no more. I was now going to be a scientist, a philosopher. He sighed: he thought it over, and with the approval of my mother, who was for every sort of education, he gave his consent.

Vocabulary

ethics   the philosophy of morals, the accepted principles of right or wrong

Discussion

1. What does Steffens mean when he says: "I was not trying to be a good boy; I was better than that: I was a curious boy"?
2. What does he mean by: "What I had was a quickening sense that I was learning a method of studying history and that every chapter of it, from the beginning of the world to the end, is crying out to be rewritten"?
   Do you agree with Steffens? Why or why not?
   Would his words as easily fit any other field of knowledge? Language study?
3. What is the cause/effect of "learning" Steffens is writing about here? Why did Steffens find a renewed interest in education?
   Examine especially the paragraph beginning with: "Nothing is done. Everything in the world remains to be done or done over."
   What does Steffens mean when he says, "They are told to learn what is known"? What does he mean when he says, "This is nothing. . . . "
4. What is, according to Steffens, "the religion of scholarship and science"?

For Further Discussion

5. In writing cause/effect essays, or in using cause/effect reasoning, we must be careful not to attribute single causes, or assume causes can be easily found. For the effects we can see, many causes are at work. Keeping an eye to this, how do you find Steffens's reasoning about the nature of knowledge?
6. You might wish to write an essay using the cause/effect organizational pattern, such as the effects of college on your intellectual or social development. How is college affecting your life?

Sylvia Plath
(1932–1963)

Sylvia Plath was born October 27, 1932, in Boston, Massachusetts. She had her first poem published when she was eight and, except for a brief guest-editorship at *Mademoiselle* magazine and a stint as an English teacher at Smith College, writing was her career. In 1955 she went to Cambridge as a Fulbright scholar, and while there met and married poet Ted Hughes. She moved to England permanently in 1959.

Known primarily as a poet, Plath's intense, confessional writing created a legend that still tends to obscure her immense talent. A. Alvarez has said she made "poetry and death inseparable." Charles Newman contends she "remains among the few women writers in recent memory to link the grand theme of womanhood with the destiny of modern civilization."

According to Ted Hughes, her early poems were written "very slowly." But with "Tulips" in 1961 she began writing "at top speed, as one might write an urgent letter. From then on, all her poems were written this way." Her novel, *The Bell Jar*, from which the following selection is taken, has been called

a "testing ground" for her poetry. She called it "an autobiographical apprentice work which I had to write in order to free myself from the past." One
month after it was published, she committed suicide by putting her head in a
gas oven.

In an interview Plath said: "I feel that in a novel, for example, you can get
in the toothbrushes and all the paraphernalia that one finds in daily life . . . in
a novel I can get more of life, perhaps not such an intense life, but certainly
more of life."

Lenny's Place

I wouldn't have missed Lenny's place for anything.

It was built exactly like the inside of a ranch, only in the middle
of a New York apartment house. He'd had a few partitions knocked
down to make the place broaden out, he said, and then had them pine-
panel the walls and fit up a special pine-paneled bar in the shape of a
horseshoe. I think the floor was pine-paneled, too.

Great white bearskins lay about underfoot, and the only furniture
was a lot of low beds covered with Indian rugs. Instead of pictures hung
up on the walls, he had antlers and buffalo horns and a stuffed rabbit
head. Lenny jutted a thumb at the meek little gray muzzle and stiff jack-
rabbit ears.

"Ran over that in Las Vegas."

He walked away across the room, his cowboy boots echoing like
pistol shots. "Acoustics," he said, and grew smaller and smaller until he
vanished through a door in the distance.

All at once music started to come out of the air on every side. Then
it stopped, and we heard Lenny's voice say "This is your twelve o'clock
disc jock, Lenny Shepherd, with a roundup of the tops in pops. Number
Ten in the wagon train this week is none other than that little yaller-
haired gal you been hearin' so much about lately . . . the one an' only
Sunflower!"

> *I was born in Kansas, I was bred in Kansas,*
> *And when I marry I'll be wed in Kansas . . .*

"What a card!" Doreen said. "Isn't he a card?"

"You bet," I said.

"Listen, Elly, do me a favor," She seemed to think Elly was who I
really was by now.

"Sure," I said.

"Stick around, will you? I wouldn't have a chance if he tried anything funny. Did you see that muscle?" Doreen giggled.

Lenny popped out of the room. "I got twenty grand's worth of
recording equipment in there." He ambled over to the bar and set out
three glasses and a silver ice bucket and a big pitcher and began to mix
drinks from several different bottles.

... to a true-blue gal who promised she would wait—
She's the sunflower of the Sunflower State.

"Terrific, huh?" Lenny came over, balancing three glasses. Big drops stood out on them like sweat, and the ice cubes jingled as he passed them around. Then the music twanged to a stop, and we heard Lenny's voice announcing the next number.

"Nothing like listening to yourself talk. Say," Lenny's eye lingered on me, "Frankie vamoosed, you ought to have somebody, I'll call up one of the fellers."

"That's okay," I said. "You don't have to do that." I didn't want to come straight out and ask for somebody several sizes larger than Frankie.

Lenny looked relieved. "Just so's you don't mind. I wouldn't want to do wrong by a friend of Doreen's." He gave Doreen a big white smile. "Would I, honeybun?"

He held out a hand to Doreen, and without a word they both started to jitterbug, still hanging onto their glasses.

I sat cross-legged on one of the beds and tried to look devout and impassive like some businessmen I once saw watching an Algerian belly dancer, but as soon as I leaned back against the wall under the stuffed rabbit, the bed started to roll out into the room, so I sat down on a bearskin on the floor and leaned back against the bed instead.

My drink was wet and depressing. Each time I took another sip it tasted more and more like dead water. Around the middle of the glass there was painted a pink lasso with yellow polka dots. I drank to about an inch below the lasso and waited a bit, and when I went to take another sip, the drink was up to lasso-level again.

Out of the air Lenny's voice boomed, "Wye oh wye did I ever leave Wyoming?"

The two of them didn't even stop jitterbugging during the intervals. I felt myself shrinking to a small black dot against all those red and white rugs and that pine paneling. I felt like a hole in the ground.

There is something demoralizing about watching two people get more and more crazy about each other, especially when you are the only extra person in the room.

It's like watching Paris from an express caboose heading in the opposite direction—every second the city gets smaller and smaller, only you feel it's really you getting smaller and smaller and lonelier and lonelier, rushing away from all those lights and that excitement at about a million miles an hour.

Every so often Lenny and Doreen would bang into each other and kiss and then swing to take a long drink and close in on each other again. I thought I might just lie down on the bearskin and go to sleep until Doreen felt ready to go back to the hotel.

Then Lenny gave a terrible roar. I sat up. Doreen was hanging on to Lenny's left earlobe with her teeth.

"Leggo, you bitch!"

Lenny stooped, and Doreen went flying up on to his shoulder, and her glass sailed out of her hand in a long, wide arc and fetched up against the pine paneling with a silly tinkle. Lenny was still roaring and whirling round so fast I couldn't see Doreen's face.

I noted, in the routine way you notice the color of somebody's eyes, that Doreen's breasts had popped out of her dress and were swinging out slightly like full brown melons as she circled belly-down on Lenny's shoulder, thrashing her legs in the air and screeching, and then they both started to laugh and slow up, and Lenny was trying to bite Doreen's hip through her skirt when I let myself out the door before anything more could happen and managed to get downstairs by leaning with both hands on the banister and half sliding the whole way.

I didn't realize Lenny's place had been air-conditioned until I wavered out onto the pavement. The tropical, stale heat the sidewalks had been sucking up all day hit me in the face like a last insult. I didn't know where in the world I was.

Discussion

1. What causes Elly (the narrator, actually named Esther) to claim: "I wouldn't have missed Lenny's place for anything"?
2. What are the causes that lead up to her leaving Lenny's?
3. How does Plath employ sensory details (words that evoke sights, sounds, smells, touch, and taste) so that the reader is not only *told* about Lenny's place, but *vicariously experiences* it?
   List as many of the descriptions that evoke a sensory response as you can find.
4. *The Bell Jar*, from which "Lenny's Place" is extracted, is a novel. "Lenny's Place" is neither expository, nor an essay. Nevertheless, one could say the entire novel is about the heroine's (Esther's) disaffection from life.
   What words and phrases reveal the causes of Esther's distancing from events surrounding her?
5. How does Plath feel toward Esther? (Show evidence from the piece itself to prove your thesis.)
   What is the tone of this piece? Funny? Sad? Bitter? Angry?
   Did it make you laugh? If so, what does this indicate about its tone?

For Further Discussion

6. You may be interested in comparing and contrasting fiction pieces. The Fitzgerald selection, "The Buchanan's Mansion," in Chapter Three and the Plath piece above afford interesting comparisons. For the sake of a class in writing, concentrate always on the words, the writing itself.
   What are the differences between Plath's words and Fitzgerald's? Can you tell which is which? How?

☐ By Comparison/Contrast

Write a risky paper I told my class: take some chances. The next day Shanna handed me a piece of typing paper jaggedly cut on three sides, the typed words running slightly uphill. "It looks like they are falling off a cliff," she said. She had broken every rule. Writing was spelled writting. There was no punctuation. Because she liked the look of the letter "g" she had invented the word garbadgegobble-gogopigs. Never mind that garbage doesn't usually have the word bad imbedded in it, her last line read why why eye eye ld.

Brian wrote a piece about himself, nostalgic yearnings for his lost soul wanderings as a young man on Venice Boulevard, date palms, and the girl in the stucco house wearing the flowered dress her mother made on the sewing machine from Sears.

I got more than I bargained for.

Communication by comparison and contrast is an everyday occurrence. My colleague Leonard Held handed me *Writing Procedures*, a collection of his students' essays. "Look at the essay called 'Secret Tears,'" he said, "and then by way of contrast read 'T.V. Family/Real Family.'" In the first, a student recalls his childhood in a broken home. "I've never understood," he writes, "how the two people I loved most in the world could possibly abuse each other so passionately." In the second essay a student compares his home life to T.V.'s "The Brady Bunch." While the Bradys "march straight up to their uncluttered bedrooms and put everything in its place," he and his siblings' "crusty shoes, wet sweatpants and sticky tee-shirts stay where they land." I can see what Leonard is getting at. Both papers are beautifully written. The first paper shows a home life filled with sorrow; the second makes a distinction between an artificial happy home, tidy and perfect, and an ideal happy home, cluttered and alive. "All of my life," the second student writes, "my family has teased me, fought with me and loved me." The first student concludes with the statement: "Though now I realize it was not my fault that my parents argued so bitterly, I still wonder upon occasion what my life would be like had their words been hidden from my young and vulnerable mind."

Comparing and contrasting as a way to explain similarities and differences in the stuff of existence is usually accomplished in one of two ways. The block method is the Shanna and Brian story, where everything is said about Shanna before anything is said about Brian. The point-by-point method is the Leonard Held story, similarities and differences in the two student essays and actual home life experience are written about side by side.

In the following section Russell Baker compares an Italian attitude toward time and the human condition with an American attitude. Everything passes, the Italians seem to say; the American, by contrast, believes human accomplishment can last forever. Donald Peattie compares the green world of chlorophyll to the restless world of blood, in an attempt to show the relationships of all life to life. Annie Dillard, in a more abstruse comparison, but rich with the clarity of detail, shows the difference between sight and insight. Like life, her sentences are filled with the stuff of living: tadpoles, mosses, creeks, bridges, and clouds. The mysterious structure of her piece echoes the mystery she finds in each thing, from Tinker Creek and her pet amoeba, to the galaxies. Finally Richard Selzer, an American physician, compares the ritual of the scientific white-coated physician to the purple and maroon-robed Eastern mystic counterpart, Yeshi Dhonden, who captivates his imagination with his spiritual ways.

What do you compare and contrast? Your favorite things, everything, your memory with a friend's, your vintage '57 hardtop Chevy with something new, yourself to Gertrude Stein.

Russell Baker

(1925–   )

Russell Baker was born August 14, 1925, in Loudoun County, Virginia. He attended Johns Hopkins University on a competitive scholarship and, on graduation with a degree in English literature, went to work as a reporter for the Baltimore *Sun*. He has been in the newspaper industry since.

Baker has written a thrice-weekly column, "Observer," for *The New York Times* since 1962. The nationally syndicated column won the Pulitzer Prize for commentary in 1979, the first humorist ever to do so. According to one biographer, the award was "largely because of the universality of his vision."

In an *Esquire* interview Baker commented: "I've always felt that journalism ought to be a little spontaneous, and I want my stuff, which is a very personal kind of journalism, to reflect how I feel at the moment." Accordingly he never researches, rarely revises, and always has a deadline. "This is daily journalism, not literature."

Italian Realism and American Delusion

Venice is sinking and nobody here seems to care. Every hundred years the city sinks another fifteen inches into the sea. At this rate, the Director of Public Works estimates, within 300 years every palace, church and hotel will be under water.

There are complicated proposals for saving it. One plan, for example, would take 150 years to complete. But though the Italian Government talks about appointing a committee to look into the problem, the interesting point is that nobody is very excited about the prospect of losing Venice to the Adriatic Sea.

Here is one of the keys to the difference between the Italian and the American character. If New York were sinking, Americans would immediately set up a multi-billion dollar crash program to defeat the sea.

We would develop an amazing set of hydraulic jacks capable of raising the whole city of New York like so much furniture on a freight elevator. Alternatively, we might devise a new method for lowering the Atlantic Ocean.

To an American a sinking city is a challenge to native ingenuity. To an Italian it is simply further evidence that all things pass and that life, therefore, should be lived in the present. These differing attitudes toward life often produce ironic results.

If New York were sinking, the Americans would surely save it, but only from sinking. Having rescued the real estate from submersion, they would go on tearing New York apart and rebuilding a new one every few years just as they do now.

The Italians are more sensible about this. Perhaps it is inborn ancient wisdom which tells them that very little that man makes, including cities, can really be saved in the end. With American mentality, they would have paved the Venetian canals years ago, sealed off the ocean, chased the pigeons out of Saint Mark's Square, cleared out those three orchestras that fill it with Strauss waltzes and fill it with Neapolitan schmaltz and put up some neon billboards in all that wasted space.

This would have saved Venice a long time ago by the simple American expedient of destroying it. The Italians seem too realistic to accept this kind of solution. The American, on the other hand, is a dreamer deluding himself.

The contrast is striking in the Italian and American attitudes toward art, and particularly painting. To the American, great painting is a priceless treasure to be stored and preserved. To the Italian, it is one of life's pleasures to be lived with while it lasts.

The American visiting an Italian museum is shocked at first by the treatment given to the old masters. They seem to be hung all over the walls, willy nilly, as though by a rather careless housewife in a hurry to get to the bridge club.

Raphaels are secreted high up in gloomy corners. Open windows let in not only blinding sunlight, making it impossible to see pictures on the shaded wall to advantage, but also flies, mosquitoes, smog and damps.

By contrast, visiting an American gallery can be a traumatic experience, like trying to negotiate a big loan at a snooty bank without collateral. The paintings are beautifully lit. They hang like treasures. The windows are sealed, the humidity scientifically controlled to protect the canvas.

□

The guard's heavy feet tramp suspiciously behind, making the visitor mindful that one false move may result in bloodshed. In a way, this is commendable of Americans. They think they are protecting these great treasures. They have an innocent faith the painting can be preserved forever.

It can't be, of course. It is the most fragile of the arts. Even a change in taste can do it in. By treating it as treasure the Americans end by destroying it as one of life's pleasures which may account for the national suspicion that it is something incomprehensible to be endured for the sake of passing as a person of "culture."

In the Italian galleries, it is something that might be found around the house, as they say on "What's My Line?," and for this reason is simply something pleasant, warm and human. The paintings in Italy's galleries may wear out faster than those in ours, but if so, why does painting in American galleries seem already dead?

The Italians may have something to tell us—namely, that everything wears out in the end, and even cities sink, and the trick is to make good use of what we have and let the next century take care of itself.

Allusions/References

Raphael   Italian Renaissance Painter and architect (1483–1520)
"What's My Line?"   game show where a panel of celebrities tried to guess the surprising or odd occupations of contestants

Discussion

1. How does the title of this essay indicate Baker's attitude toward his material?
2. What are the ways in which Baker compares the Italian character with the American?
   (Find the "skeleton" of this essay. Write down Baker's main points, paragraph by paragraph.)
3. Comparison/contrasts should include illustrations (or examples) for each point being made. Using your outline of Baker's main points, find the examples he uses for each.
4. How does the first sentence of the essay draw the reader's interest immediately?
5. With what specific quality or belief attributed to the Italians does Baker especially agree?
   Find a sentence or two where Baker states the primary differences he finds between the Italians and Americans.
   Do you agree with Baker?

Donald Peattie

(1898–1964)

Donald Peattie was born June 21, 1898, in Chicago. Both his parents were writers as were his brother, wife, and a son. Though he also wrote children's books, fiction, and biography, he was best known as a "nature writer." For many years he wrote a nature column for the *Washington Star* and later, the *Chicago Tribune*. He also worked as a "roving editor" for *Reader's Digest*.

Peattie's most successful book, *An Almanac for Moderns*, reflects his "dual activity in the fields of science and poetry, which combine, finally, in nature writing." His wife, novelist Louise Ridfield, who worked closely with him, said: "he had the keenly trained eye of the scientist, the vision of the poet."

Ultimately Peattie's interest was to write about nature in language that would engage the reader. In the foreword to *A Natural History of Trees* he writes: "Almost every tree in our sylva has made history, or witnessed it, or entered into our folkways, or usefully become a part of our daily life. To tell a little of these things is the main purpose of this book . . . (the author) has told, simply, what interested him most, stopping short (he trusts) of boring others."

Chlorophyll: The Sun Trap

What we love, when on a summer day we step into the coolness of a wood, is that its boughs close up behind us. We are escaped, into another room of life. The wood does not live as we live, restless and running, panting after flesh, and even in sleep tossing with fears. It is aloof from thoughts and instinct; it responds, but only to the sun and wind, the rock and the stream—never, though you shout yourself hoarse, to propaganda, temptation, reproach, or promises. You cannot mount a rock and preach to a tree how it shall attain the kingdom of heaven. It is already closer to it, up there, than you will grow to be. And you cannot make it see the light, since in the tree's sense you are blind. You have nothing to bring it, for all the forest is self-sufficient; if you burn it, cut, hack through it with a blade, it angrily repairs the swathe with thorns and weeds and fierce suckers. Later there are good green leaves again, toiling, adjusting, breathing—forgetting you.

For this green living is the world's primal industry; yet it makes no roar. Waving its banners, it marches across the earth and the ages, without dust around its columns. I do not hold that all of that life is pretty; it is not, in purpose, sprung for us, and moves under no compulsion to please. If ever you fought with thistles, or tried to pull up a cattail's matted root-stocks, you will know how plants cling to their own lives and defy you. The pond-scums gather in the cistern frothing and buoyed with their own gases; the storm waves fling at your feet upon the beach the limp sea-lettuce wrenched from its submarine hold—reminder that there too, where the light is filtered and refracted, there is life still to intercept and net and by it proliferate. Inland from the shore I look and see the coastal ranges clothed in chaparral—dense shrubbery and scrubbery, close-fisted, intricately branched, suffocating the rash rambler in the noon heat with its pungency. Beyond, on the deserts, under a fierce sky, between the harsh lunar ranges of unweathered rock, life still, somehow, fights its way through the year, with thorn and succulent cell and indomitable root.

Between such embattled life and the Forest of Arden, with its ancient beeches and enchanter's nightshade, there is no great biologic difference. Each lives by the cool and cleanly and most commendable virtue of being green. And though that is not biological language, it is the whole story in two words. So that we ought not speak of getting at the root of a matter, but of going back to the leaf of things. The orator who knows the way to the country's salvation and does not know that the breath of life he draws was blown into his nostrils by green leaves, had better spare his breath. And before anyone builds a new state upon the industrial proletariat, he will be wisely cautioned to discover that the source of all wealth is the peasantry of grass.

The reason for these assertions—which I do not make for metaphorical effect but maintain quite literally—is that the green leaf pigment, called chlorophyll, is the one link between the sun and life; it is the conduit of perpetual energy to our own frail organisms.

For inert and inorganic elements—water and carbon dioxide of the air, the same that we breathe out as a waste—chlorophyll can synthesize with the energy of sunlight. Every day, every hour of all the ages, as each continent and, equally important, each ocean rolls into sunlight, chlorophyll ceaselessly creates. Not figuratively, but literally, in the grand First Chapter Genesis style. One instant there are a gas and water, as lifeless as the core of earth or the chill of space; and the next they are become living tissue—mortal yet genitive, progenitive, resilient with all the dewy adaptability of flesh, ever changing in order to stabilize some unchanging ideal of form. Life, in short, synthesized, plant-synthesized, light-synthesized. Botanists say photosynthesized. So that the post-Biblical synthesis of life is already a fact. Only when man has done as much, may he call himself the equal of a weed.

Plant life sustains the living world; more precisely, chlorophyll does so, and where, in the vegetable kingdom, there is not chlorophyll or something closely like it, then that plant or cell is a parasite—no better, in vital economy, than a mere animal or man. Blood, bone and sinew, all flesh is grass. Grass to mutton, mutton to wool, wool to the coat on my back—it runs like one of those cumulative nursery rhymes, the wealth and diversity of our material life accumulating from the primal fact of chlorophyll's activity. The roof of my house, the snapping logs upon the hearth, the desk where I write, are my imports from the plant kingdom. But the whole of modern civilization is based upon a whirlwind spending of the plant wealth long ago and very slowly accu-

☐

mulated. For, fundamentally, and away back, coal and oil, gasoline and illuminating gas had green origins too. With the exception of a small amount of water power, a still smaller of wind and tidal mills, the vast machinery of our complex living is driven only by these stores of plant energy.

We, then, the animals, consume those stores in our restless living. Serenely the plants amass them. They turn light's active energy to food, which is potential energy stored for their own benefit. Only if the daisy is browsed by the cow, the maple leaf sucked of its juices by an insect, will that green leaf become of our kind. So we get the song of a bird at dawn, the speed in the hoofs of the fleeing deer, the noble thought in the philosopher's mind. So Plato's *Republic* was builded on leeks and cabbages.

Animal life lives always in the red; the favorable balance is written on the other side of life's page, and it is written in chlorophyll. All else obeys the thermodynamic law that energy forever runs down hill, is lost and degraded. In economic language, this is the law of diminishing returns, and it is obeyed by the cooling stars as by man and all the animals. They float down its Lethe stream. Only chlorophyll fights up against the current. It is the stuff in life that rebels at death, that has never surrendered to entropy, final icy stagnation. It is the mere cobweb on which we are all suspended over the abyss.

And what then is this substance which is not itself alive but is made by life and makes life, and is never found apart from life?

I remember the first time I ever held it, in the historic dimness of the old Agassiz laboratories, pure, in my hands. My teacher was an owl-eyed master, with a chuckling sense of humor, who had been trained in the greatest laboratory in Germany, and he believed in doing the great things first. So on the first day of his course he set us to extracting chlorophyll, and I remember that his eyes blinked amusement behind his glasses, because when he told us all to go and collect green leaves and most went all the way to the Yard for grass, I opened the window and stole from a vine upon the wall a handful of Harvard's sacred ivy.

We worked in pairs, and my fellow student was a great-grand-nephew or something of the sort, of Elias Fries, the founder of the study of fungi. Together we boiled the ivy leaves, then thrust them in alcohol. After a while it was the leaves which were colorless while the alcohol had become green. We had to dilute this extract with water, and then we added benzol, because this will take the chlorophyll away from the alcohol which, for its part, very conveniently retains the yellow pigments also found in leaves. This left us with a now yellowish alcohol and, floating on top of it, a thick green benzol; you could simply decant the latter carefully off into a test tube, and there you had chlorophyll extract, opaque, trembling, heavy, a little viscous and oily, and smelling, but much too rankly, like a lawn-mower's blades after a battle with rainy grass.

Then, in a darkened room where beams from a spectroscope escaped in painful darts of light as from the cracks in an old-fashioned magic lantern, we peered at our extracted chlorophyll through prisms. Just as in a crystal chandelier the sunlight is shattered to a rainbow, so in the spectroscope light is spread out in colored bands—a long narrow ribbon, sorting the white light by wave lengths into its elemental parts. And the widths, the presence or the absence, of each crossband on the ribbon, tell the tale of a chemical element present in the spectrum, much as the bands on a soldier's insignia ribbon show service in Asia, in the tropics, on the border, in what wars. When the astronomer has fixed spectroscope instead of telescope upon a distant star, he reads off the color bands as easily as one soldier reads another's, and will tell you whether sodium or oxygen, helium or iron is present.

Just so our chlorophyll revealed its secrets. The violet and blue end of the spectrum was almost completely blacked out. And that meant that chlorophyll absorbed and used these high-frequency waves. So, too, the red and orange were largely obliterated, over at the right hand side of our tell-tale bar. It was the green that came through clearly. So we call plants green because they use that color least. It is what they reject as fast as it smites the upper cells; it is what they turn back, reflect, flash into our grateful retinas.

Is was only routine in a young botanist's training to make an extraction and spectrum analysis of chlorophyll. My student friends over in the chemistry laboratories were more excited than I about it. They were working under Conant, before he became president of Harvard and had to sneak into his old laboratory at night with a key he still keeps. For chlorophyll was Conant's own problem. His diagram of its structure, displayed to me by his students, was closely worked over with symbols and signs, unfolded to something like the dimensions of a blue print of Boulder Dam, and made clear—to anyone who could understand it!—how the atoms are arranged and deployed and linked in such a tremendous molecule as $MgN_4C_{55}H_{72}O_5$.

To Otto and Alfred and Mort every jot and joint in the vast Rube Goldberg machinery of that structural formula had meaning, and more than meaning—the geometrical beauty of the one right, inevitable position for every atom. To me, a botanist's apprentice, a future naturalist, there was just one fact to quicken the pulse. That fact is the close similarity between chlorophyll and hemoglobin, the essence of our blood.

So that you may lay your hand upon the smooth flank of a beech and say, "We be of one blood, brother, thou and I."

The one significant difference in the two structural formulas is this: that the hub of every hemoglobin molecule is one atom of iron, while in chlorophyll it is one atom of magnesium.

Iron is strong and heavy, clamorous when struck, avid of oxygen and capable of corruption. It does not surprise us by its presence in our blood stream. Magnesium is a light, silvery, unresonant metal; its density is only one seventh that of iron, it has half of iron's molecular weight, and melts at half the temperature. It is rustless, ductile and pliant; it burns with a brilliant white light rich in actinic rays, and is widely distributed through the upper soil, but only, save at mineral springs, in dainty quantities. Yet the plant succeeds always in finding that mere trace that it needs, even when a chemist might fail to detect it.

How does the chlorophyll, green old alchemist that it is, transmute the dross of earth into living tissue? Its hand is swifter than the chemist's most sensitive analyses. In theory, the step from water and carbon dioxide to the formation of sugar (the first result readily discerned) must involve several syntheses; yet it goes on in a split hundredth of a second. One sunlight particle or photon strikes the chlorophyll, and instantaneously the terribly tenacious molecule of water, which we break down into its units of hydrogen and oxygen only with difficulty and expense, is torn apart; so too is the carbon dioxide molecule. Building blocks of the three elements, carbon, hydrogen and oxygen, are then whipped at lightning speed into carbonic acid; this is instantly changed over into formic acid—the same that smarts so in our nerve endings when an ant stings us. No sooner formed than formic acid becomes formaldehyde and hydrogen peroxide. This last is poisonous, but a ready enzyme in the plant probably splits it as fast as it is born into harmless water and oxygen, while the formaldehyde is knocked at top speed into a new pattern—and is grape sugar, glucose. And all before you can say Albert Einstein. Indeed, by the time you have said Theophrastus Bombastus Aureolus Paracelsus von Hohenheim, the sugar may have lost a modicum of water—and turned into starch, the first product of photosynthesis that could be detected by the methods of fifty years ago.

At this very instant, with the sun delivering to its child the earth, in the bludgeoning language of mathematics, 215×10^{15} calories per second, photosynthesis is racing along wherever the leaf can reach the light. (All else goes to waste.) True, its efficiency is very low—averaging no better than one per cent, while our machines are delivering up to twenty-five per cent of the fuel they combust. But that which they burn—coal and gas, oils and wood—was made, once, by leaves in ancient geologic times. The store of such energy is strictly finite. Chlorophyll alone is hitched to what is, for earthly purposes, the infinite.

Light, in the latest theory, is not waves in a sea of ether, or a jet from a nozzle; it could be compared rather to machine gun fire, every photo-electric bullet of energy traveling in regular rhythm, at a speed that bridges the astronomical gap in eight minutes. As each bullet hits an electron of chlorophyll it sets it to vibrating, at its own rate, just as one tuning fork when struck, will cause another to hum in the same pitch. A bullet strikes—and one electron is knocked galley west into a dervish dance like the madness of the atoms in the sun. The energy splits open chlorophyll molecules, recombines their atoms, and lies there, dormant, in foods.

The process seems miraculously adjusted. And yet, like most living processes it is not perfect. The reaction time of chlorophyll is not geared as high as the arrival of the light-bullets. Light comes too fast; plants, which are the very children of light, can get too much of it. Exposure to the sunlight on the Mojave desert is something that not a plant in my garden, no, nor even the wiry brush in the chaparral, could endure. Lids against the light plants do not have; but by torsions of the stalk some leaves may turn their blades edge-on to dazzling radiation, and present them again broadside in failing light. Within others the chlorophyll granules too, bun or pellet-shaped as they are, can roll for a side or frontal exposure toward the light. In others they can crowd to the top of a cell and catch faint rays, or sink or flee to the sides to escape a searing blast. . . .

When I began to write these pages, before breakfast, the little fig tree outside my window was rejoicing in the early morning light. It is a special familiar of my work, a young tree that has never yet borne fruit. It is but a little taller than I, has only two main branches and forty-three twigs, and the brave if not impressive sum of two hundred and sixteen leaves—I have touched every one with a counting finger. Though sparse, they are large, mitten-shaped, richly green with chlorophyll. I compute, by measuring the leaf and counting both sides, that my little tree has a leaf surface of about eighty-four square feet. This sun-trap was at work today long before I.

Those uplifted hand-like leaves caught the first sky light. It was poor for the fig's purpose, but plant work begins from a nocturnal zero. When I came to my desk the sun was full upon those leaves—and it is a wondrous thing how they are disposed so that they do not shade each other. By the blazing California noon, labor in the leaves must have faltered from very excess of light; all the still golden afternoon it went on; now as the sun sets behind a sea fog the little fig slackens peacefully at its task.

Yet in the course of a day it has made sugar for immediate burning and energy release, put by a store of starch for future use; with the addition of nitrogen and other salts brought up in water from the roots it has built proteins too—the very bricks and mortar of the living protoplasm, the perdurable stuff of permanent tissue. The annual growth ring in the wood of stem and twigs has widened an infinitesimal but a real degree. The fig is one day nearer to its coming of age, to flowering and fruiting. Then, still leafing out each spring, still toiling in the sunlight that I shall not be here to see, it may go on a century and more, growing eccentric, solidifying whimsies, becoming a friend to generations. It will be "the old fig" then. And at last it may give up the very exertion of bearing. It will lean tough elbows in the garden walks, and gardeners yet unborn will scold it and put up with it. But still it will leaf out till it dies.

Dusk is here now. So I switch on the lamp beside my desk. The powerhouse burns its hoarded tons of coal a week, and gives us this instant almost marvelous current. But that light is not new. It was hurled out of the sun two hundred million years ago, and was captured by the leaves of the Carboniferous tree-fern forests, fell with the falling plant, was buried, fossilized, dug up and resurrected. It is the same light. And, in my little fig tree as in the ancient ferns, it is the same unchanging green stuff from age to age, passed without perceptible improvement from evolving plant to plant. What it is and does, so complex upon examination, lies about us tranquil and simple, with the simplicity of a miracle.

Vocabulary

proliferate   to reproduce rapidly
proletariat   working people
conduit   a channel or pipe for conveying fluids
genitive   productive
entropy   measure of the capacity to undergo spontaneous change
benzol   benzene, a clear, colorless flammable liquid
actinic rays   rays which produce photochemical activity
dervish   whirling dances and collective ecstasy (originally of Moslem ascetics)
perdurable   extremely durable, permanent
carboniferous   producing, containing, or pertaining to carbon or coal

Allusions/References

Forest of Arden   wooded area in Warwickshire, England, site of former forest, the mythical haven of Shakespeare's *As You Like It*
Plato's *Republic*   the greatest of Plato's dialogues in which Socrates, while seeking an answer to the question *What Is Justice?* describes an ideal or perfect society
Lethe stream   the river of forgetfulness in Hades
Theophrastus, Bombastus, Paracelsus, et al.   various personages of ancient science; Theophrastus was a Greek philosopher and botanist; Paracelsus a Swiss alchemist and physician; the point is that one could not say these names fast enough before the first product of photosynthesis would occur

Discussion

1. What evidence do you find of Peattie's "Keenly trained eye of the scientist, the vision of a poet"?
   How do Peattie's ways of describing the world's "green living" differ from

scientific ways? How are they the same? (See Vocabulary and Allusions for language level and use.)

2. In order to personalize the nonpersonal, Peattie makes many comparisons to humans. How does the following use of language achieve personalizing (personifying) a tree, even though its intent is to show the tree as distinct: "You cannot mount a rock and preach to a tree how it shall attain the kingdom of heaven."?
Find other such examples throughout the text.

3. How does comparing the "green world" to the "red world," chlorophyll to hemoglobin, assist our understanding of Peattie's intentions?
To quote Theodore Roethke, the American poet: "God bless the Ground! I shall walk softly there." How might this also describe Peattie's sentiments?

4. What evidence can you find of Peattie's gentleness toward nature?

5. How do the animals, with their "restless living," compare to the plants?

6. What does the narrative of the Agassiz laboratories add to Peattie's thesis?

7. What does Peattie mean when he writes: " . . . you may lay your hand upon the smooth flank of a beech and say, 'We be of one blood, brother, thou and I' "?

8. On the last page Peattie begins to personalize the writing of this essay. He takes us into his confidence, at his desk before breakfast, " . . . the little fig tree outside . . . rejoicing in the early morning light." What does he accomplish with this narrative?
How does seeing Peattie in a personal way affect our feelings about his ideas? How might you reveal *yourself,* to enhance your ideas in a comparison/contrast essay?

Annie Dillard
(1945–   )

Annie Dillard was born April 30, 1945, in Pittsburgh, Pennsylvania. She has taught poetry and writing and has written a book of literary theory, *Living by Fiction.* She is also a contributing editor at *Harper's* magazine.

Her book *Pilgrim at Tinker Creek* won the Pulitzer Prize in nonfiction in 1974. She calls herself, "a wanderer with a background in theology and a penchant for quirky facts." The book is an account of a year spent observing nature on a tract of land in Virginia. It is full of "quirky" facts and meditations on or inspired by what she sees. Ultimately her writing is an attempt to "see" the universe. "Seeing is of course very much a matter of verbalization. Unless I call my attention to what passes before my eyes, I simply won't see it."

The following selection is from *Pilgrim at Tinker Creek.* Describing the act of writing the book she has said: "You're writing consciously, off of hundreds of index cards, often distorting the literal truth to achieve an artistic one. It's all hard, conscious, terribly frustrating work."

Strangers to Darkness

Where Tinker Creek flows under the sycamore log bridge to the tear shaped island, it is slow and shallow, fringed thinly in cattail marsh. At

this spot an astonishing bloom of life supports vast breeding populations of insects, fish, reptiles, birds, and mammals. On windless summer evenings I stalk along the creek bank or straddle the sycamore log
in absolute stillness, watching for muskrats. The night I stayed too late
I was hunched on the log staring spellbound at spreading, reflected
stains of lilac on the water. A cloud in the sky suddenly lighted as if
turned on by a switch; its reflection just as suddenly materialized on
the water upstream, flat and floating, so that I couldn't see the creek
bottom, or life in the water under the cloud. Downstream, away from
the cloud on the water, water turtles smooth as beans were gliding
down with the current in a series of easy, weightless push-offs, as men
bound on the moon. I didn't know whether to trace the progress of one
turtle I was sure of, risking sticking my face in one of the bridge's spider
webs made invisible by the gathering dark, or take a chance on seeing
the carp, or scan the mudbank in hope of seeing a muskrat or follow
the last of the swallows who caught at my heart and trailed it after
them like streamers as they appeared from directly below, under the
log, flying upstream with their tails forked, so fast.

But shadows spread and deepened and stayed. After thousands of
years we're still strangers to darkness, fearful aliens in an enemy camp
with our arms crossed over our chests. I stirred. A land turtle on the
bank, startled, hissed the air from its lungs and withdrew to its shell.
An uneasy pink here, an unfathomable blue there, gave great suggestion of lurking beings. Things were going on. I couldn't see whether
that rustle I heard was a distant rattlesnake, slit-eyed, or a nearby spar-
row kicking in the dry flood debris slung at the foot of a willow. Tremendous action roiled the water everywhere I looked, big action, inex-
plicable. A tremor welled up beside a gaping muskrat burrow in the
bank and I caught my breath, but no muskrat appeared. The ripples
continued to fan upstream with a steady, powerful thrust. Night was
knitting an eyeless mask over my face, and I still sat transfixed. A distant
airplane, a delta wing out of nightmare, made a gliding shadow on the
creek's bottom that looked like a stingray cruising upstream. At once a
black fin split the pink cloud on the water, shearing it in two. The two
halves merged together and seemed to dissolve before my eyes. Darkness pooled in the cleft of the creek and rose, as water collects in a well.
Untamed, dreaming lights flickered over the sky. I saw hints of hulking
underwater shadows, two pale splashes out of the water, and round
ripples rolling close together from a blackened center.

At last I stared upstream where only the deepest violet remained
of the cloud, a cloud so high its underbelly still glowed, its feeble color
reflected from a hidden sky lighted in turn by a sun halfway to China.
And out of that violet, a sudden enormous black body arched over the
water. Head and tail, if there was a head and tail, were both submerged
in cloud. I saw only one ebony fling, a headlong dive to darkness; then
the waters closed, and the lights went out.

I walked home in a shivering daze, up hill and down. Later I lay open-mouthed in bed, my arms flung wide at my sides to steady the whirling darkness. At this latitude I'm spinning 836 miles an hour round the earth's axis; I feel my sweeping fall as a breakneck arch like the dive of dolphins, and the hollow rushing of wind raises the hairs on my neck and the side of my face. In orbit around the sun I'm moving 64,800 miles an hour. The solar system as a whole, like a merry-go-round unhinged, spins, bobs, and blinks at the speed of 43,200 miles an hour along a course set east of Hercules. Someone has piped, and we are dancing a tarantella until the sweat pours. I open my eyes and I see dark, muscled forms curl out of water, with flapping gills and flattened eyes. I close my eyes and I see stars, deep stars giving way to deeper stars, deeper stars bowing to deepest stars at the crown of an infinite cone.

"Still," wrote Van Gogh in a letter, "a great deal of lights falls on everything." If we are blinded by darkness, we are also blinded by light. Sometimes here in Virginia at sunset low clouds on the southern or northern horizon are completely invisible in the lighted sky. I only know one is there because I can see its reflection in still water. The first time I discovered this mystery I looked from cloud to no-cloud in bewilderment, checking my bearings over and over, thinking maybe the ark of the covenant was just passing by south of Dead Man Mountain. Only much later did I learn the explanation: polarized light from the sky is very much weakened by reflection, but the light in clouds isn't polarized. So invisible clouds pass among visible clouds, till all slide over the mountains; so a greater light extinguishes a lesser as though it didn't exist.

In the great meteor shower of August, the Perseid, I wait all day for the shooting stars I miss. They're out there showering down, committing hara-kiri in a flame of fatal attraction, and hissing perhaps at last into the ocean. But at dawn what looks like a blue dome clamps down over me like a lid on a pot. The stars and planets could smash and I'd never know. Only a piece of ashen moon occasionally climbs up or down the inside of the dome, and our local star without surcease explodes on our heads. We have really only that one light, one source for all power, and yet we must turn away from it by universal decree. Nobody here on the planet seems aware of this strange, powerful taboo, that we all walk about carefully averting our faces, this way and that, lest our eyes be blasted forever.

Darkness appalls and light dazzles; the scrap of visible light that doesn't hurt my eyes hurts my brain. What I see sets me swaying. Size and distance and the sudden swelling of meanings confuse me, bowl me over. I straddle the sycamore log bridge over Tinker Creek in the summer. I look at the lighted creek bottom: snail tracks tunnel the mud in quavering curves. A crayfish jerks, but by the time I absorb what has happened, he's gone in a billowing smoke screen of silt. I look at the water: minnows and shiners. If I'm thinking minnows, a carp will fill my brain till I scream. I look at the water's surface: skaters, bubbles, and leaves sliding down. Suddenly, my own face, reflected, startles me witless. Those snails have been tracking my face! Finally, with a shuddering wrench of the will, I see clouds, cirrus clouds. I'm dizzy, I fall in.

This looking business is risky. Once I stood on a humped rock on nearby Purgatory Mountain, watching through binoculars the great autumn hawk migration below, until I discovered that I was in danger of joining the hawks on a vertical migration of my own. I was used to binoculars, but not, apparently, to balancing on humped rocks while looking through them. I reeled. Everything advanced and receded by turns; the world was full of unexplained foreshortenings and depths. A distant huge object, a hawk the size of an elephant, turned out to be the browned bough of a nearby loblolly pine. I followed a sharp-shinned hawk against a featureless sky, rotating my head unawares as it flew, and when I lowered the glass a glimpse of my own looming shoulder sent me staggering. What prevents the men on Palomar from falling, voiceless and blinded, from their tiny, vaulted chairs?

I reel in confusion; I don't understand what I see. With the naked eye I can see two million light-years to the Andromeda galaxy. Often I slop some creek water in a jar, and when I get home I dump it in a white china bowl. After the silt settles I return and see tracings of minute snails on the bottom, a planarian or two winding round the rim of water, roundworms shimmying frantically, and finally, when my eyes have adjusted to these dimensions, amoebae. At first the amoebae look like *muscae Volitantes*, those curled moving spots you seem to see in your eyes when you stare at a distant wall. Then I see the amoebae as drops of water congealed, bluish, translucent, like chips of sky in the bowl. At length I choose one individual and give myself over to its idea of an evening. I see it dribble a grainy foot before it on its wet, unfathomable way. Do its unedited sense impressions include the fierce focus of my eyes? Shall I take it outside and show it Andromeda, and blow its little endoplasm? I stir the water with a finger, in case it's running out of oxygen. Maybe I should get a tropical aquarium with motorized bubblers and lights, and keep this one for a pet. Yes, it would tell its fissioned descendants, the universe is two feet by five, and if you listen closely you can hear the buzzing music of the spheres.

Oh, it's mysterious, lamplit evenings here in the galaxy, one after the other. It's one of those nights when I wander from window to window, looking for a sign. But I can't see. Terror and a beauty insoluble are a riband of blue woven into the fringes of garments of things both great and small. No culture explains, no bivouac offers real haven or rest. But it could be that we are not seeing something. Galileo thought comets were an optical illusion. This is fertile ground: since we are certain that they're not, we can look at what our scientists have been saying with fresh hope. What if there are *really* gleaming, castellated cities hung upside-down over the desert sand? What limpid lakes and cool date palms have our caravans always passed untried? Until, one by one, by the blindest of leaps, we light on the road to these places, we must stumble in darkness and hunger. I turn from the window. I'm blind as a bat, sensing only from every direction the echo of my own thin cries.

Vocabulary

tarantella   a lively, whirling Italian dance, once thought to be a remedy for tarantism, the uncontrollable urge to dance believed to have been brought on by the bite of a tarantula
polarized   to cause light to concentrate about two conflicting positions
cirrus clouds   high altitude, tendril-like fleecy clouds
Andromeda   a constellation in the Northern Hemisphere
endoplasm   inner part of the cytoplasm (outside the nucleus) of a cell
fissioned   split into parts
castellated   furnished with turrets and battlements like a castle

Allusions/References

Van Gogh   Dutch postimpressionist painter (1853–1890)

Discussion

1. Using only the first paragraph of this piece, follow each word with your finger on the page, extracting those which describe things, or are the names for things. For example: "Tinker Creek," "Sycamore log bridge," "tear-shaped island," etc.
   What does your list say to you about the nature of Dillard's writing?
   How does description of this kind, the sensory details of her writing, add to your enjoyment of it?
2. Compare a paragraph of Dillard's writing with one of similar length by Selzer or Baker, also in this chapter. Note especially the number of sensory details, the number of words per sentence.
   How might you describe Dillard's writing as compared to theirs? Streamlike? Fluid? Terse? Cobbled with words? Thick?
3. What is the progression of this piece from the first paragraph through the fourth?
   What is the effect of beginning in the cattail marsh and ending in the solar system?
   How are the microcosm and macrocosm related?
4. What does Dillard mean by the paradox: "If we are blinded by darkness, we are also blinded by light"?
   How are the "invisible clouds" and her "reflected face" examples of this kind of light blindness?

5. The eighth paragraph begins, "This looking business is risky." How might this be Dillard's thesis?
   How is the "looking business" risky? What example does she give?
6. What is the point about amoebae? Why does she give us this little narrative?
   How is she comparing human sight to the amoeba's "sight"?
   What does she mean by "I don't understand what I see"?

For Further Discussion

7. For good comparisons of voice and style you might see Virginia Woolf's "Death of a Moth," Simone de Beauvoir's "The Discovery and Assumption of Old Age," and Anaïs Nin's "Extract From the Diary." For contrasts see Plath's "Lenny's Place," and Mitford's "To Bid the World Farewell."
   In each case, compare sample paragraphs for language use, rhythm, sensory details, and sentence length. Is there any one "female" voice?
8. Comparing what there is to see with what we see, extrapolating from what we see to what we don't see, Dillard concludes, "I'm as blind as a bat."
   What does she mean by all this?
   What has she "seen" and reported to us in this essay? How can she then conclude she is blind?
9. This essay comes from a larger piece called "Sight into Insight." How does sight differ from insight? How might the differences in the meanings of these words explain Dillard's thesis?

Richard Selzer
(1928–   )

Richard Selzer was born June 24, 1928, in Troy, New York. The son of a doctor, he has had a practice in general surgery in New Haven, Connecticut, since 1960. His writings have appeared in *Harpers, Mademoiselle* and the *New American Review*, among others.

The following selection is from *Mortal Lessons: Notes on the Art of Surgery.* In the opening chapter Selzer says he writes "to search for some meaning in the ritual of surgery, which is at once murderous, painful, healing, and full of love."

Yeshi Dhonden

On the bulletin board in the front hall of the hospital where I work, there appeared an announcement. "Yeshi Dhonden," it read, "will make rounds at six o'clock on the morning of June 10." The particulars were then given, followed by a notation: "Yeshi Dhonden is Personal Physician to the Dalai Lama." I am not so leathery a skeptic that I would knowingly ignore an emissary from the gods. Not only might such sangfroid be inimical to one's earthly well-being, it could take care of eternity as well. Thus, on the morning of June 10, I join the clutch of whitecoats waiting in the small conference room adjacent to the ward selected for the rounds. The air in the room is heavy with ill-concealed dubiety and suspicion of bamboozlement. At precisely six o'clock, he materializes, a short, golden, barrelly man dressed in a sleeveless robe of saffron and maroon. His scalp is shaven, and the only visible hair is a scanty black line above each hooded eye.

He bows in greeting while his young interpreter makes the introduction. Yeshi Dhonden, we are told, will examine a patient selected by a member of the staff. The diagnosis is as unknown to Yeshi Dhonden as it is to us. The examination of the patient will take place in our presence, after which we will reconvene in the conference room where Yeshi Dhonden will discuss the case. We are further informed that for the past two hours Yeshi Dhonden has purified himself by bathing, fasting, and prayer. I, having breakfasted well, performed only the most desultory of ablutions, and given no thought at all to my soul, glance furtively at my fellows. Suddenly, we seem a soiled, uncouth lot.

The patient had been awakened early and told that she was to be examined by a foreign doctor, and had been asked to produce a fresh specimen of urine, so when we enter her room, the woman shows no surprise. She has long ago taken on that mixture of compliance and resignation that is the facies of chronic illness. This was to be but another in an endless series of tests and examinations. Yeshi Dhonden steps to the bedside while the rest stand apart, watching. For a long time he gazes at the woman, favoring no part of her body with his eyes, but seeming to fix his glance at a place just above her supine form. I, too, study her. No physical sign nor obvious symptom gives a clue to the nature of her disease.

At last he takes her hand, raising it in both of his own. Now he bends over the bed in a kind of crouching stance, his head drawn down into the collar of his robe. His eyes are closed as he feels for her pulse. In a moment he has found the spot, and for the next half hour he remains thus, suspended above the patient like some exotic golden bird with folded wings, holding the pulse of the woman beneath his fingers, cradling her hand in his. All the power of the man seems to have been drawn down into this one purpose. It is palpation of the pulse raised to the state of ritual. From the foot of the bed, where I stand, it is as though he and the patient have entered a special place of isolation, of apartness, about which a vacancy hovers, and across which no violation is possible. After a moment the woman rests back upon her pillow. From time to time, she raises her head to look at the strange figure above her, then sinks back once more. I cannot see their hands joined in a correspondence that is exclusive, intimate, his fingertips receiving the voice of her sick body through the rhythm and throb she offers at her wrist. All at once I am envious—not of him, not of Yeshi Dhonden for his gift of beauty and holiness, but of her. I want to be held like that, touched so, *received.* And I know that I, who palpated a hundred thousand pulses, have not felt a single one.

At last Yeshi Dhonden straightens, gently places the woman's hand upon the bed, and steps back. The interpreter produces a small wooden bowl and two sticks. Yeshi Dhonden pours a portion of the urine specimen into the bowl, and proceeds to whip the liquid with the two sticks. This he does for several minutes until a foam is raised. Then, bowing above the bowl, he inhales the odor three times. He sets down the bowl and turns to leave. All this while, he has not uttered a single word. As he nears the door, the woman raises her head and calls out to him in a voice at once urgent and serene. "Thank you, doctor," she says, and touches with her other hand the place he had held on her wrist, as though to recapture something that had visited there. Yeshi Dhonden turns back for a moment to gaze at her, then steps into the corridor. Rounds are at an end.

We are seated once more in the conference room. Yeshi Dhonden speaks now for the first time, in soft Tibetan sounds that I have never heard before. He has barely begun when the young interpreter begins to translate, the two voices continuing in tandem—a bilingual fugue, the one chasing the other. It is like the chanting of monks. He speaks of winds coursing through the body of the woman, currents that break against barriers, eddying. These vortices are in her blood, he says. The last spendings of an imperfect heart. Between the chambers of her heart, long, long before she was born, a wind had come and blown open a deep gate that must never be opened. Through it charge the full waters of her river, as the mountain stream cascades in the springtime, battering, knocking loose the land, and flooding her breath. Thus he speaks, and is silent.

"May we now have the diagnosis?" a professor asks.

The host of these rounds, the man who knows, answers.

"Congenital heart disease," he says. "Interventricular septal defect, with resultant heart failure."

A gateway in the heart, I think. That must not be opened. Through it charge the full waters that flood her breath. So! Here then is the doctor listening to the sounds of the body to which the rest of us are deaf. He is more than doctor. He is priest.

I know . . . I know . . . the doctor to the gods is pure knowledge, pure healing. The doctor to man stumbles, must often wound; his patients must die, as must he.

Now and then it happens, as I make my own rounds, that I hear the sounds of his voice, like an ancient Buddhist prayer, its meaning long since forgotten, only the music remaining. Then a jubilation possesses me, and I feel myself touched by something divine.

Vocabulary

sangfroid French for "cold blood" and pronounced (san-frwa')
inimical antagonistic, harmful
desultory of ablutions haphazard and random washing and cleansing
facies outward appearance
supine lying on the back, face up
bilingual fugue two languages spoken nearly at once, one after another (in translation) like the musical style called a fugue
vortices fluid flowing around an axis like a whirlpool

Allusions/References

Dalai Lama the traditional governmental ruler and high priest of the Lamaist religion in Tibet and Mongolia
Buddhist a religion of eastern and central Asia whose great teacher was Buddha

Discussion

1. Seltzer's piece on Yeshi Dhonden is rich with subtlety. Examine the language he uses to weave his subtle comparison of Western medicine with Eastern practices.

   For instance, how do the words work in the following snippets:

   > "I am not so leathery a skeptic"

   > "the clutch of whitecoats"

   > "suspicion of bamboozlement"

   > "precisely six o'clock, he materializes"

   > "sleeveless robe of saffron and maroon"

   > "a scanty black line above each hooded eye"

   How do each of these phrases imply a comparison between the East and the West? Why is the Western attitude one of suspicion? What details above (e.g., whitecoats versus saffron-and-maroon robe), delineate the comparison?
2. The quotes above all came from the first paragraph. Find other such snippets that reveal both Selzer's love of language and his wry way with comparison.
3. Describe the process Yeshi Dhonden uses to diagnose his patient. How does this compare with a Western diagnosis?
4. How do you react to Dhonden's diagnosis? What does its language of "full waters of her river," and so on remind you most of?
   What is the irony of the professor's question following?
   Yeshi Dhonden's response shows him to be, in the truest sense, multilingual. How has he put his diagnosis in Western terms?

How do the Eastern words and the Western words used to describe the same
ailment compare? Which language do you prefer? Why?

5. How does the author, Richard Selzer, compare with his colleagues? What use
of language, of tone, in this piece indicates Selzer's position?
How do you interpret the last paragraph?

6. The physician as writer is not an uncommon phenomenon (note Chekhov
or William Carlos Williams). What in Selzer's writing tips you off to his love
of, not only medicine, but of words themselves?

☐ By Analysis

I get so excited when I come up with an idea for a chapter like this I
can hardly wait to get to work. This is when I like to write, when I
can't help myself. The trouble is the mind is analytical. A good idea
no more than lights on the page than the mind wants to whisk it
away. That's not right; that's not always true, it says. Then along
comes Writer's Block.

I don't have writer's block this time, or at least I hope I don't.
Analysis can be a wonderful thing. It allows us to take something
apart and examine it. And it allows us to put it together again with an
altogether new perspective or vision.

A "New Journalist," Tom Wolfe, reports his stories scene by
scene like a novelist. His Phil Spector speaks for himself in a device
called "third person point of view." A technique of the fiction writer,
third person point of view presents a scene through the eyes and
consciousness of a character in it. Wolfe borrows Spector's voice:

> Where does a man find friends, comrades, anything, in a world like
> that? They resent his success. But it is no better with the kids. He is so
> much more mature and more . . . eminent . . . They all want to form
> "the father thing" with him.

Wolfe allows us to analyze Spector by getting inside Spector's mind.
We experience the emotional reality of the scene as he experiences it.

X. J. Kennedy looks at the reasons Americans remain hooked on
the B-rated movie *King Kong*. Its imagery evoked in words might give
one cause enough: "dinosaurs, headhunters, riots, aerial battles,
bullets, bombs, bloodletting." Certainly these spritely words are
reason to read and reread Kennedy's essay, each time with more
enjoyment. As we evolve away from our animal selves we see in the
film a eulogy of sorts for our lost animal soul.

William Golding, author of *Lord of the Flies*, thinks about
thinking in an essay titled thoughtfully "Thinking as a Hobby." In it
he identifies three grades of thinking and classifies which kind should

fit in each grade. The essay bears the surface tone of comedy, Golding's *amour* being, for instance, the minor grade, but underneath is an analysis of human thought as scathing as any you might find.

Clarence Darrow exhibits for all to see the skeptic's position with matters of faith and God. One by one he analyzes his tenets, ending finally with a demonstration of the *faith* he has in the functioning of the analytical mind—his own. Analysis is a way of thinking.

You don't have to worship at the gate of analysis, but you can use it.

Tom Wolfe
(1931–   )

Tom Wolfe was born March 2, 1931, in Richmond, Virginia. His career as a journalist began with the *Springfield Union* in 1956. In addition to being a contributing editor to *New York* magazine and *Esquire,* he has been a contributing artist to *Harper's.*

Wolfe says his style developed when, unable to meet a deadline for an article, he decided to type quickly his notes. "I just started recording it all and inside of a couple of hours, typing like a madman, I could tell something was beginning to happen."

The notes were printed in *Esquire* as typed. This was one of the early pieces associated with "the New Journalism." Wolfe, with other journalists such as Gay Talese, Jimmy Breslin, and Joan Didion, became one of "a bunch of slick-magazine and Sunday supplement writers" who "began using all the techniques of the novelists" in journalism.

The First Tycoon of Teen

Phil Spector is here! The British have the ability to look at all sorts of rebel baddies and alienated thin young fellows and say coo and absorb them like a great soggy lukewarm, mother's poultice. The Beatles, Beatlemania, rock and roll, suddenly it is all absorbed into the center of things as if it could have been there all along if it only asked. Phil Spector arrives at London Airport and, Santa Barranza, there are photographers all over the place, for him, Phil Spector, and the next morning he is all over the center fold of the *London Daily Mirror*, the biggest newspaper in the Western World, five million circulation: "The 23-year-old American rock and roll magnate." He is in the magazines as the "U.S. Recording Tycoon." Invitations go out to come to the receptions to meet "America's outstanding hit maker, Phil Spector." And then he lands back at Idlewild and waiting are, yes, the same bunch of cheese-breath cabbies, and he takes a cab on back to 440 E. 62nd St. and goes into his beige world, the phones are ringing and it is all the same, the same—

"Cigar-smoking sharpies," says Phil Spector. He is in a livelier mood after the talk with Andrew Oldham. "They're a bunch of cigar-smoking sharpies in record distribution. They've all been in the business for years and they resent you if you're young. That's one reason so many kids go broke in this business. They're always starting new record companies, or they used to, the business is very soft right now, they start a company and pour all their money into a record, and it can be successful and they're still broke, because these characters don't even pay you until you've had three or four hit records in a row. They order the records and sell them and don't pay you. They don't pay you because they know they don't have to. You start yelling for the money and they tell you, 'Whattya mean, I have all these records coming back from the retailers and what about my right to return records, and blah-blah.' What are you going to do? Sue twenty guys in twenty different courts in the United States?

"They look at everything as a product. They don't care about the work and sweat you put into a record. They respect me now because I keep turning out hits, and after that they become sort of honest . . . in their own decayed way."

Where does a man find friends, comrades, anything, in a world like that? They resent his youth. They resent his success. But it is no better with the kids. He is so much more mature and more . . . eminent . . . they all want to form "the father thing" with him. Or else they want to fawn over him, cousin him, cajole, fall down before him, whistle, shout, stomp, bang him on the head, anything to get his attention and get "the break," just one chance. Or one more chance. Spector can't go near the Brill Building, the center of the music business, because the place is crawling with kids with winkle-picker shoes cracking in the folds, who made one hit record five years ago and still can't realize that they are now, forever, in oblivion. They crawl all over the place the way the small-time balding fatty promoters and managers used to in the days when A. J. Liebling wrote about the place as the Jollity Building. Phil Spector steps onto an elevator in the Brill Building, the elevator is packed, and suddenly he feels this arm hooking through his in the most hideously cozy way and a mouth is closing in on his ear and saying, "Phil, baby, wait'll you hear this one: 'Ooh-oom-bah-ay,'" and Phil Spector is imprisoned there with the elevator inching up, "vah ump nooby poon fang ooh-ooh ayub bah-ay—you dig that, Phil? You dig that, don't you, Phil? Phil, babes!" He walks down the hall and kids sneak up behind him and slip songs, music, lyrics into his coat pocket. He finds the stuff in there, all this ratty paper, when he gets home. Or he is leaving the Brill Building and he feels a great whack on the back of his head and wheels around and there are four kids in the singing stance, their heads angled in together, saying, "Just one bar, Phil—Say wohna love boo-uh ay-yay bubby—" while the guy on the end sings bass with his chin mashed into a pulpy squash down over his collar bone, *beh—ungggh, beh-ungggh.*

Vocabulary

poultice   a cure-all for aches and pains; a moist, soft, mealy or claylike substance spread on a cloth and applied on the inflamed part of the body
cajole   to coax or wheedle

Allusions/References

Phil Spector   rock and roll record producer, a millionaire by twenty-one; writer of such rock and roll hits as "To Know Him Is to Love Him" and "Spanish Harlem"

Discussion

1. "The First Tycoon of Teen" is actually not an essay but a piece of journalism, and is a much larger work than the extract given here would indicate. With this disclaimer, then, analyze the tone of this piece.
   To analyze you must first take it apart. How many paragraphs? What is happening in each; what is the point of each?
2. Paragraph two is mostly quotation from Phil Spector. What do you learn about Spector from what he says?
3. The first and last paragraphs convey a certain stance toward Spector and his life. What is this stance?
   Is Wolfe enjoying his subject or not? What indications in the words themselves can you find to support your view?
4. Tom Wolfe's technique has been described as New Journalism. In it is a kind of detailed realism Wolfe describes as: "Hey! Come here! This is the way people are living now—just the way I'm going to show you! It may astound you, disgust you, delight you or arouse your contempt or make you laugh . . . Nevertheless, this is what it's like! It's all right here! You won't be bored! Take a look!"
   How is this attitude evident in Wolfe's tone toward the teen tycoon?
5. One of the devices of New Journalism Wolfe describes is "third-person point of view." In it a scene is presented to the reader "through the eyes of a particular character, giving the reader the feeling of being inside the character's mind and experiencing the emotional reality of the scene as he experiences it."
   How might this explain the tone of paragraphs one and four in particular?
6. Wolfe, in a comparison to Balzac's stance as chronicler of Paris and France, compares the New Journalist to "the secretary of American society."
   What does he mean by this?
   How is Phil Spector an index of American society?
7. Even though the emphasis in this chapter is on analysis, don't forget to look back from this larger, organizational structure, to the language itself.
   What is the narrative and descriptive effect of the following words representing song in paragraph four: "vah ump nooby poon fang ooh-ooh ayub bay-ay-you dig that, Phil?"
   What does this suggest about Wolfe's eye and ear for words?

For Further Discussion

8. Analyze carefully a single paragraph, paragraph four. To analyze is to ask
   questions, to take apart.
   Why is this all one long paragraph?
   What is the point being made?
   What is the sentence length? How many sentences?
   How do such impacted sentences as the following work: " . . . to fawn over
   him, cousin him, cajole, fall down before him, whistle, shout, stomp, bang
   . . . " Why this "shotgun" approach? What pace is being suggested here?
   Then ask yourself: What do all these parts add up to? How does the form of
   this paragraph match or contradict its content, its meaning?
9. Is Wolfe analyzing Phil Spector?

X. J. Kennedy
(1929–   )

X. J. Kennedy was born Joseph Charles Kennedy (he added the X to distinguish
himself from the better-known Kennedy family) August 21, 1929, in Dover, New
Jersey. Known primarily as a poet, he began writing at an early age, publishing
a science-fiction magazine *Terrifying Test Tube Tales* at age 12.

Often called "witty" by critics, Kennedy says: "I would wish to be seriously funny." As a poet he is a traditionalist, using rhyme and meter. "To me
the old forms are where the primitive and surprising action is."

"I write a lot," he says, "but like very little that I do; and my dearest joy
is to keep every effort for a long time, pecking at its commas like a broody hen,
perpetually fussing with it."

Who Killed King Kong?

The ordeal and spectacular death of King Kong, the giant ape, undoubt-
edly have been witnessed by more Americans than have ever seen a
performance of *Hamlet, Iphigenia at Aulis*, or even *Tobacco Road*.
Since RKO-Radio Pictures first released *King Kong*, a quarter-century
has gone by; yet year after year, from prints that grow more rain-
beaten, from sound tracks that grow more tinny, ticket-buyers by thousands still pursue Kong's luckless fight against the forces of technology,
tabloid journalism, and the DAR. They see him chloroformed to sleep,
see him whisked from his jungle isle to New York and placed on show,
see him burst his chains to roam the city (lugging a frightened blonde),
at last to plunge from the spire of the Empire State Building, machine-
gunned by model airplanes.

Though Kong may die, one begins to think his legend unkillable.
No clearer proof of his hold upon the popular imagination may be seen
than what emerged one catastrophic week in March 1955, when New
York WOR-TV programmed *Kong* for seven evenings in a row (a total

of sixteen showings). Many a rival network vice-president must have scowled when surveys showed that *Kong*—the 1933 B-picture—had lured away fat segments of the viewing populace from such powerful competitors as Ed Sullivan, Groucho Marx and Bishop Sheen.

But even television has failed to run *King Kong* into oblivion. Coffee-in-the-lobby cinemas still show the old hunk of hokum, with the apology that in its use of composite shots and animated models the film remains technically interesting. And no other monster in movie history has won so devoted a popular audience. None of the plodding mummies, the stultified draculas, the white-coated Lugosis with their shiny pinball-machine laboratories, none of the invisible stranglers, berserk robots, or menaces from Mars has ever enjoyed so many resurrections.

Why does the American public refuse to let King Kong rest in peace? It is true, I'll admit, that *Kong* outdid every monster movie before or since in sheer carnage. Producers Cooper and Schoedsack crammed into it dinosaurs, headhunters, riots, aerial battles, bullets, bombs, bloodletting. Heroine Fay Wray, whose function is mainly to scream, shuts her mouth for hardly one uninterrupted minute from first reel to last. It is also true that *Kong* is larded with good healthy sadism, for those whose joy it is to see the frantic girl dangled from cliffs and harried by pterodactyls. But it seems to me that the abiding appeal of the giant ape rests on other foundations.

Kong has, first of all, the attraction of being manlike. His simian nature gives him one huge advantage over giant ants and walking vegetables in that an audience may conceivably identify with him. Kong's appeal has the quality that established the Tarzan series as American myth—for what man doesn't secretly imagine himself a huge hairy howler against whom no other monster has a chance? If Tarzan recalls the ape in us, then Kong may well appeal to that great-granddaddy primordial brute from whose tribe we have all deteriorated.

Intentionally or not, the producers of *King Kong* encourage this identification by etching the character of Kong with keen sympathy. For the ape is a figure in a tradition familiar to moviegoers: the tradition of the pitiable monster. We think of Lon Chaney in the role of Quasimodo, of Karloff in the original Frankenstein. As we watch the Frankenstein monster's fumbling and disastrous attempts to befriend a flower-picking child, our sympathies are enlisted with the monster in his impenetrable loneliness. And so with Kong. As he roars in his chains, while barkers sell tickets to boobs who gape at him, we perhaps feel something more deep than pathos. We begin to sense something of the problem that engaged Eugene O'Neill in *The Hairy Ape:* the dilemma of a displaced animal spirit forced to live in a jungle built by machines.

King Kong, it is true, had special relevance in 1933. Landscapes of the depression are glimpsed early in the film when an impressario, seeking some desperate pretty girl to play the lead in a jungle movie, visits souplines and a Woman's Home Mission. In Fay Wray—who's been caught snitching an apple from a fruitstand—his search is ended. When he gives her a big feed and a movie contract, the girl is magic-carpeted out of the world of the National Recovery Act. And when, in the film's climax, Kong smashes that very Third Avenue landscape in which Fay had wandered hungry, audiences of 1933 may well have felt a personal satisfaction.

What is curious is that audiences of 1960 remain hooked. For in the heart of urban man, one suspects, lurks the impulse to fling a bomb. Though machines speed him to the scene of his daily grind, though IBM comptometers ("freeing the human mind from drudgery") enable him to drudge more efficiently once he arrives, there comes a moment when he wishes to turn upon his machines and kick hell out of them. He wants to hurl his combination radio-alarmclock out of the bedroom window and listen to its smash. What subway commuter wouldn't love—just for once—to see the downtown express smack head-on into the uptown local? Such a wish is gratified in that memorable scene in *Kong* that opens with a wide-angle shot: interior of a railway car on the Third Avenue El. Straphangers are nodding, the literate refold their newspapers. Unknown to them, Kong has torn away a section of the trestle toward which the train now speeds. The motorman spies Kong up ahead, jams on the brakes. Passengers hurtle together like so many peas in a pail. In a window of the car appear Kong's bloodshot eyes. Women shriek. Kong picks up the railway car as if it were a rat, flips it to the street and ties knots in it, or something. To any commuter the scene must appear one of the most satisfactory pieces of celluloid ever exposed.

Yet however violent his acts, Kong remains a gentleman. Remark-able is his sense of chivalry. Whenever a fresh boa constrictor threatens Fay, Kong first sees that the lady is safely parked, then manfully thrashes her attacker. (And she, the ingrate, runs away every time his back is turned). Atop the Empire State Building, ignoring his pursuers, Kong places Fay on a ledge as tenderly as if she were a dozen eggs. He fondles her, then turns to face the Army Air Force. And Kong is per-haps the most disinterested lover since Cyrano: his attentions to the lady are utterly without hope of reward. After all, between a five-foot blonde and a fifty-foot ape, love can hardly be more than an intellectual flirtation. In his simian way King Kong is the hopelessly yearning lover of Petrarchan convention. His forced exit from his jungle, in chains, results directly from his single-minded pursuit of Fay. He smashes a Broadway theater when the notion enters his dull brain that the flash-bulbs of photographers somehow endanger the lady. His perilous shin-nying up a skyscraper to pluck Fay from her boudoir is an act of the kindliest of hearts. He's impossible to discourage even though the love of his life can't lay eyes on him without shrieking murder.

The tragedy of King Kong then, is to be the beast who at the end of the fable fails to turn into the handsome prince. This is the conviction that the scriptwriters would leave with us in the film's closing line. As Kong's corpse lies blocking traffic in the street, the entrepreneur who brought Kong to New York turns to the assembled reporters and proclaims: "That's your story, boys—it was Beauty killed the Beast!" But greater forces than those of the screaming Lady have combined to lay Kong low, if you ask me. Kong lives for a time as one of those persecuted near-animal souls bewildered in the middle of an industrial order, whose simple desires are thwarted at every turn. He climbs the Empire State Building because in all New York it's the closest thing he can find to the clifftop of his jungle isle. He dies, a pitiful dolt, and the army brass and publicity-men cackle over him. His death is the only possible outcome to as neat a tragic dilemma as you can ask for. The machineguns do him in, while the manicured human hero (a nice clean Dartmouth boy) carries away Kong's sweetheart to the altar. O, the misery of it all. There's far more truth about upper-middle-class American life in *King Kong* than in the last seven dozen novels of John P. Marquand. . . .

Every day in the week on a screen somewhere in the world, King Kong relives his agony. Again and again he expires on the Empire State Building, as audiences of the devout assist his sacrifice. We watch him die, and by extension kill the ape within our bones, but these little deaths of ours occur in prosaic surroundings. We do not die on a tower, New York before our feet, nor do we give our lives to smash a few flying machines. It is not for us to bring to a momentary standstill the civilization in which we move. King Kong does this for us. And so we kill him again and again, in much-spliced celluloid, while the ape in us expires from day to day, obscure, in desperation.

Vocabulary

stultified   crippled, ineffectual
pterodactyls   any of various extinct flying reptiles
simian   apelike
primordial   the earliest stage of development, original
impresario   one who sponsors or produces entertainment
entrepreneur   a person who, at considerable risk, organizes and manages
    some enterprise
prosaic   ordinary, matter-of-fact
disinterested   unbiased (this word does not mean uninterested)

Allusions/References

Hamlet   the hero of Shakespeare's play by the same name, a long-time favorite
    of audiences partly because of his enigmatic nature
Iphigenia at Aulis   a tragedy by Eurypides about a young woman (Iphigenia)
    who is sacrificed so that the Greeks can sail against Troy

□

Tobacco Road a popular Erskine Caldwell novel, also a play and film

DAR Daughters of the American Revolution, a patriotic and conservative society of women descended from Americans of the Revolution

Quasimodo the name of the hunchback in Victor Hugo's *The Hunchback of Notre Dame*

Frankenstein a movie made from the Mary Shelley (wife of Percy Bysshe Shelley) book; Boris Karloff became famous as Frankenstein

Discussion

1. Let us analyze X. J. Kennedy's analysis of the popularity of *King Kong*. Remember, analysis asks that you "take apart" and then look at the parts. Kennedy's thesis is presented as a question in the beginning of the fourth paragraph: "Why does the American public refuse to let King Kong rest in peace?"

   How do the three paragraphs preceding this function? What information is contained in them?

   How is this information important to the remainder of the piece?

2. How does the fourth paragraph function? What information is conveyed in it?

   How does Kennedy, in this paragraph, *show* you what he means rather than only *tell?*

   How is this paragraph pivotal to the rest of the piece?

3. On a piece of paper write Kennedy's thesis statement. (You may wish to rewrite the thesis as a statement rather than as a question.)

   Next outline the points Kennedy makes to support his thesis, paragraph by paragraph. Your outline could begin with the first sentence of the fifth paragraph: "Kong has, first of all, the attraction of being manlike." (Again, you may wish to put these points in your own words, or summarize them—the attraction of being manlike.)

   How is Kennedy's essay built from the foundation of his thesis to the support of the evidence he has collected?

4. What does Kennedy mean, finally, by the statement: " . . . the ape in us expires from day to day, obscure, in desperation."?

5. Do you agree with Kennedy? Is he right about why we refuse to willingly let the movie *King Kong* die?

   (Since you have taken apart his essay and reduced to its barest bones the outline structure Kennedy fleshed out with his writing, you should base your answer to the question above on your *analysis* of his facts. Are his facts sound? Do they sound reasonable? Where do you agree or disagree with him? What would you add or subtract?)

6. Analysis obviously calls for an astute mind, and for ample support or evidence. Analyze Kennedy's Kong for details, for facts and words that add support to the points he is making.

   In this analysis you might use your outline as your map. Fill in the outline with lists of the examples and detail Kennedy uses for support.

   Is his essay well supported?

7. Finally, let us try a third analysis, this time for language. What descriptive and narrative elements can you find here?

□

How do the little narratives of the movie itself add interest for the reader? How many such narratives can you find? (A common writing problem for beginners lies in forgetting to fill the reader in on what is being analyzed. Even if the audience has seen the movie, or read the book, or keeps up with current events, a good essayist always refreshes their memory, makes the subject vivid in the reader's mind. Use your narrative skills.)

8. Every writer creates a little universe in written words, and then populates it with the things of existence. Beginning again with the opening of this essay, follow each word with your finger, collecting those which name things. For instance, paragraph four: dinosaurs, headhunters, riots, aerial battles, bullets, bombs, bloodletting, etc.

   What have you found in the universe of Kennedy's words?

   How is your appetite for this essay increased by being able to *see these words* as well as by seeing the imagery (the real thing) the words stand for or evoke? In other words, it's fun to read such words as *straphanger, bloodshot, rat, mummy, machineguns, sweetheart, pterodactyls, boobs, berserk, cackle, shinnying, bomb, flips, hurtle,* and *smash,* isn't it?

9. How do Kennedy's words make his essay pleasurable in the same way that "Kong's" images make the movie pleasurable, a surface of fun with an undercurrent of deeper significance?

William Golding
(1911–   )

William Golding was born September 19, 1911, in Cornwall, England. While he has written essays, reviews, and poetry, he is known primarily as a novelist. *Lord of the Flies,* 1954, was his first published novel and is still his most widely read book. His own early favorite was *The Inheritors,* 1955, which was told from the point of view of a Neanderthal man.

Though Golding's stories are often called fables by critics, he would prefer they be called myth, a fable being "an invented thing on the surface whereas myth is something which comes out from the roots of things in the ancient sense of being the key to existence, the whole meaning of life, and experience as a whole."

Golding, who as a youth collected words "like stamps or bird's eggs," considers the Greek classics his literary parentage. To him the writer's primary function is to help people "understand their own humanity."

Thinking as a Hobby

While I was still a boy, I came to the conclusion that there were three grades of thinking; and since I was later to claim thinking as my hobby, I came to an even stranger conclusion—namely, that I myself could not think at all.

I must have been an unsatisfactory child for grownups to deal with. I remember how incomprehensible they appeared to me at first, but not, of course, how I appeared to them. It was the headmaster of my grammar school who first brought the subject of thinking before me—though neither in the way, nor with the result he intended. He had some statuettes in his study. They stood on a high cupboard behind his desk. One was a lady wearing nothing but a bath towel. She seemed frozen in an eternal panic lest the bath towel slip down any farther; and since she had no arms, she was in an unfortunate position to pull the towel up again. Next to her, crouched the statuette of a leopard, ready to spring down at the top drawer of a filing cabinet labeled A-AH. My innocence interpreted this as the victim's last despairing cry. Beyond the leopard was a naked, muscular gentleman, who sat, looking down, with his chin on his fist and his elbow on his knee. He seemed utterly miserable.

Some time later, I learned about these statuettes. The headmaster had placed them where they would face delinquent children, because they symbolized to him the whole of life. The naked lady was the Venus of Milo. She was Love. She was not worried about the towel. She was just busy being beautiful. The leopard was nature, and he was being natural. The naked, muscular gentleman was not miserable. He was Rodin's Thinker, an image of pure thought. It is easy to buy small plaster models of what you think life is like.

I had better explain that I was a frequent visitor to the headmaster's study, because of the latest thing I had done or left undone. As we now say, I was not integrated. I was, if anything, disintegrated; and I was puzzled. Grownups never made sense. Whenever I found myself in a penal position before the headmaster's desk, with the statuettes glimmering whitely above him, I would sink my head, clasp my hands behind my back and writhe one shoe over the other.

The headmaster would look opaquely at me through flashing spectacles.

"What are we going to do with you?"

Well, what *were* they going to do with me? I would writhe my shoe some more and stare down at the worn rug.

"Look up, boy! Can't you look up?"

Then I would look up at the cupboard, where the naked lady was frozen in her panic and the muscular gentleman comtemplated the hindquarters of the leopard in endless gloom. I had nothing to say to the headmaster. His spectacles caught the light so that you could see nothing human behind them. There was no possibility of communication.

"Don't you ever think at all?"

No, I didn't think, wasn't thinking, couldn't think—I was simply waiting in anguish for the interview to stop.

"Then you'd better learn—hadn't you?"

On one occasion the headmaster leaped to his feet, reached up and plunked Rodin's masterpiece on the desk before me.

"That's what a man looks like when he's really thinking."

I surveyed the gentleman without interest or comprehension.

"Go back to your class."

Clearly there was something missing in me. Nature had endowed the rest of the human race with a sixth sense and left me out. This must be so, I mused, on my way back to the class, since whether I had broken a window, or failed to remember Boyle's Law, or been late for school, my teachers produced me one, adult answer: "Why can't you think?"

As I saw the case, I had broken the window because I had tried to hit Jack Arney with a cricket ball and missed him; I could not remember Boyle's Law because I had never bothered to learn it; and I was late for school because I preferred looking over the bridge into the river. In fact, I was wicked. Were my teachers, perhaps, so good that they could not understand the depths of my depravity? Were they clear, untormented people who could direct their every action by this mysterious business of thinking? The whole thing was incomprehensible. In my earlier years, I found even the statuette of the Thinker confusing. I did not believe any of my teachers were naked, ever. Like someone born deaf, but bitterly determined to find out about sound, I watched my teachers to find out about thought.

There was Mr. Houghton. He was always telling me to think. With a modest satisfaction, he would tell me that he had thought a bit himself. Then why did he spend so much time drinking? Or was there more sense in drinking than there appeared to be? But if not, and if drinking were in fact ruinous to health—and Mr. Houghton was ruined, there was no doubt about that—why was he always talking about the clean life and the virtues of fresh air? He would spread his arms wide with the action of a man who habitually spent his time striding along mountain ridges.

"Open air does me good, boys—I know it!"

Sometimes, exalted by his own oratory, he would leap from his desk and hustle us outside into a hideous wind.

"Now, boys! Deep breaths! Feel it right down inside you—huge draughts of God's good air!"

He would stand before us, rejoicing in his perfect health, an open-air man. He would put his hands on his waist and take a tremendous breath. You could hear the wind, trapped in the cavern of his chest and struggling with all the unnatural impediments. His body would reel with shock and his ruined face go white at the unaccustomed visitation. He would stagger back to his desk and collapse there, useless for the rest of the morning.

Mr. Houghton was given to high-minded monologues about the good life, sexless and full of duty. Yet in the middle of one of these monologues, if a girl passed the window, tapping along on her neat little feet, he would interrupt his discourse, his neck would turn of itself and he would watch her out of sight. In this instance, he seemed to me ruled not by thought but by an invisible and irresistible spring in his nape.

His neck was an object of great interest to me. Normally it bulged a bit over his collar. But Mr. Houghton had fought in the First World War alongside both Americans and French, and had come—by who knows what illogic?—to a settled detestation of both countries. If either country happened to be prominent in current affairs, no argument could make Mr. Houghton think well of it. He would bang the desk, his neck would bulge still further and go red. "You can say what you like," he would cry, "but I've thought about this—and I know what I think!"

Mr. Houghton thought with his neck.

There was Miss Parsons. She assured us that her dearest wish was our welfare, but I knew even then, with the mysterious clairvoyance of childhood, that what she wanted most was the husband she never got. There was Mr. Hands—and so on.

I have dealt at length with my teachers because this was my introduction to the nature of what is commonly called thought. Through them I discovered that thought is often full of unconscious prejudice, ignorance and hypocrisy. It will lecture on disinterested purity while its neck is being remorselessly twisted toward a skirt. Technically, it is about as proficient as most businessmen's golf, as honest as most politicians' intentions, or—to come near my own preoccupation—as coherent as most books that ever get written. It is what I came to call grade-three thinking, though more properly, it is feeling, rather than thought.

True, often there is a kind of innocence in prejudices, but in those days I viewed grade-three thinking with an intolerant contempt and an incautious mockery. I delighted to confront a pious lady who hated the Germans with the proposition that we should love our enemies. She taught me a great truth in dealing with grade-three thinkers; because of her, I no longer dismiss lightly a mental process which for nine-tenths of the population is the nearest they will ever get to thought. They have immense solidarity. We had better respect them, for we are outnumbered and surrounded. A crowd of grade-three thinkers, all shouting the same thing, all warming their hands at the fire of their own prejudices, will not thank you for pointing out the contradictions in their beliefs. Man is a gregarious animal, and enjoys agreement as cows will graze all the same way on the side of a hill.

Grade-two thinking is the detection of contradictions. I reached grade two when I trapped the poor, pious lady. Grade-two thinkers do not stampede easily, though often they fall into the other fault and lag behind. Grade-two thinking is a withdrawal, with eyes and ears open. It became my hobby and brought satisfaction and loneliness in either hand. For grade-two thinking destroys without having the power to create. It set me watching the crowds cheering His Majesty the King and asking myself what all the fuss was about, without giving me any-

□

thing positive to put in the place of that heady patriotism. But there were compensations. To hear people justify their habit of hunting foxes and tearing them to pieces by claiming that the foxes liked it. To hear our Prime Minister talk about the great benefit we conferred on India by jailing people like Pandit Nehru and Gandhi. To hear American politicians talk about peace in one sentence and refuse to join the League of Nations in the next. Yes, there were moments of delight.

But I was growing toward adolescence and had to admit that Mr. Houghton was not the only one with an irresistible spring in his neck. I, too, felt the compulsive hand of nature and began to find that pointing out contradiction could be costly as well as fun. There was Ruth, for example, a serious and attractive girl. I was an atheist at the time. Grade-two thinking is a menace to religion and knocks down sects like skittles. I put myself in a position to be converted by her with an hypocrisy worthy of grade three. She was a Methodist—or at least, her parents were, and Ruth had to follow suit. But, alas, instead of relying on the Holy Spirit to convert me, Ruth was foolish enough to open her pretty mouth in argument. She claimed that the Bible (King James Version) was literally inspired. I countered by saying that the Catholics believed in the literal inspiration of Saint Jerome's *Vulgate*, and the two books were different. Argument flagged.

At last she remarked that there were an awful lot of Methodists, and they couldn't be wrong, could they—not all those millions? That was too easy, said I restively (for the nearer you were to Ruth, the nicer she was to be near to) since there were more Roman Catholics than Methodists anyway; and they couldn't be wrong, could they—not all those hundreds of millions? An awful flicker of doubt appeared in her eyes. I slid my arm round her waist and murmured breathlessly that if we were counting heads, the Buddhists were the boys for my money. But Ruth had *really* wanted to do me good, because I was so nice. She fled. The combination of my arm and those countless Buddhists was too much for her.

That night her father visited my father and left, red-cheeked and indignant. I was given the third degree to find out what had happened. It was lucky we were both of us only fourteen. I lost Ruth and gained an undeserved reputation as a potential libertine.

So grade-two thinking could be dangerous. It was in this knowledge, at the age of fifteen, that I remember making a comment from the heights of grade two, on the limitations of grade three. One evening I found myself alone in the school hall, preparing it for a party. The door of the headmaster's study was open. I went in. The headmaster had ceased to thump Rodin's Thinker down on the desk as an example to the young. Perhaps he had not found any more candidates, but the statuettes were still there, glimmering and gathering dust on top of the cupboard. I stood on a chair and rearranged them. I stood Venus in her bath towel on the filing cabinet, so that now the top drawer caught its

□

breath in a gasp of sexy excitement. "A-ah!" The portentous Thinker I placed on the edge of the cupboard so that he looked down at the bath towel and waited for it to slip.

Grade-two thinking, though it filled life with fun and excitement, did not make for content. To find out the deficiencies of our elders bolsters the young ego but does not make for personal security. I found that grade two was not only the power to point out contradictions. It took the swimmer some distance from the shore and left him there, out of his depth. I decided that Pontius Pilate was a typical grade-two thinker. "What is truth?" he said, a very common grade-two thought, but one that is used always as the end of an argument instead of the beginning. There is a still higher grade of thought which says, "What is truth?" and sets out to find it.

But these grade-one thinkers were few and far between. They did not visit my grammar school in the flesh though they were there in books. I aspired to them, partly because I was ambitious and partly because I now saw my hobby as an unsatisfactory thing if it went no further. If you set out to climb a mountain, however high you climb, you have failed if you cannot reach the top.

I *did* meet an undeniably grade-one thinker in my first year at Oxford. I was looking over a small bridge in Magdelen Deer Park, and a tiny mustached and hatted figure came and stood by my side. He was a German who had just fled from the Nazis to Oxford as a temporary refuge. His name was Einstein.

But Professor Einstein knew no English at that time and I knew only two words of German. I beamed at him, trying wordlessly to convey by my bearing all the affection and respect that the English felt for him. It is possible—and I have to make the admission—that I felt here were two grade-one thinkers standing side by side; yet I doubt if my face conveyed more than a formless awe. I would have given my Greek and Latin and French and a good slice of my English for enough German to communicate. But we were divided; he was as inscrutable as my headmaster. For perhaps five minutes we stood together on the bridge, undeniable grade-one thinker and breathless aspirant. With true greatness, Professor Einstein realized that any contact was better than none. He pointed to a trout wavering in midstream.

He spoke, "Fisch."

My brain reeled. Here I was, mingling with the great, and yet helpless as the veriest grade-three thinker. Desperately I sought for some sign by which I might convey that I, too, revered pure reason. I nodded vehemently. In a brilliant flash I used up half of my German vocabulary. "*Fisch. Ja. Ja.*"

For perhaps another five minutes we stood side by side. Then Professor Einstein, his whole figure still conveying good will and amiability, drifted away out of sight.

I, too, would be a grade-one thinker. I was irreverent at the best of times. Political and religious systems, social customs, loyalties and traditions, they all came tumbling down like so many rotten apples off a tree. This was a fine hobby and a sensible substitute for cricket, since you could play it all the year round. I came up in the end with what must always remain the justification for grade-one thinking, its sign, seal and charter. I devised a coherent system for living. It was a moral system, which was wholly logical. Of course, as I readily admitted, conversion of the world to my way of thinking might be difficult, since my system did away with a number of trifles, such as big business, centralized government, armies, marriage. . . .

It was Ruth all over again. I had some very good friends who stood by me, and still do. But my acquaintances vanished, taking the girls with them. Young women seemed oddly contented with the world as it was. They valued the meaningless ceremony with a ring. Young men, while willing to concede the chaining sordidness of marriage, were hesitant about abandoning the organizations which they hoped would give them a career. A young man on the first rung of the Royal Navy, while perfectly agreeable to doing away with big business and marriage, got as red-necked as Mr. Houghton when I proposed a world without any battleships in it.

Had the game gone too far? Was it a game any longer? In those prewar days, I stood to lose a great deal, for the sake of a hobby.

Now you are expecting me to describe how I saw the folly of my ways and came back to the warm nest, where prejudices are so often called loyalties, where pointless actions are hallowed into custom by repetition, where we are content to say we think when all we do is feel.

But you would be wrong. I dropped my hobby and turned professional.

If I were to go back to the headmaster's study and find the dusty statuettes still there, I would arrange them differently. I would dust Venus and put her aside, for I have come to love her and know her for the fair things she is. But I would put the Thinker, sunk in his desperate thought, where there were shadows before him—and at his back, I would put the leopard, crouched and ready to spring.

Vocabulary

opaquely obscurely, not clear or lucid, dully
draughts British variant spelling for drafts
impediments obstructions, obstacles
disinterested unbiased (this word does not mean uninterested)
gregarious friendly, outgoing
libertine morally or sexually unrestrained; a freethinker, commonly thought to be profligate, a rake
aspirant one who seeks a career, but used also as an auditory pun by Golding; see Discussion question #5
portentous ominously significant

□

Allusions/References

Boyle's Law from thermodynamics, the principle that, for relatively low pressures, the pressure of an ideal gas kept at a constant temperature varies inversely with the volume of the gas

Pontius Pilate early 1st Century A.D. Roman official of Judea who tried and condemned Jesus Christ

Discussion

1. While Golding is busy analyzing thinking, let's analyze his thinking about thinking. Remember always that analysis asks that you first take something apart.

   What are the three grades of thinking Golding indentifies?

   How do these three grades function as the structural bases of this essay? (Find the areas of the essay where each grade is primarily discussed, and fence them off as fields of idea.)

2. Narrative is always a mainstay of good writing. Find the narratives used to exemplify each of the three grades of thinking.

   How do these narratives work toward clarifying Golding's thesis?

   How do they work toward maintaining reader interest?

3. How does the narrative about the statuettes work?

   How, structurally, does this essay succeed in "swallowing" itself? How does it end where it began?

   Or does it? What does the shift in the statuettes' positioning indicate about Golding's thesis?

4. What comparisons are implied in the following:

   > "neck . . . remorsely twisted toward a skirt"

   > "all warming their hands at the fire"

   > "grade-two thinkers do not stampede"

   > "knocks down sects like skittles"

   How many more can you find?

   How effective is Golding's use of comparisons in engaging your attention? In supporting his ideas?

5. Finally, let's look at the descriptive elements of Golding's prose. How does he use words that involve the reader's total person, the senses as well as the intellect?

   What do you hear, see, touch, smell, taste, in this essay?

   Examine the following:

   > "hustle us outside in the hideous wind"

   > "to thump Rodin's Thinker down"

   > "breathless aspirant"

   What do you *hear?*

   Find other examples of Golding's use of sensuous language.

6. What conclusions can you reach about this piece now that you have examined its parts? (This is the difficult question, students. Reach into your own deep responses. What do you make of Mr. Golding and this essay? This would be your thesis, were you to write a formal analysis of "Thinking as a Hobby." Your data, collected by careful scrutiny and analysis, would be your support. Why not try it?)
7. What is Golding's tone, attitude toward his material, his audience?

Clarence Darrow
(1857–1938)

While Clarence Darrow is best known as an attorney (see "Crime and Criminals," Chapter Six), his importance as a writer is also clear. In all he wrote eight books, including an autobiography, *The Story of My Life*.

Perhaps his greatest concern in life and writing was how the law treated those who ran afoul of it. To him the criminal was "a human being, like all others, neither perfect nor entirely worthless." To Darrow, the attitude that the criminal was outside society and acting by "free will" was ridiculous. "Nothing in the universe is outside the law, whether mineral, vegetable, or animal. Free-will is the doctrine of despair. It means that man would live day to day governed by his transient will, instead of being moved and virtually controlled by every experience and influence of his life."

Why I Am an Agnostic

An agnostic is a doubter. The word is generally applied to those who doubt the verity of accepted creeds of faith. Everyone is an agnostic as to the beliefs or creeds they do not accept. Catholics are agnostic to the Protestant creeds, and the Protestants are agnostic to the Catholic creed. Anyone who thinks is an agnostic about something, otherwise he must believe that he is possessed of all knowledge. And the proper place for such a person is in the madhouse or the home for the feeble-minded. In a popular way, in the western world, an agnostic is one who doubts or disbelieves the main tenets of the Christian faith.

I would say that belief in at least three tenets is necessary to the faith of a Christian: a belief in God, a belief in immortality, and a belief in a supernatural book. Various Christian sects require much more, but it is difficult to imagine that one could be a Christian, under any intelligent meaning of the word, with less. Yet there are some people who claim to be Christians who do not accept the literal interpretation of all the Bible, and who give more credence to some portions of the book than to others.

I am an agnostic as to the question of God. I think it is impossible for the human mind to believe in an object or thing unless it can form a mental picture of such object or thing. Since man ceased to worship openly an anthropomorphic God and talked vaguely and not intelligently about some force in the universe, higher than man, that is responsible for the existence of man and the universe, he cannot be said to believe in God. One cannot believe in a force excepting as a force that pervades matter and is not an individual entity. To believe in a thing, an image of the thing must be stamped on the mind. If one is asked if he believes in such an animal as a camel, there immediately arises in his mind an image of a camel. This image has come from experience or knowledge of the animal gathered in some way or another. No such image comes, or can come, with the idea of a God who is described as a force.

Man has always speculated upon the origin of the universe, including himself. I feel, with Herbert Spencer, that whether the universe had an origin—and if it had—what the origin is will never be known by man. The Christian says that the universe could not make itself; that there must have been some higher power to call it into being. Christians have been obsessed for many years by Paley's argument that if a person passing through a desert should find a watch and examine its spring, its hands, its case and its crystal, he would at once be satisfied that some intelligent being capable of design had made the watch. No doubt this is true. No civilized man would question that someone made the watch. The reason he would not doubt it is because he is familiar with watches and other appliances made by man. The savage was once unfamiliar with a watch and would have had no idea upon the subject. There are plenty of crystals and rocks of natural formation that are as intricate as a watch, but even to intelligent man they carry no implication that some intelligent power must have made them. They carry no such implication because no one has any knowledge or experience of someone having made these natural objects which everywhere abound.

To say that God made the universe gives us no explanation of the beginning of things. If we were told that God made the universe, the question immediately arises: Who made God? Did he always exist, or was there some power back of that? Did he create matter out of nothing, or is his existence co-extensive with matter? The problem is still there. What is the origin of it all? If, on the other hand, one says that the universe was not made by God, that it always existed, he has the same difficulty to confront. To say that the universe was here last year, or millions of years ago, does not explain its origin. This is still a mystery. As to the question of the origin of things, man can only wonder and doubt and guess.

As to the existence of the soul, all people may either believe or disbelieve. Everyone knows the origin of the human being. They know that it came from a single cell in the body of the mother, and that the cell was one out of ten thousand in the mother's body. Before gestation the cell must have been fertilized by a spermatozoön from the body of the father. This was one out of perhaps a billion spermatozoa that was the capacity of the father. When the cell is fertilized a chemical process begins. The cell divides and multiplies and increases into millions of cells, and finally a child is born. Cells die and are born during the life of the individual until they finally drop apart, and this is death.

If there is a soul, what is it, and where did it come from, and where does it go? Can anyone who is guided by his reason possibly imagine a soul independent of a body, or the place of its residence, or the character of it, or anything concerning it? If man is justified in any belief or disbelief on any subject, he is warranted in the disbelief in a soul. Not one scrap of evidence exists to prove any such impossible thing.

Many Christians base the belief of a soul and God upon the Bible. Strictly speaking, there is no such book. To make the Bible, sixty-six books are bound into one volume. These books were written by many people at different times, and no one knows the time or identity of any author. Some of the books were written by several authors at various times. These books contain all sorts of contradictory concepts of life and morals and the origin of things. Between the first and the last nearly a thousand years intervened, a longer time than has passed since the discovery of America by Columbus.

When I was a boy the theologians used to assert that the proof of the divine inspiration of the Bible rested on miracles and prophecies. But a miracle means a violation of natural law, and there can be no proof imagined that could be sufficient to show the violation of a natural law; even though proof seemed to show violation, it would only show that we were not acquainted with all natural laws. One believes in the truthfulness of a man because of his long experience with the man, and because the man has always told a consistent story. But no man has told so consistent a story as nature.

If one should say that the sun did not rise, to use the ordinary expression, on the day before, his hearer would not believe it, even though he had slept all day and knew that his informant was a man of the strictest veracity. He would not believe it because the story is inconsistent with the conduct of the sun in all the ages past.

Primitive and even civilized people have grown so accustomed to believing in miracles that they often attribute the simplest manifestations of nature to agencies of which they know nothing. They do this when the belief is utterly inconsistent with knowledge and logic. They believe in old miracles and new ones. Preachers pray for rain, knowing full well that no such prayer was ever answered. When a politician is sick, they pray for God to cure him, and the politician almost invariably dies. The modern clergyman who prays for rain and for the health of the politician is no more intelligent in this matter than the primitive man who saw a separate miracle in the rising and setting of the sun, in the birth of an individual, in the growth of a plant, in the stroke of lightning, in the flood, in every manifestation of nature and life.

As to prophecies, intelligent writers gave them up long ago. In all prophecies facts are made to suit the prophecy, or the prophecy was made after the facts, or the events have no relation to the prophecy. Weird and strange and unreasonable interpretations are used to explain simple statements, that a prophecy may be claimed.

Can any rational person believe that the Bible is anything but a human document? We now know pretty well where the various books came from, and about when they were written. We know that they were written by human beings who had no knowledge of science, little knowledge of life, and were influenced by the barbarous morality of primitive times, and were grossly ignorant of most things that men know today. For instance, Genesis says that God made the earth, and he made the sun to light the day and the moon to light the night, and in one clause disposes of the stars by saying that "he made the stars also." This was plainly written by someone who had no conception of the stars. Man, by the aid of his telescope, has looked out into the heavens and found stars whose diameter is as great as the distance between the earth and the sun. We now know that the universe is filled with stars and suns and planets and systems. Every new telescope looking further into the heavens only discovers more and more worlds and suns and systems in the endless reaches of space. The men who wrote Genesis believed, of course, that this tiny speck of mud that we call the earth was the center of the universe, the only world in space, and made for man, who was the only being worth considering. These men believed that the stars were only a little way above the earth, and were set in the firmament for man to look at, and for nothing else. Everyone today knows that this conception is not true.

The origin of the human race is not as blind a subject as it once was. Let alone God creating Adam out of hand, from the dust of the earth, does anyone believe that Eve was made from Adam's rib—that the snake walked and spoke in the Garden of Eden—that he tempted Eve to persuade Adam to eat an apple, and that it is on that account that the whole human race was doomed to hell—and for four thousand years there was no chance for any human to be saved, though none of them had anything whatever to do with the temptation; and that finally men were saved only through God's son dying for them, and that unless human beings believed this silly, impossible and wicked story they were doomed to hell? Can anyone with intelligence really believe that a child born today should be doomed because the snake tempted Eve and Eve tempted Adam? To believe that is not God-worship; it is devil-worship.

Can anyone call this scheme of creation and damnation moral? It defies every principle of morality, as man conceives morality. Can anyone believe today that the whole world was destroyed by flood, save only Noah and his family and a male and female of each species of animal that entered the Ark? There are almost a million species of insects alone. How did Noah match these up and make sure of getting male and female to reproduce life in the world after the flood had spent its force? And why should all the lower animals have been destroyed? Were they included in the sinning of man? This is a story which could not beguile a fairly bright child of five years of age today.

Do intelligent people believe that the various languages spoken by man on earth came from the confusion of tongues at the Tower of Babel, some four thousand years ago? Human languages were dispersed all over the face of the earth long before that time. Evidences of civilizations are in existence now that were old long before the date that romancers fix for the building of the Tower, and even before the date claimed for the flood.

Do Christians believe that Joshua made the sun stand still, so that the day could be lengthened, that a battle might be finished? What kind of person wrote that story, and what did he know about astronomy? It is perfectly plain that the author thought that the earth was the center of the universe and stood still in the heavens, and that the sun either went around it or was pulled across its path each day, and that the stopping of the sun would lengthen the day. We know now that had the sun stopped when Joshua commanded it, and had it stood still until now, it would not have lengthened the day. We know that the day is determined by the rotation of the earth upon its axis, and not by the movement of the sun. Everyone knows that this story simply is not true, and not many even pretend to believe the childish fable.

What of the tale of Balaam's ass speaking to him, probably in Hebrew? Is it true, or is it a fable? Many asses have spoken, and doubtless some in Hebrew, but they have not been that breed of asses. Is salvation to depend on a belief in a monstrosity like this?

Above all the rest, would any human being today believe that a child was born without a father? Yet this story was not at all unreasonable in the ancient world; at least three or four miraculous births are recorded in the Bible, including John the Baptist and Samson. Immaculate conceptions were common in the Roman world at the time and at the place where Christianity really had its nativity. Women were taken to the temples to be inoculated of God so that their sons might be heroes, which meant, generally, wholesale butchers. Julius Caesar was a miraculous conception—indeed, they were common all over the world. How many miraculous-birth stories is a Christian now expected to believe?

In the days of the formation of the Christian religion, disease meant the possession of human beings by devils. Christ cured a sick man by casting out the devils, who ran into the swine, and the swine ran into the sea. Is there any question but what that was simply the attitude and belief of a primitive people? Does anyone believe that sickness means the possession of the body by devils, and that the devils must be cast out of the human being that he may be cured? Does anyone believe that a dead person can come to life? The miracles recorded in the Bible are not the only instances of dead men coming to life. All over the world one finds testimony of such miracles; miracles which no person is expected to believe, unless it is his kind of a miracle. Still at Lourdes today, and all over the present world, from New York to Los Angeles and up and down the lands, people still believe in miraculous occurrences, and even in the return of the dead. Superstition is everywhere prevalent in the world. It has been so from the beginning, and most likely will be so unto the end.

The reasons for agnosticism are abundant and compelling. Fantastic and foolish and impossible consequences are freely claimed for the belief in religion. All the civilization of any period is put down as a result of religion. All the cruelty and error and ignorance of the period has no relation to religion. The truth is that the origin of what we call civilization is not due to religion but to skepticism. So long as men accepted the miracles without question, so long as they believed in original sin and the road to salvation, so long as they believed in a hell where man would be kept for eternity on account of Eve, there was no reason whatever for civilization: life was short, and eternity was long, and the business of life was preparation for eternity.

When every event was a miracle, when there was no order or system or law, there was no occasion for studying any subject, or being interested in anything excepting a religion which took care of the soul. As man doubted the primitive conceptions about religion, and no longer accepted the literal, miraculous teachings of ancient books, he set himself to understand nature. We no longer cure disease by casting out devils. Since that time, men have studied the human body, have built hospitals and treated illness in a scientific way. Science is responsible for the building of railroads and bridges, of steamships, of telegraph lines, of cities, towns, large buildings and small, plumbing and sanitation, for the food supply, and countless thousands of useful things that we now deem necessary to life. Without skepticism and doubt, none of these things could have been given to the world.

The fear of God is not the beginning of wisdom. The fear of God is the death of wisdom. Skepticism and doubt lead to study and investigation, and investigation is the beginning of wisdom.

The modern world is the child of doubt and inquiry, as the ancient world was the child of fear and faith.

Vocabulary

verity   the condition or quality of being real, accurate
anthropomorphic   attributing human characteristics to nonhuman things
theologians   those who study God and man's relation to God

Allusions/References

Herbert Spencer British philosopher who attempted to apply evolutionary theory to all branches of knowledge (1820–1903)

Discussion

The following questions form the basis for an *analysis* of Darrow:

1. What evidence is there that Darrow has come to think of the *locus* of himself as the human mind? Show evidence from the text that demonstrates Darrow's faith in reason, in the mind.

2. How is it he feels the origin of the universe will never be known to man? Through what faculty does Darrow *know?*

   If Darrow's mind should fail at knowing the origins of the universe (despite the accumulated spiritual and physical explanations of mankind), then it is unknowable?

   Is the mind the only way?

3. What is the logic of the story of the watch? How is it a parable for the larger issue of whether all phenomena of existence have a maker?

4. "Can anyone who is guided by his reason possibly imagine . . . ?" Darrow asks. The two key words here are "reason" and "imagine." Is the imagination guided by reason? (If it were, could you imagine?)

   Is there any other possible guide but reason? What do you think? Speculate.

5. Why doesn't Darrow believe in miracles? Find the passages in the text that explain his position.

6. How is belief needed to believe in knowledge and logic, as much as to believe in belief?

7. Notice Darrow's language use here: "As to prophecies, intelligent writers gave them up long ago. In all prophecies facts are made to suit the prophecy, or the prophecy was made after the facts, or the events have no relation to the prophecy."

   What does the repetition of the word prophecy and its positioning in the passage above remind you most of, logic or poetry?

8. What does Darrow think of the primitive? How do you know?

   How is it that Darrow has faith in the superiority of today?

9. Is to *believe* in facts the same thing as to *believe* in fables? What does Darrow think? (Show by retelling his interpretation of one or two of the biblical tales.)

10. If two thousand years of accumulated knowledge make the old stories and explanations preposterous to Darrow, what will a thousand years more make Darrow's accumulated explanations?

11. How many examples does Darrow use to prove the inferiority of the past to now—in knowledge and beliefs?

12. Examine closely the last three paragraphs in this piece.

    (a) How is it that Darrow's argument about Science's achievements—railroads, bridges, steamships, cities, etc., reminds us of religion's claims expressed just a paragraph before?

□

"All the civilization of any period is put down as a result of religion."

"Without skepticism and doubt, none of these things could have been given to the world."

(b) Are not religion and science claiming the same things?

(c) Does science willingly list its "cruelty and error and ignorance"?

(d) What is and what is not "the beginning of wisdom" to Darrow?

(e) How is his last sentence both true and ironic at the same time? What does "child" imply, for then and *now?*

13. "An agnostic is a doubter." Does Darrow doubt science and reason, the human mind? Why not?

The *method* of analysis can be used to analyze anything, even man's faith and dependence upon being analytical. It merely requires that you ask the question, why?

By Emotion
By Logic
By Ethics

6

Argumentation: To Persuade

You're not arguing logically, he said. You are too emotional. She *was* getting emotional hearing him say that, she said. What's so good about logic anyway?

No kind of argument but emotional, Ross said, no other kind. I pondered this a while. I was feeling pretty emotional about logic.

Are you making any sense of this? It is an overheard line of thought about argumentation. Where shall we go from here? I'm not writing logically, I am following some other way. In this culture logic is a valued art. Where does that leave me? Lost. Lost. I'm sorry to be writing a poem. I wanted to write you a song. A poem is a song is not logical. This is a textbook. A textbook is straight words, columns, and lines all even at the edges. For a minute I could see it there, the way out. When you run blind and trust it this is the way it is. A ride man tired. Maybe you can close your eyes. Back to where you belong logic. Stop making sense. Fight the impulse. Could I persuade you of *this?* No. Then let me lay it out for you.

□

There are three kinds of argument: by emotion, by logic, and by ethics. It is impossible to find any one in a pure form since the human being cannot so easily sort himself out. In essence, to argue by emotion is to appeal directly to your readers' senses, to get them to feel on their pulses your argument. The idea is that if others can be stimulated to feel as you do, certainly they will be persuaded. At its best, emotional argument is an effective and moral appeal. At its worst, it is used to manipulate others, to get them to feel some way for purposes of gain.

Logic is as powerful a tool and as easily corrupted. At its best, logic is a form for thoughts agreed upon by others. No one plays checkers against an opponent playing chess. An idea can be examined inside of the parameters of the form we call logic, and agreed upon by others following the rules. Emotion is at a disadvantage in this because it has been so often scorned as a subject of serious thought. Its parameters have not been mapped and it seems, therefore, the more perilous journey. Logic, on the other hand, is a highly developed civilization of thought. At its worst, it becomes a weapon with which to bludgeon those whose arguments come from a different court.

Ethics is the highest-order argument. Man is much admired when he reaches the level of maturity where a moral system has been internalized and informs his every thought and action. Ethics is a system of morality, or moral choices. Logic can be used in the service of any system, but once one has committed oneself to an ethic, only that ethic will serve. This is why we value so highly the person who argues from a moral point of view. We sense in the act a commitment to a way of seeing things, a vision through which the individual acts of humans are explained. If we like the ethic we like the individual and thus his or her argument. At its worst, arguing from ethics allows no other possible explanation. It is a closed system paid office to by commitment and faith. This is why human beings are always in trouble with one another over beliefs that appear eternally in contradiction.

Remember, no one argues from one kind of argument only. Each is a branch on the same tree. From the study of such famous persuasions as Pericles's funeral oration, Shakespeare's Antony, "I come to bury Caesar, not to praise him," and Winston Churchill's World War II addresses, rhetoricians have identified certain common features you might want to use in structuring your argumentative essays. Open with a snappy first line: earth is a grain of cosmic dust; white cotton bedsheets are a sin; there is no political solution. Save your best support for last: emotional, logical, or ethical. Begin your argument with the second best reason you have for believing what you believe. Bury your less promising, but still strong, arguments in the middle of your paper. Ending on a strong note is the only way. What is last is remembered. Or at least it seems logical.

□ By Emotion

In this chapter are many compelling voices. Cleveland Amory in
"Little Brother of the Wolf" appeals to our humanness, our instinct on
the side of life over death, to get us to reconsider our war on the
coyote. Even Amory's designation of the coyote as "little brother of
the wolf," is witness to how Amory uses the connotative emotional
value of words: "little" makes us feel protective, small ourselves if we
bully; "brother" is a word connoting one of the closest of human
bonds, blood of our blood; "wolf" is a noble animal, not at all skulky
or mangy. The coyote is transformed into a smaller wolf, blood
brother, and has cast upon it the same mythological glow. At least this
is what Amory hopes for in this compassionate essay, which actually
reveals a logic of its own and an ethic informing the author with his
humanistic stance.

Larry Woiwode, in an essay on guns, demonstrates the terrible
fascination and even beauty humans find in matters of life and death,
in having within their province the power of this decision over other
living forms. Woiwode's words raise the hairs on our arm. While
arguing against the use of guns, he is revealing that which is within
him, within man, an undeniable attraction to blood.

Lawrence Langer in "The Human Use of Language" argues from
the personal instance. He sees in the injustice toward a single person,
the metaphor for the injustice toward us all. When language is used
as a barrier between us, behind which we "lie concealed, unwilling
or unable to hear a human voice and return a human echo," it is, says
Langer, inhuman. As Woiwode's stance is one of risk and vulnerabil-
ity, so is Langer's. To open the heart in argumentation takes courage.

Darwin once wrote in his journals that he regretted one thing,
that he did not read enough literature. It exercises the emotions, was
his conclusion, and emotions not exercised atrophy. This is the
function of emotion in argument. It urges us to *feel* human.

Cleveland Amory
(1917–   )

Cleveland Amory was born September 2, 1917, in Nahaut, Massachusetts. He is
a social historian and novelist. As a student at Harvard he worked on the student daily, the *Harvard Crimson,* becoming its president in his senior year.
After graduation he remained in journalism and gained a reputation for exper-
tise with the "institutional article," profiles of American institutions that
reveal the nature of society.

In addition to his articles, which have appeared in many major magazines, he has written several books. Of particular interest to him is society's treatment of animals. And even here, on a subject he feels strongly about, he is known for his great humor.

He has said: "Writing, in case you don't know it, is hard work—good writing, that is, like you're reading right now." The following selection is from *Mankind?*

Little Brother of the Wolf

"Next to God," goes the Mexican saying, "the coyote is the smartest person on earth." Even if this is exaggerated, the fact remains that the coyote, if not the most intelligent of all animals, is certainly the cleverest. He would have to be.

Man has made his very name suspect. The second definition for the word "coyote" in the new *American Heritage Dictionary* is "contemptible sneak." For two hundred years, the coyote has faced a steadily increasing campaign to eradicate him from the face of the earth. Many animals have faced such campaigns, but against no other animal has the campaign reached such heights of cruelty.

In the old days, the coyote was hunted for his pelt. When pelts dropped in price, he was hunted because he was supposed to be a cattle killer. When it was proven he wasn't a cattle killer—he lives almost exclusively on mice, moles, rabbits, insects, snakes and even eats fruit for dessert—he was hunted because he was supposed to be a sheep killer. Finally, when it was proven he wasn't a sheep killer, he was hunted because—well, he was supposed to hunt what man wanted to hunt. The coyote is classed, simply, as a "varmint."

As such, there is no season for hunting coyote. For him, it is always open season. He is hunted by land and by air. He has learned that the air can be dangerous; when he hears or sees a plane he takes cover, and like a trained guerilla fighter, camouflages himself. The coyote is regularly jack-hunted by light at night, something forbidden by law for most animals. "Most hunters," says one hunting magazine, "clamp a powerful light directly to their guns and keep it on at all times."

In the winter, snowmobiles hunt the coyote down, with the hunters signaling to each other by walkie-talkies. In the summer, trained hunting dogs run him down in relays. Often, the coyote is chased by dogs riding in automobiles. When he begins to tire, the automobiles are stopped and the dogs are released.

In such situations, the coyote's only hope lies in his cleverness. And stories of coyotes outwitting hunters are legion. Coyotes will work in teams, alternately resting and running to escape dogs set upon them. They have even been known to jump on automobiles and flat cars to escape dogs. And they have also successfully resisted bombing. Lewis Nordyke reports that once when a favorite coyote haunt in Texas became a practice range for bombing, the coyotes left—temporarily. Soon they were back to investigate and found that the bombing kept people out. They decided to stay. Meanwhile, they learned the bombing schedule and avoided bombs.

Many a coyote has gotten along with its lower jaw shot off. Joe Van Wormer reports a coyote in Idaho whose mouth had been cruelly wired shut. It was able to open it only half an inch, but nonetheless had been able to survive. A coyote in Montana also had her jaw wired shut—she was used by a hunter to "train" his dogs. And a female coyote killed in Tule Lake in northern California was found to have four healthy pups in her den. She had managed to fend for them although she herself had been shot in both eyes with a shotgun and was totally blind.

From some hunts, of course, there is no escape. John Farrar, in his *Autobiography of a Hunter*, writes of an all too typical hunt in the sandhill region of Nebraska. It was, he writes, "a well-planned military maneuver," with a plane overhead to spot the coyotes and, below, hundreds of hunters."They came in pickups," he says, "armed with shortwave radios, powerful engines, clinging snow tires . . . each nervously fingering a high-powered rifle with telescopic sight."

> At the next section line 12 men awaited [the coyote's] approach. At 100 yards head-on, it began. His faltering speed spared him as bullets churned the snow ahead. As he reached the ditch he sank shoulder deep and floundered desperately. Astonished, ashamed or angry, no one fired. As he struggled across the road and into the next section, he seemed to crawl. As if he were shielded, 30 or more rounds left him untouched. In a weedy draw he could run no further. In cover no more than 12 inches high, he disappeared.
>
> The plane circled and then the men closed in afoot. Talk of letting this one go passed idly. Twenty-five armed men closed in on one terrified, exhausted animal. The enclosed area dwindled to the size of a football field and less. Still no coyote.
>
> Then he appeared, staggering, worn, mouth agape. He weaved pitifully up the hill among the hunters, as if defying death, or seeking it.
>
> Then man, the rational animal, the pinnacle of evolution, the great humanitarian, gunned him down.
>
> There was little laughing or joking, little back slapping. Just a sickening, nauseating silence. The day ended. With it ended my coyote hunting.

When the coyote is not hunted, he is trapped. For the coyote, there are especially horrible traps—to match his ingenuity. So-called "passion bait" is soaked in a piece of wool and put under a pan. When the coyote investigates, the slightest pressure releases the deadly steel leghold.

Once the coyote is caught, he has been known to chew off his own

☐

leg rather than remain in the trap. Literally thousands of coyotes have existed for life on three legs. Also, amazingly, there are thousands of two-legged coyotes. One female coyote in Michigan had only stubs for front legs—she ran like a kangaroo—and yet, when killed, was bearing five unborn pups. A coyote in Colorado existed for more than a year missing two feet—the left front and right hind. In New Mexico, a coyote got along somehow with both feet missing from his right side, and still managed to raise a family. Trapper Art Cooper once caught a coyote in two traps at once. One trap caught him by a front foot, one by a hind. The two-trap set was fastened to an iron drag, and when Cooper and a companion came upon the coyote he was trying to cross a plowed field. Seeing the man, the coyote grabbed the drag in his mouth and took off.

Marguerite Smelser tells an even more remarkable coyote-trapping story. Two government trappers spent weeks tracking down and trying to kill a whole coyote family. First the nursing mother was trapped, then released after the trappers had fastened a collar and tire chain to her. By the trail of the dragging chain, the trappers expected to follow her to her den where they could then wipe out the pups.

But for two weeks the mother coyote did not betray her family. Her mate brought food to her at night and kept the pups fed. And so, after days of frustration, convinced the mother would never endanger her young, the trappers tracked her down and killed her.

Later, however, they did get a chance at the pups. The trappers came upon them playing at the far side of the dam. At this juncture, however, the father coyote suddenly appeared and, acting as a decoy, managed to divert the trappers' attention until he was shot. His young had safely disappeared into the brush.

I have on my desk something called a "Humane Coyote-Getter," which is advertised as the "Marvel of the 20th Century." Humane? It is literally a whole trap gun. A bait is soaked in urine and covered with a jacket, then placed over a bullet cartridge, the whole being set in the ground. When the coyote investigates, the bullet is set off by a spring and shoots the coyote in the mouth with sodium cyanide. This in turn, on contact with the moisture in the coyote's mouth, or eyes, or wherever it hits him, releases gas and the coyote gases himself to death.

This Coyote-Getter is, by coyote-getting standards, actually humane—at least compared to the more general way of killing coyotes. That is, plainly and simply, by poisoning them. One state, for example, put out in one year 300,000 strychnine tablets—tablets which are slipped into an inch-square of suet made out of sheep fat. But even strychnine is as nothing compared to the dread Compound 1080 or sodium fluoroacetate. This is a poison so lethal that there is no known antidote. It is chain-reacting. Thus, when a meadow mouse eats it and is in turn eaten by a larger animal, who is in turn eaten by a coyote, who is in turn eaten by a mountain lion, 1080 will have poisoned them all.

Perhaps the most horrible thing about Compound 1080 is that it is administered in small doses. Not because it is expensive—unfortunately it isn't, it is cheap. But it is administered in small doses so that the coyote will get as far away from the bait as possible before he dies and thus his body will not be able to warn other possible victims. Coyotes have been known to travel over twenty miles to die—in agony.

The United States government has poisoned more than a million coyotes. The real irony, though, is not that poisoning is done by the government, it is that it is done on public land. After the findings of the Leopold Report, the government's "Predator and Rodent Control Board" had to change its name to "Wildlife Services." But still, the sheep men graze their sheep on public land, which they do for a nominal fee, and then have the government poison coyotes merely on the suspicion that they kill their sheep. And this despite the Leopold Report's warning, "For every person whose sheep may be molested by a coyote, there are perhaps a thousand others who would thrill to hear a coyote chorus in the night."

Texas rancher Arthur Lytton, who for forty years has run a 20,000-acre spread, said, "I would never allow a predator to be killed on my land. They are necessary for the balance of nature. Kill them and you're in for nothing but trouble from rabbits and rodents and everything."

In 1971, the coyote poisoning program cost the public over $8 million. And, of course, the program didn't just poison coyotes. In a typical year, the wildlife "body count" was as follows: 89,653 coyotes, 24,273 foxes, 20,780 bobcats, 19,052 skunks, 10,078 raccoons, 7,615 opossums, 6,941 badgers, 6,685 porcupines, 2,771 red wolves, 1,170 beavers and 842 bears.

Finally, after years of effort by the Defenders of Wildlife, Audubon, the Fund for Animals and other societies, President Nixon issued his now-historic Executive Order 11643, in February, 1972, banning the use of most predator poisons on public lands. The order continues to be opposed by the National Wool Growers Association and others. Coyote hunters, meanwhile, seemed to be redoubling their efforts. One hunt in particular, out of Karval, Colorado, which boasted nine pickup trucks with specially bred "coyote dogs" (mixes of greyhounds with Irish and Russian wolfhounds) penned in quick-release cages in the back, was billed as "The Biggest Coyote Hunt in Colorado History." Scores of hunters and dozens of dogs hunted all day. Their total kill—five coyotes.

Such hunts—this latter hunt even included an official "observer" from the department of the Interior—have outraged coyote friends. The Fund for Animals announced a reward of $500 for prior information which led to the stopping of any such hunt, and also announced that it would back any group engaged in breaking up such hunts by any means short of actual violence. One such group, the Defenders of the Coyote, already includes more than a hundred college and high school students as well as businessmen and housewives.

In the long run, some coyote friends believe the only answer is to make a pet out of him—and there has been signal success in this regard, the coyote's charm and loyalty overcoming all difficulties. Others believe that the answer is to meet the coyote literally halfway. Have him, in other words, as he is, half pet and half wild. One who believes this is Los Angeles' Gerald Coward, a man who, on a lonely walk up a canyon a few years ago, managed to make a lasting friend of a coyote. Coward, a photographer and writer, gave up his job and from that day on, every day for two and a half years, he walked up his canyon. And every day, for two and a half years, his coyote faithfully met him. All day they played, romped and explored together, learning about each other—and then, at the end of each day, they said goodbye. When the coyote mated, he even brought his companion to Coward at the same rendezvous. It was a remarkable idyll that existed until the terrible Los Angeles fire—when Mr. Coward saw his coyote no more. "The coyote," he said, "is the greatest animal there is."

Vocabulary

agape mouth open

Discussion

1. An argumentative essay is often opened by a strong statement of intent—an aphorism, a tersely phrased opinion—so that the reader's interest is immediately enlisted. How does Amory draw us immediately into his thesis and, therefore, into his argument?
2. How does the argument end on a similar note?
   (It is best never to end an argumentative essay with: "in summary," or "in conclusion." End as you begin, with thoughtfulness and snap.)
3. Find the structure of Amory's argument. Summarize each point he makes and the evidence he has collected for support, paragraph by paragraph. What is the nature of his evidence? Testimonial? Data? Fact?
4. In assembling the details, the facts and descriptions that lend credence to your argument, you might consider how their arrangement affects your reader. One plan might be to save your best piece of evidence for last, to end the piece on your strongest note, allowing your reader to leave with your strongest point still fresh in mind. (In this strategy, you might begin with your second best reason for believing what you do, leaving your weakest points embedded in the middle of the essay.)
   Look over Amory's arrangement of his defense of the coyote. What is his strongest statement? What kind of a statement is it? Fact? Testimonial?
   What is Amory's weakest point? What kind of a statement is it?
5. How strongly does Amory convince you that the coyote is a much maligned creature?

6. How does the narrative about John Farrar's coyote hunt function in this piece?

What other narratives are at work here and what do they add to Amory's argument?

(How might you use narrative in a persuasive piece?)

For Further Discussion

7. Examine Amory's use of descriptive language (words that appeal to the senses, to sight, smell, touch, etc.) in this piece.

How does description contribute toward convincing the reader that the argument is worthy? (Remember, description appeals to the total person, not just the intellect.)

8. Compare Amory's persuasive techniques with Clarence Darrow's "Crime and Criminals." What marks the difference between an argument whose support is primarily emotional, appealing to our human sensitivity, and one which is primarily ethical, appealing to the human use of reason, of principles of good conduct?

What differences do you find in the use of language?

Larry Woiwode
(1941–   )

Larry Woiwode was born October 30, 1941, in Sykeston, North Dakota. He has been a freelance writer since 1964 and writes poems, short stories, reviews, and novels. His work has appeared in many periodicals, including *Atlantic Monthly, New Yorker,* and *The New York Times.*

Critics often refer to Woiwode's "poetic gifts." John Gardner said of *Beyond the Bedroom Wall,* "nothing more beautiful and moving has been written in years." Memory plays a large part in Woiwode's writing, and he speaks of "words that have been on my tongue so long they're mangled and broken."

Guns

Once in the middle of a Wisconsin winter I shot a deer, my only one, while my wife and daughter watched. It had been hit by a delivery truck along a country road a few miles from where we lived and one of its rear legs was torn off at the hock; a shattered shin and hoof lay steaming in the red-beaded snow. The driver of the truck and I stood and watched as it tried to leap a fence, kicked a while at the top wire it was entangled in, flailing the area with fresh ropes of blood, and then went hobbling across a pasture toward a wooded hill. Placid cows followed it with a curious awe. "Do you have a rifle with you?" the driver asked. "No, not with me. At home." He looked once more at the deer, then got in his truck and drove off.

I went back to our Jeep where my wife and daughter were waiting, pale and withdrawn, and told them what I was about to do, and suggested that they'd better stay at home. No, they wanted to be with me, they said; they wanted to watch. My daughter was three and a half at the time. I got my rifle, a .22, a foolishly puny weapon to use on a deer but the only one I had, and we came back and saw that the deer was lying in some low brush near the base of the hill; no need to trail its blatant spoor. When I got about a hundred yards off, marveling at how it could have made it so far in its condition through snow that came over my boot tops, the deer tried to push itself up with its front legs, then collapsed. I aimed at the center of its skull, thinking, *This will be the quickest*, and heard the bullet ricochet off and go singing through the woods.

The deer was on its feet, shaking its head as though stung, and I fired again at the same spot, quickly, and apparently missed. It was now moving at its fastest hobble up the hill, broadside to me, and I took my time to sight a heart shot. Before the report even registered in my mind, the deer went down in an explosion of snow and lay struggling there, spouting blood from its stump and a chest wound. I was shaking by now. Deer are color-blind as far as science can say, and as I went toward its quieting body to deliver the coup de grace, I realized I was being seen in black and white, and then the deer's eye seemed to home in on me, and I was struck with the understanding that I was its vision of approaching death. And then I seemed to enter its realm through its eye and saw the countryside and myself in shades of white and grey. *But I see the deer in color*, I thought.

A few yards away, I aimed at its head once more, and there was the crack of a shot, the next-to-last round left in the magazine. The deer's head came up, and I could see its eye clearly now, dark, placid, filled with an appeal, it seemed, and then felt the surge of black and white surround and subsume me again. The second shot, or one of them, had pierced its neck; a grey-blue tongue hung out over its jaw; urine was trickling from below its tail; a doe. I held the rifle barrel inches from its forehead, conscious of my wife's and daughter's eyes on me from behind, and as I fired off the final and fatal shot, felt myself drawn by them back into my multicolored, many-faceted world again.

I don't remember my first gun, the heritage is so ingrained in me, but know I've used a variety of them to kill birds, reptiles, mammals, amphibians, plant life, insects (bees and butterflies with a shotgun), fish that came too close to shore—never a human being, I'm quick to interject, although the accumulated carnage I've put away with bullets since boyhood is probably enough to add up to a couple of cows, not counting the deer; and have fired, at other targets living and fairly inert, an old ten gauge with double hammers that left a welt on my shoulder that lasted a week, a Mauser, a twelve-gauge sawed-off shotgun, an M-16, at least a dozen variations on the .22-pump, bolt action, lever action, target pistols, special scopes and sights and stocks—a .410 over-and-under, a zip gun that blew up and scattered shrapnel that's still imbedded in my arm, an Italian carbine, a Luger, and, among others, a fancily engraved, single-trigger, double-barreled twenty gauge at snowballs thrown from behind my shoulder out over a bluff; and on that same bluff on the first day of this year, after some wine and prodding, I found myself at the jittering rim of stutters from a paratrooper's lightweight machine gun with a collapsible, geometrically reinforced metal stock, watched the spout of its trajectory of tangible tracers go off across the night toward the already-set sun, and realized that this was perhaps the hundredth weapon I'd had performing in my hands.

I was raised in North Dakota, near the edge of the West, during the turbulence and then the aftermath of the Second World War, which our country ended in such an unequivocal way there was a sense of vindication about our long-standing fetish for guns, not to say pride in it, too. "Bang! Bang! You're dead," returns to me from that time without the least speck of friction or reflection. When we weren't playing War, or Cowboys and Indians, or Cops and Robbers, we were reading War Comics (from which you could order for less than a dollar little cardboard chests of plastic weaponry and soldiers to stage your own debacles), or Westerns, or listening to *The Lone Ranger* and *Richard Diamond, Private Detective* and other radio shows—all of which openly glorified guns, and the more powerful the better.

My fantasies, when I was frustrated, angry, or depressed, were rife with firearms of the most lethal sort, flying shot, endless rounds of shattering ammunition; the enemy bodies blown away and left in bloody tableaux. And any gun was an engineered instrument—much more far-ranging and accurate than bows and arrows or slingshots—that detached you from your destructiveness or crime or sometimes even from being a source of death.

I've only owned three firearms in my life as an adult. Two I brought back to the shops within a week after I'd bought them, realizing I was trying to reach out in some archaic way, and the limits to my maturity and imagination that that implied, plus the bother to my daughter of their powing sounds; and the third, the .22, after trembling over it a few years and using it to shoot holes in the floor to enact a between-the-legs suicide, I gave away. To my younger brother. Who was initiated into the buck-fever fraternity in the forests of northern Wisconsin when he was an adolescent by a seasoned local who said to him, "If you see anything moving out there tomorrow, boy, *shoot* it. You can check out later what it is. Nobody gives a shit up here." And on a hunting trip years later, an acquaintance from the village my brother lived in then, a lawyer, was shot in the head with a deer rifle, but somehow survived. And even went back to practicing law. It was thought to be an accident at first, what with all the bullets embroidering the air that day, and then rumor had it that another member of the party hunting on adjoining land, an old friend of the lawyer's had

□

found out a week before the season that the lawyer had been having
his wife for a while. The two men were polite enough to one another
in the village after that, my brother said, but not such good friends, of
course. Just balanced, justice-balanced males.

For months and seasons after I'd shot the crippled doe, every time
we passed the field in our Jeep, my daughter would say, "Here's where
Daddy shooted the deer." In exactly that manner, using the tone and
detachment of a storyteller or tourist guide. And I'd glance into the rear-
view mirror and see her in her car seat, studying the hill with troubled
and sympathetic eyes. One day I stopped. "Does it bother you so much
that I shot it?" I asked. There was no answer, and then I saw that she
was nodding her head, her gaze still fixed on the hill.

"Well, if I wouldn't have, it could have suffered a long time. You
saw how badly hurt it was. It couldn't have lived that way. I didn't like
doing it, either, but it was best for the deer. When I told the game war-
den about it, he even thanked me and said, 'Leave it for the foxes and
crows.' They have to eat, too, you know, and maybe the deer made the
winter easier for them." And I thought, Oh, what a self-justifying fool
and ass and pig you are. Why didn't you leave her at home? Why didn't
you go to the farmer whose land the deer was on, which would have
been as quick or quicker than going back for the .22—a man who
would have had a deer rifle, or at least a shotgun with rifled slugs, and
would have put the deer away with dispatch in one shot and might
have even salvaged the hide and venison? And who could say it
wouldn't have lived, the way some animals do after tearing or chewing
off a limb caught in a trap? Who was to presume it wouldn't have preferred to die a slow death in the brush, looking out over the pasture, as
the crimson stain widening in the snow drew away and dimmed its
colorless world until all went black? Why not admit that I was a common backcountry American and, like most men of my mold, had used
an arsenal of firearms to kill and was as excited about putting away a
deer as moved by compassion for its suffering? Then again, given my
daughter's understanding and the person I am, perhaps she sensed this,
and more.

I once choked a chicken to death. It was my only barefaced, not
to say barehanded, confrontation with death and the killer in me and
happened on my grandparents' farm. I couldn't have been more than
nine or ten and no firearms were included or necessary. I was on my
knees and the chicken fluttered its outstretched wings with the last of
the outraged protest. I gripped, beyond release, above its swollen crop,
its beak gaping, translucent eyelids sliding up and down. An old molt-
ing specimen. A hen, most likely; a worse loss, because of eggs, than a
capon or cock. My grandfather, who was widely traveled and world-
wise, in his eighties then, and had just started using a cane from earlier
times, came tapping at that moment around the corner of the chicken

coop and saw what I was doing and started gagging at the hideousness of it, did a quick assisted spin away and never again, hours later nor for the rest of his life, for that matter, ever mentioned the homicidal incident to me. Keeping his silence, he seemed to understand; and yet whenever I'm invaded by the incident, the point of it seems to be his turning away from me.

My wife once said she felt I wanted to kill her. A common enough feeling among long-married couples, I'm sure, and not restricted to either sex (I know, for instance, that there were times when she wanted to kill me), but perhaps with firsthand experience infusing the feeling, it became too much to endure. I now live in New York City, where the clock keeps moving toward my suitcase, alone, and she and my daughter in the Midwest. The city has changed in the seven years since the three of us lived here together. There are more frivolous and not-so-frivolous wares—silk kerchiefs, necklaces and rings, roach clips, rolling papers, socks, a display of Florida coral across a convertible top, books of every kind—being sold in the streets than anybody can remember seeing in recent years. People openly saying that soon it will be like the Thirties once were, with us *all* in the streets selling our apples, or whatever, or engaged in a tacit and friendly sort of gangsterism to survive. Outside my window, a spindly deciduous species has a sign strung on supporting posts on either side of it, in careful hand-lettering, that reads, THIS TREE GIVES OXYGEN. GIVE IT LOVE. More dogs in the streets and parks than they'd remembered, and more canine offal sending up its open-ended odor; at least half the population giving up cigarette smoking, at last, for good, they say, and many actually are. The mazed feeling of most everywhere now of being in the midst of a slowly forging and forgiving reciprocity. An air of bravura about most everybody in maintaining one's best face, with a few changes of costumish clothing to reflect it, perhaps, no matter what might yet evolve. A unisex barbershop or boutique on nearly every other block, it seems.

Sometimes I think this is where I really belong. Then a man is gunned down in a neighborhood bar I used to drop into and the next day a mob leader assassinated, supposedly by members of his own mob. *Perhaps this is where I'm most at home*, I equivocate again and have an image of myself in a Stetson traveling down a crosstown street at a fast-paced and pigeon-toed shamble toward the setting sun (setting this far east, but not over my wife and daughter yet), my eyes cast down and shoulders forward, hands deep in my empty Levi pockets, a suspect closet-faggot-cowboy occasionally whistled at by queens.

I won't (and can't) refute my heritage, but I doubt that I'll use a firearm again, or, if I do, only in the direst sort of emergency. Which I say to protect my flanks. The bloody, gun-filled fantasies seldom return now, and when they do they're reversed: I'm the one being shot, or shot at, or think I am.

Vocabulary

spoor   track or trail of a wild animal
debacles   sudden, disastrous collapses, ruins
rife   frequent, widespread occurrence
tableaux   striking incidental scenes, graphic descriptions
reciprocity   interchanged, mutual action

Discussion

1. An argument should draw the reader in from the first view of the words across the line. How does this essay capture your interest?
   How do the first four paragraphs (a personal narration) work on you? Do you read with dispassion or with passionate involvement?
   How do you feel about being so drawn up in Woiwode's description? Does the enlisting of *feeling* aid or hinder an argument?
2. Examine closely the paragraphs beginning after the narrative about the deer, paragraphs five, "I don't remember my first gun . . . ," through eight, "I've only owned three firearms in my life as an adult." What is the function of these paragraphs? Why is Woiwode listing his experience with guns?
3. A thesis can be either stated or unstated. Woiwode's is subtle. What is it?
   What is Woiwode getting at here with all his talk of killing and of guns?
4. Does Woiwode argue from principles of human conduct or does he argue from inside, from the personal, from human nature? Testimonial?
   How effective is this kind of argument to you?
5. How is turning the essay away from deer and chickens to humans an unnerving turn in the argument?
   (An interesting tension exists in this essay between the attempt to show violence as unnecessary, and the fascination Woiwode admits he feels for it exemplified in the graphic nature of his words/illustrations.)
   How is Woiwode's thesis a risky one? Does it invite judgment and rebuff?
6. What does Woiwode mean by his final words: "I won't (and can't) refute my heritage. . . "?
   How satisfactory do you find this conclusion?

For Further Discussion

7. This essay is filled with sensory details, with language that appeals to the senses. Examine the phrases below. (And others you find.) How does Woiwode's language work *to show* the reader rather than *to tell* the reader what is meant?

   "at the jittering rim of stutters"

   "bullets embroidering the air"

   "just balanced, justice balanced males."

8. You may wish to compare Woiwode with Kerouac's "The Bullfight," in Chapter Eight.

9. See also "The Saturday Night Special," by Robert Sherrill, for another essay on guns and the myth of the American "cowboy" and "outlaw."

Lawrence Langer
(1929–   )

Lawrence L. Langer was born June 20, 1929, in New York City. He has taught English in the United States and been a Fulbright lecturer for a year in Austria. In addition he has written criticism on various contemporary authors and has had a continuing interest in the "moral and material imagination" of post-Civil War America.

A concern that words can restrict as well as facilitate communication can be found in the following selection reprinted from *The Chronicle of Higher Education*. "It is little wonder that human beings have so much trouble saying what they feel, when they are told that there is a specialized vocabulary for saying what they think."

The Human Use of Language

A friend of mine recently turned in a paper to a course on behavior modification. She had tried to express in simple English some of her reservations about this increasingly popular approach to education. She received it back with the comment: "Please rewrite this in behavioral terms."

It is little wonder that human beings have so much trouble saying what they feel, when they are told that there is a specialized vocabulary for saying what they think. The language of simplicity and spontaneity is forced to retreat behind the barricades of an official prose developed by a few experts who believe that jargon is the most precise means of communication. The results would be comic, if they were not so poisonous; unfortunately, there is an attitude toward the use of language that is impervious to human need and drives some people back into silence when they realize the folly of risking human words on insensitive ears.

The comedy is easy to come by. Glancing through my friend's textbook on behavior modification, I happened on a chapter beginning with the following challenging statement: "Many of the problems encountered by teachers in the daily management of their classes could be resolved if. . . ." Although I was a little wary of the phrase "daily management," I was encouraged to plunge ahead, because as an educator I have always been interested in ideas for improving learning. So I plunged. The entire sentence reads: "Many of the problems encountered by teachers in the daily management of their classes could be resolved if the emission of desirable student behaviors was increased."

Emission? At first I thought it was a misprint for "omission," but the omission of desirable student behaviors (note the plural) hardly seemed an appropriate goal for educators. Then I considered the possibility of metaphor, both erotic and automotive, but these didn't seem to fit, either. A footnote clarified the matter: "'Emission' is a technical term used in behavioral analysis. The verb, 'to emit,' is used specifically with a certain category of behavior called 'operant behavior.' Operant behaviors are modified by their consequences. Operant behaviors correspond closely to the behavior colloquially referred to as voluntary." Voluntary? Is jargon then an attack on freedom of the will?

Of course, this kind of abuse of language goes on all the time—within the academic world, one regrets to say, as well as outside it. Why couldn't the author of this text simply say that we need to motivate students to learn willingly? The more I read such non-human prose, and try to avoid writing it myself, the more I am convinced that we must be in touch with ourselves before we can use words to touch others.

Using language meaningfully requires risk; the sentence I have just quoted takes no risks at all. Much of the discourse that poses as communication in our society is really a decoy to divert our audience (and often ourselves) from that shadowy plateau where our real life hovers on the precipice of expression. How many people, for example, have the courage to walk up to someone they like and actually *say* to them: "I'm very fond of you, you know"?

Such honesty reflects the use of language as revelation, and that sort of revelation, brimming with human possibilities, is risky precisely because it invites judgment and rebuff. Perhaps this is one reason why, especially in academe, we are confronted daily with not much neutral prose: Our students are not yet in touch with themselves; not especially encouraged by us, their instructors, to move in that direction; they are encouraged indeed to expect judgment and hence perhaps rebuff, too, in our evaluation of them. Thus they instinctively retreat behind the anonymity of abstract diction and technical jargon to protect themselves against us—but also, as I have suggested, against themselves.

This problem was crystallized for me recently by an encounter only peripherally related to the issue. As part of my current research, I have been interviewing children of concentration-camp survivors. One girl I have been meeting with says that her mother does not like to talk about the experience, *except with other survivors*. Risk is diminished when we know in advance that our audience shares with us a sympathy for our theme. The nakedness of pain *and* the nakedness of love require gentle responses. So this survivor is reticent, except with fellow victims.

But one day a situation arose which tempted her to the human use of language although she could not be sure, in advance, of the reception her words would receive. We all recognize it. This particular woman, at the age of 40, decided to return to school to get a college degree. Her first assignment in freshman composition was to write a paper on something that was of great importance to her personally. The challenge was immense; the risk was even greater. For the first time in 20 years, she resolved to confront a silence in her life that she obviously needed to rouse to speech.

She was 14 when the Germans invaded Poland. When the roundup of the Jews began a year later, some Christian friends sent their young daughter to "call for her" one day, so that they might hide her. A half hour later, the friends went themselves to pick up her parents, but during that interval, a truck had arrived, loaded aboard the Jewish mother and father—and the daughter never saw them or heard from them again. Their fate we can imagine. The girl herself was eventually arrested, survived several camps, and after the war came to America. She married, had children of her own, and except for occasional reminiscences with fellow survivors, managed to live adequately without diving into her buried personal past. Until one day her instructor in English composition touched a well-insulated nerve, and it began to throb with a painful impulse to express. I present verbatim the result of that impulse, a paper called "People I Have Forgotten":

"Can you forget your own Father and Mother? If so—how or why?

"I thought I did. To mention their names, for me is a great emotional struggle. The brutal force of this reality shakes my whole body and mind, wrecking me into ugly splinters; each crying to be mended anew. So the silence I maintain about their memory is only physical and valid as such but not true. I could never forget my parents, nor do I want to do it. True, I seldom talk about them with my husband or my children. How they looked, who they were, why they perished during the war. The love and sacrifices they have made for me during their lifetime, never get told.

"The cultural heritage to which each generation is entitled to have access to seems to be nonexistant [sic], since I dare not talk about anything relating to my past, my parents.

"This awful, awesome power of non-remembering, this heartbreaking sensation of the conspiracy of silence is my dilemma.

"Often, I have tried to break through my imprisoning wall of irrational silence, but failed: now I hope to be able to do it.

"Until now, I was not able to face up to the loss of my parents, much less talk about them. The smallest reminder of them would set off a chain reaction of results that I could anticipate but never direct. The destructive force of sadness, horror, fright would then become my master. And it was this subconscious knowledge that kept me paralyzed with silence, not a conscious desire to forget my parents.

"My silent wall, my locked shell existed only of real necessity; I needed time.

"I needed time to forget the tragic loss of my loved ones, time to heal my emotional wound so that there shall come a time when I can again remember the people I have forgotten."

The essay is not a confrontation, only a prelude, yet it reveals qualities which are necessary for the human use of language: In trying to reach her audience, the author must touch the deepest part of herself. She risks self-exposure—when we see the instructor's comment, we will realize how great was her risk—and she is prepared for judgment and perhaps even rebuff, although I doubt whether she was prepared for the form they took. This kind of prose, for all its hesitant phraseology, throws down a gauntlet to the reader, a challenge asking him to understand that life is pain as well as plenty, chaos as well as form. Its imagery of locked shells and imprisoning walls hints at a silent world of horror and sadness far less enchanting than the more familiar landscape of love where most of us dwell. Language is a two-edged tool, to pierce the wall which hides that world, or build high abstract barriers to protect us from its threats.

The instructor who graded the paper I have just read preferred walls to honest words. At the bottom of the last page she scrawled a large "D-minus," emphatically surrounded by a circle. Her only comment was: "Your theme is not clear—you should have developed your 1st paragraph. You talk around your subject." At this moment, two realms collide: a universe of unarticulated feeling seeking expression (and the courage and encouragement to express) and a nature made so immune to feeling by heaven-knows-what that she hides behind the tired, tired language of the professional theme-corrector.

Suddenly we realize that reading as well as writing requires risks, and that the metaphor of insulation, so central to the efforts of the Polish woman survivor to re-establish contact with her past, is a metaphor governing the response of readers, too. Some writing, like "the emission of desirable student behaviors," thickens the insulation that already separates the reader from the words that throw darts at his armor of indifference. But even when language unashamedly reveals the feeling that is hidden behind the words, it must contend with a different kind of barrier, the one behind which our instructor lies concealed, unwilling or unable to hear a human voice and return a human echo of her own.

Ironically, the victor in this melancholy failure at communication is the villain of the piece, behavior modification. For the Polish survivor wrote her next theme on an innocuous topic, received a satisfactory grade, and never returned to the subject of her parents. The instructor, who had encountered a problem in the daily management of her class in the form of an essay which she could not respond to in a human way, altered the attitude of her student by responding in a non-human way, thus resolving her problem by increasing the emission of desirable student behavior. The student now knows how vital it is to develop her first paragraph, and how futile it is to reveal her first grief.

Even more, she has learned the danger of talking around her subject: She not only refuses to talk *around* it now, she refuses to talk *about* it. Thus the human use of language leads back to silence—where perhaps it should have remained in the first place.

Vocabulary

jargon   a vocabulary peculiar to a particular trade, profession, or group
reticent   disposed to be silent, not inclined to speak freely
gauntlet   to receive severe criticism, an ordeal
innocuous   not harmful or injurious, harmless

Discussion

1. Langer writes, " . . . we must be in touch with ourselves before we can use words to touch others." How is this the thesis of his essay?
   What kinds of evidence, and how much evidence, does he use to support his thesis? (Look carefully at each paragraph and extract his support.)
2. Langer further says, "using language meaningfully requires risk."
   Again, what kinds of evidence, and how much evidence, does he use to support this statement?
3. What is "that shadowy plateau where our real life hovers on the precipice of expression"?
4. What does Langer mean by "the human use of language" in his last line: "Thus the human use of language leads back to silence—where perhaps it should have remained in the first place"?
   Does he mean what he is saying here?
   If so, what does it indicate about his faith in human nature, his faith in how much "in touch" with themselves most people are?
5. What is the function of the two narratives embedded in this piece: the friend's textbook and the Jewish woman's essay?
   Think not only of how these narratives add or subtract from Langer's argument, but how they work to create or quell a reader's interest in the piece.
6. Is Langer attempting to convince the reader by personal experience alone?
   How is Langer's own argument an illustration of taking risks? In this essay, is Langer standing behind a barrier of data, facts?
7. How does Langer's essay invite "judgment and rebuff"? Do you feel that this helps or hinders his case? Why do you feel about it the way you do?

□ By Logic

Logic has it that all can be known through a system of thought. To argue logically is to honor this system by staying within its parameters. As a tool for organizing and systematizing thoughts, logic has no parallel. Will it illuminate the unknown? Anne Roiphe argues that if men are to become nicer, so then must women in "Confessions of a Female Chauvinist Sow." Andy Rooney delineates the attractions of war to mankind in "An Essay on War." Would it be logical to have war if there was no pleasure in it?

Under each of these arguments, reasoned as they are, you will find the voice of emotion. Roiphe wants to, but cannot quite, believe it is possible for males and females to drop the charges against each other, as evidenced by how much she calls forth the hurts and causes in her confessions.

Andy Rooney's stance is that of the ironist. The irony is that we get the message. Under that news journalist's objectivity is the voice of a concerned man. Can logic ever explain away war?

Anne Roiphe
(1935–   )

Anne Roiphe was born December 25, 1935, in New York and has lived there all her life. She has been a writer since 1966. The primary concern in her several novels is contemporary woman's place in society. The conflict marriage and motherhood brings to personhood is a common theme, though she said in 1979 that it already seemed a "dated problem."

Roiphe says she became a writer because "I felt I could do it better than I could do anything else." Though she feels criticism of an author's work can be "very hurtful, and it can certainly affect self-confidence," she contends that "The only criticism I won't accept is the one that says 'she should stop.' Anything else—I hear it."

Confessions of a Female Chauvinist Sow

I once married a man I thought was totally unlike my father and I imagined a whole new world of freedom emerging. Five years later it was clear even to me—floating face down in a wash of despair—that I had simply chosen a replica of my handsome daddy-true. The updated version spoke English like an angel but—good God!—underneath he was my father exactly: wonderful, but not the right man for me.

Most people I know have at one time or another been fouled up by their childhood experiences. Patterns tend to sink into the unconscious only to reappear, disguised, unseen, like marionette strings, pulling us this way or that. Whatever ails people—keeps them up at night, tossing and turning—also ails movements no matter how historically huge or politically important. The women's movement cannot remake consciousness, or reshape the future, without acknowledging and shedding all the unnecessary and ugly baggage of the past. It's easy enough now to see where men have kept us out of clubs, baseball games, graduate schools; it's easy enough to recognize the hidden directions that limit Sis to cake-baking and Junior to bridge-building; it's now possible for even Miss America herself to identify what *they* have done to us, and, of course, *they* have and *they* did and *they* are. . . . But along the way we also developed our own hidden prejudices, class assumptions and an anti-male humor and collection of expectations that gave us, like all oppressed groups, a secret sense of superiority (co-existing with a poor self-image—it's not news that people can believe two contradictory things at once).

Listen to any group that suffers materially and socially. They have a lexicon with which they tease the enemy: ofay, goy, honky, gringo. "Poor pale devils," said Malcolm X loud enough for us to hear, although blacks had joked about that to each other for years. Behind some of the women's liberation thinking lurk the rumors, the prejudices, the defense systems of generations of oppressed women whispering in the kitchen together, presenting one face to their menfolk and another to their card clubs, their mothers and sisters. All this is natural enough but potentially dangerous in a revolutionary situation in which you hope to create a future that does not mirror the past. The hidden anti-male feelings, a result of the old system, will foul us up if they are allowed to persist.

During my teen years I never left the house on my Saturday night dates without my mother slipping me a few extra dollars—mad money, it was called. I'll explain what it was for the benefit of the new generation in which people just sleep with each other: the fellow was supposed to bring me home, lead me safely through the asphalt jungle, protect me from slithering snakes, rapists and the like. But my mother and I knew young men were apt to drink too much, to slosh down so many rye-and-gingers that some hero might well lead me in front of an oncoming bus, smash his daddy's car into Tiffany's window or, less gallantly, throw up on my new dress. Mad money was for getting home on your own, no matter what form of insanity your date happened to evidence. Mad money was also a wallflower's rope ladder; if the guy you came with suddenly fancied someone else, well, you didn't have to stay there and suffer, you could go home. Boys were fickle and likely to be unkind; my mother and I knew that, as surely as we knew they tried to make you do things in the dark they wouldn't respect you for afterwards, and in fact would spread the word and spoil your rep. Boys liked to be flattered; if you made them feel important they would eat out of your hand. So talk to them about their interests, don't alarm them with displays of intelligence—we all knew that, we groups of girls talking into the wee hours of the night in a kind of easy companionship we thought impossible with boys. Boys were prone to have a good time, get you pregnant, and then pretend they didn't know your name when you came knocking on their door for finances or comfort. In

☐

short, we believed boys were less moral than we were. They appeared to be hypocritical, self-seeking, exploitative, untrustworthy and very likely to be showing off their precious masculinity. I never had a girl friend I thought would be unkind or embarrass me in public. I never expected a girl to lie to me about her marks or sports skill or how good she was in bed. Altogether—without anyone's directly coming out and saying so—I gathered that men were sexy, powerful, very interesting, but not very nice, not very moral, humane and tender, like us. Girls played fairly while men, unfortunately, reserved their honor for the battlefield.

Why are there laws insisting on alimony and child support? Well, everyone knows that men don't have an instinct to protect their young and, given half a chance, with the moon in the right phase, they will run off and disappear. Everyone assumes a mother will not let her child starve, yet it is necessary to legislate that a father must not do so. We are taught to accept the idea that men are less than decent; their charms may be manifold but their characters are riddled with faults. To this day I never blink if I hear that a man has gone to find his fortune in South America, having left his pregnant wife, his blind mother and taken the family car. I still gasp in horror when I hear of a woman leaving her asthmatic infant for a rock group in Taos because I can't seem to avoid the assumption that men are naturally heels and women the ordained carriers of what little is moral in our dubious civilization.

My mother never gave me mad money thinking I would ditch a fellow for some other guy or that I would pass out drunk on the floor. She knew I would be considerate of my companion because, after all, I was more mature than the boys that gathered about. Why was I more mature? Women just are people-oriented; they learn to be empathetic at an early age. Most English students (students interested in humanity, not artifacts) are women. Men and boys—so the myth goes—conceal their feelings and lose interest in anybody else's. Everyone knows that even little boys can tell the difference between one kind of a car and another—proof that their souls are mechanical, their attention directed to the nonhuman.

I remember shivering in the cold vestibule of a famous men's athletic club. Women and girls are not permitted inside the club's door. What are they doing in there, I asked? They're naked, said my mother, they're sweating, jumping up and down a lot, telling each other dirty jokes and bragging about their stock market exploits. Why can't we go in? I asked. Well, my mother told me, they're afraid we'd laugh at them.

The prejudices of childhood are hard to outgrow. I confess that every time my business takes me past that club, I shudder. Images of large bellies resting on massage tables and flaccid penises rising and falling with the Dow Jones average flash through my head. There it is, chauvinism waving its cancerous tentacles from the depths of my psyche.

Minorities automatically feel superior to the oppressor because, after all, they are not hurting anybody. In fact, they feel they are morally better. The old canard that women need love, men need sex— believed too long by both sexes—attributes moral and spiritual superiority to women and makes of men beasts whose urges send them prowling into the night. This false division of good and bad, placing deforming pressures on everyone, doesn't have to contaminate the future. We know that the assumptions we make about each other become a part of the cultural air we breathe and, in fact, become social truths. Women who want equality must be prepared to give it and to believe in it, and in order to do that it is not enough to state that you are as good as any man, but also it must be stated that he is as good as you and both will be humans together. If we want men to share in the care of the family in a new way, we must assume them as capable of consistent loving tenderness as we.

I rummage about and find in my thinking all kinds of anti-male prejudices. Some are just jokes and others I will have a hard time abandoning. First, I share an emotional conviction with many sisters that women given power would not create wars. Intellectually I know that's ridiculous; great queens have waged war before; the likes of Lurleen Wallace, Pat Nixon and Mrs. General Lavelle can be depended upon in the future to guiltlessly condemn to death other people's children in the name of some ideal of their own. Little girls, of course, don't take toy guns out of their hip pockets and say "Pow, pow" to all their neighbors and friends like the average well-adjusted little boy. However, if we gave little girls the six-shooters, we would soon have double the pretend body count.

Aggression is not, as I secretly think, a male-sex-linked characteristic: brutality is masculine only by virtue of opportunity. True, there are 1,000 Jack the Rippers for every Lizzie Borden, but that surely is the result of social forms. Women as a group are indeed more masochistic than men. The practical result of this division is that women seem nicer and kinder, but when the world changes, women will have a fuller opportunity to be just as rotten as men and there will be fewer claims of female moral superiority.

Now that I am entering early middle age, I hear many women complaining of husbands and ex-husbands who are attracted to younger females. This strikes the older woman as unfair, of course. But I remember a time when I thought all boys around my age and grade were creeps and bores. I wanted to go out with an older man: a senior or, miraculously, a college man. I had a certain contempt for my coevals, not realizing that the freshman in college I thought so desirable, was some older girl's creep. Some women never lose that contempt for men of their own age. That isn't fair either and may be one reason why some sensible men of middle years find solace in young women.

I remember coming home from school one day to find my mother's card game dissolved in hysterical laughter. The cards were floating in black rivers of running mascara. What was so funny? A woman named Helen was lying on a couch pretending to be her husband with a cold. She was issuing demands for orange juice, aspirin, suggesting a call to a specialist, complaining of neglect, of fate's cruel finger, of heat, of cold, of sharp pains on the bridge of the nose that might indicate brain involvement. What was so funny? The ladies explained to me that all men behave just like that with colds, they are reduced to temper tantrums by simple nasal congestion, men cannot stand any little physical discomfort—on and on the laughter went.

The point of this vignette is the nature of the laughter—us laughing at them, us feeling superior to them, us ridiculing them behind their backs. If they were doing it to us we'd call it male chauvinist pigness; if we do it to them, it is inescapably female chauvinist sowness and, whatever its roots, it leads to the same isolation. Boys are messy, boys are mean, boys are rough, boys are stupid and have sloppy handwriting. A cacophony of childhood memories rushes through my head, balanced, of course, by all the well-documented feelings of inferiority and envy. But the important thing, the hard thing, is to wipe the slate clean, to start again without the meanness of the past. That's why it's so important that the women's movement not become anti-male and allow its most prejudiced spokesmen total leadership. The much-chewed-over abortion issue illustrates this. The women's-liberation position, insisting on a woman's right to determine her own body's destiny, leads in fanatical extreme to a kind of emotional immaculate conception in which the father is not judged even half-responsible—he has no rights, and no consideration is to be given to his concern for either the woman or the fetus.

Woman, who once was abandoned and disgraced by an unwanted pregnancy, has recently arrived at a new pride of ownership or disposal. She has traveled in a straight line that still excludes her sexual partner from an equal share in the wanted or unwanted pregnancy. A better style of life may develop from an assumption that men are as human as we. Why not ask the child's father if he would like to bring up the child? Why not share decisions, when possible, with the male? If we cut them out, assuming an old-style indifference on their part, we perpetuate the ugly divisiveness that has characterized relations between the sexes so far.

Hard as it is for many of us to believe, women are not really superior to men in intelligence or humanity—they are only equal.

Vocabulary

empathetic understanding so intimate that the feelings, thoughts, and motives of one are readily comprehended by another

□

Discussion

1. How does Roiphe's first paragraph work as a reinforcement of her thesis: "The women's movement cannot remake consciousness, or reshape the future, without acknowledging and shedding all the unnecessary and ugly baggage of the past"?
2. What is "all the unnecessary and ugly baggage of the past"?
3. Paragraph by paragraph outline Roiphe's main points. What are the "hidden anti-male feelings" ... "that will foul us up if they are allowed to persist"?
4. Roiphe says, "In short, we believed boys were less moral than we were." How does her argument refute that belief?
5. Does her accumulated detail castigating males (the hidden anti-male feelings) work somehow against her stated purpose here, to clear the air? Or is it necessary to get these feelings all out in the open before one can go on?
6. In a classroom of men and women, some men are likely to react with suspicion and negativity to Roiphe's thesis. Why is that when she is purportedly on their side?
7. How does narrative, the use of little stories from the past, work in this piece? How many narratives are included here? Examine each one and show how they contribute to Roiphe's argument.
8. Roiphe states: "Women who want equality must be prepared to give it and to believe in it, and in order to do that it is not enough to state that you are as good as any man, but also it must be stated that he is as good as you and both will be humans together."
   Does Roiphe show (or state by examples in her essay) that men are as good as women?
   Why or why not?
9. Why does Roiphe compare the women's movement with "any group that suffers materially and socially"?
10. How logical is Roiphe's argument? Use your outline here. What evidence does she marshal to support her points? Does the evidence fit the thesis? (For instance, what does Roiphe mean by the following: "Aggression is not, as I secretly think, a male-sex-linked characteristic." How does that "as I secretely think" work? Is Roiphe begging the question?)

Andy Rooney
(1919–   )

Andy Rooney was born January 14, 1919, in Albany, New York. Primarily a writer and producer for television, he also has a nationally syndicated newspaper column. But to most Americans he is known for his humorous commentary on the CBS show "60 Minutes."

Rooney, who "started dreaming of being a writer when I was twelve," realizes a television personality can sell books regardless of their merit. But he says, "it is unsatisfactory for a writer to have his words said once and then disappear forever into the air. Seeing our names in print leads to the dream all of us have of immortality. You can't ask for more from something than immortality and money next week."

An Essay on War

We are all inclined to believe that our generation is more civilized than the generations that preceded ours.

From time to time, there is even some substantial evidence that we hold in higher regard such civilized attributes as compassion, pity, remorse, intelligence and a respect for the customs of people different from ourselves.

Why war then?

Some pessimistic historians think the whole society of man runs in cycles and that one of the phases is war.

The optimists, on the other hand, think war is not like an eclipse or a flood or a spell of bad weather. They believe that it is more like a disease for which a cure could be found if the cause were known.

Because war is the ultimate drama of life and death, stories and pictures of it are more interesting than those about peace. This is so true that all of us, and perhaps those of us in television more than most, are often caught up in the action of war to the exclusion of the ideas of it.

If it is true, as we would like to think it is, that our age is more civilized than ages past, we must all agree that it's very strange that in the twentieth century, our century, we have killed more than 70 million of our fellowmen on purpose, at war.

It is very, very strange that since 1900 more men have killed more other men than in any other seventy years in history.

Probably the reason we are able to do both—that is, believe on one hand that we are more civilized and on the other hand wage war to kill—is that killing is not so personal an affair in war as it once was. The enemy is invisible. One man doesn't look another in the eye and run him through with a sword. The enemy, dead or alive, is largely unseen. He is killed by remote control: a loud noise, a distant puff of smoke and then . . . silence.

The pictures of the victim's wife and children, which he carries in his breast pocket, are destroyed with him. He is not heard to cry out. The question of compassion or pity or remorse does not enter into it. The enemy is not a man, he is a statistic. It is true, too, that more people are being killed at war now than previously because we're better at doing it than we used to be. One man with one modern weapon can kill thousands.

The world's record for killing was set on August 6, 1945, at Hiroshima.

There have been times in history when one tribe attacked another for no good reason except to take its land or its goods, or simply to prove its superiority. But wars are no longer fought without some ethical pretension. People want to believe they're on God's side and he on theirs. One nation does not usually attack another anymore without first having propagandized itself into believing that its motives are honorable. The Japanese didn't attack Pearl Harbor with any sense in their own minds that they were scheming, deceitful or infamous.

Soldiers often look for help to their religion. It was in a frenzy of religious fervor that Japanese Kamikaze pilots died in World War II with eternal glory on their minds. Even a just God, though, listening to victory prayers from both sides, would be understandably confused.

It has always seemed wrong to the people who disapprove of war that we have spent much of our time and half of our money on anti-creation. The military budget of any major power consumes half of everything and leaves us half to live on.

It's interesting that the effective weapons of war aren't developed by warriors, but by engineers. In World War I they made a machine that would throw five hundred pounds of steel fifty miles. They compounded an ingeniously compressed package of liquid fire that would burn people like bugs. The engineers are not concerned with death, though.

The scientist who splits an atom and revolutionizes warfare isn't concerned with warfare; his mind is on that fleck of matter.

And so we have a machine gun a man can carry that will spit out two hundred bullets a minute, each capable of ripping a man in two, although the man who invented it, in all probability, loves his wife, children, dogs, and probably wouldn't kill a butterfly.

Plato said that there never was a good war or a bad peace, and there have always been people who believed this was true. The trouble with the theory is that the absence of war isn't necessarily peace. Maybe the worst thing Adolf Hitler did was to provide evidence for generations to come that any peace is *not* better than any war. Buchenwald wasn't war.

The generation that had found Adolf Hitler hard to believe, was embarrassed at how reluctant it had been to go help the people of the world who needed help so desperately. That generation determined not to be slow with help again and as a result may have been too quick. A younger generation doesn't understand why the United States went into Vietnam. Having gotten into the war, all it wanted to consider itself a winner was to get out. Unable to make things the way it wanted them, but unwilling to accept defeat, it merely changed what is wanted.

> DWIGHT EISENHOWER, 1962: "I think it's only defense, self-defense, that's all it is." JOHN KENNEDY, 1963: "In the final analysis it's their war. They're the ones that have to win it or lose it." LYNDON JOHNSON, 1969: "But America has not changed her essential position. And that purpose is peaceful settlement." RICHARD NIXON, 1974: "But the time has come to end this war."

☐

There are a lot of reasons for the confusion about a war. One of them is that the statesmen who make the decisions never have to fight one themselves. Even the generals don't fight the battles.

Professional soldiers often say they hate war, but they would be less than human if they did not, just once, want to play the game they spent a lifetime practicing. How could you go to West Point for four years and not be curious about whether you'd be any good in a war?

Even in peacetime, nations keep huge armies. The trouble with any peacetime all-volunteer army is that the enlisted men in one are often no smarter than the officers. During a war when the general population takes up arms, the character of an army changes and for the better.

In the twentieth century there is open rebellion between the people who decide about whether to fight or not and some of the young men being asked to do the fighting. It hasn't always been that way. Through the years, even the reluctant draftees have usually gone to battle with some enthusiasm for it. Partially the enthusiasm comes from the natural drama of war and the excitement of leaving home on a crusade. It's a trip to somewhere else, and with the excitement inherent in an uncertain return. It is a great adventure, with the possibility of being killed the one drawback to an otherwise exciting time in life.

There have been just and unjust wars throughout history but there is very little difference in the manner in which people have been propagandized to believe in them. Patriotism, sometimes no more knowing or sophisticated than pride in a high school football team, is the strongest motivator. With flags enough and martial music enough, anyone's blood begins to boil.

Patriotic has always been considered one of the good things to be in any nation on earth, but it's a question whether patriotism has been a force for good or evil in the world.

Once the young men of a country get into a battle, most of them are neither heroes nor cowards. They're swept up in a movement that includes them and they go where they're told to go, do what they're told to do. It isn't long before they're tired and afraid and they want to go home.

True bravery is always highly regarded because we recognize that someone has done something that is good for all of us, certainly at the risk and possibly at the expense of his own life. But in war, the mantle of virtue is pressed on every soldier's head as though they were all heroes. This is partly because everyone else is grateful to him and wants to encourage him to keep at it. All soldiers who come home alive are heaped with the praise that belongs to very few of them . . . and often to the dead they left behind.

In part, at least, this accounts for why so many men like being ex-soldiers. Once the war and the fighting are done with and they are safe at home, it matters not that they may have served in the 110th emergency shoe-repair battalion. In their own eyes, they are heroes of the front lines.

Even in retrospect, though, a nation has always felt an obligation to honor its warriors. The face of the earth is covered with statuary designed for this purpose which is so bad in many cases that were it not in honor of the dead, it would evoke not tears but laughter.

During and since World War II, the United States alone has bestowed ten million medals and ribbons of honor on its soldiers, many of them for acts calling for as little courage as living a year in Paris.

Bravery is as rare in war as it is in peace. It isn't just a matter of facing danger from which you would prefer to run. If a man faces danger because the alternative to doing that is worse or because he doesn't understand the danger, this may make him a good soldier but it is something other than bravery. Stupidity faces danger easier than intelligence.

The average bright young man who is drafted hates the whole business because an army always tries to eliminate the individual differences in men. The theory is that a uniformity of action is necessary to achieve a common goal. That's good for an army but terrible for an individual who likes himself the way he is.

Some men, of course, like the order imposed on them. They like the freedom from making hard decisions that mindless submission to authority gives them.

There is always more precision on the drill field back home than there is on the battlefield. Uniformity of action becomes less precise as an army approaches the front. At the front it usually disappears altogether. It is not always, or even usually, the best marchers who make the best fighters.

Everyone talks as though there was nothing good about war, but there are some good things and it's easy to see why so many people are attracted by it. If there were no good things about war, the chances are we would find a way not to have another.

A nation at war feels a unity it senses at no other time. Even the people not fighting are bound together. There is a sense of common cause missing in peacetime. Accomplishments are greater, change is quicker . . . and if progress is motion, there is more of it in wartime. A nation at peace is busy gratifying itself, overeating, overdressing, lying in the sun until it's time to eat and drink again.

If war brings out the worst in people as it has been assumed it does, it also brings out the very best. It's the ultimate competition. Most of us live our lives at half speed, using only as much of our ability as is absolutely necessary to make out. But at war if a man is actually fighting it, he uses all his brain and all his muscle. He explores depths of his emotions he didn't know were down there and might never have occasion to use again in his lifetime. He lives at full speed, finding strength he didn't know he had accomplishing things he didn't know he could do.

The best thing about war is hard to describe, is never talked about. Most of us get a warm sense of fellow feeling when we act in close and successful relationship with others, and maybe that happens more in war than any other time. There is a lonesomeness about life that no one who has experienced it likes to talk about, and acting together for a common cause, men often come closest to what they ought to be at their very best.

It is paradoxical but true that in war when man is closest to death, he is also closest to complete fulfillment and farthest from loneliness. He is dependent, dependable, loved and loving.

And there is another thing about war. If there is love in us, there is hate too and it's apparent that hate springs from the same well as love and just as quickly. No one is proud of it but hate is not an unpleasant emotion and there is no time other than wartime when we are encouraged to indulge ourselves in an orgy of hate.

The worst of war is hell but there isn't much of the worst of it and not many soldiers experience even that much.

A soldier at war doesn't feel the need to answer any questions about it. He is exhausted by the battle.

He is busy destroying and it does not occur to him that he will have to help rebuild the world he is pulling down.

He often mistakes the exultation of victory for a taste of what things will be like for the rest of his life.

And they are only like that for a very short time.

Discussion

1. Follow the line of Rooney's logic from first paragraph to last. How does he move from a discussion about being "civilized" to "the exultation of victory"?
2. Outline Rooney's main points from paragraph to paragraph. (You will have to do this for this one; the essay has an organic form.)
3. Rooney terms war "the ultimate drama of life and death." How does this add to its attractiveness?
   (What other things might be termed "the ultimate drama of life and death? For instance, a hospital comes to mind, but has it the scale of a war?)
4. Rooney writes: "There are a lot of reasons for confusion about a war." What are they? Find those that Rooney identifies.
5. What are some of the "good things" about war that Rooney enumerates? Do you agree or disagree?
   (See also Michael Herr's "Breathing In" in Chapter Four for another view on war.)
6. How does Rooney's essay end? On an optimistic or a pessimistic note? Indif-

ferent? Objective? What would you say, finally, is Rooney's point of view about war?

7. What is Rooney's thesis in this essay? Can you state it in one sentence? (Look carefully over your outline of his main points before you attempt this. It is not a simple proposition to make a thesis statement from an essay such as this. What is Rooney trying to persuade us of here?)

□ By Ethics

If a square turned us in, X said, we didn't do anything about it, because they don't know the code or anything. But if one of us did it, we showed no mercy. Such was the ethic of the onetime outlaw X who happens to be a friend of mine. He was talking about honor among thieves.

In "Crime and Criminals" Clarence Darrow explains to prisoners the inevitability of crime, given a planet where an ethic allows the rich to take it all.

"As long as there is poverty there will be gods," say Will and Ariel Durant in "Religion and History." They trace the historical reasons for religion and find in it a consciousness that has "been indispensable in every land and age" in the civilizing of mankind. This is a generous admission from two historians who considered themselves skeptics. They said, "a natural ethic is too weak to withstand the savagery that lies under civilization and emerges in our dreams, crimes and wars." Loren Eiseley, in "The Last Magician," dives inside to find God "couched in the body of man." His is the ethic of transcendance, "a turning toward some inner light." To believe in yourself despite "human inadequacy and weakness" is, perhaps, the most difficult ethic of all.

Loren Eiseley
(1907–1977)

Loren Eiseley was born in 1907 in Lincoln, Nebraska. Like Jacob Bronowski, he was a scientist, in this case an anthropologist, who was also a poet. A 1933 graduate of the University of Nebraska, he was one of the first editors of *Prairie Schooner,* a literary journal that started there.

But it is for his writing in the area of science that he is most widely known. Beginning with *The Immense Journey* in 1957, Eiseley established his gift of writing about science with beauty and clarity. He was most interested in what scientific inquiry revealed about ourselves, and about how we should move into the future. "The most enormous extension of vision of which life is capable," he once said, "is the projection of itself into other lives. This is the lonely, magnificent power of humanity."

The Last Magician

There is [an] aspect of man's mental life which demands the utmost attention, even though it is manifest in different degrees in different times and places and among different individuals; this is the desire for transcendence—a peculiarly human trait. Philosophers and students of comparative religion have sometimes remarked that we need to seek for the origins of the human interest in the cosmos, "a cosmic sense" unique to man. However this sense may have evolved, it has made men of the greatest imaginative power conscious of human inadequacy and weakness. There may thus emerge the desire for "rebirth" expressed in many religions. Stimulated by his own uncompleted nature, man seeks a greater role, restructured beyond nature like so much in his aspiring mind. Thus we find the Zen Buddhist, in the words of the scholar Suzuki, intent upon creating "a realm of Emptiness or Void where no conceptualism prevails" and where "rootless trees grow." The Buddhist, in a true paradox, would empty the mind in order that the mind may adequately receive or experience the world. No other creature than man would question his way of thought or feel the need of sweeping the mind's cloudy mirror in order to unveil its insight.

Man's life, in other words, is felt to be unreal and sterile. Perhaps a creature of so much ingenuity and deep memory is almost bound to grow alienated from his world, his fellows, and the objects around him. He suffers from a nostalgia for which there is no remedy upon earth except as it is to be found in the enlightenment of the spirit—some ability to have a perceptive rather than an exploitive relationship with his fellow creatures.

After man had exercised his talents in the building of the first neolithic cities and empires, a period mostly marked by architectural and military triumphs, an intellectual transformation descended upon the known world, a time of questioning. This era is fundamental to an understanding of man, and has engaged the attention of such modern scholars as Karl Jaspers and Lewis Mumford. The period culminates in the first millennium before Christ. Here in the great centers of civilization, whether Chinese, Indian, Judaic, or Greek, man had begun to abandon inherited gods and purely tribal loyalties in favor of an inner world in which the pursuit of earthly power was ignored. The destiny of the human soul became of more significance than the looting of a province. Though these dreams are expressed in different ways by such divergent men as Christ, Buddha, Lao-tse, and Confucius, they share many things in common, not the least of which is respect for the dignity of the common man.

The period of the creators of transcendent values—the axial think-ers, as they are called—created the world of universal thought that is our most precious human heritage. One can see it emerging in the mind of Christ as chronicled by Saint John. Here the personalized tribal deity of earlier Judaic thought becomes transformed into a world deity. Christ, the Good Shepherd, says: "Other sheep I have, which are not of this fold: them also I must bring, and they shall hear my voice; and there shall be one fold and one shepherd. . . . My sheep hear my voice . . . and they follow me."

These words spoken by the carpenter from Nazareth are those of a world changer. They passed boundaries, whispered in the ears of gal-lery slaves: "One fold, one shepherd. Follow me." These are no longer the wrathful words of a jealous city ravager, a local potentate god. They mark instead, in the high cultures, the rise of a new human image, a rejection of purely material goals, a turning toward some inner light. As these ideas diffused, they were, of course, subject to the wear of time and superstition, but the human ethic of the individual prophets and thinkers has outlasted empires.

Such men speak to us across the ages. In their various approaches to life they encouraged the common man toward charity and humility. They did not come with weapons; instead they bespoke man's purpose to subdue his animal nature and in so doing to create a radiantly new and noble being. These were the dreams of the first millennium B.C. Tormented man, arising, falling, still pursues those dreams today.

Earlier I mentioned Plato's path into the light that blinds the man who has lived in darkness. Out of just such darkness arose the first humanizing influence. It was genuinely the time of the good shepherds. No one can clearly determine why these prophets had such profound effects within the time at their disposal. Nor can we solve the mystery of how they came into existence across the Euro-Asiatic land mass in diverse cultures at roughly the same time. As Jaspers observes, he who can solve this mystery will know something common to all mankind.

In this difficult era we are still living in the inspirational light of a tremendous historical event, one that opened up the human soul. But if the neophytes were blinded by the light, so, perhaps, the prophets were in turn confused by the human darkness they encountered. The scientific age replaced them. The common man, after brief days of enlightenment, turned once again to escape, propelled outward first by the world voyagers, and then by the atom breakers. We have called up vast powers which loom menacingly over us. They await our bidding, and we turn to outer space as though the solitary answer to the unspo-ken query must be flight, such flight as ancient man engaged in across ice ages and vanished game trails—the flight from nowhere.

The good shepherds meantime have all faded into the darkness of history. One of them, however, left a cryptic message: "My doctrine is not mine but his that sent me." Even in the time of unbelieving this carries a warning. For He that sent may still be couched in the body of man awaiting the end of the story.

VOCABULARY

transcendence above human limitation, material experience, and the universe; (passing beyond)

conceptualism the doctrine that universals, or abstract concepts, exist only in the mind and have no external reality

nostalgia a longing for things that are no longer present

axial a hub, an imaginary line around which an object may be conceived to rotate

potentate one who has the power to rule over others

neophytes recent converts

cryptic hidden, secret, mysterious meaning

Discussion

1. What does Eiseley mean by the "desire for transcendence"? What does this desire lead humans to do?
2. What does Eiseley imply by the following: "He suffers from a nostalgia for which there is no remedy upon earth except as it is to be found in the enlightenment of the spirit—some ability to have a perceptive rather than an exploitive relationship with his fellow creatures." What is this "nostalgia" for which there is no cure?

   What is a "perceptive" relationship in Eiseley's terms? Perceptive of what? (Examine Eiseley's meaning here at all levels. This is the crux of his argument.)
3. What is "the inner light" Eiseley speaks of? The "inner world"?
4. Outline Eiseley's argument from the first paragraph to the last, paragraph by paragraph. List the main points and the main supporting evidence. What is Eiseley saying here?

   What ethic (rules of moral conduct) is he arguing for?
5. What is the meaning of Eiseley's last lines: "Even in the time of unbelieving this carries a warning. For He that sent may still be couched in the body of man awaiting the end of the story."

   According to Eiseley, what is the nature of man? (Use your outline to discuss this. Essays in this section are difficult because of the maturity of thought and vision. To argue from an ethic, a code of human morality, is a high-order thing. What is Eiseley's vision of man? What is he saying here? Do you agree or disagree? Why?)

   See also Huston Smith's 'The Story of Lao Tzu," in Chapter 5. For the sake of rebuttal, see Clarence Darrow's "Why I Am an Agnostic," also in Chapter 5.

These essays would make a wonderful unit of discussion on writers and their views of humankind.

Will and Ariel Durant
(1885–1981)
(1898–1981)

William Durant was born November 5, 1885, in North Adams, Massachusetts. Ariel was born Ida Kaufman in Proskurov, Russia, May 10, 1898. Together they collaborated on the eleven-volume series *The Story of Civilization,* in which they strove to interrelate the developments of art, literature, science, politics, religion, and economics of the past 6,000 years. Their tenth volume, *Rousseau and Revolution,* won the 1968 Pulitzer Prize for general nonfiction.

The purpose of what Will called their "absurd enterprise" was, he said, "to tell as much as I can, in as little space as I can, of the contribution genius and labor have made to the cultural heritage of mankind." Together they would work fourteen-hour days, seven days a week, Will doing the writing. The final volume was published in 1975. Will died in November 1981, less than two weeks after Ariel's death.

Religion and History

Even the skeptical historian develops a humble respect for religion, since he sees it functioning, and seemingly indispensable, in every land and age. To the unhappy, the suffering, the bereaved, the old, it has brought supernatural comforts valued by millions of souls as more precious than any natural aid. It has helped parents and teachers to discipline the young. It has conferred meaning and dignity upon the lowliest existence, and through its sacraments has made for stability for transforming human covenants into solemn relationships with God. It has kept the poor (said Napoleon) from murdering the rich. For since the natural inequality of men dooms many of us to poverty or defeat, some supernatural hope may be the sole alternative to despair. Destroy that hope, and class war is intensified. Heaven and utopia are buckets in a well: when one goes down the other goes up; when religion declines Communism grows.

Religion does not seem at first to have any connection with morals. Apparently (for we are merely guessing, or echoing Petronius, who echoed Lucretius) "it was fear that first made the gods"—fear of hidden forces in the earth, rivers, oceans, trees, winds, and sky. Religion became the propitiatory worship of these forces through offerings, sacrifice, incantation, and prayer. Only when priests used these fears and rituals to support morality and law did religion become a force vital and rival to the state. It told the people that the local code of morals and laws had been dictated by the gods. It pictured the god Thoth giving laws to Menes for Egypt, the god Shamash giving Hammurabi a code for Babylonia, Yahveh giving the Ten Commandments and 613 precepts to Moses for the Jews, and the divine nymph Egeria giving Numa Pompilius laws for Rome. Pagan cults and Christian creeds proclaimed that earthly rulers were appointed and protected by the gods. Gratefully nearly every state shared its lands and revenues with the priests.

Some recusants have doubted that religion ever promoted morality, since immorality has flourished even in the ages of religious domination. Certainly sensuality, drunkenness, coarseness, greed, dishonesty, robbery, and violence existed in the Middle Ages, but probably the moral disorder born of half a millennium of barbarian invasion, war, economic devastation, and political disorganization would have been much worse without the moderating effect of the Christian ethic, priestly exhortations, saintly exemplars, and a calming, unifying ritual. The Roman Catholic Church labored to reduce slavery, family feuds, and national strife, to extend the intervals of truce and peace, and to replace trial by combat or ordeal with the judgments of established courts. It softened the penalties exacted by Roman or barbarian law, and vastly expanded the scope and organization of charity.

Though the Church served the state, it claimed to stand above all states, as morality should stand above power. It taught men that patriotism unchecked by a higher loyalty can be a tool of greed and crime. Over all the competing governments of Christendom it promulgated one moral law. Claiming divine origin and spiritual hegemony, the Church offered itself as an international court to which all rulers were to be morally responsible. The Emperor Henry IV recognized this claim by submitting to Pope Gregory VII at Canossa (1077); and a century later Innocent III raised the authority and prestige of the papacy to a height where it seemed that Gregory's ideal of a moral superstate had come to fulfillment.

The majestic dream broke under the attacks of nationalism, skepticism, and human frailty. The Church was manned with men, who often proved biased, venal, or extortionate. France grew in wealth and power, and made the papacy her political tool. Kings became strong enough to compel a pope to dissolve that Jesuit order which had so devotedly supported the popes. The Church stooped to fraud, as with pious legends, bogus relics, and dubious miracles; for centuries it profited from a mythical "Donation of Constantine" that had allegedly bequeathed Western Europe to Pope Sylvester I (r. 314–35), and from "False Decretals" (c. 842) that forged a series of documents to give a sacred antiquity to papal omnipotence. More and more the hierarchy spent its energies in promoting orthodoxy rather than morality, and the Inquisition almost fatally disgraced the Church. Even while preaching peace the Church fomented religious wars in sixteenth-century France and the Thirty Years' War in seventeenth-century Germany. It played only a modest part in the outstanding advance of modern morality—the abolition of slavery. It allowed the philosophers to take the lead in the humanitarian movements that have alleviated the evils of our time.

History has justified the Church in the belief that the masses of mankind desire a religion rich in miracle, mystery, and myth. Some minor modifications have been allowed in ritual, in ecclesiastical costume, and in espiscopal authority; but the Church dares not alter the doctrines that reason smiles at, for such changes would offend and disillusion the millions whose hopes have been tied to inspiring and consolatory imaginations. No reconciliation is possible between religion and philosophy except through the philosophers' recognition that they have found no substitute for the moral function of the Church, and the ecclesiastical recognition of religious and intellectual freedom.

Does history support a belief in God? If by God we mean not the creative vitality of nature but a supreme being intelligent and benevolent, the answer must be a reluctant negative. Like other departments of biology, history remains at bottom a natural selection of the fittest individuals and groups in a struggle wherein goodness receives no favors, misfortunes abound, and the final test is the ability to survive. Add to the crimes, wars, and cruelties of man the earthquakes, storms, tornadoes, pestilences, tidal waves, and other "acts of God" that periodically desolate human and animal life, and the total evidence suggests either a blind or impartial fatality, with incidental and apparently haphazard scenes to which we subjectively ascribe order, splendor, beauty, or sublimity. If history supports any theology this would be a dualism like the Zoroastrian or Manichaean; a good spirit and an evil spirit battling for control of the universe and men's souls. These faiths and Christianity (which is essentially Manichaean) assured their followers that the good spirit would win in the end; but of this consummation history offers no guarantee. Nature and history do not agree with our conceptions of good and bad; they define good as that which survives, and bad as that which goes under; and the universe has no prejudice in favor of Christ as against Genghis Khan.

The growing awareness of man's miniscule place in the cosmos has furthered the impairment of religious belief. In Christendom we may date the beginning of the decline from Copernicus (1543). The process was slow, but by 1611 John Donne was mourning that the earth had become a mere "suburb" in the world, and that "new philosophy calls all in doubt"; and Francis Bacon, while tipping his hat occasionally to the bishops, was proclaiming science as the religion of modern emancipated man. In that generation began the "death of God" as an external deity.

So great an effect required many causes beside the spread of science and historical knowledge. First, the Protestant Reformation, which originally defended private judgment. Then the multitude of

Protestant sects and conflicting theologies, each appealing to both Scriptures and reason. Then the higher criticism of the Bible, displaying that marvelous library as the imperfect work of fallible men. Then the deistic movement in England, reducing religion to a vague belief in a God hardly distinguishable from nature. Then the growing acquaintance with other religions, whose myths, many of them pre-Christian, were distressingly similar to the supposedly factual bases of one's inherited creed. Then the Protestant exposure of Catholic miracles, the deistic exposure of Biblical miracles, the general exposure of frauds, inquisitions, and massacres in the history of religion. Then the replacement of agriculture—which had stirred men to faith by the annual rebirth of life and the mystery of growth—with industry, humming daily a litany of machines, and suggesting a world machine. And meanwhile the bold advance of skeptical scholarship, as in Bayle, and of pantheistic philosophy, as in Spinoza; the massive attack of the French Enlightenment upon Christianity; the revolt of Paris against the Church during the French Revolution. And, in our own time, the indiscriminate slaughter of civilian populations in modern war. Finally, the awesome triumph of scientific technology, promising man omnipotence and destruction, and challenging the divine command of the skies.

In one way Christianity lent a hand against itself by developing in many Christians a moral sense that could no longer stomach the vengeful God of the traditional theology. The idea of hell disappeared from educated thought, even from pulpit homilies. Presbyterians became ashamed of the Westminster Confession, which had pledged them to belief in a God who had created billions of men and women despite his foreknowledge that, regardless of their virtues and crimes, they were predestined to everlasting hell. Educated Christians visiting the Sistine Chapel were shocked by Michelangelo's picture of Christ hurling offenders pell-mell into an inferno whose fires were never to be extinguished; was this the "gentle Jesus, meek and mild," who had inspired our youth? Just as the moral development of the Hellenes had weakened their belief in the quarrelsome and adulterous deities of Olympus ("A certain proportion of mankind," wrote Plato, "do not believe at all in the existence of the gods"), so the development of the Christian ethic slowly eroded Christian theology. Christ destroyed Jehovah.

The replacement of Christian with secular institutions is the culminating and critical result of the Industrial Revolution. That states should attempt to dispense with theological supports is one of the many crucial experiments that bewilder our brains and unsettle our ways today. Laws which were once presented as the decrees of a god-given king are now frankly the confused commands of fallible men. Education, which was the sacred province of god-inspired priests, becomes the task of men and women shorn of theological robes and awe, and relying on reason and persuasion to civilize young rebels who fear only the policeman and may never learn to reason at all. Colleges once allied to churches have been captured by businessmen and scientists. The propaganda of patriotism, capitalism or Communism succeeds to the inculcation of a supernatural creed and moral code. Holydays give way to holidays. Theaters are full even on Sundays, churches are half empty. In Anglo-Saxon families religion has become a social observance and protective coloration; in American Catholic families it flourishes; in upper- and middle-class France and Italy religion is "a secondary sexual characteristic of the female." A thousand signs proclaim that Christianity is undergoing the same decline that fell upon the old Greek religion after the coming of the Sophists and the Greek Enlightenment.

Catholicism survives because it appeals to imagination, hope, and the senses: because its mythology consoles and brightens the lives of the poor; and because the commanded fertility of the faithful slowly regains the lands lost to the Reformation. Catholicism has sacrificed the adherence of the intellectual community, and suffers increasing defections through contact with secular education and literature; but it wins converts from souls wearied with the uncertainty of reason, and from others hopeful that the Church will stem internal disorder and the Communist wave.

If another great war should devastate Western civilization, the resultant destruction of cities, the dissemination of poverty, and the disgrace of science may leave the Church, as in A.D. 476, the sole hope and guide of those who survive the cataclysm.

One lesson of history is that religion has many lives and a habit of resurrection. How often in the past have God and religion died and been reborn! Ikhnaton used all the powers of a pharaoh to destroy the religion of Amon; within a year of Ikhnaton's death the religion of Amon was restored. Atheism ran wild in the India of Buddha's youth, and Buddha himself founded a religion without a god; after his death Buddhism developed a complex theology including gods, saints, and hell. Philosophy, science, and education depopulated the Hellenic pantheon, but the vacuum attracted a dozen Oriental faiths rich in resurrection myths. In 1793 Hebert and Chaumette, wrongly interpreting Voltaire, established in Paris the atheistic worship of the Goddess of Reason; a year later Robespierre, fearing chaos and inspired by Rousseau, set up the worship of the Supreme Being; in 1801 Napoleon, versed in History, signed a concordat with Pius VII, restoring the Catholic Church in France. The irreligion of eighteenth-century England disappeared under the Victorian compromise with Christianity: the state agreed to support the Anglican Church, and the educated class would muffle their skepticism, on the tacit understanding that the Church would accept subordination to the state, and the parson would humbly serve the squire. In America the rationalism of the Founding Fathers gave place to a religious revival in the nineteenth century.

Puritanism and paganism—the repression and the expression of the senses and desires—alternate in mutual reaction in history. Generally religion and puritanism prevail in periods when the laws are feeble and morals must bear the burden of maintaining social order; skepticism and paganism (other factors being equal) progress as the rising power of law and government permits the decline of the church, the family, and morality without basically endangering the stability of the state. In our time the strength of the state has united with the several forces listed above to relax faith and morals, and to allow paganism to resume its natural sway. Probably our excesses will bring another reaction; moral disorder may generate a religious revival; atheists may again (as in France after the debacle of 1870) send their children to Catholic schools to give them the discipline of religious belief. Hear the appeal of the agnostic Renan in 1866:

> Let us enjoy the liberty of the sons of God, but let us take care lest we become accomplices in the diminution of virtue which would menace society if Christianity were to grow weak. What should we do without it? . . . If Rationalism wishes to govern the world without regard to the religious needs of the soul, the experience of the French Revolution is there to teach us the consequences of such a blunder.

Does history warrant Renan's conclusions that religion is necessary to morality—that a natural ethic is too weak to withstand the savagery that lurks under civilization and emerges in our dreams, crimes, and wars? Joseph de Maistre answered: "I do not know what the heart of a rascal may be; I know what is in the heart of an honest man; it is horrible." There is no significant example in history, before our time, of a society successfully maintaining moral life without the aid of religion. France, the United States, and some other nations have divorced their governments from all churches, but they have had the help of religion in keeping social order. Only a few Communist states have not merely dissociated themselves from religion but have repudiated its aid; and perhaps the apparent and provisional success of this experiment in Russia owes much to the temporary acceptance of Communism as the religion (or, as the skeptics would say, the opium) of the people, replacing the church as the vendor of comfort and hope. If the socialist regime should fail in its efforts to destroy relative poverty among the masses, this new religion may lose its fervor and efficacy, and the state may wink at the restoration of supernatural beliefs as an aid in quieting discontent. "As long as there is poverty there will be gods."

Vocabulary

covenants   a compact; God's promises to man as recorded in the Old and New
Testaments
propitiatory   offered, a conciliatory offering

recusants dissenters, nonconformists
hegemony predominance, a preponderant influence of one state over others
venal corruptible, susceptible to betraying honor for a price
extortionate one who uses official powers to obtain money or patronage, or something to which one is not entitled
inculcation to instill or teach by forceful urging

Allusions/References

Petronius Roman courtier and wit of the first century A.D.; author of the *Satyricon*, a novel that exists only in fragments
Lucretius Roman poet and philosopher (96?–55 B.C.)
Zoroastrian a religious system, founded in Persia, in which is seen the universal struggle between the forces of light and darkness
Manichaean the philosophy of Zoroastrian, taught by the Persian prophet Manes about the third century; any dualistic philosophy
deistic movement a movement based on the belief of reason
Bayle French philosopher and critic (1647–1706)
Spinoza Dutch philosopher and theologian (1632–1677)
Sophists a pre-Socratic school of philosophy in ancient Greece
Ikhnaton (Akhenaton) king of Egypt and religious reformer; husband of Nefertiti (1375–1358 B.C.)
Amon (Amen) the god of life and reproduction, represented as a man with a ram's head
Hellenic pantheon Greek gods

Discussion

1. One glance at the allusions in this piece by the Durants will indicate to you that you are in the presence of scholarly writing. Do not despair if many of the references are unfamiliar to you. Read the first time for meaning; the second reading should allow you to look up each of the unfamiliar referents. (See Allusions/References)
2. Who are Thoth and Menes, Shamash and Hammurabi, Yahveh and Moses, Egeria and Numa Pompilius? A good dictionary can answer this question for you.
3. Let us examine two statements from the text. The first is the Durants' first sentence: "Even the skeptical historian develops a humble respect for religion, since he sees it functioning, and seemingly indispensable, in every land and age." The second comes later, in the last paragraph of the essay: "Does history warrant Renan's conclusions that religion is necessary to morality—that a natural ethic is too weak to withstand the savagery that lurks under civilization and emerges in our dreams, crimes, and wars"?
   How is the Durant essay a working out of these two ideas?
4. How does the essay progress, paragraph by paragraph, in an exploration of the function of religion in history?
5. How do you respond to the statement by Joseph de Maistre: "I do not know

what the heart of a rascal may be; I know what is in the heart of an honest man; it is horrible"?

Would you agree or disagree? (Search your own heart for the answer here.) What does this indicate about the hope of a "natural" ethic as opposed to a "religious" ethic?

6. What does the last line of the essay mean: "As long as there is poverty there will be gods"?

For Further Discussion

7. Compare and contrast Loren Eiseley's "The Last Magician" with this essay. What evidence does Eiseley use to support his thesis? What is the nature of the Durant evidence? How does the evidence used by each, the "vision" of these authors, determine their conclusions?

   What is the difference between looking outside and looking inside? Does one view necessarily create a skeptic and the other view a believer?

Clarence Darrow
(1857–1938)

Clarence Darrow was born April 18, 1857 in Ferndale, Ohio. Darrow is probably one of the most well-known attorneys of this century. His controversial cases included defenses of Socialist Eugene V. Debs, murderers Leopold and Loeb, and a schoolteacher in the Scopes "Monkey Trial."

In taking cases that attracted public attention, Darrow hoped to reform unjust and inhumane laws and educate people on issues he felt strongly about. First as a labor lawyer and later in criminal law he adopted the causes of the underdog. He believed criminals were victims of environment who were further victimized by the law. "Nothing is so cruel as the belief in sin. Given the cause, the effect cannot be avoided."

(See also "Why I Am an Agnostic," Chapter 5.)

Crime and Criminals

If I looked at jails and crimes and prisoners in the way the ordinary person does, I should not speak on this subject to you. The reason I talk to you on the question of crime, its cause and cure, is because I really do not in the least believe in crime. There is no such thing as a crime as the word is generally understood. I do not believe there is any sort of distinction between the real moral condition of the people in and out of jail. One is just as good as the other. The people here can no more help being here than the people outside can avoid being outside. I do not believe that people are in jail because they deserve to be. They are in jail simply because they can not avoid it on account of circumstances which are entirely beyond their control and for which they are in no way responsible.

I suppose a great many people on the outside would say I was doing you harm if they should hear what I say to you this afternoon, but you can not be hurt a great deal anyway, so it will not matter. Good people outside would say that I was really teaching you things that were calculated to injure society, but it's worthwhile now and then to hear something different from what you ordinarily get from preachers and the like. These will tell you that you should be good and then you get rich and be happy. Of course we know that people do not get rich by being good, and that is the reason why so many of you people try to get rich some other way, only you do not understand how to do it quite as well as the fellow outside.

There are people who think that everything in this world is an accident. But really there is no such thing as an accident. A great many folks admit that many of the people in jail ought to be there, and many who are outside ought to be in. I think none of them ought to be here. There ought to be no jails, and if it were not for the fact that the people on the outside are so grasping and heartless in their dealings with the people on the inside, there would be no such institution as jails.

I do not want you to believe that I think all you people here are angels. I do not think that. You are people of all kinds, all of you doing the best you can, and that is evidently not very well—you are people of all kinds and conditions and under all circumstances. In one sense everybody is equally good and equally bad. We all do the best we can under the circumstances. But as to the exact things for which you are sent here, some of you are guilty and did the particular act because you needed the money. Some of you did it because you are in the habit of doing it, and some of you because you are born to it, and it comes to be as natural as it does, for instance, for me to be good.

Most of you probably have nothing against me, and most of you would treat me the same as any other person would; probably better than some of the people on the outside would treat me, because you think I believe in you and they know I do not believe in them. While you would not have the least thing against me in the world you might pick my pockets. I do not think all of you would, but I think some of you would. You would not have anything against me, but that's your profession, a few of you. Some of the rest of you, if my doors were unlocked, might come in if you saw anything you wanted—not out of any malice to me, but because that is your trade. There is no doubt there are quite a number of people in this jail who would pick my pockets. And still I know this, that when I get outside pretty nearly everybody picks my pocket. There may be some of you who would hold up a man on the street, if you did not happen to have something else to do, and needed the money; but when I want to light my house or my office the gas company holds me up. They charge me one dollar for something that is worth twenty-five cents, and still all these people are good people, they are pillars of society and support the churches, and they are respectable.

When I ride on the streetcars, I am held up—I pay five cents for a ride that is worth two-and-a half cents, simply because a body of men have bribed the city council and the legislature, so that all the rest of us have to pay tribute to them.

If I do not want to fall into the clutches of the gas trust and choose to burn oil instead of gas, then good Mr. Rockefeller holds me up, and he uses a certain portion of his money to build universities and support churches which are engaged in telling us how to be good.

Some of you are here for obtaining property under false pretenses—yet I pick up a great Sunday paper and read the advertisements of a merchant prince—"Shirtwaists for 39¢, marked down from $3."

When I read the advertisements in the paper I see they are all lies. When I want to get out and find a place to stand anywhere on the face of the earth, I find that it has all been taken up long ago before I came here, and before you came here, and somebody says, "Get off, swim into the lake, fly into the air; go anywhere, but get off." That is because these people have the police and they have the jails and the judges and the lawyers and the soldiers and all the rest of them to take care of the earth and drive everybody off that comes in their way.

A great many people will tell you that all this is true, but that it does not excuse you. These facts do not excuse some fellow who reaches into my pocket and takes out a five-dollar bill; the fact that the gas company bribes the members of the legislature from year to year, and fixes the law, so that all you people are compelled to be "fleeced" whenever you deal with them; the fact that the streetcar companies and the gas companies have control of the streets and the fact that the landlords own all the earth, they say, has nothing to do with you.

Let us see whether there is any connection between the crimes of the respectable classes and your presence in the jail. Many of you people are in jail because you have really committed burglary. Many of you, because you have stolen something: in the meaning of the law, you have taken some other person's property. Some of you have entered a store and carried off a pair of shoes because you did not have the price. Possibly some of you have committed murder. I can not tell what all of you did. There are a great many people here who have done some of these things who really do not know themselves why they did them. I think I know why you did them—every one of you; you did these things because you were bound to do them. It looked to you at the time as if you had a chance to do them or not, as you saw fit, but still after all you had no choice. There may be people here who had some money in their pockets and who still went out and got some more money in a way society forbids. Now you may not yourselves see exactly why it was you did this thing, but if you look at the question deeply enough and carefully enough you would see that there were circumstances that drove you to do exactly the thing which you did. You could not help it any more than we outside can help taking the positions that we take. The reformers who tell you to be good and you will be happy, and the people on the outside who have property to protect—they think that the only way to do it is by building jails and locking you up in cells on weekdays and praying for you Sundays.

I think that all of this has nothing whatever to do with right conduct. I think it is very easily seen what has to do with right conduct. Some so-called criminals—and I will use this word because it is handy, it means nothing to me—I speak of the criminals who get caught as distinguished from the criminals who catch them—some of these so-called criminals are in jail for the first offenses, but nine-tenths of you are in jail because you did not have a good lawyer and of course you did not have a good lawyer because you did not have enough money to pay a good lawyer. There is no very great danger of a rich man going to jail.

Some of you may be here for the first time. If we would open the doors and let you out, and leave the laws as they are today, some of you would be back tomorrow. This is about as good a place as you can get anyway. There are many people here who are so in the habit of coming that they would not know where else to go. There are people who are born with the tendency to break into jail every chance they get, and they can not avoid it. You can not figure out your life and see why it was, but still there is a reason for it, and if we were all wise and knew all the facts we could figure it out.

In the first place, there are a good many more people who go to jail in the winter time than in summer. Why is this? Is it because people are more wicked in winter? No, it is because the coal trust begins to get in its grip in the winter. A few gentlemen take possession of the coal, and unless the people will pay $7 or $8 a ton for something that is worth $3, they will have to freeze. Then there is nothing to do but to break into jail, and so there are many more in jail in the winter than in summer. It costs more for gas in the winter because the nights are longer, and people go to jail to save gas bills. The jails are electric-lighted. You may not know it, but these economic laws are working all the time, whether we know it or do not know it.

There are more people who go to jail in hard times than in good times—few people comparatively go to jail except when they are hard up. They go to jail because they have no other place to go. They may not know why, but it is true all the same. People are not more wicked in hard times. That is not the reason. The fact is true all over the world that in hard times more people go to jail than in good times, and in winter more people go to jail than in summer. Of course it is pretty hard times for people who go to jail at any time. The people who go to jail are almost always poor people—people who have no other place

□

to live first and last. When times are hard then you find large numbers of people who go to jail who would not otherwise be in jail.

Long ago, Mr. Buckle, who was a great philosopher and historian, collected facts and he showed that the number of people who are arrested increased just as the price of food increased. When they put up the price of gas ten cents a thousand I do not know who will go to jail, but I do know that a certain number of people will go. When the meat combine raises the price of beef I do not know who is going to jail, but I know that a large number of people are bound to go. Whenever the Standard Oil Company raises the price of oil, I know that a certain number of girls who are seamstresses, and who work night after night long hours for somebody else, will be compelled to go out on the streets and ply another trade, and I know that Mr. Rockefeller and his associates are responsible and not the poor girls in the jails.

First and last, people are sent to jail because they are poor. Sometimes, as I say, you may not need money at the particular time, but you wish to have thrifty forehanded habits, and do not always wait until you are in absolute want. Some of you people are perhaps plying the trade, the profession, which is called burglary. No man in his right senses will go into a strange house in the dead of night and prowl around with a dark lantern through unfamiliar rooms and take chances of his life if he has plenty of the good things of the world in his own home. You would not take any such chances as that. If a man had clothes in his clothes-press and beefsteak in his pantry, and money in the bank, he would not navigate around nights in houses where he knows nothing about the premises whatever. It always requires experience and education for this profession, and people who fit themselves for it are no more to blame than I am for being a lawyer. A man would not hold up another man on the street if he had plenty of money in his own pocket. He might do it if he had one dollar or two dollars, but he wouldn't if he had as much money as Mr. Rockefeller has. Mr. Rockefeller has a great deal better holdup game than that.

The more that is taken from the poor by the rich, who have the chance to take it, the more poor people there are who are compelled to resort to these means for a livelihood. They may not understand it, they may not think so at once, but after all they are driven into that line of employment.

There is a bill before the legislature of this State to punish kidnaping children, with death. We have wise members of the Legislature. They know the gas trust when they see it and they always see it—they can furnish light enough to be seen, and this Legislature thinks it is going to stop kidnaping children by making a law punishing kidnapers of children with death. I don't believe in kidnaping children, but the Legislature is all wrong. Kidnaping children is not a crime, it is a profession. It has been developed with the times. It has been developed with our modern industrial conditions. There are many ways of making money—many new ways that our ancestors knew nothing about. Our ancestors knew nothing about a billion-dollar trust; and here comes some poor fellow who has no other trade and he discovers the profession of kidnaping children.

This crime is born, not because people are bad; people don't kidnap other people's children because they want the children or because they are devilish, but because they see a chance to get some money out of it. You cannot cure this crime by passing a law punishing by death kidnapers of children. There is one way to cure it. There is one way to cure all the offenses, and that is to give the people a chance to live. There is no other way, and there never was any other way since the world began, and the world is so blind and stupid that it will not see. If every man and woman and child in the world had a chance to make a decent, fair, honest living, there would be no jails, and no lawyers and no courts. There might be some persons here or there with some peculiar formation of their brain, like Rockefeller, who would do these things simply to be doing them; but they would be very, very few, and those should be sent to a hospital and treated, and not sent to jail; and they would entirely disappear in the second generation, or at least in the third generation.

I am not talking pure theory. I will just give you two or three illustrations.

The English people once punished criminals by sending them away. They would load them on a ship and export them to Australia. England was owned by lords and nobles and rich people. They owned the whole earth over there, and the other people had to stay in the streets. They could not get a decent living. They used to take their criminals and send them to Australia—I mean the class of criminals who got caught. When these criminals got over there, and nobody else had come, they had the whole continent to run over, and so they could raise sheep and furnish their own meat, which is easier than stealing it; these criminals then became decent, respectable people because they had a chance to live. They did not commit any crimes. They were just like the English people who sent them there, only better. And in the second generation the descendants of those criminals were as good and respectable a class of people as there were on the face of the earth, and then they began building churches and jails themselves.

A portion of this country was settled in the same way, landing prisoners down on the southern coast; but when they got here and had a whole continent to run over and plenty of chances to make a living, they became respectable citizens, making their own living just like any other citizen in the world; but finally these descendants of the English aristocracy, who sent the people over to Australia, found out they were getting rich, and so they went over to get possession of the earth as they always do, and they organized land syndicates and got control of the land and ores, and then they had just as many criminals in Australia as they did in England. It was not because the world had grown bad; it was because the earth had been taken away from the people.

Some of you people have lived in the country. It's prettier than it is here. And if you have ever lived on a farm you understand that if you put a lot of cattle in a field, when the pasture is short they will jump over the fence; but put them in a good field where there is plenty of pasture, and they will be law-abiding cattle to the end of time. The human animal is just like the rest of the animals, only a little more so. The same thing that governs in the one governs in the other.

Everybody makes his living along the lines of least resistance. A wise man who comes into a country early sees a great undeveloped land. For instance, our rich men twenty-five years ago saw that Chicago was small and knew a lot of people would come here and settle, and they readily saw that if they had all the land around here it would be worth a good deal, so they grabbed the land. You cannot be a landlord because somebody has got it all. You must find some other calling. In England and Ireland and Scotland less than 5 percent own all the land there is, and the people are bound to stay there on any kind of terms the landlords give. They must live the best they can, so they develop all these various professions—burglary, picking pockets and the like.

Again, people find all sorts of ways of getting rich. These are diseases like everything else. You look at people getting rich, organizing trusts, and making a million dollars, and somebody gets the disease and he starts out. He catches it just as a man catches the mumps or the measles; he is not to blame, it is in the air. You will find men speculating beyond their means, because the mania of money-getting is taking possession of them. It is simply a disease; nothing more, nothing less. You can not avoid catching it; but the fellows who have control of the earth have the advantage of you. See what the law is; when these men get control of things, they make the laws. They do not make the laws to protect anybody; courts are not instruments of justice; when your case gets into court it will make little difference whether you are guilty or innocent; but it's better if you have a smart lawyer. And you can not have a smart lawyer unless you have money. First and last it's a question of money. Those men who own the earth make the laws to protect what they have. They fix up a sort of fence or pen around what they have, and they fix the law so the fellow on the outside can not get in. The laws are really organized for the protection of the men who rule the world. They were never organized or enforced to do justice. We have no system for doing justice, not the slightest in the world.

Let me illustrate: Take the poorest person in this room. If the community had provided a system of doing justice the poorest person in this room would have as good a lawyer as the richest, would he not? When you went into court you would have just as long a trial, and just as fair a trial as the richest person in Chicago. Your case would not be tried in fifteen or twenty minutes, whereas it would take fifteen days to get through with a rich man's case.

Then if you were rich and were beaten, your case would be taken to the Appellate Court. A poor man can not take his case to the Appellate Court; he has not the price; and then to the Supreme Court, and if he were beaten there he might perhaps go to the United States Supreme Court. And he might die of old age before he got into jail. If you are poor, it's a quick job. You are almost known to be guilty, else you would not be there. Why should any one be in the criminal court if he were not guilty? He would not be there if he could be anywhere else. The officials have not time to look after all these cases. The people who are on the outside, who are running banks and building churches and making jails, they have no time to examine six hundred or seven hundred prisoners each year to see whether they are guilty or innocent. If the courts were organized to promote justice the people would elect somebody to defend all these criminals, somebody as smart as the prosecutor—and give him as many detectives and as many assistants to help, and pay as much money to defend you as to prosecute you. We have a very able man for State's Attorney, and he has many assistants, detectives and policemen without end, and judges to hear the cases—everything handy.

Most of our criminal code consists in offenses against property. People are sent to jail because they have committed a crime against property. It is of very little consequence whether one hundred people more or less go to jail who ought not to go—you must protect property, because in this world property is of more importance than anything else.

How is it done? These people who have property fix it so they can protect what they have. When somebody commits a crime it does not follow that he has done something that is morally wrong. The man on the outside who has committed no crime may have done something. For instance: to take all the coal in the United States and raise the price two dollars or three dollars when there is no need of it, and thus kill thousands of babies and send thousands of people to the poorhouse and tens of thousands to jail, as is done every year in the United States—this is a greater crime than all the people in our jails ever committed, but the law does not punish it. Why? Because the fellows who control the earth make the laws. If you and I had the making of the laws, the first thing we would do would be to punish the fellow who gets control of the earth. Nature put this coal in the ground for me as well as for them and nature made the prairies up here to raise wheat for me as well as for them, and then the great railroad companies came along and fenced it up.

Most of all the crimes for which we are punished are property crimes. There are a few personal crimes, like murder—but they are very few. The crimes committed are mostly those against property. If this punishment is right the criminals must have a lot of property. How much money is there in this crowd? And yet you are all here for crimes against property. The people up and down the Lake Shore have not

☐

committed crimes, still they have so much property they don't know what to do with it. It is perfectly plain why those people have not committed crimes against property; they make the laws and therefore do not need to break them. And in order for you to get some property you are obliged to break the rules of the game. I don't know but what some of you may have had a very nice chance to get rich by carrying the hod for one dollar a day, twelve hours. Instead of taking that nice, easy profession, you are a burglar. If you had been given a chance to be a banker you would rather follow that. Some of you may have had a chance to work as a switchman on a railroad where you know, according to statistics, that you can not live and keep all your limbs more than seven years, and you can get fifty dollars or seventy-five dollars a month for taking your lives in your hands, and instead of taking that lucrative position you choose to be a sneak thief, or something like that. Some of you made that sort of choice. I don't know which I would take if I was reduced to this choice. I have an easier choice.

I will guarantee to take from this jail, or any jail in the world, five hundred men who have been the worst criminals and lawbreakers who ever got into jail, and I will go down to our lowest streets and take five hundred of the most abandoned prostitutes, and go out somewhere where there is plenty of land, and will give them a chance to make a living, and they will be as good people as the average in the community.

There is a remedy for the sort of condition we see here. The world never finds it out, or when it does find it out it does not enforce it. You may pass a law punishing every person with death for burglary, and it will make no difference. Men will commit it just the same. In England there was a time when one hundred different offenses were punishable with death, and it made no difference. The English people strangely found out that so fast as they repealed the severe penalties and so fast as they did away with punishing men by death, crime decreased instead of increased; that the smaller the penalty the fewer the crimes.

Hanging men in our county jails does not prevent murder. It makes murderers.

And this has been the history of the world. It's easy to see how to do away with what we call crime. It is not so easy to do it. I will tell you how to do it. It can be done by giving the people a chance to live by destroying special privileges. So long as big criminals can get the coal fields, so long as the big criminals have control of the city council and get the public streets for streetcars and gas rights, this is bound to send thousands of poor people to jail. So long as men are allowed to monopolize all the earth, and compel others to live on such terms as these men see fit to make, then you are bound to get into jail.

The only way in the world to abolish crime and criminals is to abolish the big ones and the little ones together. Make fair conditions of life. Give men a chance to live. Abolish the right of private ownership of land, abolish monopoly, make the world partners in production, partners in the good things of life. Nobody would steal if he could get something of his own some easier way. Nobody will commit burglary when he has a house full. No girl will go out on the streets when she has a comfortable place at home. The man who owns a sweatshop or a department store may not be to blame himself for the condition of his girls, but when he pays them five dollars, three dollars, and two dollars a week, I wonder where he thinks they will get the rest of their money to live. The only way to cure these conditions is by equality. There should be no jails. They do not accomplish what they pretend to accomplish. If you would wipe them out there would be no more criminals than now. They terrorize nobody. They are a blot upon any civilization, and a jail is an evidence of the lack of charity of the people on the outside who make the jails and fill them with the victims of their greed.

Discussion

1. Who is Darrow's audience for this essay? How do you know?
2. What is Darrow's thesis statement? Read paragraph by paragraph for support of his thesis.
3. Upon what is he basing his argument, what moral reasoning? (Find a statement or two in the text that shows Darrow's ethic in this piece.) Do you agree or disagree. Why?
4. What does a statement such as the following indicate about Darrow's beliefs: "I think I know why you did them—every one of you; you did these things because you were bound to do them."?
5. How would Darrow define "criminal"? Find evidence in the text to support your views.
6. Why does Darrow call robbery a trade, a profession?
7. What do you think: Is Darrow correct? If every man, woman, and child in the world "had a chance to make a decent, fair, honest living, there would be no jails, and no lawyers and no courts."?
   What, would you say, is Darrow's view of man? Is man intrinsically good or bad?
8. How does Darrow's statement, "Everybody makes his living along the lines of least resistance," add or detract from his view of man? (Remember, you are judging Darrow by your own system of moral values. Try to work hard to extract his from yours so that each can be given its full integrity. Why do you believe what you believe? Darrow is demonstrating the reasons he has for believing his way.)
9. What does Darrow call the business of getting rich?
   How does he find avarice the source of all crime?

For Further Discussion

10. How has Darrow's audience affected the shape and form and the very words of this essay? Give examples from the text that illustrate the influence of the audience on this piece.

☐

(You might like to compare Darrow's writing in another essay, "Why I Am an Agnostic," in Chapter 5, By Analysis. How does "Crime and Criminals" compare to "Why I Am an Agnostic"?)

11. How do your own moral values shape your arguments?

(Look especially at Darrow's argument. How have his beliefs shaped the way he *sees* things and, therefore, the way he presents what he sees? You can be certain your beliefs, formed and unformed, contribute as identifiable a shape to your written thoughts. Begin to look at your writing as a reflection of yourself. Find yourself in it, your own unique voice.)

7 Humor and Irony

Humor and irony are two sides of a coin. Many people find the comic voice more comfortable than the serious. They like the irreverence of saying the opposite of what they mean, of crossing the boundaries of "good taste" and of the expected.

Each of us has the comic voice inside. We are often surprised and amused at its emergence on even serious occasions. Humor is a way to look at the difficult and to laugh. It is not a way of avoiding it. Humor crosses all social barriers; it is profound and profane, coarse and refined. It is a way to release us for a moment's stay, from the seriousness of our living.

Irony adds an element of intellect. It is primarily a mental form of comedy. While humor resides more commonly with the senses, with the cream pie in the face, irony deliberately chooses the mind. It states untruths when it actually means the opposite. Is Thurber, in "The Ladies of Orlon," being ironic when he writes: "Woman's day, on the other hand, is, by every sign and token, just beginning. It couldn't happen to a nicer sex."? Or is irony the undertone of Mark Twain's "Advice to Youth" when he writes: "For the history of our race, and each individual's experience, are sown thick with evidence that a truth is not hard to kill and that a lie told well is immortal."?

The spirit behind irony is sometimes hard to detect, in fact, it sometimes fools us completely. Woody Allen's "My Speech to the Graduates," has the delivery of a standup comic routine: "But not every air conditioner. Not my sister Henny's for instance." It wracks up a score of horrible accusations about man's existence like an indictment, then resorts to the form of a sloppy college theme: "Summing up, it is clear the future holds great opportunities." These are clearly not the voices of men unable to face existence.

In this chapter you will begin again to think about how surprise, contrariness, the preposterous, and laughter, among many other attitudes, inform the human condition, instruct us and release us from tensions of all kinds. Those who would be good humorist writers should look carefully for the tricks of the trade. And all writers should especially note the words invited into play. Language itself can afford us a good laugh. Goodnight Mr. Preston, wherever you are.

Mark Twain
(1835–1910)

Mark Twain (Samuel Langhorne Clemens) was born November 30, 1835, in Florida, Missouri, and grew up in Hannibal, Missouri, the Mississippi River setting of many of his writings. At age twelve he began working as a printer and worked in that field until 1887 when he apprenticed as a steamboat pilot. He remained on the Mississippi as a journeyman pilot until the Civil War when, after no success at mining in Nevada, he returned to journalism, this time as a feature writer. Within a few years pieces such as "The Celebrated Jumping Frog of Calavenas County," and the book *Innocents Abroad,* had established his reputation as a popular humorist.

One biographer writes of Twain," . . . though his mind grew up, his heart remained always that of a child. Hot-tempered, profane, wreathed in tobacco smoke, enthralled by games and gadgets, extravagant, sentimental, superstitious, chivalrous to the point of the ridiculous. . . ."

Twain did not try for a cultivated, educated readership, " . . . but always hunted for bigger game—the masses. I have seldom deliberately tried to instruct them but have done my best to entertain them. . . ." He said: "My books are water; those of the great geniuses are wine. Everybody drinks water." Twain's writing relied on the sound and rhythms of speech. Here he describes his approach to his autobiography: "Start it at no particular time in your life; talk only about the thing which interests you for the moment; drop it the moment its interest threatens to pale; and turn your talk upon the new and more interesting thing that has intruded itself into your mind."

□

Advice to Youth

Being told I would be expected to talk here, I inquired what sort of a talk I ought to make. They said it should be something suitable to youth—something didactic, instructive, or something in the nature of good advice. Very well. I have a few things in my mind which I have often longed to say for the instruction of the young; for it is in one's tender early years that such things will best take root and be most enduring and most valuable. First, then, I will say to you, my young friends—and I say it beseechingly, urgingly—

Always obey your parents, when they are present. This is the best policy in the long run, because if you don't they will make you. Most parents think they know better than you do, and you can generally make more by humoring that superstition than you can by acting on your own better judgment.

Be respectful to your superiors, if you have any, also to strangers, and sometimes to others. If a person offend you, and you are in doubt as to whether it was intentional or not, do not resort to extreme measures; simply watch your chance and hit him with a brick. That will be sufficient. If you shall find that he had not intended any offense, come out frankly and confess yourself in the wrong when you struck him; acknowledge it like a man and say you didn't mean to. Yes, always avoid violence; in this age of charity and kindliness, the time has gone by for such things. Leave dynamite to the low and unrefined.

Go to bed early, get up early—this is wise. Some authorities say get up with the sun; some others say get up with one thing, some with another. But a lark is really the best thing to get up with. It gives you a splendid reputation with everyone to know that you get up with the lark; and if you get the right kind of a lark, and work at him right, you can easily train him to get up at half past nine, every time—it is no trick at all.

Now as to the matter of lying. You want to be very careful about lying; otherwise you are nearly sure to get caught. Once caught, you can never again be, in the eyes of the good and the pure, what you were before. Many a young person has injured himself permanently through a single clumsy and illfinished lie, the result of carelessness born of incomplete training. Some authorities hold that the young ought not to lie at all. That, of course, is putting it rather stronger than necessary; still, while I cannot go quite so far as that, I do maintain, and believe I am right, that the young ought to be temperate in the use of this great art until practice and experience shall give them that confidence, elegance, and precision which alone can make the accomplishment graceful and profitable. Patience, diligence, painstaking attention to detail—these are the requirements; these, in time, will make the student perfect; upon these, and upon these only, may he rely as the sure foundation for future eminence. Think what tedious years of study, thought, practice, experience, went to the equipment of that peerless old master who was able to impose upon the whole world the lofty and sounding maxim that "truth is mighty and will prevail"—the most majestic compound fracture of fact which any of woman born has yet achieved. For the history of our race, and each individual's experience, are sown thick with evidence that a truth is not hard to kill and that a lie told well is immortal. There is in Boston a monument of the man who discovered anaesthesia; many people are aware, in these latter days, that the man didn't discover it at all, but stole the discovery from another man. Is this truth mighty, and will it prevail? Ah no, my hearers, the monument is made of hardy material, but the lie it tells will outlast it a million years. An awkward, feeble, leaky lie is a thing which you ought to make it your unceasing study to avoid; such a lie as that has no more real permanence than an average truth. Why, you might as well tell the truth at once and be done with it. A feeble, stupid, preposterous lie will not live two years—except it be a slander upon somebody. It is indestructible, then, of course, but that is no merit of yours. A final word: begin your practice of this gracious and beautiful art early— begin now. If I had begun earlier, I could have learned how.

Never handle firearms carelessly. The sorrow and suffering that have been caused through the innocent but heedless handling of firearms by the young! Only four days ago, right in the next farmhouse to the one where I am spending the summer, a grandmother, old and gray and sweet, one of the loveliest spirits in the land, was sitting at her work, when her young grandson crept in and got down an old, battered, rusty gun which had not been touched for many years and was supposed not to be loaded, and pointed it at her, laughing and threatening to shoot. In her fright she ran screaming and pleading toward the door on the other side of the room; but as she passed him he placed the gun almost against her very breast and pulled the trigger! He had supposed it was not loaded. And he was right—it wasn't. So there wasn't any harm done. It is the only case of that kind I ever heard of. Therefore, just the same, don't you meddle with old unloaded firearms; they are the most deadly and unerring things that have ever been created by man. You don't have to take any pains at all with them; you don't have to have a rest, you don't have to have any sights on the gun, you don't have to take aim, even. No, you just pick out a relative and bang away, and you are sure to get him. A youth who can't hit a cathedral at thirty yards with a Gatling gun in three-quarters of an hour, can take up an old empty musket and bag his grandmother every time, at a hundred. Think what Waterloo would have been if one of the armies had been boys armed with old muskets supposed not to be loaded, and the other army had been composed of their female relations. The very thought of it makes one shudder.

There are many sorts of books; but good ones are the sort for the young to read. Remember that. They are a great, an inestimable, an unspeakable means of improvement. Therefore be careful in your selection, my young friends; be very careful; confine yourself exclusively to Robertson's Sermons, Baxter's *Saint's Rest*, *The Innocents Abroad*, and works of that kind.

But I have said enough. I hope you will treasure up the instructions which I have given you, and make them a guide to your feet and a light to your understanding. Build your character thoughtfully and painstakingly upon the precepts, and by and by, when you have got it built, you will be surprised and gratified to see how nicely and sharply it resembles everybody else's.

Vocabulary

didactic   intended to teach or moralize
eminence   a position of superiority in achievement
anaesthesia   variant of anesthesia, drug induced unconsciousness
precepts   rules imposing a particular standard of conduct

Discussion

1. Where is the first sentence of evidence that this piece is pulling your leg?
2. Notice the structure of the sentence: "Always obey your parents, when they are present." How does one part work against the other?
3. Find other examples of being led down the primrose path only to find the opposite of what you are led to expect.
4. How does this element of surprise add to what we find funny? Why does being surprised make one laugh?
5. How are "the brick" and "the lark" incidents preposterous, contrary to common sense?
   Why does what is contrary to common sense make one laugh?
6. Find other examples of the preposterous in this piece.
7. Here is, perhaps, a harder question. Where is the first piece of evidence that Twain's advice isn't all that humorous at all, but is actually a kind of indictment on the follies of mankind?
   After this undertone is first discovered, do you move quickly into it on a second reading?
8. Twain said his writing " . . . seldom deliberately tried to instruct." Can we always believe what a writer tells us? (Twain also said: "My books are water. . . .")

For Further Discussion

9. We call the undertone of Twain's writing irony. Irony is the use of words to employ a deliberate contrast between intended and apparent meaning. While the effect is often humor, what other purpose besides laughter does irony serve?

□

10. What purpose does laughter serve? Compare and contrast Woody Allen's "Speech to the Graduates" with Twain's "Advice." Does Allen's purpose seem also larger than laughs?
11. Think about these devices of humor and your own humor and humorous writing. Do you also write humor as an entertaining surface to a larger and more serious intent?

R. Emmett Tyrrell

(1943–   )

R. Emmett Tyrrell was born December 14, 1943, in Chicago. In 1966 he founded *The Alternative* at Indiana University. In 1970 he changed its name to the *American Spectator* and went national. The *Spectator* has become a small but respected journal of conservative opinion. In addition to Tyrrell's own monthly column, the magazine has included articles from such conservatives as William F. Buckley and Daniel Patrick Moynihan. Ronald Reagan and James Schlesinger are among its subscribers.

The magazine has never been profitable and survives only by support from its conservative readers. Tyrrell has said: "No little magazine is financially viable unless it is trash. I successfully deluded myself into thinking I could get good writers and the readership of intellectuals. No use going for the ultimate delusion that we could make money."

Robert Preston: Awash in History's Wake

No yokel in American history has quite so artlessly flummoxed an appointment with fame, prosperity, and power as Mr. Robert Preston, the audacious young grease monkey who became the first person ever to lead an aerial assault on the White House when he attempted to ram it with his pilfered UH-1 (Huey) helicopter.

The exact date of his tryst was February 17, 1974, and, so far as my staff has been able to ascertain, Jehovah reserved that date for him with no strings attached. Nonetheless, Mr. Preston blew it. While looking a gift horse in the mouth he fell into a funk, and the wheel of history ground on. By the time he had come to, his hour had passed. Back into the shadows he had slipped, there to stumble through a meaningless existence with the millions of other patheticoes who grouse about the "good fortune" of their betters.

Jehovah must have been appalled, and surely many sharp public relations men still shake their heads as they muse upon the tidy fortune poor Mr. Preston could have earned for them. It was as though haberdasher Harry Truman had turned down the call to public service and continued to bankrupt himself, or the Pope had snubbed the summons of the angels and opened a spaghetti parlor. Not since a youthful

Edward Kennedy turned his back on driver's education classes has a mortal so thumpingly sealed his own fate. ROBERT PRESTON . . . you will probably never hear his name again. *Au revoir*, oaf.

What this poor fish did was, in this glorious era, well-nigh unthinkable. He committed a mischievous and indeed felonious act and did not make the faintest gesture to embroider it with noble purpose or high-toned symbolism. He merely stepped from his wounded helicopter and confessed to the assembled reporters and secret servicemen: "There wasn't anything else to do"—not a word about political repression, ecological suicide, or alienation and the search for one's sexuality. Preston could have mentioned the cruel conditions of our women, the political castration of our homosexuals, the impending demise of the black-footed ferret, or the heartbreak of psoriasis. Rather, he grinned. And though *Newsweek* described it as a "cryptic" grin, it was a grin nevertheless. Had he possessed the astuteness to boom for any one of the aforementioned causes he would be a free man today with a gorgeous publishing contract, a decade's lecturing engagements on the college Chautauqua circuit, and an office in Washington paid for by some occult rivulet of the Department of Health, Education and Welfare. Instead, he grinned.

Not only is he a grinning ignoramus, but he is also selfish. Any of a dozen just causes could have been put over on the American people had he but uttered a threatening declaration. He had a two-way radio; why did he not use it? Why not a clenched fist when he emerged from the Huey? Imagine what would have become of the Black Panthers had they merely grinned after a shoot-up. Would Mr. Huey P. Newton ever have achieved celebrity and riches had he admitted that he shot cops and tortured fellow blacks because "there wasn't anything else to do"? Consider the rise of artsy pornography. If the aesthetes who began producing renderings of man's goatish impulses in the 1960s had stated at the outset that they wanted to create salacious movies so that they could make mounds of money, how many opportunities do you suppose we would have to appreciate sadism, bestiality, and masochism today? The pioneers of adult theater had to loosen up the Supreme Court with a few shots of the First Amendment. They had to address themselves to a worthy cause, the cause of free expression and art. Presto, progress was at hand, the greatest advance in art since John Cage heard fingernails scratch across a blackboard.

So let us wash our hands of this wretch. He committed an audacious act and fouled it with a stupid and irresponsible grin. Had he called a press conference and announced that his flight was meant to symbolize the immediate need to impeach Richard Nixon he would have made the cover of every newsweekly in the country. He could have become *Time*'s "Man of the Year." Instead he grinned and admitted to having a vacant mind. No other eminento of recent years was so foolhardy, and none had a briefer stay in the limelight.

☐
Vocabulary

flummoxed   slang for confused, perplexed
tryst   an appointed station in hunting
patheticoes   pathetic ones
cryptic   mysterious, secret, enigmatic
salacious   stimulating to the sexual imagination
eminento   superior one

Allusions/References

Chautauqua   annual summer educational assembly since 1847 at Chautauqua
   Lake, New York
John Cage   American composer, born 1912

Discussion

1. From the first two words you know that something is happening in this
   piece, that is, if you *listen* to words. How could anyone write a highly somber
   piece beginning, "No Yokel"?
   Look also at the word "flummoxed." Not only does it *look* odd, even funny,
   but it *sounds* preposterous.
   How do the looks and shapes and sounds of words become the subject of
   laughter with a humorist?
2. Diction is a term we use to indicate word choices. We often divide our word
   choices into high, middle, or low diction. High diction includes all of our
   bookish words, the language of the cultured and the refined; middle diction
   is the middle way, the more casual words of the middle class; low diction,
   as you might already have supposed, is the slang and colloquialism of the
   street.
   Writers are told not to mix diction, not to choose bookish language primarily,
   and then inexplicably throw in slang. How is mixed diction a stock trick of
   the humorist?
   Find as many examples of mixed diction in this piece as you can. How do
   they add to the humor?
3. If Robert Preston is to be totally forgotten, why is Emmett Tyrrell writing
   about him?
   Notice the sentence: "ROBERT PRESTON . . . you will probably never hear
   his name again." Not only does the typography shout at us, but *do* we ever
   hear his name again?
   How does a deliberate contradiction of the reader's expectation cause a chuc-
   kle or two?
4 Humorist writers, like comedians, are rebels. They relish breaking as many
   rules as they can. They like pushing back boundaries. Does this give any clue
   as to why Robert Preston might be a kind of perfect goof to Tyrrell?
5. Why is the sentence "*Au revoir,* oaf," funny? (Look at its diction, its appearance, and the *sounds* of those words.)

6. Name-calling in the right mood can be funny. What "names" are given Mr. Robert Preston?
7. Why are "high" words, words from the diction of the educated and elite, funny in a joke?

   Why is calling Preston's aborted attempt to ram the White House a "tryst" funny?

   What other examples of high diction used preposterously, for effect, can you find?
8. Is there a high purpose for this "low piece"? Does Tyrrell have any underlying reason for telling us about Preston? Is there a serious intent?

   What would it be?

   (The root of comedy, it has been said, is serious. The comedian is always exhorting mankind to be better by pointing out its follies.)
9. How is Tyrrell making a comment on the human tendency to "embroider" one's acts "with noble purpose or high-toned symbolism"?

Woody Allen
(1935–   )

Allen Stewart Konigsberg (Woody Allen) was born in New York City. In addition to being an essayist he is a comedian, jazz clarinetist, actor, and an Academy Award-winning director and screenwriter. (See other Woody Allen write-ups in Chapter 1.)

To the question of *redeeming social value* in his work, Allen replies: "To me all art—comedy, opera, painting, anything—is a diversion, an entertainment. So I view my own work in the same way. I don't think it needs to be redeemed . . . in the end it's all entertainment. I don't believe in art as a social force."

My Speech to the Graduates

More than any other time in history, mankind faces a crossroads. One path leads to despair and utter hopelessness. The other, to total extinction. Let us pray we have the wisdom to choose correctly. I speak, by the way, not with any sense of futility, but with a panicky conviction of the absolute meaninglessness of existence which could easily be misinterpreted as pessimism. It is not. It is merely a healthy concern for the predicament of modern man. (Modern man is here defined as any person born after Nietzsche's edict that "God is dead," but before the hit recording "I Wanna Hold Your Hand.") This "predicament" can be stated one of two ways, though certain linguistic philosophers prefer to reduce it to a mathematical equation where it can be easily solved and even carried around in the wallet.

Put in its simplest form, the problem is: How is it possible to find meaning in a finite world given my waist and shirt size? This is a very difficult question when we realize that science has failed us. True, it has

☐

conquered many diseases, broken the genetic code, and even placed human beings on the moon, and yet when a man of eighty is left in a room with two eighteen-year-old cocktail waitresses nothing happens. Because the real problems never change. After all, can the human soul be glimpsed through a microscope? Maybe—but you'd definitely need one of those very good ones with two eyepieces. We know that the most advanced computer in the world does not have a brain as sophisticated as that of an ant. True, we could say that of many of our relatives but we only have to put up with them at weddings or special occasions. Science is something we depend on all the time. If I develop a pain in the chest I must take an X-ray. But what if the radiation from the X-ray causes me deeper problems? Before I know it, I'm going in for surgery. Naturally, while they're giving me oxygen an intern decides to light up a cigarette. The next thing you know I'm rocketing over the World Trade Center in bed clothes. Is this science? True, science has taught us how to pasteurize cheese. And true, this can be fun in mixed company—but what of the H-bomb? Have you ever seen what happens when one of those things falls off a desk accidentally? And where is science when one ponders the eternal riddles? How did the cosmos originate? How long has it been around? Did matter begin with an explosion or by the word of God? And if by the latter, could He not have begun it just two weeks earlier to take advantage of some of the warmer weather? Exactly what do we mean when we say, man is mortal? Obviously it's not a compliment.

Religion too has unfortunately let us down. Miguel de Unamuno writes blithely of the "eternal persistence of consciousness," but this is no easy feat. Particularly when reading Thackeray. I often think how comforting life must have been for early man because he believed in a powerful benevolent Creator who looked after all things. Imagine his disappointment when he saw his wife putting on weight. Contemporary man, of course, has no such peace of mind. He finds himself in the midst of a crisis of faith. He is what we fashionably call "alienated." He has seen the ravages of war, he has known natural catastrophes, he has been to singles bars. My good friend Jacques Monod spoke often of the randomness of the cosmos. He believed everything in existence occurred by pure chance with the possible exception of his breakfast, which he felt certain was made by his housekeeper. Naturally belief in a divine intelligence inspires tranquility. But this does not free us from our human responsibilities. Am I my brother's keeper? Yes. Interestingly, in my case I share that honor with the Prospect Park Zoo. Feeling godless then, what we have done is made technology God. And yet can technology really be the answer when a brand new Buick, driven by my close associate, Nat Zipsky, winds up in the window of Chicken Delight causing hundreds of customers to scatter? My toaster has never once worked properly in four years. I follow the instructions and push two slices of bread down in the slots and seconds later they rifle upward. Once they broke the nose of a woman I loved very dearly. Are we counting on nuts and bolts and electricity to solve our problems? Yes, the telephone is a good thing—and the refrigerator—and the air-conditioner. But not every air conditioner. Not my sister Henny's, for instance. Hers makes a loud noise and still doesn't cool. When the man comes over to fix it, it gets worse. Either that or he tells her she needs a new one. When she complains, he says not to bother him. This man is truly alienated. Not only is he alienated but he can't stop smiling.

The trouble is, our leaders have not adequately prepared us for a mechanized society. Unfortunately our politicians are either incompetent or corrupt. Sometimes both on the same day. The Government is unresponsive to the needs of the little man. Under five-seven, it is impossible to get your Congressman on the phone. I am not denying that democracy is still the finest form of government. In a democracy at least, civil liberties are upheld. No citizen can be wantonly tortured, imprisoned, or made to sit through certain Broadway shows. And yet this is a far cry from what goes on in the Soviet Union. Under their form of totalitarianism, a person merely caught whistling is sentenced to thirty years in a labor camp. If, after fifteen years, he still will not stop whistling, they shoot him. Along with this brutal fascism we find its handmaiden, terrorism. At no other time in history has man been so afraid to cut into his veal chop for fear that it will explode. Violence breeds more violence and it is predicted that by 1990 kidnapping will be the dominant mode of social interaction. Overpopulation will exacerbate problems to the breaking point. Figures tell us there are already more people on earth than we need to move even the heaviest piano. If we do not call a halt to breeding, by the year 2000 there will be no room to serve dinner unless one is willing to set the table on the heads of strangers. Then they must not move for an hour while we eat. Of course energy will be in short supply and each car owner will be allowed only enough gasoline to back up a few inches.

Instead of facing these challenges we turn instead to distractions like drugs and sex. We live in far too permissive a society. Never before has pornography been this rampant. And those films are lit so badly! We are a people who lack defined goals. We have never learned to love. We lack leaders and coherent programs. We have no spiritual center. We are adrift alone in the cosmos wreaking monstrous violence on one another out of frustration and pain. Fortunately, we have not lost our sense of proportion. Summing up, it is clear the future holds great opportunities. It also holds pitfalls. The trick will be to avoid the pitfalls, seize the opportunities, and get back home by six o'clock.

Vocabulary

pessimism   a tendency to take the gloomiest possible view of a situation
linguistic   of or relating to language; a specialist in analysis of language is a
    linguist

☐

genetic code   the mechanism of hereditary transmission
wantonly   maliciously cruel; mercilessly
totalitarianism   a state in which one political party has absolute control
fascism   a system of government of the extreme right that advocates a dicta-
     torship, together with belligerent nationalism
rampant   extending unchecked, unrestrained, widespreading
exacerbate   increase the severity of: aggravate

Allusions/References

Nietzsche   A German philosopher, poet and critic 1844–1900; often credited
     with the edict: "God is dead."
Miguel de Unamuno   A contemporary Spanish philosopher, poet and essayist
Thackeray   English novelist, 1811–1863
"I wanna hold your hand"   Beatles' tune popular in early 60s

Discussion

1. After glancing at Allen's word choices and allusions above, what kind of an
   audience do you feel he was writing for? (In answering this question you
   might consider how you see your intended audience for essays in this class,
   and how your audience will affect your use of language.)
2. In the second paragraph Allen asks the question: "How is it possible to find
   meaning in a finite world given my waist and shirt size?" What are the problems he sees as central to this question, and how do they give his essay form?
3. Although Allen claims his works are merely diversions, "it's all entertainment," what indications are there in his question and its answers that his
   concerns go deeper?

For Further Discussion

4. Allen admits he has been "influenced by Kafka, Rilke, the *Bible, A Boy's
   Guide to Forestry*, and *Advanced Sexual Positions—How to Achieve Them
   Without Laughing.*" What other Allenesque "influences" do you find in his
   "Speech to the Graduates"?
5. Another familiar college experience that Allen mocks in his book *Getting
   Even* is the college catalogue:

   > Philosophy XXIX-B: Introduction to God. Confrontation with the Crea-
   > tor of the universe through informal lectures and field trips.

   > Yeats and Hygiene, A Comparative Study: The poetry of William Butler
   > Yeats is analyzed against a background of proper dental care. (Course
   > open to a limited number of students.)

   What does this suggest about the original impulse that might drive Allen (any
   writer—*you*) to write?

6. If you are interested in writing humor, you might find it entertaining and informative to compare humorists' approaches. Mark Twain's "Advice to Youth," also in this chapter, compares well with this essay.

James Thurber
(1894–1961)

James Thurber was born December 8, 1894, in Columbus, Ohio. He began his career as a reporter for the *Columbus Dispatch* in 1920. He went on to become one of the great humorists and illustrators of the twentieth century.

He was most often associated with the *New Yorker* magazine, where he was something of a legend. His friend Mark Van Doren said of him: "He was an extraordinary man . . . gentle and fierce, fascinating and boring, sophisticated and boorish, kind and cruel, broadminded and parochial. You can't explain Thurber."

Thurber wrote voluminously, rewriting most things several times. "One reason you go over and over it is to make the piece sound less as if you were having a lot of fun yourself. You try to play it down." And though he loved writing, even rewriting, in later years it was a great effort. His eyesight became so bad that he was able to put only twenty words to a page.

Never one to plot his story beforehand, Thurber "found out" what he would write at the typewriter. "I don't believe the writer should know too much where he's going. If he does, he runs into old man blueprint—old man propaganda."

The Ladies of Orlon

Surgical science, still achieving, still pursuing, has successfully replaced a section of the femoral artery in a human leg with a tube made of nylon, and the medical profession confidently prophesies for the near future a practicable aorta made of the fabric known as orlon. We are all so used to the heart as a lyrical organ, made of the stuff that breaks, that a metaphorical shift to a heart made of the stuff that tears, or rips, or has to be hemstitched, may have a strange and disastrous effect on writers and composers. It has already had its effect on me, getting into my daydreams and nightmares. In one of the latter, a bearded doctor, fiercely grinning, asked me, "Do you know how to tell your wife from the children's toys?" and startled me wide awake just before dawn. This fragment of dream was probably the associative product of the orlon surgical technique and Eugene Field's creatures of gingham and calico. (It wasn't until later that I heard about the new orlon-filled toys.) All I need to make a chaos out of my already tormented nights is a dream world of patchwork girls, indestructibly fabricated females with a disconcerting froufrou deep inside their organdie in place of the old-fashioned pulse beat.

One night, I dreamed I was at this party. A young lady had been carelessly flung onto the sofa beside me, her long legs loosely inter-twined and her stuffing showing plainly at one shoulder seam. 'You're losing your sawdust," I told her anxiously. "Nonsex," she said, and I suddenly realized that she and all the other women guests were dolls. Such a dream could be construed as meaning that I have reached the time of life when I seek to deny the actuality of the American Woman and to reduce her to the level of an insentient plaything. Actually, the latent meaning of this dream goes far deeper than that, and consists of a profound anxiety on my part as to what would happen to our world if the stature of Woman decreased.

A lovely woman with a taffeta xiphisternum might conceivably make this artificiality a part of her mysterious allure—I have known the kind of lady whose charm could even take the ugliness out of a thrug sutured with silk to her thisbe—but a gentleman of like kidney, let us say, could surely never regain the position he held in our com-petitive society before his operation. Man is used to being repaired with silver plates and pins, and it is doubtful whether his ego could long sus-tain a body consisting largely, or in part, of dress material. It may be, then, that a gradual textilization of the human species is one of the des-perate strategies of Nature in her ceaseless effort to save our self-destructive race from the extinction of which it seems so massively enamored. Nature and I have long felt that the hope of mankind is womankind, that the physically creative sex must eventually dominate the physically destructive sex if we are to survive on this planet. The simplest things last longest, the microbe outlives the mastodon, and the female's simple gift of creativity happily lacks the ornaments and hand-icaps of male artifice, pretension, power, and balderdash.

Nature (I do not say God, because I think protective Providence washed Its hands of us long ago) realizes that we have to be turned into something as durable as the toughest drygoods if we are to endure the wear and tear caused by the frightened tempo of our time. Men and women—the former because they think the Devil is after them, the lat-ter merely to hold their own—make the revolving doors of our office buildings whirl at a dangerous and terrifying rate of speed as they rush lickety-split to their lunches, return hellbent to their desks, and fling themselves recklessly homeward at twilight to their separate sorrows. It is the men who are the casualties of this pell-mell, the men who are caught in the doors and flung to the floors, and it is the women who pick them up, or at least it is the women who pick *me* up. Once the ladies have become compounded largely of bland but durable textiles, they will outlive the once stronger sex even more easily than they do now. Nature, prefiguring the final disappearance of the male, has aided science in solving the problem of the continuation of the human being with her usual foresight, by establishing the ingenious, if admittedly stuffy, technique of artificial insemination. It is only a question of time before the male factor in the perpetuation of the species becomes a matter of biological deep freeze, an everlasting laboratory culture, labelled, controlled, and supervised by women technicians.

The male, continuously preoccupied with his own devices and his own mythical destiny, polysyllabically boasting of his power and purposes, seems blithely unconscious of the conspiracy of Nature and women to do him in. He does not seem to know that he is doomed to go out like a light unless he abandons the weapons and the blue-prints of annihilation. Woman says little about it, but she does not intend to be annihilated by Man, even if she has to get rid of him first to save herself. This is not going to be as difficult for her to face as one might think, for her ancient dependence on the male began slowly to turn into disdain about A.D. 135, according to Dr. Rudolph Horch, who makes the astounding statement that the female's sexual interest in her mate has decreased seventeen and two-tenths per cent since September, 1929. The female has greater viability than the male, Dr. Horch reminds us, and the male knows this when he puts his mind to it, which he naturally does not like to do. I once asked a distinguished obstetrician which he would rather be called upon to deliver, male quintuplets or female quintuplets. He began with the usual masculine circumlocutions, pointing out that there are no dependable statistics, on a large scale, dealing with the relative viability of the sexes. "Let me put it this way," I said. "Two women are about to give birth to quintuplets, and by means of some hypothetical prescience it has become known that one is going to have five boys and the other five girls. Which would you rather deliver if you were called upon to make a choice?" "The girls," he said.

It may come down, in the end, to a highly dramatic sex crisis. Man is forever discovering some new and magnificent miracle weapon or miracle drug, and it is possible that he may soon stumble upon an undreamed-of mineral, of which there will be just enough in the world to create a drug that could cure everybody of everything or to manufacture a bomb capable of blowing the planet into fragments the size of Cuba. The ultimate struggle for possession of the precious material would divide men and women into two warring camps. I have the confidence to believe that the creative females would defeat the destructive males and gain control of the miracle substance.

I no longer see the faces of men and women at the parties I attend, or in the streets I walk along, or the hotel lobbies I sit in, but I hear their voices more clearly than ever. The voices of the women, it seems to me, have taken on a new and quiet quality—a secret conspiratorial tone, the hopeful and reassuring note of a sex firmly dedicated to the principle of not being blown into fragments. For centuries Woman has been quietly at work achieving her present identity. Not many years ago the Encyclopaedia Britannica listed nothing under "Woman," but merely said "See Man." The latest Oxford English Dictionary, however, gives woman twelve columns to man's fifteen. The development of her name

from Old English through Middle English to Modern English is fascinating to trace in the O.E.D. She began as "wife," became "wifman" and
underwent seventeen other changes until the word "woman" came
into use about the year 1400. Most writers, glibly discussing the origin
of the word over their brandy, contend that it derives from the derog-
atory phrase "with man" or the physiological "wombman." They don't
know what they are talking about. Earlier male writers, equally mistaken, declared the word derived from "woe to man" or "wee man."
Some of them were serious, others merely kidding, in the immemorial
manner of the superior male.

I'm glad to report that the feminist Flecknor took a fairer view in
1653 when he wrote: "Say of Woman worst ye can, what prolongs their
woe, but man?" In the past three hundred years the importance of
women has often been derided by men from J. Clarke's "A Woman,
asse, and walnut-tree, the more you beat the better be" to Noel Coward's "A woman should be struck regularly like a gong." But there were
wiser men who spoke of the female of the species with proper respect,
and even fear. It was Congreve who wrote the almost invariably mis-
quoted "Heav'n has no Rage, like Love to Hatred turn'd, Nor Hell a Fury,
like a Woman scorned," and in 1835 Hook recognized the stature of the
female with "A girl of seventeen is a woman when a man of seventeen
is a boy." Thirty-two years later, English law under Queen Victoria for-
mally defined the female: "Woman shall mean a Female of the Age of
Eighteen Years or Upwards," and twenty years after that, the British
female legally became a woman at the age of sixteen, while males of
the same age were still regarded as schoolchildren.

It was in the 1890's that the old-fashioned dependent woman was
scornfully rejected by her own sex as the "cow-woman," and "new
woman" and even "new womandom" came into common and spirited
use. Ninety years before the decade of the self-assertive woman, J.
Brown had arrogantly written, "No ecclesiastical power can reside in a
heathen, a woman, or child." Fortunately for his peace of mind, he
didn't live to see the female become the residence of practically any
power you can name. She is now definitely here to stay, whereas the
decline of the male, even the actual decadence of the insecure sex, has
been observed by alarmed scientists in a score of other species. A certain scorpion, for example, disappears with his mate after a ritualistic
courtship dance, and is never seen again. The female, though, emerges
from the honeymoon, fit as a fiddle and fresh as a daisy. And there is a
certain female fish in the waters of the sea who has reduced the male
to the status of a mere accessory. She actually carries him about with
her, for occasional biological use, in the casual way that a woman carries a compact or a cigarette lighter in her handbag. There are dozens
of other significant instances of dwindling of the male in the animal
kingdom, but I am much too nervous to go into them here. Some
twenty years ago, a gloomy scientist reported, "Man's day is done."

Woman's day, on the other hand, is by every sign and token, just beginning. It couldn't happen to a nicer sex.

In case you have always wondered why the *o* in women is pronounced differently from the *o* in woman, the Oxford Dictionary has a theory about that, as about everything else. The change is the result of associative influence of certain other pairs of words, singular and plural, such as foot and feet, and tooth and teeth. The women will now please keep their seats until the men have left the auditorium. They need, God knows, a head start.

Vocabulary

froufrou   fussy dress or ornament
insentient   inanimate, without sensation
xiphisternum   the smallest of three divisions of the breastbone
circumlocutions   roundabout speech, evasion in writing or speech
viability   capable of living
ecclesiastical power   priestly power

Discussion

1. How does Thurber's first sentence portend a work of "heavy seriousity"? Why is the pretension to grand themes a humorous beginning to this piece?
2. Notice the structure of the third sentence beginning: "We are all so used to the heart as a lyrical organic. . . ." How does it progress from what appears to be common sense to the preposterous?
   How many cues have you had in this sentence that its ending was to completely reverse into the humorous?
3. Why does the reader feel delight at the sudden turns and twists of comedy? Consider how much, in order to facilitate communication with others, writers stay to the middle way, the smooth ride, providing transitions between one thought and another. The humorist takes us on another kind of ride? Which kind of ride excites your senses most?
4. How much does our reason enjoy being teased with the unreasonable? Notice the bearded doctor's statement: "Do you know how to tell your wife from the children's toys?"
   What other examples of the absurd can you find in this piece?
5. What is Thurber doing with such language use as the following: " 'Nonsex,' she said"; and "a thrug sutured with silk to her thisbe"?
   A pun is a play on words. Why is it fun to play with words?
6. Words can be teased by appearance, by meaning, and by sound. How many examples of each of these ways can you find?
   What is the "gradual textilization of the human species"? What word does the word "textilization" look and sound like? Why is this phrase funny to us if not that we delight in seeing words fooled with, played with, and not just treated somberly and with "respect." (Somehow play indicates close-

ness, that we feel as comfortable with our words as we do members of our own family.)

7. By the bottom of paragraph three Thurber's intent seems clear: "Nature and I have long felt that the hope of mankind is womankind, that the physically creative sex must eventually dominate the physically destructive sex if we are to survive on this planet."
   How does he twist and turn this thesis throughout his piece?
   How does this twisting and turning add up to an exhilarating reading journey and, therefore, fun—humor?

8. Thurber writes about man: "He does not seem to know that he is doomed to go out like a light unless he abandons the weapons and the blue-prints of annihilation." Does he mean this, or is this overstatement for comic effect?
   He writes of woman, on the other hand: "Woman says little about it, but she does not intend to be annihilated by man. . . ." Does he mean this also? Is the addition of " . . . even if she has to get rid of him first to save herself" a disclaimer? Does it reduce his entire thesis to humor?

9. Humor is the ability to laugh at ourselves; at least that's what we've always been told. How does laughing at ourselves help? What is its function?

For Further Discussion

10. What language devices do writers use to make their readers laugh? After reading the four essays in this chapter and the questions for discussion, how many more devices of written humor can you find or invent? See below.

    the words themselves, their sounds, shapes, meanings, juxtapositions
    the structure information is conveyed in, how ideas are arranged in a sentence, paragraph, essay; how radical the structure is, how many infractions or twists on the expected (the rules) it makes, its rhythm
    the ideas conveyed, their sounds, shapes, meanings, juxtapositions

A Study of
Four Writers

Here is your opportunity to look more closely at the prose style of four authors. While the bird's-eye view of an anthology, surveying as many essays as possible, is certainly both necessary and rewarding, nothing feels quite the same as an in-depth look at just a few essays written by the same author, looking for the writer's fingerprint, so to speak. George Orwell, John McPhee, Joan Didion, and Jack Kerouac are presented here for your further study and enjoyment.

George Orwell (1903–1950) was born in Bengal, India, and raised in England. He was an impoverished writer committed to use his "gift" in the service of political reform, always a champion of the poor and downtrodden. His essays are rich with exotic location and detail: Marrakech, Morocco, Burma, bamboo huts, donkeys, and gazelles. His is, perhaps, for the sake of comparison, the voice of the European intellectual. His prose is cultured and gracious, at the same time flooded with a romantic sensibility and a heightened sense of the word as poetry.

□

John McPhee (1931–   ) was born in Princeton, New Jersey. He is a Princeton University graduate and a staff writer for the *New Yorker* magazine. Primarily known as a journalist, McPhee writes on a range of subjects that take him to such locations as the Pine Barrens, a patch of wild land near the largest city in the United States, and to the Colorado River for a raft trip with a man who would dam it and a man who insists it be left wild. His is the refined and gentlemanly prose of east coast culture and intelligence. He writes in a style that is clean and shapely, rich in detail, and above all, readable. His interest is always in his subject and in his craft. John McPhee stays politely out of sight, objective, and impersonal.

By way of contrast the other two Americans included here, Joan Didion and Jack Kerouac, are highly autobiographical writers. Joan Didion (1934–   ) was born on the west coast of a pioneer family of five generations. Hers is the landscape and detail of Death Valley, the Sacramento Valley, coyotes, the code of the West, rattlesnakes, and the dream of the cabin by the bend of the river. She writes from a sense of the mythic, man eating man on a snowbound pass.

Jack Kerouac (1922–1969) was born in Lowell, Massachusetts, the son of a working-class, French-Canadian family. His is the restless spirit of America, the American version of *The Odyssey*, the coast to coast wanderer. His theory of spontaneous prose, "swimming in a sea of language," suits his landscape of jazz nights, bum hotels, car journeys, and riding the rails. "Tap from yourself the song of yourself," he said, and all his writings consist of one long personal narrative, written "on the run."

You might want to think about how life circumstances have contributed to making these writers' voices uniquely their own. And you? What is it that makes *your* voice unique?

George Orwell
(1903–1950)

George Orwell (Eric Hugh Blair) was born in Bengal, India, in 1903 and raised in England. His family was "lower-upper-middle class," according to Orwell, and he attended Eton on a scholarship.

In 1927 Orwell decided to become a writer and worked for years in destitution. These years of poverty formed the basis of his writing and contributed to a growing involvement in political concerns. He began to see the place of the writer as an influence on society and was committed to serving the cause of the poor and downtrodden.

Marrakech

As the corpse went past the flies left the restaurant table in a cloud and rushed after it, but they came back a few minutes later.

The little crowd of mourners—all men and boys, no women—
threaded their way across the market place between the piles of pome-
granates and the taxis and the camels, wailing a short chant over and
over again. What really appeals to the flies is that the corpses here are
never put into coffins, they are merely wrapped in a piece of rag and
carried on a rough wooden bier on the shoulders of four friends. When
the friends get to the burying ground they hack an oblong hole a foot
or two deep, dump the body in it and fling over it a little of the dried
up, lumpy earth, which is like broken brick. No gravestone, no name,
no identifying mark of any kind. The burying ground is merely a huge
waste of hummocky earth, like a derelict building lot. After a month or
two no one can even be certain where his own relatives are buried.

When you walk through a town like this—two hundred thousand
inhabitants, of whom at least twenty thousand own literally nothing
except the rags they stand up in—when you see how the people live,
and still more how easily they die, it is always difficult to believe that
you are walking among human beings. All colonial empires are in reality founded upon that fact. The people have brown faces—besides,
there are so many of them! Are they really the same flesh as yourself?
Do they even have names? Or are they merely a kind of undifferentiated brown stuff, about as individual as bees or coral insects? They rise
out of the earth, they sweat and starve for a few years, and then they
sink back into the nameless mounds of the graveyard and nobody
notices that they are gone. And even the graves themselves soon fade
back into the soil. Sometimes, out for a walk, as you break your way
through the prickly pear, you notice that it is rather bumpy underfoot,
and only a certain regularity in the bumps tells you that you are walking over skeletons.

I was feeding one of the gazelles in the public gardens.

Gazelles are almost the only animals that look good to eat when
they are still alive, in fact, one can hardly look at their hindquarters
without thinking of a mint sauce. The gazelle I was feeding seemed to
know that this thought was in my mind, for though it took the piece of
bread I was holding out it obviously did not like me. It nibbled rapidly
at the bread, then lowered its head and tried to butt me, then took
another nibble and then butted again. Probably its idea was that if it
could drive me away the bread would somehow remain hanging in
mid-air.

An Arab navvy working on the path nearby lowered his heavy
hoe and sidled slowly towards us. He looked from the gazelle to the
bread and from the bread to the gazelle, with a sort of quiet amazement, as though he had never seen anything quite like this before.
Finally he said shyly in French:

"I could eat some of that bread."

I tore off a piece and he stowed it gratefully in some secret place
under his rags. This man is an employee of the Municipality.

When you go through the Jewish quarters you gather some idea of what the medieval ghettoes were probably like. Under their Moorish rulers the Jews were only allowed to own land in certain restricted areas, and after centuries of this kind of treatment they have ceased to bother about overcrowding. Many of the streets are a good deal less than six feet wide, the houses are completely windowless, and sore-eyed children cluster everywhere in unbelievable numbers, like clouds of flies. Down the centre of the street there is generally running a little river of urine.

In the bazaar huge families of Jews, all dressed in the long black robe and little black skull-cap, are working in dark fly-infested booths that look like caves. A carpenter sits crosslegged at a prehistoric lathe, turning chair-legs at lightning speed. He works the lathe with a bow in his right hand and guides the chisel with his left foot, and thanks to a lifetime of sitting in this position his left leg is warped out of shape. At his side his grandson, aged six, is already starting on the simpler parts of the job.

I was just passing the coppersmiths' booths when somebody noticed that I was lighting a cigarette. Instantly, from the dark holes all round, there was a frenzied rush of Jews, many of them old grandfathers with flowing grey beards, all clamouring for a cigarette. Even a blind man somewhere at the back of one of the booths heard a rumour of cigarettes and came crawling out, groping in the air with his hand. In about a minute I had used up the whole packet. None of these people, I suppose, works less than twelve hours a day, and every one of them looks on a cigarette as a more or less impossible luxury.

As the Jews live in self-contained communities they follow the same trades as the Arabs, except for agriculture. Fruit-sellers, potters, silversmiths, blacksmiths, butchers, leatherworkers, tailors, water-carriers, beggars, porters—whichever way you look you see nothing but Jews. As a matter of fact there are thirteen thousand of them, all living in the space of a few acres. A good job Hitler wasn't here. Perhaps he was on his way, however. You hear the usual dark rumours about the Jews, not only from the Arabs but from the poorer Europeans.

"Yes *mon vieux*, they took my job away from me and gave it to a Jew. The Jews! They're the real rulers of this country, you know. They've got all the money. They control the banks, finance—everything."

"But," I said, "isn't it a fact that the average Jew is a labourer working for about a penny an hour?"

"Ah, that's only for show! They're all money lenders really. They're cunning, the Jews."

In just the same way, a couple of hundred years ago, poor old women used to be burned for witchcraft when they could not even work enough magic to get themselves a square meal.

All people who work with their hands are partly invisible, and the more important the work they do, the less visible they are. Still, a

□

white skin is always fairly conspicuous. In northern Europe, when you see a labourer ploughing a field, you probably give him a second glance. In a hot country, anywhere south of Gibraltar or east of Suez, the chances are that you don't even see him. I have noticed this again and again. In a tropical landscape one's eye takes in everything except the human beings. It takes in the dried-up soil, the prickly pear, the palm tree and the distant mountain, but it always misses the peasant hoeing at his patch. He is the same colour as the earth, and a great deal less interesting to look at.

It is only because of this that the starved countries of Asia and Africa are accepted as tourist resorts. No one would think of running cheap trips to the Distressed Areas. But where the human beings have brown skins their poverty is simply not noticed. What does Morocco mean to a Frenchman? An orange grove or a job in Government service. Or to an Englishman? Camels, castles, palm trees, Foreign Legionnaires, brass trays, and bandits. One could probably live there for years without noticing that for nine-tenths of the people the reality of life is an endless, back-breaking struggle to wring a little food out of an eroded soil.

Most of Morocco is so desolate that no wild animal bigger than a hare can live on it. Huge areas which were once covered with forest have turned into a treeless waste where the soil is exactly like broken-up brick. Nevertheless a good deal of it is cultivated, with frightful labour. Everything is done by hand. Long lines of women, bent double like inverted capital L's, work their way slowly across the fields, tearing up the prickly weeds with their hands, and the peasant gathering lucerne for fodder pulls it up stalk by stalk instead of reaping it, thus saving an inch or two on each stalk. The plough is a wretched wooden thing, so frail that one can easily carry it on one's shoulder, and fitted underneath with a rough iron spike which stirs the soil to a depth of about four inches. This is as much as the strength of the animals is equal to. It is usual to plough with a cow and a donkey yoked together. Two donkeys would not be quite strong enough, but on the other hand two cows would cost a little more to feed. The peasants possess no harrows, they merely plough the soil several times over in different directions, finally leaving it in rough furrows, after which the whole field has to be shaped with hoes into small oblong patches to conserve water. Except for a day or two after the rare rainstorms there is never enough water. Along the edges of the fields channels are hacked out to a depth of thirty or forty feet to get at the tiny trickles which run through the subsoil.

Every afternoon a file of very old women passes down the road outside my house, each carrying a load of firewood. All of them are mummified with age and the sun, and all of them are tiny. It seems to be generally the case in primitive communities that women, when they get beyond a certain age, shrink to the size of children. One day a poor

□

old creature who could not have been more than four feet tall crept past me under a vast load of wood. I stopped her and put a five-sou piece (a little more than a farthing) into her hand. She answered with a shrill wail, almost a scream, which was partly gratitude but mainly surprise. I suppose that from her point of view, by taking any notice of her, I seemed almost to be violating a law of nature. She accepted her status as an old woman, that is to say as a beast of burden. When a family is travelling it is quite usual to see a father and a grown-up son riding ahead on donkeys, and an old woman following on foot, carrying the baggage.

But what is strange about these people is their invisiblity. For several weeks, always at about the same time of day, the file of old women had hobbled past the house with their firewood, and though they had registered themselves on my eyeballs I cannot truly say that I had seen them. Firewood was passing—that was how I saw it. It was only that one day I happened to be walking behind them, and the curious up and down motion of a load of wood drew my attention to the human being beneath it. Then for the first time I noticed the poor old earth-coloured bodies, bodies reduced to bones and leathery skin, bent double under the crushing weight. Yet I suppose I had not been five minutes on Moroccan soil before I noticed the overloading of the donkeys and was infuriated by it. There is no question that the donkeys are damnably treated. The Moroccan donkey is hardly bigger than a St. Bernard dog, it carries a load which in the British Army would be considered too much for a fifteen-hands mule, and very often its packsaddle is not taken off its back for weeks together. But what is peculiarly pitiful is that it is the most willing creature on earth, it follows its master like a dog and does not need either bridle or halter. After a dozen years of devoted work it suddenly drops dead, whereupon its master tips it into the ditch and the village dogs have torn its guts out before it is cold.

This kind of thing makes one's blood boil, whereas—on the whole—the plight of the human beings does not. I am not commenting, merely pointing to a fact. People with brown skins are next door to invisible. Anyone can be sorry for the donkey with its galled back, but it is generally owing to some kind of accident if one even notices the old woman under her load of sticks.

As the storks flew northward the Negroes were marching southward—a long, dusty column, infantry, screw-gun batteries, and then more infantry, four or five thousand men in all, winding up the road with a clumping of boots and a clatter of iron wheels.

They were Senegalese, the blackest Negroes in Africa, so black that sometimes it is difficult to see whereabouts on their necks the hair begins. Their splendid bodies were hidden in reach-me-down khaki uniforms, their feet squashed into boots that looked like blocks of wood,

□

and every tin hat seemed to be a couple of sizes too small. It was very hot and the men had marched a long way. They slumped under the weight of their packs and the curiously sensitive black faces were glistening with sweat.

As they went past, a tall, very young Negro turned and caught my eye. But the look he gave me was not in the least the kind of look you might expect. Not hostile, not contemptuous, not sullen, not even inquisitive. It was the shy, wide-eyed Negro look, which actually is a look of profound respect. I saw how it was. This wretched boy, who is a French citizen and has therefore been dragged from the forest to scrub floors and catch syphilis in garrison towns, actually has feelings of reverence before a white skin. He has been taught that the white race are his masters, and he still believes it.

But there is one thought which every white man (and in this connection it doesn't matter twopence if he calls himself a socialist) thinks when he sees a black army marching past. "How much longer can we go on kidding these people? How long before they turn their guns in the other direction?"

It was curious, really. Every white man there had this thought stowed somewhere or other in his mind. I had it, so had the other onlookers, so had the officers on their sweating chargers and the white N.C.O.'s marching in the ranks. It was a kind of secret which we all knew and were too clever to tell; only the Negroes didn't know it. And really it was like watching a flock of cattle to see the long column, a mile or two miles of armed men, flowing peacefully up the road, while the great white birds drifted over them in the opposite direction, glittering like scraps of paper.

Vocabulary

pomegranate   an edible fruit from a shrubby tree, with a tough, reddish rind and many seeds in a juicy red pulp
bier   a stand on which a corpse is carried to the grave
hummocky   moundy (earth)
derelict   social outcast, vagrant
undifferentiated   no differences made, no distinctions
gazelle   a slender-necked, hooved, deerlike animal known for its bounding gait
navvy   a laborer, especially one employed in construction
lucerne   an alfalfa plant
harrow   a farm instrument with teeth or discs to break up and even off plowed ground
farthing   a British coin worth about one-fourth of a penny
galled   embittered

□

Allusions/References

the Municipality the British governing body
mon vieux well (what about it), or old chap

Discussion

1. The true beauty of the first sentence eludes the reader until halfway into the second paragraph. What strange effect is achieved by Orwell's focus on the flies?
   First sentences in your own writing ought to be strong. Since many of us tend to need a "warm up" before the impulse behind our words makes itself known, one tip to follow is to, afterward, after all your words on a subject, go back and edit. Take away all sentences before the one where you finally "felt" the strength of your idea take over. This sentence is your: "As the corpse went past the flies left the restaurant table in a cloud and rushed after it, but they came back a few minutes later." Don't worry about a preamble. This is where a good writer starts.
2. How does Orwell's statement in the third paragraph, " . . . it is always difficult to believe that you are walking among human beings . . . " further clarify the choice to begin with the flies?
   Orwell describes the peoples of colonial empires as "a kind of undifferentiated brown stuff." Again, how are his stylistic choices (word choices, metaphors) all contributing to a point he is trying to make about colonialism?
   Good descriptive writing makes you *experience* the scene, not just learn about it. When *your* eyes and ears, when *your* senses become Orwell's, in whose shoes are you walking? (I'm not trying to be funny here, only to ask you a question of some complexity. Orwell was a political writer. His stance here is that of a man disapproving very much of man's inhumanity to man, but at the same time showing us how it can occur.)
3. Notice the transition between the third paragraph and the single sentence fourth paragraph. " . . . only a certain regularity in the bumps tells you that you are walking over skeletons." From this evocation of the *wasteland* to " . . . I was feeding one of the gazelles in the public *gardens*."
   As in a good film cut, many meanings become evident in this sudden change of scene. Discuss some of them. Notice also how the shapes and sounds of words can serve as echos or repeated images from one scene to the next (one paragraph to the next). The "prickly pear" and the "public gardens" are juxtaposed to our eye and ear much as a cut, from polishing fingernails to a gloxinia in bloom in the next scene, might be accomplished in film. The same, somehow, with "skeleton" and "gazelle," those sound-alike, awkwardly skeletal-shaped words. Such language choice is a matter of craft and art. Look carefully at other such transitions or cuts.
4. How do the "clouds of flies" come back at us again? In what sort of metamorphoses?
5. Listen to the sounds of the bazaar in paragraphs nine and ten beginning: "In the bazaar huge families of Jews . . . " How do words like "long black robe and little black skull-cap" and "dark fly-infested booths that look like caves,"

□

work both to convey information and to convey sounds clacking like the life of the bazaar?

Look again at the "long black robe and little black skull-cap." How do those "l's" and 'k's" echo each other in our eye?

Does a writer really care about such things? Of course. They are his brushstrokes.

6. One more look at the *look* of Orwell's words.

> "Long line of women, bent double like inverted capital L's . . . "

> " . . . peasant gathering lucerne for fodder pulls it up stalk by stalk . . . "

> " . . . to plough with a cow and a donkey . . . "

> "Two donkeys . . . two cows . . . "

> " . . . a long, dusty column, infantry, screw-gun batteries, and then more infantry, four or five thousand men in all, winding up the road with a clumping of boots and a clatter of iron wheels."

How in each of the lines above are you *shown* the thing being described and not merely told about it?

What other examples of words that *look like* what they are saying (a visual onomatopoeia) can you find?

7. Now reread Orwell's essay. At first, awareness of these "fine details" may seem to get in the way of your understanding. In truth, they will add to it immeasurably.

George Orwell
(1903–1950)

Orwell went to Spain as a journalist in 1936 to cover the Spanish Civil War and instead joined a combat unit and was seriously wounded. This involvement had a profound influence on him. In 1947 he wrote: "Every line of serious work that I have written since 1936 has been written, directly or indirectly, against totalitarianism and for democratic socialism."

He went on to write his most famous works *Animal Farm* ("the first book in which I tried . . . to fuse political purpose and artistic purpose") and *1984*. Orwell died of tuberculosis at age 46.

A Hanging

It was in Burma, a sodden morning of the rains. A sickly light, like yellow tinfoil, was slanting over the high walls into the jail yard. We were waiting outside the condemned cells, a row of sheds fronted with double bars, like small animal cages. Each cell measured about ten feet by ten and was quite bare within except for a plank bed and a pot of drinking water. In some of them brown silent men were squatting at the inner bars, with their blankets draped round them. These were the condemned men, due to be hanged within the next week or two.

One prisoner had been brought out of his cell. He was a Hindu, a puny wisp of a man, with a shaven head and vague liquid eyes. He had a thick, sprouting mustache, absurdly too big for his body, rather like the mustache of a comic man on the films. Six tall Indian warders were guarding him and getting him ready for the gallows. Two of them stood by with rifles and fixed bayonets, while the others handcuffed him, passed a chain through his handcuffs and fixed it to their belts, and lashed his arms tight to his sides. They crowded very close about him, with their hands always on him in a careful, caressing grip, as though all the while feeling him to make sure he was there. It was like men handling a fish which is still alive and may jump back into the water. But he stood quite unresisting, yielding his arms limply to the ropes, as though he hardly noticed what was happening.

Eight o'clock struck and a bugle call, desolately thin in the wet air, floated from the distant barracks. The superintendent of the jail, who was standing apart from the rest of us, moodily prodding the gravel with his stick, raised his head at the sound. He was an army doctor, with a gray toothbrush mustache and a gruff voice. "For God's sake hurry up, Francis," he said irritably. "The man ought to have been dead by this time. Aren't you ready yet?"

Francis, the head jailer, a fat Dravidian in a white drill suit and gold spectacles, waved his black hand. "Yes sir, yes sir," he bubbled. "All iss satisfactorily prepared. The hangman iss waiting. We shall proceed."

"Well, quick march, then. The prisoners can't get their breakfast till this job's over."

We set out for the gallows. Two warders marched on either side of the prisoner, with their rifles at the slope; two others marched close against him, gripping him by arm and shoulder, as though at once pushing and supporting him. The rest of us, magistrates and the like, followed behind. Suddenly, when we had gone ten yards, the procession stopped short without any order or warning. A dreadful thing had happened—a dog, come goodness knows whence, had appeared in the yard. It came bounding among us with a loud volley of barks, and leapt round us wagging its whole body, wild with glee at finding so many human beings together. It was a large woolly dog, half Airedale, half pariah. For a moment it pranced round us, and then, before anyone could stop it, it had made a dash for the prisoner, and jumping up tried to lick his face. Everyone stood aghast, too taken aback even to grab at the dog.

"Who let that bloody brute in here?" said the superintendent angrily. "Catch it, someone!"

A warder, detached from the escort, charged clumsily after the dog, but it danced and gambolled just out of his reach, taking everything as part of the game. A young Eurasian jailer picked up a handful of gravel and tried to stone the dog away, but it dodged the stones and came after us again. Its yaps echoed from the jail walls. The prisoner, in the grasp of the two warders, looked on incuriously, as though this was another formality of the hanging. It was several minutes before someone managed to catch the dog. Then we put my handkerchief through its collar and moved off once more, with the dog still straining and whimpering.

It was about forty yards to the gallows. I watched the bare brown back of the prisoner marching in front of me. He walked clumsily with his bound arms, but quite steadily, with that bobbing gait of the Indian who never straightens his knees. At each step his muscles slid nearly into place, the lock of hair on his scalp danced up and down, his feet printed themselves on the wet gravel. And once, in spite of the men who gripped him by each shoulder, he stepped slightly aside to avoid a puddle on the path.

It is curious, but till that moment I had never realized what it means to destroy a healthy, conscious man. When I saw the prisoner step aside to avoid the puddle, I saw the mystery, the unspeakable wrongness, of cutting a life short when it is in full tide. This man was not dying, he was alive just as we were alive. All the organs of his body were working—bowels digesting food, skin renewing itself, nails growing, tissues forming—all toiling away in solemn foolery. His nails would still be growing when he stood on the drop, when he was falling through the air with a tenth of a second to live. His eyes saw the yellow gravel and the gray walls, and his brain still remembered, foresaw, reasoned—reasoned even about puddles. He and we were a party of men walking together, seeing, hearing, feeling, understanding the same world; and in two minutes, with a sudden snap, one of us would be gone—one mind less, one world less.

The gallows stood in a small yard, separate from the main grounds of the prison, and overgrown with tall prickly weeds. It was a brick erection like three sides of a shed, with planking on top, and above that two beams and a crossbar with the rope dangling. The hangman, a gray-haired convict in the white uniform of the prison, was waiting beside his machine. He greeted us with a servile crouch as we entered. At a word from Francis the two warders, gripping the prisoner more closely than ever, half led, half pushed him to the gallows and helped him clumsily up the ladder. Then the hangman climbed up and fixed the rope round the prisoner's neck.

We stood waiting, five yards away. The warders had formed in a rough circle round the gallows. And then, when the noose was fixed, the prisoner began crying out on his god. It was a high, reiterated cry of "Ram! Ram! Ram! Ram!", not urgent and fearful like a prayer or a cry for help, but steady, rhythmical, almost like the tolling of the bell. The dog answered the sound with a whine. The hangman, still stand-

□

ing on the gallows, produced a small cotton bag like a flour bag and
drew it down over the prisoner's face. But the sound, muffled by the
cloth, still persisted, over and over again: "Ram! Ram! Ram! Ram!
Ram!"

The hangman climbed down and stood ready, holding the lever.
Minutes seemed to pass. The steady, muffled crying from the prisoner
went on and on, "Ram! Ram! Ram!" never faltering for an instant. The
superintendent, his head on his chest, was slowly poking the ground
with his stick; perhaps he was counting the cries, allowing the prisoner
a fixed number—fifty, perhaps, or a hundred. Everyone had changed
color. The Indians had gone gray like bad coffee, and one or two of the
bayonets were wavering. We looked at the lashed, hooded man on the
drop, and listened to his cries—each cry another second of life;
the same thought was in all our minds: oh, kill him quickly, get it over,
stop that abominable noise!

Suddenly the superintendent made up his mind. Throwing up his
head he made a swift motion with his stick. "Chalo!" he shouted almost
fiercely.

There was a clanking noise, and then dead silence. The prisoner
had vanished, and the rope was twisting on itself. I let go of the dog,
and it galloped immediately to the back of the gallows; but when it got
there it stopped short, barked, and then retreated into a corner of the
yard, where it stood among the weeds, looking timorously out at us.
We went round the gallows to inspect the prisoner's body. He was dangling with his toes pointed straight downwards, very slowly revolving,
as dead as a stone.

The superintendent reached out with his stick and poked the bare
body; it oscillated slightly. "*He's* all right," said the superintendent. He
backed out from under the gallows, and blew out a deep breath. The
moody look had gone out of his face quite suddenly. He glanced at his
wrist-watch. "Eight minutes past eight. Well, that's all for this morning,
thank god."

The warders unfixed bayonets and marched away. The dog, sob-
ered and conscious of having misbehaved itself, slipped after them. We
walked out of the gallows yard, past the condemned cells with their
waiting prisoners, into the big central yard of the prison. The convicts,
under the command of warders armed with lathis, were already
receiving their breakfast. They squatted in long rows, each man holding a tin pannikin, while two warders with buckets marched round
ladling out rice; it seemed quite a homely, jolly scene, after the hanging.
An enormous relief had come upon us now that the job was done. One
felt an impulse to sing, to break into a run, to snigger. All at once everyone began chattering gaily.

The Eurasian boy walking beside me nodded towards the way we
had come, with a knowing smile: "Do you know, sir, our friend (he
meant the dead man), when he heard his appeal had been dismissed,

he pissed on the floor of his cell. From fright.—Kindly take one of my cigarettes, sir. Do you not admire my new silver case, sir? From the box-wallah, two rupees eight annas. Classy European style."

Several people laughed—at what, nobody seemed certain.

Francis was walking by the superintendent, talking garrulously: "Well, sir, all hass passed off with the utmost satisfactoriness. It wass all finished—flick! like that. It iss not always so—oah, no! I have known cases where the doctor wass obliged to go beneath the gallows and pull the prisoner's legs to ensure decease. Most disagreeable!"

"Wriggling about, eh? That's bad," said the superintendent.

"Ach, sir, it iss worse when they become refractory! One man, I recall, clung to the bars of hiss cage when we went to take him out. You will scarcely credit, sir, that it took six warders to dislodge him, three pulling at each leg. We reasoned with him. 'My dear fellow,' we said, 'think of all the pain and trouble you are causing to us!' But no, he would not listen! Ach, he wass very troublesome!"

I found that I was laughing quite loudly. Everyone was laughing. Even the superintendent grinned in a tolerant way. "You'd better all come out and have a drink," he said quite genially. "I've got a bottle of whisky in the car. We could do with it."

We went through the big double gates of the prison, into the road. "Pulling at his legs!" exclaimed a Burmese magistrate suddenly, and burst into a loud chuckling. We all began laughing again. At that moment Francis's anecdote seemed extraordinarily funny. We all had a drink together, native and European alike, quite amicably. The dead man was a hundred yards away.

Vocabulary

sodden   thoroughly soaked
Dravidian   a member of the aboriginal population of southern India
pariah   member of low caste, social outcast
aghast   shocked by something horrible
gambolled   leapt about playfully
abominable   thoroughly unpleasant
timorously   full of apprehensiveness
oscillated   back and forth in a steady, uninterrupted rhythm
lathis   a heavy stick, often of bamboo, bound with iron; used in India as a weapon, especially by police
pannikin   a small saucepan or metal cup
box wallah   peddler
rupee   basic monetary unit; equal to 100 cents
anna   a copper coin equal to $\frac{1}{16}$ of a rupee
garrulously   habitually talkative
refractory   obstinant, unmanageable
amicably   friendly, peaceably

□

Discussion

1. Again let's begin with a closer look at Orwell's word choices:

> "a sodden morning of rains"
>
> "light, like yellow tinfoil"
>
> "the mustache of a comic man"
>
> "hands . . . in a careful, caressing grip"
>
> "like men handling a fish"

   In each case is an implied or stated comparison. How do these comparisons put the reader into the scene like it or not? And "like it or not" is the way it is with this piece, isn't it? Orwell puts the reader into a position of complicity with the wardens and the hangman—a voyeur at a hanging. Why? What does Orwell hope will be gained by our vicarious experiencing of this event?

2. An oxymoron is a figure of speech in which two words of seeming contradiction are paired—for instance, bitter sweet or caressing grip. Orwell is fond of the oxymoron. When the man is brought to the gallows and Orwell reflects on his life and consciousness, he writes "the organs of his body were working . . . in *solemn foolery.*" These seeming incongruities of language are paralleled by Orwell's theme.

   How is this tendency toward the paradoxical shown in matters also of theme? What is Orwell showing us about man's humanity to man? How is it that everything ends with the ring of laughter? What kind of laughter is this? What kind of ending for Orwell's essay? Effective?

3. As in music, every piece of writing has a sound, the sound of its notes (the words) and the rhythm created by its sentences and paragraphs, sound and interval. Orwell is particularly conscious of the rhythms leading up to the gallows and those that follow after. You might wish to divide the essay thusly and look (listen) closely to the pacing and mood escalation of the first part as juxtaposed to the last. Why does the last part *sound* so matter-of-fact? How does it, almost insidiously, lead you into the hysteria?

John McPhee
(1931–   )

John McPhee was born March 8, 1931, in Princeton, New Jersey. While in college at Princeton University, McPhee wrote for several student publications. After graduate study at Cambridge University he worked briefly as a television playwright and then for several years as an associate editor at *Time* magazine. Since 1964 he has been a staff writer for *New Yorker* magazine.

Most properly considered a "journalist," there are more than fifteen books of McPhee's writing in print. His range of subjects is amazing: animals, athletes, colleges, canoes, science, travel, and even oranges, to list just a few. As one reviewer wrote: "Sometimes it seems that McPhee deliberately chooses unpromising subjects, just to show what he can do with them."

The Pine Barrens

Fred Brown's house is on an unpaved road that curves along the edge of a wide cranberry bog. What attracted me to it was the pump that stands in his yard. It was something of a wonder that I noticed the pump, because there were, among other things, eight automobiles in the yard, two of them on their sides and one of them upside down, all ten years old or older. Around the cars were old refrigerators, vacuum cleaners, partly dismantled radios, cathode-ray tubes, a short wooden ski, a large wooden mallet, dozens of cranberry pickers' boxes, many tires, an orange crate dated 1946, a cord or so of firewood, mandolins, engine heads, and maybe a thousand other things. The house itself, two stories high, was covered with tarpaper that was peeling away in some places, revealing its original shingles, made of Atlantic white cedar from the stream courses of the surrounding forest. I called out to ask if anyone was home, and a voice called back, "Come in. Come in. Come on the hell in."

I walked through a vestibule that had a dirt floor, stepped up into a kitchen, and went on into another room that had several overstuffed chairs in it and a porcelain-topped table, where Fred Brown was seated, eating a pork chop. He was dressed in a white sleeveless shirt, ankle-top shoes, and undershorts. He gave me a cheerful greeting and, without asking why I had come or what I wanted, picked up a pair of khaki trousers that had been tossed onto one of the overstuffed chairs and asked me to sit down. He set the trousers on another chair, and he apologized for being in the middle of his breakfast, explaining that he seldom drank much but the night before he had had a few drinks and this had caused his day to start slowly. "I don't know what's the matter with me, but there's got to be something the matter with me, because drink don't agree with me anymore," he said. He had a raw onion in one hand, and while he talked he shaved slices from the onion and ate them between bites of the chop. He was a muscular and well-built man, with short, bristly white hair, and he had bright, fast-moving eyes in a wide-open face. His legs were trim and strong, with large muscles in the calves. I guessed that he was about sixty, and for a man of sixty he seemed to be in remarkably good shape. He was actually seventy-nine. "My rule is: Never eat except when you're hungry," he said, and he ate another slice of the onion.

In a straight-backed chair near the doorway to the kitchen sat a young man with long black hair, who wore a visored red leather cap that had darkened with age. His shirt was coarse-woven and had eyelets down a V neck that was laced with a thong. His trousers were made of canvas, and he was wearing gum boots. His arms were folded, his legs were stretched out, he had one ankle over the other, and as he sat there he appeared to be sighting carefully past his feet, as if his toes were the outer frame of a gunsight and he could see some sort of target in the floor. When I had entered, I had said hello to him, and he had nodded without looking up. He had a long, straight nose and high cheekbones, in a deeply tanned face that was, somehow, gaunt. I had no idea whether he was shy or hostile. Eventually, when I came to know him, I found him to be as shy a person as I have ever had a chance to know. His name is Bill Wasovwich, and he lives alone in a cabin about half a mile from Fred. First his father, then his mother left him when he was a young boy, and he grew up depending on the help of various people in the pines. One of them, a cranberry grower, employs him and has given him some acreage, in which Bill is building a small cranberry bog of his own, "turfing it out" by hand. When he is not working in the bogs, he goes roaming, as he puts it, setting out cross-country on long, looping journeys, hiking about thirty miles in a typical day, in search of what he calls "events"—surprising a buck, or a gray fox, or perhaps a poacher or a man with a still. Almost no one who is not native to the pines could do this, for the woods have an undulating sameness, and the understory—huckleberries, sheep laurel, sweet fern, high-bush blueberry—is often so dense that a wanderer can walk in a fairly tight circle and think that he is moving in a straight line. State forest rangers spend a good part of their time finding hikers and hunters, some of whom have vanished for days. In his long, pathless journeys, Bill always emerges from the woods near his cabin—and about when he plans to. In the fall, when thousands of hunters come into the pines, he sometimes works as a guide. In the evenings, or in the daytime when he is not working or roaming, he goes to Fred Brown's house and sits there for hours. The old man is a widower whose seven children are long since gone from Hog Wallow, and he is as expansively talkative and worldly as the young one is withdrawn and wild. Although there are fifty-three years between their ages, it is obviously fortunate for each of them to be the other's neighbor.

That first morning, while Bill went on looking at his outstretched toes, Fred got up from the table, put on his pants, and said he was going to cook me a pork chop, because I looked hungry and ought to eat something. It was about noon, and I was even hungrier than I may have looked, so I gratefully accepted his offer, which was a considerable one. There are two or three small general stores in the pines, but for anything as fragile as a fresh pork chop it is necessary to make a round trip from Fred's place of about fifty miles. Fred went into the kitchen and dropped a chop into a frying pan that was crackling with hot grease. He has a fairly new four-burner stove that uses bottled gas. He keeps water in a large bowl on a table in the kitchen and ladles some when he wants it. While he cooked the meat, he looked out a window through a stand of pitch pines and into the cranberry bog. "I saw a big buck out here last night with velvet on his horns," he said. "Them horns is soft when they're in velvet." On a nail high on one wall of the room that Bill and I were sitting in was a large meat cleaver. Next to it was a billy club. The wall itself was papered in a flower pattern, and the wallpaper continued out across the ceiling and down the three other walls, lending the room something of the appearance of the inside of a gift box. In some parts of the ceiling, the paper had come loose. "I didn't paper this year." Fred said. "For the last couple months, I've had sinus." The floor was covered with old rugs. They had been put down in random pieces, and in some places as many as six layers were stacked up. In winter, when the temperature approaches zero, the worst cold comes through the floor. The only source of heat in the house is a wood-burning stove in the main room. There were seven calendars on the walls, all current and none with pictures of nudes. Fading into pastel on one wall was a rotogravure photograph of President and Mrs. Eisenhower. A framed poem read:

God hath not promised

Sun without rain

Joy without sorrow

Peace without pain.

Noticing my interest in all this, Fred reached into a drawer and showed me what appeared to be a postcard. On it was a photograph of a woman, and Fred said with a straight face that she was his present girl, adding that he meets her regularly under a juniper tree on a road farther south in the pines. The woman, whose appearance suggested strongly that she had never been within a great many miles of the Pine Barrens, was wearing nothing at all.

I asked Fred what all those cars were doing in his yard, and he said that one of them was in running condition and the rest were its predecessors. The working vehicle was a 1956 Mercury. Each of the seven others had at one time or another been his best car, and each, in turn, had lain down like a sick animal and had died right there in the yard, unless it had been towed home after a mishap elsewhere in the pines. Fred recited, with affection, the history of each car. Of one old Ford, for example, he said, "I upset that up to Speedwell in the creek." And of an even older car, a station wagon, he said, "I busted that one up in the snow. I met a car on a little hill, and hit the brake, and hit a tree." One of the cars had met its end at a narrow bridge about four miles from Hog Wallow, where Fred had hit a state trooper, head on.

The pork was delicious and almost crisp. Fred gave me a potato with it, and a pitcher of melted grease from the frying pan to pour over the potato. He also handed me a loaf of bread and a dish of margarine, saying, "Here's your bread. You can have one piece or two. Whatever you want."

Fred apologized for not having a phone, after I asked where I would have to go to make a call, later on. He said, "I don't have no phone because I don't have no electric. If I had electric, I would have had a phone in here a long time ago." He uses a kerosene lamp, a propane lamp, and two flashlights.

He asked where I was going, and I said that I had no particular destination, explaining that I was in the pines because I found it hard to believe that so much unbroken forest could still exist so near the big Eastern cities, and I wanted to see it while it was still there. "Is that so?" he said three times. Like many people in the pines, he often says things three times. "Is that so? Is *that* so?"

I asked him what he thought of a plan that has been developed by Burlington and Ocean counties to create a supersonic jetport in the pines, connected by a spur of the Garden State Parkway to a new city of two hundred and fifty thousand people, also in the pines.

"They've been talking about that for three years, and they've never give up," Fred said.

"It'd be the end of these woods," Bill said. This was the first time I heard Bill speak. I had been there for an hour, and he had not said a word. Without looking up, he said again, "It'd be the end of these woods, I can tell you that."

Fred said, "They could build ten jetports around me. I wouldn't give a damn."

"You ain't going to be around very long," Bill said to him. "It would be the end of these woods."

Fred took that as a fact, and not as an insult. "Yes, it would be the end of these woods," he said. "But there'd be people here you could do business with."

Bill said, "There ain't no place like this left in the country, I don't believe—and I travelled around a little bit, too."

Eventually, I made the request I had intended to make when I walked in the door. "Could I have some water?" I said to Fred. "I have a jerry can and I'd like to fill it at the pump."

"Hell, yes," he said. "That isn't my water. That's God's water. That's God's water. That right, Bill?"

"I *guess* so," Bill said, without looking up. "It's good water, I can tell you that."

"That's God's water," Fred said again. "Take all you want."

Vocabulary

vestibule   a small entrance hall

Discussion

1. McPhee introduces Bill Wasovwich to the reader as "he sat there . . . sighting carefully past his feet." Note how McPhee then gives intervening informa-

tion before returning to "that first morning, while Bill went on looking at his outstretched toes." Find other examples of McPhee's craftsmanship, the delicate spans he builds between the "now" and the "further information" he wishes to add.

2. McPhee does not use tape recorders when he interviews. He finds them mechanical and obtrusive. He wishes to capture the words of the occasion, however, and through voluminous notes and memory he gives us his recreations. What indications do you get from this piece of his amazing ear for dialogue?

3. How does McPhee's withholding of some pertinent detail in a catalogue of details recreate for the reader the sense of astonishment or delight that he himself must have felt? (Don't *tell* your readers, *show* them.) See, for example, the paragraph following the framed poem. It begins: "Noticing my interest in all this. . . ." What other examples of displacements, or tiny surprises, can you find?

4. Notice the "is that so" paragraph. Why does McPhee repeat "is that so" twice in a row? Why not three times? How many times do your eyes *see* it on the page?
Examine the closing of this excerpt. How are the repeated phrases finally amusing?

John McPhee
(1931–   )

In his introduction to *The John McPhee Reader* William Howarth writes, "McPhee is a craftsman; he understands that his work must always have inherent form." Howarth describes the laborious process McPhee employs involving travel, elaborate note-taking and interviewing, the complex method of development and organization of material, all this preceding the writing of drafts.

As Howarth notes: "As the reader begins a piece, he can be certain that McPhee always knew how it would end. He also knew where the center was, and how that middle would span its opposite structural members." It is from this development of structural order that he manages to produce works that are rich in detail and absolutely readable.

from The Curve of Binding Energy

I once asked Ted Taylor if he was at all worried about people making hydrogen bombs in their basements and, if so, how they might go about it.

He said, "I can't tell you anything at all about that except that my opinion is that a homemade H-bomb is essentially an impossibility. One can't even hint at the principles involved, beyond saying that it requires heating some material up to a terribly high temperature, which is why it is called a thermonuclear bomb. There are by now several thousand people who know how this is done, so the secret of the H-bomb will out somewhere along the line, but, even when it does, the fact remains: to make an H-bomb is not a basement operation. The project would take a large, well-organized group of people a great deal of time. The secret, incidentally, is not a matter of materials. It is a matter of design."

The design was hit upon by Stanislaw Ulam and Edward Teller in 1951. In the pages of a patent application they were described as the bomb's "inventors." After a long period of getting nowhere—an effort by many scientists, under considerable pressure from Washington—Ulam one day asked Teller to sit down in private with him and listen to an idea. They closed the door of Teller's office at Los Alamos and talked. Teller was much impressed with Ulam's idea and at once thought of a better way to do the kind of thing Ulam had in mind. The two men came out of the room with the answer to the problem of the hydrogen bomb. The rest was detail, albeit on a major scale—computer calculations, design, fabrication. The better part of two years went by before a task force was ready to go—in the fall of 1952—to Eniwetok to test the theory.

Not all Los Alamos theories could be tested. Long popular within the Theoretical Division was, for example, a theory that the people of Hungary are Martians. The reasoning went like this: The Martians left their own planet several aeons ago and came to Earth; they landed in what is now Hungary; the tribes of Europe were so primitive and barbarian that it was necessary for the Martians to conceal their evolutionary difference or be hacked to pieces. Through the years, the concealment had on the whole been successful, but the Martians had three characteristics too strong to hide; their wanderlust, which found its outlet in the Hungarian gypsy; their language (Hungarian is not related to any of the languages spoken in surrounding countries); and their unearthly intelligence. One had only to look around to see the evidence; Teller, Wigner, Szilard, von Neumann—Hungarians all. Wigner had designed the first plutonium-production reactors. Szilard had been among the first to suggest that fission could be used to make a bomb. Von Nuemann had developed the digital computer. Teller—moody, tireless, and given to fits of laughter, bursts of anger—worked long hours and was impatient with what he felt to be the excessively slow advancement of Project Panda, as the hydrogen-bomb development was known. Kindly to juniors, he had done much to encourage Ted Taylor in his work. His impatience with his peers, however, eventually caused him to leave Los Alamos and establish a rival laboratory at Livermore, in California. Teller had a thick Martian accent. He also had a sense of humor that could penetrate bone. Dark-haired, heavy-browed, he limped pronouncedly. In Europe, one of his feet had been mangled by a streetcar.

Ulam was a Pole and had no inclination to feel thunderstruck in the presence of Hungarians, whatever their origins. His wife was vivacious and French. He worked short hours. He was heroically lazy. He was considered lazy by all of his colleagues, and he did not disagree. The pressures of the Cold War were almost as intense at Los Alamos as the pressures of the war that preceded it, but these pressures were resisted by Ulam. Mornings, he never appeared for work before ten, and in the afternoons he was gone at four. When Enrico Fermi organized hikes on Sundays, Ulam went along to the foot of the trail. Fermi, Hans Bethe, George Bell, Ted Taylor—up the talus slopes they went while Ulam sat below and watched them through binoculars. Many years after the first thermonuclear bomb had been successfully tested, Ulam's secretary cut out and tacked to a bulletin board a cartoon in which two cavemen were talking about a third caveman, who was standing off by himself. The caption was "He's been unbearable since he invented fire."

The object that had been sent out to Eniwetok was distinguished by its plainness and its size. It was a cylinder with somewhat convex ends. It was twenty-two feet long and five and a half feet in diameter. It was the result of Project Panda, and it was called Mike. It looked something like the tank on a railway tank car, and it weighed twenty-one tons. Inside it was at least one fission bomb, and a great deal of heavy hydrogen. Mike was placed in a building with metal siding which had been constructed for the purpose on an island called Elugelab, in the northern sector of the atoll. After Mike had exploded, nothing whatever remained where the island had been but seawater. The island had disappeared from the earth. The yield of the Hiroshima bomb had been thirteen kilotons. The theoretical expectation for Mike was a few thousand kilotons—a few megatons. The fireball spread so far and fast that it terrified observers who had seen many tests before. The explosion, in the words of Ted Taylor, who was not there, "was so huge, so brutal—as if things had gone too far. When the heat reached the observers, it stayed and stayed and stayed, not for seconds but for minutes." The yield of the bomb was ten megatons. It so unnerved Norris Bradbury, the Los Alamos director, that for a brief time he wondered if the people at Eniwetok should somehow try to conceal from their colleagues back in New Mexico the magnitude of what had happened. Few hydrogen bombs subsequently exploded by the United States have been allowed to approach that one in yield. The Russians, however, in their own pursuit of grandeur, eventually detonated one that reached just under sixty megatons—more than four thousand times the explosive yield of the Hiroshima bomb. Taylor guessed that if the Russians had wrapped a uranium blanket around it they could have got a hundred megatons, but he imagined they were afraid to go that far. Whatever the size of the big bombs—ten, sixty, or a hundred megatons—they had begun to dismay him long before they were tested. (In seven years at Los Alamos he would work on the design of only one hydrogen bomb.) He was even sorry that he had designed the Super Oralloy Bomb, for the belief he had once held in the "deterrent posture" of such huge explosions had eventually dissolved in the thought that if they ever were used they would be "too all-killing"— that the destruction they would effect across hundreds of square miles would be so indiscriminate that the existence of such a weapon could not be justified on any moral ground. He reached the conclusion that an acceptable deterrent posture could only be achieved by making small bombs with a capacity for eradicating specific small targets. The laboratory's almost total emphasis in the other direction—toward the H-bomb—bothered him deeply. He began wondering just how small and light a nuclear explosive could be—how much yield could be got out of something with the over-all size of a softball. With George Gamow, he wrote a scientific paper called "What the World Needs Is a Good Two-Kiloton Bomb."

In 1953, Taylor was sent by Los Alamos at full pay to Cornell, to spend a year and a half getting his Ph.D. His mentor there was Bethe, who had long since become a close friend and counsellor—a relationship that continues. When Taylor returned to Los Alamos, he resumed the conception of a number of bombs whose names unmistakably indicate the direction of his effort: Bee, Hornet, Viper, the Puny Plutonium Bomb. The test of that last one was called "the P.P. shot," and it was the first known complete failure in the history of nuclear testing. "Now you're making progress," Fermi said. "You've finally fired a dud." The bomb had plenty of high explosive around an amount of plutonium so small that it remains secret, for the figure is somewhere near the answer to the root question: How small can a nuclear bomb be? In the absence of precise numbers, the answer would have to be: Pretty small. Fiddling around on this lightweight frontier, Taylor once designed an implosion bomb that weighed twenty pounds, but it was never tested.

Studying ordinary artillery shells, he replicated their external dimensions in conceiving fission bombs that could be fired out of guns. Being longitudinal in shape, these were not implosion bombs, of the Nagasaki type, but gun-type bombs—the kind that had been dropped over Hiroshima. The basic idea was to fire one piece of metallic uranium down a shaft and into another piece of metallic uranium, turning what had been two subcritical masses into one supercritical mass that would explode. Taylor called this exercise "whacking away at Hiroshima," and he performed it successfully, but he was not much interested in gun-type bombs. The Hiroshima bomb, which had been designed by a committee, was overloaded with uranium, and Taylor's summary desciption of it was that it was "a stupid bomb." Possibilities were so much greater in implosion systems. The Nagasaki bomb's nuclear core had been designed by Robert Christy, who taught physics and astrophysics at the California Institute of Technology, and returned frequently to Los Alamos as a consultant. Taylor, in his own words, would "light up" when he found that Christy had come to town.

□

Christy showed great interest in what Taylor was trying to do, and gave him much encouragement.

As the bombs grew smaller, the yield did, too. So the obvious next step was to try to get the yield back up while retaining the diminutions of size and weight. Taylor incorporated an essentially new feature that might do just that. It was put into Bee and Hornet. At the sound and the sight of each of them—the big fireball, the loud bang—he knew at once that the feature had worked.

"What feature?" I asked him once.

"I can't say," he answered. "So far as that part of the discussion goes, we have come to a dead end."

While Ted's bombs grew smaller, some of his other ideas grew to epic proportions. He spent a lot of time walking aimlessly from corridor to corridor thinking about the slow production of plutonium. The A.E.C.'s plants at Hanford and Savannah River were literally dripping it out, and Ted thought he saw a way to make a truly enormous amount of plutonium in a short time. He wanted to wrap up an H-bomb in a thick coat of uranium and place it deep in arctic ice. When it was detonated, the explosion would make plutonium-239 by capturing neutrons in uranium-238—exactly what happened in a reactor. The explosion would also turn a considerable amount of ice into a reservoir of water, which could easily be pumped out to a chemical plant on the surface, where the plutonium would be separated out. Why not? Why not make tritium in the same way? Tritium, the heaviest isotope of hydrogen (one proton, two nuetrons), is the best fuel for a thermonuclear explosion, and the most expensive (eight hundred thousand dollars a kilogram). Tritium is everywhere—in the seven seas, in the human body—but in such small proportions to ordinary hydrogen that collecting tritium in quantity from the natural world is completely impractical. So it is made, slowly, in production reactors. Ted wanted to do it a short way. Put a considerable amount of lithium around a thermonuclear bomb and emplace it under ten thousand feet of ice. Boom. An underground lake full of heavy isotopes. "That idea did not fly," said Carson Mark, in summary. "It properly received a lot of exploratory thought. It was a good idea. It would work, but it was too hard to do." These arctic ideas of Ted's became known as MICE—megaton ice-contained explosions. He found a serious supporter in John von Neumann, who was by then an A.E.C. commissioner. Von Neumann died two years later, in 1957, and the support died with him. Alternatively, Ted wanted to spread out on the ground somewhere a uranium blanket four hundred feet square. Then he would detonate a thermonuclear bomb in the air above it. Instantly on the ground there would be tons of plutonium. That idea did not even crawl.

Ted's imagination was given limited assignments as well as unlimited freedom. He was, after all, working for the government, and, as

□

Marshall Rosenbluth remembers those days, "admirals and generals were forever calling up begging for appointments." One time, for example, Ted was asked to see how well he could do "in a certain yield range" in terms of "high efficiency, high compressions, high criticality"—no fancy innovations, just the best implosion bomb he could make within the parameters given. The result was Hamlet, the most efficient pure-fission bomb ever exploded in the kiloton range.

Driving around Los Alamos with him once, when I went along on a visit he made there in 1972, I asked him what he had done to occupy himself during the flat periods between projects, the lulls that would come in any pattern of conceptual work. He said, "Between bombs, we messed around, in one way or another. We bowled snowballs the size of volleyballs down the E Building corridor to see what would happen. We played shuffleboard with icicles." He supposed it helped relieve the tension, of which there was a fair amount from time to time. During the strain of preparation for the Mike shot, for example, a well-known theoretical physicist picked up an inkwell, threw it at a colleague, and hit him in the chest. He could be excused. His job was to make sure that the hydrogen bomb did not ignite the atmosphere. After the Livermore laboratory began making bombs in competition with Los Alamos, a rivalry developed that was at least as intense as the football rivalry between, say, Michigan and Michigan State. Each laboratory had its stars. Johnny Foster was the fission-bomb star of Livermore. Groups of scientists from the one laboratory would attend the other's bomb tests, and there was a distant sense of locomotive cheering in the air, of chrysanthemums and hidden flasks. If a Livermore bomb succeeded only in knocking off the top of its own tower, or a Los Alamos bomb was a dud, no one actually cheered, but some people felt better. Once, at Eniwetok, somebody decided to steal Livermore's flag, which was pinned to a wall in Livermore's barracks and included in its heraldry a California golden bear. From the central flagpole, Headquarters, Joint Task Force Seven, Eniwetok Atoll, the flag of Rear Admiral B. Hall Hanlon, commander of the task force, was removed in the dead of night. Hoisted in its place was the Livermore bear. The Admiral's flag was then pinned to the wall in the Livermore barracks. In the morning, Admiral Hanlon reacted as expected, personally yielding four kilotons, one from each nostril and one from each ear. What is that bear doing on my flagpole? Where is my flag? Where? God damn it, where? Captains, colonels were running around like rabbits under hawk shadow—and, of course, they found the Admiral's flag. Los Alamos had triumphed without a shot being fired.

An explosion, however large, was a "shot." The word "bomb" was almost never used. A bomb was a "device" or a "gadget." Language could hide what the sky could not. The Los Alamos Scientific Laboratory was "the Ranch." Often, it was simply called "the hill." An implosion bomb was made with "ploot." A hundred-millionth of a second was a "shake"—a shake of a lamb's tail. A "jerk" was ten quadrillion ergs—a unit of energy equivalent to a quarter of a ton of high explosive. A "kilojerk" was a quarter of a kiloton. A "megajerk" was a quarter of a megaton. A cross-section for neutron capture was expressed in terms of the extremely small area a neutron had to hit in order to enter a nucleus—say, one septillionth of a square centimetre—and this was known as a "barn." Two new elements—numbers 99 and 100—were discovered in the debris resulting from Project Panda, the Mike shot. Some wanted to call element 99 pandamonium. The name it got was einsteinium.

Conversations were more likely to be in an idiom of numbers, though. Numbers, volumes, densities were the stuff of working thought, and of daydreams as well. Ulam announced one day that the entire population of Los Alamos could be crammed into the town water tower. Taylor figured out that the Valle Grande, a huge caldera in the mountains above Los Alamos, had been created by a thousand mega-tons of volcanic explosion. His conversation to this day is laced with phrases such as "of the order of" and "by a factor of," and around the top of his mind runs a frieze of bizzare numbers. He will say out of nowhere that his wife has baked a hundred and eighteen birthday cakes in the past twenty-five years, or that the mean free path of a neu-tron through a human being is eight inches. "The mean free path of a neutron is greater than the diameter of the earth. They go right through the world." He says there are some numbers that are so large or so small that they are never seen, because they refer to nothing. "You never see a number larger than ten to the hundred and twenty-fourth, for example."

"Why not?"

"Because there is nothing bigger than that. That is the volume of the known universe in cubic fermis. A fermi is the smallest dimension that makes any sense to talk about—ten to the minus thirteen centi-metres. That's about the diameter of an electron. Nothing we know of is smaller than that."

When I asked him how many atoms there were in his own body, he said, right back, "Eight times ten to the twenty-sixth."

We had lunch in the Los Alamos cafeteria one day with, among others, Ulam, who was now teaching mathematics at the University of Colorado, but kept a house in Santa Fe and worked as a consultant at Los Alamos several months each year. Ulam began wondering aloud about the surface of a billiard ball and what it would look like if the billiard ball were magnified until its diameter were equal to the earth's. Would the irregularities of the surface be as high as the Himalayas? He decided they would. He asked Ted to come home for dinner with him and his wife, Françoise, and to bring me along. He drew a map of his neighborhood in Santa Fe and said he could not wait to lead the way because he had to leave the laboratory at four.

Ulam's house, behind a high wrought-iron gate in a warren of adobe, might have been the retreat of a minor grandee in the old quarter of Seville. It was on several levels, the lowest of which was the living room—down a few steps and into an outreaching white space that was at once expansive, under a fourteen-foot ceiling, and compact, with a tearshaped white fireplace built into one corner. Logs were burning. They had been stood on end, and were leaning against the back of the fireplace. Cottonwood smoke was in the air. Stretched out on a large daybed during much of the evening—looking into the fire, or, with quick glances of interest or amusement, into the eyes of his wife and his visitors—was Ulam, inventor of the hydrogen bomb. A great variety of books in French and English lined the room. A grand piano stood in one corner, and on a tripod near it was a white telescope about five feet long. Ulam, always interested in the stars, had been connected with Los Alamos since 1943, and one of the earliest potentialities that occurred to him when he began to work on the Manhattan Project was that nuclear-explosive force could be used to drive vehicles from Earth into distant parts of space—an external-combustion engine, fuelled with bombs. Trim, tan across his bald head, obviously well rested, Ulam was sixty-two at the time. He looked no older than Taylor, who was forty-eight. He asked about the independent research Ted had been doing for many years in the field of nuclear-materials safeguards and was much absorbed by a story Ted told him about the attempted blackmailing in 1970 of a city in Florida. The blackmailer promised not to bomb the city out of existence in return for a million dollars and safe custody out of the United States. A day later, the threat was repeated, and with it came a diagram of a hydrogen bomb. Taylor described the diagram to Ulam—a cylinder filled with lithium hydride wrapped in cobalt, an implosion system at one end of it—and nothing in Ulam's face or Taylor's manner indicated that such a diagram might not be credible. The threat, though, had been a hoax, perpetrated by a fourteen-year-old boy. The police chose not to reveal to the public that the bomb in the threat was nuclear. A judge, after sentencing the boy, suspended the sentence and put him under the guidance of two scientists in the area, saying that talent such as the boy had should be channelled in a positive direction, and not a negative one, as might happen in a prison.

Taylor asked Ulam what was new in mathematics, and Ulam said that the properties in infinity were of much philosophical interest, that there was a lot of work being done on combinatorial mathematics as it applies to biology, and that it was now possible to prove that there are some theorems that can be neither proved nor disproved. Ulam's mind wandered on to Shakespeare, to Gaudí, to Joseph Conrad—who, like Ulam, was a Pole, and first learned English when he was about twenty years old. Ulam wondered if it was possible to discern Conrad's origins in an unlabelled quantity of Conrad's prose. "I never actually read sentences," he said. "I have a good memory, I look at a page and see what is there. But I think I miss a lot." He recalled his first arrival, many years ago, at Cambridge University, and his first visit to Trinity Great Court and the college room of Isaac Newton. He said, "I almost fainted."

Before we left, Ulam found a moment to say, out of Taylor's earshot, "I have known hundreds of people in science, and he is one of the very few most impressive and inventive. I as a boy was always reading Jules Verne. It was where I got my ideas of Americans. When I met Ted, he fitted the ideas I formed as a boy of Americans, as represented by Jules Verne. The trait I noticed immediately was inventiveness. Scientists are of different types. Some follow rules and techniques that exist. Some have imagination, larger perspectives. Often, Ted had the attitude of 'Ours not to reason why.' He was intense, high-strung, introspective. 'If something is possible, let's do it' was Ted's attitude. He did things without seeing all the consequences. So much of science is like that."

Driving away from the lights of Santa Fe and up into the mountains toward Los Alamos, Taylor fell into a ruminative mood, and eventually said, "The theorist's world is a world of the best people and the worst of possible results." He said he now saw all his work on light weapons as nothing but an implementation of "pseudo-rational military purposes." He said his belief in deterrent postures had eroded to zero. "I thought I was doing my part for my country. I thought I was contributing to a permanent state of peace. I no longer feel that way. I wish I hadn't done it. The whole thing was wrong. Rationalize how you will, the bombs were designed to kill many, many people. I sometimes can't blame people if they wish all scientists were lined up and shot. If it were possible to wave a wand and make fission impossible—fission of any kind—I would quickly wave the wand. I have a total conviction—now—that nuclear weapons should not be used under any circumstances. At any time. Anywhere. Period. If I were king. If the Russians bombed New York. I would not bomb Moscow."

Vocabulary

talus a sloping face of a wall, narrow at top, wide at base
kiloton the explosive force of 1,000 tons of TNT
plutonium a radioactive, metallic chemical element similar to uranium and neptunium used as fuel in nuclear weapons
diminution lessening, decrease
megaton the explosive force of a million tons of TNT
fermis a unit of length equal to 10^{-13} centimeter

Discussion

1. You might wish to begin exploring McPhee's writing in this piece by noting the way he is juxtapositioning the ridiculous with the sublime, the intelli-

□

gence of these scientists with the theory of Hungarians being Martians, for example. What other incidents of this kind of juxtaposition, large and small, can you find?

2. Having lived under the threat of the bomb all your life, how does McPhee's method of reporting on the bomb's creators confirm or deny your deepest concerns?

McPhee's book, *The Curve of Binding Energy*, from which this excerpt is taken, was a nominee for a National Book Award in 1975. Theodore B. Taylor, the theoretical physicist who has designed many of our atomic bombs, was McPhee's science teacher. McPhee's reporting of the various aspects of this man's character (and of the other scientists') is amazingly objective. How does one revelation counterbalance another?

3. A good companion piece to this might be Robert Sherrill's, "The Saturday Night Special" in Chapter 5. How is the language of guns and bombs as affecting as any language you are likely to read? How do the names of weapons and bombs, and those who use language describing matter-of-factly implements of death, affect you to some real emotional response, a visceral response? (Most words have been worn smooth; by contrast note how the words in McPhee and Sherrill seem sharp-edged.)

4. At least two smaller narratives are enclosed in this larger piece about Taylor. One concerns the boy in Florida who threatened the city and the other about the hypothetical bombing of the World Trade Center in New York City. How do these narratives serve to further McPhee's intention with the piece?

What *is* McPhee's intention with the piece? What evidence can you marshal from this excerpt to support your view?

What do you make of the ending statements by Taylor?

Joan Didion
(1934–   )

Joan Didion is a novelist, short story writer, essayist, journalist, and magazine editor. In 1956, the year she graduated from college, she won Vogue's Prix de Paris award and worked for the magazine as associate feature editor until 1963. Her first novel, *Run River*, was published that year.

Besides her novels and books of essays, Didion is a frequent contributor of articles and stories to magazines, and has collaborated with her husband, John Gregory Dunne, on several screenplays. These include "The Panic in Needle Park" and "True Confessions."

Of her writing she says; " . . . there is always a point in the writing of a piece when I sit in a room literally papered with false starts and cannot put one word after another and imagine that I have suffered a small stroke, leaving me apparently undamaged but actually aphasic."

On Morality

As it happens I am in Death Valley, in a room at the Enterprise Motel and Trailer Park, and it is July, and it is hot. In fact it is 119°. I cannot seem to make the air conditioner work, but there is a small refrigerator, and I can wrap ice cubes in a towel and hold them against the small of my back. With the help of the ice cubes I have been trying to think, because *The American Scholar* asked me to, in some abstract way about "morality," a word I distrust more every day, but my mind veers inflexibly toward the particular.

Here are some particulars. At midnight last night, on the road in from Las Vegas to Death Valley Junction, a car hit a shoulder and turned over. The driver, very young and apparently drunk, was killed instantly. His girl was found alive but bleeding internally, deep in shock. I talked this afternoon to the nurse who had driven the girl to the nearest doctor, 185 miles across the floor of the Valley and three ranges of lethal mountain road. The nurse explained that her husband, a talc miner, had stayed on the highway with the boy's body until the coroner could get over the mountains from Bishop, at dawn today. "You can't just leave a body on the highway," she said. "It's immoral."

It was one instance in which I did not distrust the word, because she meant something quite specific. She meant that if a body is left alone for even a few minutes on the desert, the coyotes close in and eat the flesh. Whether or not a corpse is torn apart by coyotes may seem only a sentimental consideration, but of course it is more: one of the promises we make to one another is that we will try to retrieve our casualties, try not to abandon our dead to the coyotes. If we have been taught to keep our promises—if, in the simplest terms, our upbringing is good enough—we stay with the body, or have bad dreams.

I am talking, of course, about the kind of social code that is sometimes called, usually pejoratively, "wagon-train morality." In fact that is precisely what it is. For better or worse, we are what we learned as children: my own childhood was illuminated by graphic litanies of the grief awaiting those who failed in their loyalties to each other. The Donner-Reed Party, starving in the Sierra snows, all the ephemera of civilization gone save that one vestigial taboo, the provision that no one should eat his own blood kin. The Jayhawkers, who quarreled and separated not far from where I am tonight. Some of them died in the Funerals and some of them died down near Badwater and most of the rest of them died in the Panamints. A woman who got through gave the Valley its name. Some might say that the Jayhawkers were killed by the desert summer, and the Donner Party by the mountain winter, by circumstances beyond control; we were taught instead that they had somewhere abdicated their responsibilities, somehow breached their primary loyalties, or they would not have found themselves helpless in the mountain winter or the desert summer, would not have given way to acrimony, would not have deserted one another, would not have failed. In brief, we heard such stories as cautionary tales, and they still suggest the only kind of "morality" that seems to me to have any but the most potentially mendacious meaning.

You are quite possibly impatient with me by now; I am talking,

☐

you want to say, about a "morality" so primitive that it scarcely deserves the name, a code that has as its point only survival, not the attainment of the ideal good. Exactly. Particularly out here tonight, in this country so ominous and terrible that to live in it is to live with anti-matter, it is difficult to believe that "the good" is a knowable quantity. Let me tell you what it is like out here tonight. Stories travel at night on the desert. Someone gets in his pickup and drives a couple of hundred miles for a beer, and he carries news of what is happening, back wherever he came from. Then he drives another hundred miles for another beer, and passes along stories from the last place as well as from the one before; it is a network kept alive by people whose instincts tell them that if they do not keep moving at night on the desert they will lose all reason. Here is a story that is going around the desert tonight: over across the Nevada line, sheriff's deputies are diving in some underground pools, trying to retrieve a couple of bodies known to be in the hole. The widow of one of the drowned boys is over there; she is eighteen, and pregnant, and is said not to leave the hole. The divers go down and come up, and she just stands there and stares into the water. They have been diving for ten days but have found no bottom to the caves, no bodies and no trace of them, only the black 90° water going down and down and down, and a single translucent fish, not classified. The story tonight is that one of the divers has been hauled up incoherent, out of his head, shouting—until they got him out of there so that the widow could not hear—about water that got hotter instead of cooler as he went down, about light flickering through the water, about magma, about underground nuclear testing.

That is the tone stories take out here, and there are quite a few of them tonight. And it is more than the stories alone. Across the road at the Faith Community Church a couple of dozen old people, come here to live in trailers and die in the sun, are holding a prayer sing. I cannot hear them and do not want to. What I can hear are occasional coyotes and a constant chorus of "Baby the Rain Must Fall" from the jukebox in the Snake Room next door, and if I were also to hear those dying voices, those Midwestern voices drawn to this lunar country for some unimaginable atavistic rites, *rock of ages cleft for me*, I think I would lose my own reason. Every now and then I imagine I hear a rattlesnake, but my husband says that it is a faucet, a paper rustling, the wind. Then he stands by a window, and plays a flashlight over the dry wash outside.

What does it mean? It means nothing manageable. There is some sinister hysteria in the air out here tonight, some hint of the monstrous perversion to which any human idea can come. "I followed my own conscience." "I did what I thought was right." How many madmen have said it and meant it? How many murderers? Klaus Fuchs said it, and the men who committed the Mountain Meadows Massacre said it, and Alfred Rosenberg said it. And, as we are rotely and rather pre-

sumptuously reminded by those who would say it now, Jesus said it.
Maybe we have all said it, and maybe we have been wrong. Except on
that most primitive level—our loyalties to those we love—what could
be more arrogant than to claim the primacy of personal conscience?
("Tell me," a rabbi asked Daniel Bell when he said, as a child, that he
did not believe in God. "Do you think God cares?") At least some of the
time, the world appears to me as a painting by Hieronymous Bosch;
were I to follow my conscience then, it would lead me out onto the
desert with Marion Faye, out to where he stood in *The Deer Park* looking east to Los Alamos and praying, as if for rain, that it would happen:
*" . . . let it come and clear the rot and the stench and the stink, let it come
for all of everywhere, just so it comes and the world stands clear in the
white dead dawn."*

Of course you will say that I do not have the right, even if I had
the power, to inflict that unreasonable conscience upon you; nor do I
want you to inflict your conscience, however reasonable, however
enlightened, upon me. ("We must be aware of the dangers which lie in
our most generous wishes," Lionel Trilling once wrote. "Some paradox
of our nature leads us, when once we have made our fellow men the
objects of our enlightened interest, to go on to make them the objects of
our pity, then of our wisdom, ultimately of our coercion.") That the
ethic of conscience is intrinsically insidious seems scarcely a revelatory
point, but it is one raised with increasing infrequency; even those who
do raise it tend to *segue* with troubling readiness into the quite contradictory position that the ethic of conscience is dangerous when it is
"wrong," and admirable when it is "right."

You see I want to be quite obstinate about insisting that we have
no way of knowing—beyond that fundamental loyalty to the social
code—what is "right" and what is "wrong," what is "good" and what
"evil." I dwell so upon this because the most disturbing aspect of
"morality" seems to me to be the frequency with which the word now
appears; in the press, on television, in the most perfunctory kinds of
conversation. Questions of straightforward power (or survival) politics,
questions of quite indifferent public policy, questions of almost anything: they are all assigned these factitious moral burdens. There is
something facile going on, some self-indulgence at work. Of course we
would all like to "believe" in something, like to assuage our private
guilts in public causes, like to lose our tiresome selves; like, perhaps, to
transform the white flag of defeat at home into the brave white banner
of battle away from home. And of course it is all right to do that; that is
how, immemorially, things have gotten done. But I think it is all right
only so long as we do not delude ourselves about what we are doing,
and why. It is all right only so long as we remember that all the *ad hoc*
committees, all the picket lines, all the brave signatures in *The New
York Times*, all the tools of agitprop straight across the spectrum, do
not confer upon anyone *ipso facto* virtue. It is all right only so long as

we recognize that the end may or may not be expedient, may or may not be a good idea, but in any case has nothing to do with "morality." Because when we start deceiving ourselves into thinking not that we want something or need something, not that it is a pragmatic necessity for us to have it, but that it is a *moral imperative* that we have it, then is when we join the fashionable madmen, and then is when the thin whine of hysteria is heard in the land, and then is when we are in bad trouble. And I suspect we are already there.

Vocabulary

pejoratively   tending to make or become worse, disparaging
litanies   any repetitive recital, prayer
ephemera   something short-lived or transitory
vestigial   a trace, evidence or sign of something that once existed
acrimony   bitterness or ill-natured in speech or manner
mendacious   false, untrue
lunar   moonlike
atavistic   "throwback," a reversion
rotely   unthinking repetition
coercion   compelled, forced to act or think in a given manner
intrinsically insidious   essentially harmful
perfunctory   done routinely with little care
factitious   contrived, artificial
facile   easy
assuage   ease, make less burdensome
agitprop   propaganda, slogans chalked on walls

Allusions/References

Donner-Reed Party   a group of 87 California-bound settlers trapped by snow at Truckee Lake in 1846; 47 survived the winter in part by resorting to cannibalism
Jayhawkers   free-soil guerrilla raiders of Kansas and Missouri during the border disputes of 1857–1859
Klaus Fuchs   escaped Nazi Germany in 1933; sent to the U.S. as a scientist to work on the atomic bomb and convicted in 1950 of disclosing nuclear secrets to Russia
Daniel Bell   writer and educator in the area of social science
Hieronymous Bosch   a Dutch painter of the surreal; original name van Aeken
The Deer Park   a novel by Norman Mailer
Lionel Trilling   literary critic and scholar
segue   continue at once with the next section
ad hoc   for this specific purpose
ipso facto   by the fact itself, by the very nature of the deed

Discussion

1. What exactly does Joan Didion mean by "wagon-train morality"? A writer's point of view is often determined by a sense of place, of being British in India or American in the Far West. Didion's family has lived in the Sacramento Valley for five generations. How is this "pioneer spirit" exemplified in her writing? Notice the number of allusions she makes to historical incidents particular to the west. (How does this spirit of the west infuse both of Didion's essays anthologized here?)
2. What does Didion mean by the ethic of conscience? How is this different from "wagon-train morality"? How is this essay structured around the difference between the ethic of conscience and "wagon-train morality"? How is each of these a response to the magazine article on "morality" that Didion was reading in Death Valley?
3. Would Didion's response to the word "morality" have been a different one had she been reading the journal in a Paris flat or in a New York apartment? We can only speculate on this, yet there is, in Didion, such a sense of the "ominous and terrible" landscape of the desert.
   How is "morality" determined?
4. Speculate on the nature of Joan Didion's audience. (Why so many words and references to be glossed?)

Joan Didion
(1934–   )

Some critics have found fault with Didion's tendency to expose her "personal neurosis" even in her journalistic writing. But for her the written word is her way of dealing with life. "I'm only myself in front of a typewriter."

Much of her writing has been directly autobiographical or concerned with personal experiences. Her approach is to reveal everything, no matter how personal. She says: "If you want to write about yourself, you have to give them [the readers] something."

Didion's childhood and California's Central Valley, where her family has lived for five generations, are common elements in her writing.

Going Home

I am home for my daughter's first birthday. By "home" I do not mean the house in Los Angeles where my husband and I and the baby live, but the place where my family is, in the Central Valley of California. It is a vital although troublesome distinction. My husband likes my family but is uneasy in their house, because once there I fall into their ways, which are difficult, oblique, deliberately inarticulate, not my husband's ways. We live in dusty houses ("D-U-S-T," he once wrote with his finger on surfaces all over the house, but no one noticed it) filled with mementos quite without value to him (what could the Canton dessert plates mean to him? how could he have known about the assay scales, why should he care if he did know?), and we appear to talk exclusively about people we know who have been committed to mental hospitals, about people we know who have been booked on drunk-driving charges, and about property, particularly about property, land, price per acre and C-2 zoning and assessments and freeway access. My brother does not understand my husband's inability to perceive the advantage in the rather common real-estate transaction known as "sale-leaseback," and my husband in turn does not understand why so many of the people he hears about in my father's house have recently been committed to mental hospitals or booked on drunk-driving charges. Nor does he understand that when we talk about sale-leasebacks and right-of-way condemnations we are talking in code about the things we like best, the yellow fields and the cottonwoods and the rivers rising and falling and the mountain roads closing when the heavy snow comes in. We miss each other's points, have another drink and regard the fire. My brother refers to my husband, in his presence, as "Joan's husband." Marriage is the classic betrayal.

Or perhaps it is not any more. Sometimes I think that those of us who are now in our thirties were born into the last generation to carry the burden of "home," to find in family life the source of all tension and drama. I had by all objective accounts a "normal" and "happy" family situation, and yet I was almost thirty years old before I could talk to my family on the telephone without crying after I had hung up. We did not fight. Nothing was wrong. And yet some nameless anxiety colored the emotional charges between me and the place that I came from. The question of whether or not you could go home again was a very real part of the sentimental and largely literary baggage with which we left home in the fifties; I suspect that it is irrelevant to the children born of the fragmentation after World War II. A few weeks ago in a San Francisco bar I saw a pretty young girl on crystal take off her clothes and dance for the cash prize in an "amateur-topless" contest. There was no particular sense of moment about this, none of the effect of romantic degradation, of "dark journey," for which my generation strived so assiduously. What sense could that girl possibly make of, say, *Long Day's Journey into Night?* Who is beside the point?

That I am trapped in this particular irrelevancy is never more apparent to me than when I am home. Paralyzed by the neurotic lassitude engendered by meeting one's past at every turn, around every corner, inside every cupboard, I go aimlessly from room to room. I decide to meet it head-on and clean out a drawer, and I spread the contents on the bed. A bathing suit I wore the summer I was seventeen. A letter of rejection from *The Nation*, an aerial photograph of the site for a shopping center my father did not build in 1954. Three teacups hand-painted with cabbage roses and signed "E.M.," my grandmother's initials. There is no final solution for letters of rejection from *The Nation* and teacups hand-painted in 1900. Nor is there any answer to snapshots of one's grandfather as a young man on skis, surveying around Donner Pass in the year 1910. I smooth out the snapshot and look into his face, and do and do not see my own. I close the drawer, and have another cup of coffee with my mother. We get along very well, veterans of a guerrilla war we never understood.

Days pass. I see no one. I come to dread my husband's evening call, not only because he is full of news of what by now seems to me our remote life in Los Angeles, people he has seen, letters which require attention, but because he asks what I have been doing, suggests uneasily that I get out, drive to San Francisco or Berkeley. Instead I drive across the river to a family graveyard. It has been vandalized since my last visit and the monuments are broken, overturned in the dry grass. Because I once saw a rattlesnake in the grass I stay in the car and listen to a Country-and-Western station. Later I drive with my father to a ranch he has in the foothills. The man who runs his cattle on it asks us to the roundup, a week from Sunday, and although I know that I will be in Los Angeles I say, in the oblique way my family talks, that I will come. Once home I mention the broken monuments in the graveyard. My mother shrugs.

I go to visit my great-aunts. A few of them think now that I am my cousin, or their daughter who died young. We recall an anecdote about a relative last seen in 1948, and they ask if I still like living in New York City. I have lived in Los Angeles for three years, but I say that I do. The baby is offered a horehound drop, and I am slipped a dollar bill "to buy a treat." Questions trail off, answers are abandoned, the baby plays with the dust motes in a shaft of afternoon sun.

It is time for the baby's birthday party: a white cake, strawberry-marshmallow ice cream, a bottle of champagne saved from another party. In the evening, after she has gone to sleep, I kneel beside the crib and touch her face, where it is pressed against the slats, with mine. She is an open and trusting child, unprepared for and unaccustomed to the ambushes of family life, and perhaps it is just as well that I can offer her little of that life. I would like to give her more. I would like to promise her that she will grow up with a sense of her cousins and of rivers and of her great-grandmother's teacups; would like to pledge her a picnic on a river with fried chicken and her hair uncombed, would like to give her *home* for her birthday, but we live differently now and I can promise her nothing like that. I give her a xylophone and a sundress from Madeira, and promise to tell her a funny story.

Vocabulary

oblique   indirect or evasive
assay   analysis or examination (of an ore)

crystal   "speed"; any amphetamine taken to produce euphoria
degradation   degeneration; lowered in moral or intellectual character
assiduously   diligently, industriously
neurotic lassitude   weariness, exhaustion caused by nerves
engendered   brought into existence, propogated

Allusions/References

Canton dessert plates   made in Canton, China
horehound drop   a candy made from the extract of a horehound plant, used
as cough drop
Madeira   an island in an archipelago in the Atlantic Ocean about 400 miles
west of Morocco; Portuguese

Discussion

1. What does Didion mean when she writes, "I think that those of us who are now in our thirties were born into the last generation to carry the burden of home. . . . "?
2. Again, what does Didion mean when she writes, "Paralyzed by the neurotic lassitude engendered by meeting one's past at every turn. . . . "? How does her essay show you both the "lassitude" and the "past at every turn"? Follow the essay paragraph by paragraph; what is it that leads Didion from one to the next? How does the structure of this essay become, in itself, an example of exactly what she means when she calls her family "oblique"?
3. How about gifts to her child? Why does Didion end the essay with them? What do you make of each of them? Do they indicate the passing of the very "home" Didion is talking about? How else can you defend this as an ending to Didion's essay?

Jack Kerouac
(1922–1969)

Jack Kerouac was born in Lowell, Massachusetts. He attended college in New York City on a football scholarship. There he met the group of friends who would form the nucleus of the "beat generation." Instead of fame as a football hero, Kerouac became legendary "father" of the beats and chronicler of an era.

The following selection is from *Lonesome Traveler,* in which he tells the story of the years when he was writing the books that fascinated (and outraged) the reading public. "The Bullfight" is a good example of Kerouac's theory of spontaneous prose where the writer writes: "excitedly, swiftly, with writing-or-typing cramps—swimming in a sea of language—to relaxed and said."

"I got sick and tired of the conventional English sentence which seemed so ironbound in its rules," Kerouac said.

The Bullfight

A few weeks later I go to see my first bullfight, which I must confess is a *novillera*, a novice fight, and not the real thing they show in the winter which is supposed to be so artistic. Inside it is a perfect round bowl with a neat circle of brown dirt being harrowed and raked by expert loving rakers like the man who rakes second base in Yankee Stadium only this is Bite-the-Dust Stadium.—When I sat down the bull had just come in and the orchestra was sitting down again.—Fine embroidered clothes tightly fitted to boys behind a fence.—Solemn they were, as a big beautiful shiny black bull rushed out gallumphing from a corner I hadnt looked, where he'd been apparently mooing for help, black nostrils and big white eyes and outspread horns, all chest no belly, stove polish thin legs seeking to drive the earth down with all that locomotive weight above—some people sniggered—bull galloped and flashed, you saw the riddled-up muscle holes in his perfect prize skin.—Matador stepped out and invited and the bull charged and slammed in, matador sneered his cape, let pass the horns by his loins a foot or two, got the bull revolved around by cape, and walked away like a Grandee—and stood his back to the dumb perfect bull who didnt charge like in "Blood & Sand" and lift Señor Grandee into the upper deck. Then business got underway. Out comes the old pirate horse with patch on eye, picador KNIGHT aboard with a lance, to come and dart a few slivers of steel in the bull's shoulderblade who responds by trying to lift the horse but the horse is mailed (thank God)—a historical and crazy scene except suddenly you realize the picador has started the bull on his interminable bleeding. The blinding of the poor bull in mindless vertigo is continued by the brave bowlegged little dart man carrying two darts with ribbon, here he comes head-on at the bull, the bull head-on for him, wham, no head-on crash for the dart man has stung with dart and darted away before you can say boo (& I did say boo), because a bull is hard to dodge? Good enough, but the darts now have the bull streaming with blood like Marlowe's Christ in the heavens.—An old matador comes out and tests the bull with a few capes' turn then another set of darts, a battleflag now shining down the living breathing suffering bull's side and everybody *glad*.—And now the bull's charge is just a stagger and so now the serious hero matador comes out for the kill as the orchestra goes one boom-lick on bass drum, it gets quiet like a cloud passing over the sun, you hear a drunkard's bottle smash a mile away in the cruel Spanish green aromatic countryside—children pause over tortas—the bull stands in the sun head-bowed, panting for life, his sides actually *flapping* against his ribs, his shoulders barbed like San Sebastian.—The careful footed matador youth, brave enough in his own right, approaches and curses and the bull rolls around and comes stoggling on wobbly feet at the red cape, dives in with blood streaming everywhichaway and the boy just accommodates him through the

□

imaginary hoop and circles and hangs on tiptoe, knockkneed. And Lord, I didnt want to see his smooth tight belly ranted by no horn.—He rippled his cape again at the bull who just stood there thinking "O why cant I go home?" and the matador moved closer and now the animal bunched tired legs to run but one leg slipped throwing up a cloud of dust.—But he dove in and flounced off to rest.—The matador draped his sword and called the humble bull with glazed eyes.—The bull pricked his ears and didnt move.—The matador's whole body stiffened like a board that shakes under the trample of many feet—a muscle showed in his stocking.—Bull plunged a feeble three feet and turned in dust and the matador arched his back in front of him like a man leaning over a hot stove to reach for something on the other side and flipped his sword a yard deep into the bull's shoulderblade separation.—Matador walked one way, bull the other with sword to hilt and staggered, started to run, looked up with human surprise at the sky & sun, and then gargled—O go see it folks!—He threw up ten gallons of blood into the air and it splashed all over—he fell on his knees choking on his own blood and spewed and twisted his neck around and suddenly got floppy doll and his head blammed flat.—He still wasnt dead, an extra idiot rushed out and knifed him with a wren-like dagger in the neck nerve and still the bull dug the sides of his poor mouth in the sand and chewed old blood.—His eyes! O his eyes!—Idiots sniggered because the dagger did this, as though it would not.—A team of hysterical horses were rushed out to chain and drag the bull away, they galloped off but the chain broke and the bull slid in dust like a dead fly kicked unconsciously by a foot.—Off, off with him!—He's gone, white eyes staring the last thing you see.—Next bull!—First the old boys shovel blood in a wheel-barrow and rush off with it. The quiet raker returns with his rake—"Ole!," girls throwing flowers at the animal-murder in the fine britches.—And I saw how everybody dies and nobody's going to care, I felt how awful it is to live just so you can die like a bull trapped in a screaming human ring.—

Jai Alai, Mexico, Jai Alai!

Vocabulary

beat generation a group belonging to the generation coming to maturity after World War II that asserted a loss of faith in Western cultural traditions and rejected conventional norms of dress and behavior
grandee a nobleman of the highest rank
picador a horseman in a bullfight who lances the bull's neck muscles so that it will tend to keep its head low for the subsequent stages
mail(ed) flexible armor covering the horse to protect it
vertigo a whirling, confused, disoriented state of mind
tortas cookies

□

Allusions/References

Christopher Marlowe   English dramatist and poet (1569–1593)

Discussion

1. What evidence is there of Kerouac's unconventional attitude toward the English sentence? How many paragraphs in this piece?
2. Examine Kerouac's use of punctuation (especially periods, commas, apostrophes, and dashes). How does his punctuation contribute to the sense of his sentences? Again, is there evidence of a rebellion against the conventional? (Kerouac explains his use of the dash as a way to separate variations on a theme, much in the same way that a bop musician might add statement after statement to the melodic line of a song.)
3. The critic Warren Tallman has pointed out that the movement or "sound" of Kerouac's prose is always commenting on its theme.
   What is the theme of "The Bullfight"?
   How does this "breathless, hectic rush of words" comment on Kerouac's perceptions of the living experience that generated them?

For Further Discussion

4. You might wish to compare Ernest Hemingway's "Killing a Bull," in Chapter 5: Exposition, with Kerouac's "The Bullfight." Which seems the more informative? Which is the more convincing?
   Look at the words used by each author (follow each word on a line across a page). What can you say about Kerouac's words as compared with Hemingway's? Which do you prefer? Why?

Jack Kerouac
(1922–1969)

Kerouac's first novel, *The Town and The City,* was published in 1950. It was to be his only "traditional" book. It was seven years before his next book, *On the Road,* was published. In the intervening years of developing his mature style, he worked at many jobs including fruit picker, merchant marine, railroad brakeman, and fire lookout.

Though considered fiction, Kerouac's writing was actually personal narrative. "My work comprises one vast book like Proust's *Remembrance of Things Past,* except that my remembrances are written on the run instead of afterwards in a sick bed."

Kerouac died before he could see his many books brought together in "The Duluoz Legend" he envisioned.

□

The Flop Hotel

So there I am in dawn in my dim cell—2½ hours to go till the time I
have to stick my railroad watch in my jean watchpocket and cut out
allowing myself exactly 8 minutes to the station and the 7:15 train No.
112 I have to catch for the ride five miles to Bayshore through four tunnels, emerging from the sad Rath scene of Frisco gloom gleak in the
rainymouth fogmorning to a sudden valley with grim hills rising to the
sea, bay on left, the fog rolling in like demented in the draws that have
little white cottages disposed real-ecstatically for come-Christmas blue
sad lights—my whole soul and concomitant eyes looking out on this
reality of living and working in San Francisco with that pleased semi-
loin-located shudder, energy for sex changing to pain at the portals of
work and culture and natural foggy fear.—There I am in my little room
wondering how I'll really manage to fool myself into feeling that these
next 2½ hours will be well filled, fed, with work and pleasure
thoughts.—It's so thrilling to feel the coldness of the morning to wrap
around my thickquilt blankets as I lay there, watch facing and ticking
me, legs spread in comfy skidrow soft sheets with soft tears or sew lines
in 'em, huddled in my own skin and rich and not spending a cent on—
I look at my littlebook—and I stare at the words of the Bible.—On the
floor I find last red afternoon Saturday's *Chronicle* sports page with
news of football games in Great America the end of which I bleakly see
in the gray light entering.—The fact that Frisco is built of wood satisfies
me in my peace, I know nobody'll disturb me for 2½ hours and all bums
are asleep in their own bed of eternity awake or not, bottle or not—it's
the joy I feel that counts for me.—On the floor's my shoes, big lumber-
boot flopjack workshoes to colomp over rockbed with and not turn the
ankle—solidity shoes that when you put them on, yokewise, you know
you're working now and so for same reason shoes not be worn for any
reason like joys of restaurants and shows.—Night-before shoes are on
the floor beside the clunkershoes a pair of blue canvas shoes à la 1952
style, in them I'd trod soft as ghost the indented hill sidewalks of Ah Me
Frisco all in the glitter night, from the top of Russian Hill I'd looked
down at one point on all the roofs of North Beach and the Mexican
nightclub neons, I'd descended to them on the old steps of Broadway
under which they were newly laboring a mountain tunnel—shoes fit
for watersides, embarcaderos, hill and plot lawns of park and tiptop
vista.—Workshoes covered with dust and some oil of engines—the
crumpled jeans nearby, belt, blue railroad hank, knife, comb, keys,
switch keys and caboose coach key, the knees white from Pajaro Riv-
erbottom finedusts, the ass black from slick sandboxes in yardgoat after
yardgoat—the gray workshorts, the dirty undershirt, sad shorts, tortured socks of my life.—And the Bible on my desk next to the peanut
butter, the lettuce, the raisin bread, the crack in the plaster, the stiff-
with-old-dust lace drape now no longer laceable but hard as—after all

those years of hard dust eternity in that Cameo skid inn with red eyes
of rheumy oldmen dying there staring without hope out on the dead
wall you can hardly see thru windowdusts and all you heard lately in
the shaft of the rooftop middle way was the cries of a Chinese child
whose father and mother were always telling him to shush and then
screaming at him, he was a pest and his tears from China were most
persistent and worldwide and represented all our feelings in broken-
down Cameo tho this was not admitted by bum one except for an occasional harsh clearing of throat in the halls or moan of nightmarer—by
things like this and neglect of a hard-eyed alcoholic oldtime chorusgirl
maid the curtains had now absorbed all the iron they could take and
hung stiff and even the dust in them was iron, if you shook them they'd
crack and fall in tatters to the floor and splatter like wings of iron on
the bong and the dust would fly into your nose like filings of steel and
choke you to death, so I never touched them. My little room at 6 in the
comfy dawn (at 4:30) and before me all that time, that fresh-eyed time
for a little coffee to boil water on my hot plate, throw some coffee in,
stir it, French style, slowly carefully pour it in my white tin cup, throw
sugar in (not California beet sugar like I should have been using but
New Orleans cane sugar, because beet racks I carried from Oakland out
to Watsonville many's the time, a 80-car freight train with nothing but
gondolas loaded with sad beets looking like the heads of decapitated
women).—Ah me how but it was a hell and now I had the whole thing
to myself, and make my raisin toast by sitting it on a little wire I'd especially bent to place over the hotplate, the toast crackled up, there, I
spread the margarine on the still red hot toast and it too would crackle
and sink in golden, among burnt raisins and this was my toast.—Then
two eggs gently slowly fried in soft margarine in my little skidrow
frying pan about half as thick as a dime in fact less, a little piece of tiny
tin you could bring on a camp trip—the eggs slowly fluffled in there
and swelled from butter steams and I threw garlic salt on them, and
when they were ready the yellow of them had been slightly filmed
with a cooked white at the top from the tin cover I'd put over the frying
pan, so now they were ready, and out they came. I spread them out on
top of my already prepared potatoes which had been boiled in small
pieces and then mixed with the bacon I'd already fried in small pieces,
kind of raggely mashed bacon potatoes, with eggs on top steaming, and
on the side lettuce, with peanut butter dab nearby on side.—I had
heard that peanut butter and lettuce contained all the vitamins you
should want, this after I had originally started to eat this combination
because of the deliciousness and nostalgia of the taste—my breakfast
ready at about 6:45 and as I eat already I'm dressing to go piece by piece
and by the time the last dish is washed in the little sink at the boiling
hotwater tap and I'm taking my lastquick slug of coffee and quickly
rinsing the cup in the hot water spout and rushing to dry it and plop it
in its place by the hot plate and the brown carton in which all the gro-

☐

ceries sit tightly wrapped in brown paper, I'm already picking up my brakeman's lantern from where it's been hanging on the door handle and my tattered timetable's long been in my backpocket folded and ready to go, everything tight, keys, timetable, lantern, knife, handkerchief, wallet, comb, railroad keys, change and myself. I put the light out on the sad dab mad grub little dining room and hustle out into the fog of the flow, descending the creak hall steps where the old men are not yet sitting with Sunday morn papers because still asleep or some of them I can now as I leave hear beginning to disfawdle to wake in their rooms with their moans and yorks and scrapings and horror sounds, I'm going down the steps to work, glance to check time of watch with clerk cage clock.—A hardy two or three oldtimers sitting already in the dark brown lobby under the tockboom clock, toothless, or grim, or elegantly mustached—what thought in the world swirling in them as they see the young eager brakeman bum hurrying to his thirty dollars of the Sunday —what memories of old homesteads, built without sympathy, hornyhanded fate dealt them the loss of wives, childs, moons—libraries collapsed in their time —oldtimers of the telegraph wired wood Frisco in the fog gray top time sitting in their brown sunk sea and will be there when this afternoon my face flushed from the sun, which at eight'll flame out and make sunbaths for us at Redwood, they'll still be here the color of paste in the green underworld and still reading the same editorial over again and wont understand where I've been or what for or what.—I have to get out of there or suffocate, out of Third Street or become a worm, it's alright to live and bed-wine in and play the radio and cook little breakfasts and rest in but O my I've got to go now to work, I hurry down Third to Townsend for my 7:15 train— it's 3 minutes to go, I start in a panic to jog, goddam it I didnt give myself enough time this morning, I hurry down under the Harrison ramp to the Oakland-Bay Bridge, down past Schweibacker-Frey the great dim red neon printshop always spectrally my father the dead executive I see there, I run and hurry past the beat Negro grocery stores where I buy all my peanut butter and raisin bread, past the redbrick railroad alley now mist and wet, across Townsend, the train is leaving!

Vocabulary

rheumy wet-eyed
disfaudle Kerouac's making this up, isn't he? Say the word. What is the character of its sound, its shape on the page?
yorks same with this one . . .

Discussion

1. Okay. This is it. You asked for words and you've got them. Better read out loud and careful not to trip your tongue: "—On the floor's my shoes, big lum-

berboot flopjack workshoes to colomp over rockbed with and not turn the ankle—" Have you just "colomped" over these words in the same manner Kerouac suggests those boots "colomp over rockbed"? What is that word "colomp"?

Take any line (not sentence but typed line) and look at the words without the sense. We have here a lover of words.

2. Here is the next question: Do Kerouac's words get in the way of what he is saying, do they contribute to what he is saying, or—and this is the big one— are they *what* he is saying? Everyone who has ever read Kerouac has an opinion on this. What's yours?

3. Not only is Kerouac's punctuation unconventional but his style of composing is also uniquely his own. (For comparison you might read a McPhee piece afterward and note how McPhee puts together his essays.) Kerouac says write "excitedly, swiftly ... swimming in a sea of language." Follow thoughts from *sentence* to sentence, as conventionally denoted by a period. Especially try out the string of words beginning "—Workshoes covered with dust and some oil of engines—." When do you get out of the sea? How effective do you find this writing device, this "swimming"? What is its effect on the reader?

4. In the chapter on description you learned that descriptive writing employed the senses in such a way as to give the reader the actual experience of being there rather than merely to tell about the experience. What senses are appealed to in Kerouac's description of the curtains excerpted below? Specifically, what words let you hear, see, smell, touch these curtains?

> ... the curtains had now absorbed all the iron they could take and hung stiff and even the dust in them was iron, if you shook them they'd crack and fall in tatters to the floor and spatter like wings of iron on the bong and the dust would fly into your nose like filings of steel and choke you to death, so I never touched them.

5. Lines such as "I put the light out on the sad dab mad grub little dining room and hustle out into the fog of the flow ... " may sound more like poetry than prose. Compare Dylan Thomas's (Chapter Two) use of words with Kerouac's. Dylan Thomas had a marvelous voice and was much loved and admired as a reader of poems. You might get an opportunity to hear both Kerouac, also a man of fine voice, and Dylan Thomas some day. Your college library may have tapes or records of Thomas. A good experience would be to see the film "A Child's Christmas in Wales," narrated by Thomas from his own writing, and "Pull My Daisy," an "underground" film in which Jack Kerouac, spontaneously narrates during the filming. Both men's voices demonstrate their feeling for words. Good films and good for hearing language.

Jack Kerouac
(1922–1969)

At first critical response to Kerouac's writing was cool. *Time* magazine called him a "cut-rate Thomas Wolfe." Truman Capote said his style wasn't writing, "it's typing." The literary establishment still takes little notice. But his influence on a generation and on many writers who have followed him gives a hint of the recognition that may yet come.

Kerouac felt the prose of the future would come from "the conscious top and unconscious bottom of the mind, limited only by the limitations of time flying by as our mind flies with it." He called his technique "sketching," an unedited, unrevised " . . . undisturbed flow from the mind of personal secret idea-words, blowing (as per jazz musician) on subject of image."

The following excerpt from *On the Road* is a good example of his approach. " . . . tap from yourself the song of yourself, blow!—now!—Your way is your only way—good—bad—always honest. . . . "

Frisco Jazz

Out we jumped in the warm, mad night, hearing a wild tenorman bawling horn across the way, going "EE-YAH! EE-YAH! EE-YAH!" and hands clapping to the beat and folks yelling, "Go, go go!" Dean was already racing across the street with his thumb in the air, yelling, "Blow, man, blow!" A bunch of colored men in Saturday-night suits were whooping it up in front. It was a sawdust saloon with a small bandstand on which the fellows huddled with their hats on, blowing over people's heads, a crazy place; crazy floppy women wandered around sometimes in their bathrobes, bottles clanked in alleys. In back of the joint in a dark corridor beyond the splattered toilets scores of men and women stood against the wall drinking wine-spodiodi and spitting at the stars—wine and whisky. The behatted tenorman was blowing at the peak of a wonderfully satisfactory free idea, a rising and falling riff that went from "EE-yah!" to a crazier "EE-de-lee-yah!" and blasted along to the rolling crash of butt-scarred drums hammered by a big brutal Negro with a bullneck who didn't give a damn about anything but punishing his busted tubs, crash, rattle-ti-boom, crash. Uproars of music and the tenorman *had it* and everybody knew he had it. Dean was clutching his head in the crowd, and it was a mad crowd. They were all urging that tenorman to hold it and keep it with cries and wild eyes, and he was raising himself from a crouch and going down again with his horn, looping it up in a clear cry about the furor. A six-foot skinny Negro woman was rolling her bones at the man's hornbell, and he just jabbed it at her, "Ee! ee! ee!"

Everybody was rocking and roaring. Galatea and Marie with beer in their hands were standing on their chairs, shaking and jumping. Groups of colored guys stumbled in from the street, falling over one another to get there. "Stay with it, man!" roared a man with a foghorn voice, and let out a big groan that must have been heard clear out in Sacramento, ah-haa! "Whoo!" said Dean. He was rubbing his chest, his belly; the sweat splashed from his face. Boom, kick, that drummer was kicking his drums down the cellar and rolling the beat upstairs with his murderous sticks, rattlety-boom! A big fat man was jumping on the platform, making it sag and creak. "Yoo!" The pianist was only pound-

□

ing the keys with spread-eagled fingers, chords, at intervals when the great tenorman was drawing breath for another blast—Chinese chords, shuddering the piano in every timber, chink, and wire, boing! The tenorman jumped down from the platform and stood in the crowd, blowing around; his hat was over his eyes; somebody pushed it back for him. He just hauled back and stamped his foot and blew down a hoarse, baughing blast, and drew breath, and raised the horn and blew high, wide, and screaming in the air. Dean was directly in front of him with his face lowered to the bell of the horn, clapping his hands, pouring sweat on the man's keys, and the man noticed and laughed in his horn a long quivering crazy laugh, and everybody else laughed and they rocked and rocked; and finally the tenorman decided to blow his top and crouched down and held a note in high C for a long time as everything else crashed along and the cries increased and I thought the cops would come swarming from the nearest precinct. Dean was in a trance. The tenorman's eyes were fixed straight on him; he had a madman who not only understood but cared and wanted to understand more and much more than there was, and they began dueling for this; everything came out of the horn, no more phrases, just cries, cries, "Baugh" and down to "Beep!" and up to *EEEEE!* and down to clinkers and over to sideways-echoing horn-sounds. He tried everything, up, down, sideways, upside down, horizontal, thirty degrees, forty degrees, and finally he fell back in somebody's arms and gave up and everybody pushed around and yelled, "Yes! Yes! He blowed that one!" Dean wiped himself with his handkerchief.

Then up stepped the tenorman on the bandstand and asked for a slow beat and looked sadly out the open door over people's heads and began singing "Close Your Eyes." Things quieted down a minute. The tenorman wore a tattered suede jacket, a purple shirt, cracked shoes, and zoot pants without press; he didn't care. He looked like a Negro Hassel. His big brown eyes were concerned with sadness, and the singing of songs slowly and with long, thoughtful pauses. But in the second chorus he got excited and grabbed the mike and jumped down from the bandstand and bent to it. To sing a note he had to touch his shoetops and pull it all up to blow, and he blew so much he staggered from the effect, and only recovered himself in time for the next long slow note. "Mu-u-u-usic pla-a-a-a-a-ay!" He leaned back with his face to the ceiling, mike held below. He shook, he swayed. Then he leaned in, almost falling with his face against the mike. "Ma-a-a-ake it dream-y for dancing"—and he looked at the street outside with his lips curled in scorn, Billie Holiday's hip sneer—"while we go ro-man-n-n-cing"—he staggered sideways—"Lo-o-o-ove's holi-da-a-ay"—he shook his head with disgust and weariness at the whole world—"Will make it seem"—what would it make it seem? everybody waited; he mourned—"O-kay." The piano hit a chord. "So baby come on just clo-o-o-ose your pretty little ey-y-y-y-yes"—his mouth quivered, he looked at us, Dean and me, with

☐

an expression that seemed to say, Hey now, what's this thing we're all doing in this sad brown world?—and then he came to the end of his song, and for this there had to be elaborate preparations, during which time you could send all the messages to Garcia around the world twelve times and what difference did it make to anybody? because here we were dealing with the pit and prunejuice of poor beat life itself in the god-awful streets of man, so he said it and sang it, "Close—your—" and blew it way up to the ceiling and through to the stars and on out—"Ey-y-y-y-y-y-es"—and staggered off the platform to brood. He sat in the corner with a bunch of boys and paid no attention to them. He looked down and wept. He was the greatest.

Dean and I went over to talk to him. We invited him out to the car. In the car he suddenly yelled, "Yes! ain't nothing I like better than good kicks! Where do we go?" Dean jumped up and down in the seat, giggling maniacally. "Later! later! said the tenorman. "I'll get my boy to drive us down to Jamson's Nook, I got to sing. Man, I *live* to sing. Been singing 'Close Your Eyes' for two weeks—I don't want to sing nothin else. What are you boys up to? We told him we were going to New York in two days. "Lord, I ain't never been there and they tell me it's a real jumpin town but I ain't got no cause complainin where I am. I'm married, you know."

"Oh yes?"said Dean, lighting up. "And where's the darling tonight?"

"What do you *mean?*" said the tenorman, looking at him out of the corner of his eye. "I tole you I was *married* to her, didn't I?"

"Oh yes, oh yes," said Dean. "I was just asking. Maybe she has friends? or sisters? A ball, you know, I'm just looking for a ball."

"Yah, what good's a ball, life's too sad to be ballin all the time," said the tenorman, lowering his eye to the street. "Shh-eee-it!" he said "I ain't got no money and I don't care tonight."

We went back in for more. The girls were so disgusted with Dean and me for gunning off and jumping around that they had left and gone to Jamson's Nook on foot; the car wouldn't run anyway. We saw a horrible sight in the bar; a white hipster fairy had come in wearing a Hawaiian shirt and was asking the big drummer if he could sit in. The musicians looked at him suspiciously. "Do you blow?" He said he did, mincing. They looked at one another and said, "Yeah, yeah, that's what the man does, shhh-ee-it!" So the fairy sat down at the tubs and they started the beat of a jump number and he began stroking the snares with soft goofy bop brushes, swaying his neck with that complacent Reichianalyzed ecstasy that doesn't mean anything except too much tea and soft foods and goofy kicks on the cool order. But he didn't care. He smiled joyously into space and kept the beat, though softly, with bop subtleties, a giggling, rippling background for big solid foghorn blues the boys were blowing, unaware of him. The big Negro bullneck drummer sat waiting for his turn. "What that man doing?' he said. "Play the music!" he said. "What in hell!" he said. "Shh-ee-eet!" and looked away, disgusted.

The tenorman's boy showed up; he was a little taut Negro with a great big Cadillac. We all jumped in. He hunched over the wheel and blew the car clear across Frisco without stopping once, seventy miles an hour, right through traffic and nobody even noticed him, he was so good. Dean was in ecstasies. "Dig this guy, man! dig the way he sits there and don't move a bone and just balls that jack and can talk all night while he's doing it, only thing is he doesn't bother with talking, ah, man, the things, the things I could—I wish—oh, yes. Let's go, let's not stop—go now! Yes!" And the boy wound around a corner and bowled us right in front of Jamson's Nook and was parked. A cab pulled up; out of it jumped a skinny, withered little Negro preacherman who threw a dollar at the cabby and yelled, "Blow!" and ran into the club and dashed right through the downstairs bar, yelling, "Blowblow-blow!" and stumbled upstairs, almost falling on his face, and blew the door open and fell into the jazz-session room with his hands out to support him against anything he might fall on, and he fell right on Lamp-shade, who was working as a waiter in Jamson's Nook that season, and the music was there blasting and blasting and he stood transfixed in the open door, screaming, "Blow for me, man, blow!" And the man was a little short Negro with an alto horn that Dean said obviously lived with his grandmother just like Tom Snark, slept all day and blew all night, and blew a hundred choruses before he was ready to jump for fair, and that's what he was doing.

"It's Carlo Marx!" screamed Dean above the fury.

And it was. This little grandmother's boy with the taped-up alto had beady, glittering eyes; small, crooked feet, spindly legs; and he hopped and flopped with his horn and threw his feet around and kept his eyes fixed on the audience (which was just people laughing at a dozen tables, the room thirty by thirty feet and low ceiling), and he never stopped. He was very simple in his ideas. What he liked was the surprise of a new simple variation of a chorus. He'd go from "ta-tup-tader-rara . . . ta-tup-tader-rara," repeating and hopping to it and kissing and smiling into his horn, to "ta-tup-EE-da-de-dera-RUP! ta-tup-EE-da-de-dera-RUP!" and it was all great moments of laughter and understanding for him and everyone else who heard. His tone was clear as a bell, high, pure, and blew straight in our faces from two feet away. Dean stood in front of him, oblivious to everything else in the world, with his head bowed, his hands socking in together, his whole body jumping on his heels and the sweat, always the sweat, pouring and splashing down his tormented collar to lie actually in a pool at his feet. Galatea and Marie were there, it took us five minutes to realize it. Whoo, Frisco nights, the end of the continent and the end of doubt, all dull doubt and tomfoolery, good-by. Lampshade was roaring around with his trays of beer; everything he did was in rhythm; he yelled at the waitress with the beat: "Hey now, babybaby, make a way, make a way, it's Lampshade comin your way," and he hurled by her with the beers in the air and roared through the swinging doors into the kitchen and danced with the cooks and came sweating back. The hornman sat absolutely motionless at a corner table with an untouched drink in front of him, staring gook-eyed into space, his hands hanging at his sides till they almost touched the floor, his feet outspread like lolling tongues, his body shriveled into absolute weariness and entranced sorrow and what-all was on his mind: a man who knocked himself out every evening and let the others put the quietus to him in the night. Everything swirled around him like a cloud. And that little grandmother's alto, that little Carlo Marx, hopped and monkeydanced with his magic horn and blew two hundred choruses of blues, each one more frantic than the other, and no signs of failing energy or willingness to call anything a day. The whole room shivered.

Vocabulary

baughing   it's the sound of this word that Kerouac was after
Reichianalyzed   analyzed by the Reichian School of Psychiatry
quietus   release (an interesting word in all its connotations. You may wish to
     look it up in a dictionary and note if Kerouac meant the word to resonate
     in its various meanings.)

Allusions/References

Hassel   one of the characters in *On the Road*
Carlo Marx   Kerouac's name for the poet, Alan Ginsberg; in the excerpt the
     reference is to a jazz musician who reminds Kerouac and Dean (Neal Cassady) of Ginsberg

Discussion

1. Kerouac liked to compare his writing to jazz. (See also Chapter Five for more on this in Kerouac's "The Origins of the Beat Generation.") In "Frisco Jazz" we hear "a wild tenorman bawling horn across the way, going 'EE-YAH! EE-YAH!'" Or a "taped-up alto go from 'ta-tup-tader-rara ... ta-tuptader-rara,' repeating and hopping to it and kissing and smiling into his horn. . . . "
   How is Kerouac both representing the sounds of jazz and imitating its rhythms and its free flow of ideas in his own writing? Do his words make music? How do his words restore the sense of live, improvised music?
2. Kerouac says, " . . . tap from yourself the song of yourself, blow!—now!" How is the form of "Frisco Jazz" like "blowing at the peak of a wonderfully satisfactory free idea. . . . "?

□

3. Do you agree with Truman Capote? Is Kerouac's writing only "typing"? Yes or no. Support your view with evidence/words from the text.

For Further Discussion

5. You may wish to try Kerouac's "sketching" technique yourself—with or without music. Remember, you must write fast, without editing, in an undisturbed flow. Try it, it's fun—and good practice too, even though its use in a class where the polished essay is the objective may be limited. Anything that gets you to write, and with enthusiasm, should never be entirely dismissed.

Glossary

The following is an unscholarly, but not irreverent, glossary of terms that have appeared in *The Writer's Voice*.

allegory
A literary form in which the apparent sense only parallels and illustrates a deeper sense.

authentic words
The words of your own experience. The words you use that identify you like a fingerprint.

cacophony
The clattering sound of consonantal words, used to create a din so your reader will listen to your idea.

cobbled A description of a kind of writing where words crash against each other without break of adjectives or helping modifiers. Here's a cobbled line from Kerouac: "I put the light out on the sad dab mad grub little dining room and hustle out into the fog of the flow."

description A kind of writing that attempts to convey in words a picture or experience. The words of description come from the language of the senses. Description is like a snapshot. It is an impression of scene, sensation, character, and of whatever exists in space. The first stroke of description is a word.

essay A form for expression, a field of words; a thing that needs expressing in itself.

extraneous matter It is unlikely an essay will have much because of limitations on length. Everything must mean something or further the meaning of the piece.

eye rhymes Words that look alike: balloon and floor and igloo.

first sentences First sentences in your writing ought to be strong. Randomly leaf through *The Writer's Voice* reading only first sentences. Since many of us tend to need a "warm up" before the real impulse behind our words becomes manifest, write freely and edit afterwards. Take away all sentences before the one where you finally "felt" the strength of your idea take over. This is where a good writer starts: in the thick of it all.

form   The shape of an essay, its structure. Writers rarely write from the trigger of a form. Instead they allow their ideas to take shape in ways natural to them.

human experience   Revealing human experience is the reason for words and words are the reason for essays.

imagination   A writer's best friend. Einstein felt imagination was more important than intellect. The poet Richard Hugo always said: "You might not want to invite Hitler to lunch but the imagination does." Imagination creates the future.

impressionism   Sights, sounds, smells evoked subjectively. Language used subjectively rather than as an attempt to recreate objective reality.

juxtaposition   A word often used in the humanities to indicate the placing of contradictory things side by side, the ridiculous with the sublime, progress with wilderness; the juxtapositioning of two ideas.

language   Language is the subject of good writing, not just the vehicle for thought.

length of an idea   The natural rhythm of an idea that when found is art.

love of words   What every writer has to have, for shape, for shine, for meaning. Language is a lovable thing. What would we be without it? Mute.

mixed diction   Essentially there are three neighborhoods of words: high, middle, and low. Conventionally the middle way is considered the temperate course. But

□

sometimes writers like to liven up things a bit by taking the multisyllabic out for fish 'n chips.

onomatopoeia Echoic words like zipper, crash, slit, cockadoodledo, whip and snap.

oxymoron A figure of speech in which two words of seeming contradiction are paired, creating a tension between them: solemn foolery, hideous laughter. A good writer, like George Orwell who was fond of the oxymoron, uses this incongruity of language to parallel a deeper incongruity in theme, or meaning, in existence itself.

parallelism The repetition of words and sounds and structure.

repetition All writing is made up of repetition and variation. The eye delights in it, and the ear delights in it too.

restlessness The vague uneasiness that leads a writer to write.

rhythm Some writers are naturals. Others rely on the conventional rules for good taste. Rhythm can be counted by number of words, sentence length, patterns of repetition and variation, among other ways. Writers should consider also the rhythm of attention span.
Some writers have experimented by writing to music or by using the natural rhythms of speech. Rhythm is a sound and sound is a wave that can be felt. Get to know your own rhythm of words.

roundness and angularity The shapes of letters that make up words. Writers are using the

☐

whole word, its shape, sound and meaning to convey experience. Skeletal is as angular as the actual thing it represents: it is a visual echo. Moon is also round.

The shapes of most words, like the sounds of words, are infrequently echoic or onomatopoetic. However, the more you actually look at words, the more they do take on the face of their referent. Language is the subject, not just the vehicle for thought.

sentence
A line of rhythm on which to hang your words.

show don't tell
A cardinal rule for writers. They won't believe it until they see it with their own eyes. Populate your writing with the concrete words, the names for things that can be perceived by the senses.

silences
In writing, the white space on a page. We give the reader a moment's silence between words, at the ends of sentences and paragraphs, and with margins. Do not neglect the negative space of the written word. Give your reader a break.

smooth and sharp-edged words
Like rocks on a beach, most words through tides of use have been worn smooth. The reader does not flinch. Sharp-edged words, hatchet, jagged, still have the power to raise the hair.

spoken word
The spoken word is the word, according to linguists. Writing is always attempting to record the spoken voice. The written voice is more considered, more economical.

staccato notes
The click of crisp words. Short sentences.

time cues	Transitional words like first, second, next, and finally.
transitions	Delicate spans between words, sentences, paragraphs, and ideas themselves. Word cues that allow the reader to follow smoothly from one point to the next. Some authors deliberately take the reader on a wild journey, only implying transitions at best, or asking the reader to make a "leap." It is best to remain moderate in your English composition class, however. Build bridges.
tree-shaped essay	Organic shape, asymmetrical, growing as the words grow.
ugly words	Ugliness is in the eye and ear of the beholder. There are no ugly words. (See H. Allen Smith)
vase-shaped essay	Symmetrical, planned in advance with words that fit the form.
voice	Voice in writing is like a fingerprint. Each writer's voice is unique. Phrasing, rhythms and viewpoint all help to identify a writer's voice. You should be finding your own voice. This is very difficult to do because there is no other voice like it out there. Imitating others' voices might help on this search, but knowing yourself helps more. Writing is the discovery of voice. Read yourself. Who is that speaking there?

Rhetorical Table of Contents

345

☐ ## Argumentation: To Persuade

□

Thematic
Table
of Contents

The following listing is not meant to be comprehensive, but is
included because two things may be gained by organizing a writing
class around theme. First, it becomes apparent that the primary
reason for writing is to find wisdom on important matters. Secondly,
various voices on the same theme demonstrate a range of human
response and experience. Students and teachers are encouraged to
make further applications of these writings to theme.

☐ *On Death and Extinction*

On Education

On Human Dignity, Custom, Culture

On Humor

On Imagination, Art, and Creativity

Suggestions
for Themes

1 Paint a portrait of yourself in words, close up or from a distance. Think of how a camera works. Stay with the outside of yourself. Let external details represent the inner you. Don't directly discuss your feelings, beliefs, those things the camera cannot see. Can you show the inside of a subject by describing only the outside?

2 Paint a portrait of yourself in words from the inside out. What kind of a person are you?

Compare and contrast your outer portrait with your inner portrait. Which has the more descriptive (appealing directly to the senses) words?

3 Tell your funniest story. Use no introduction to it other than the line you would ordinarily use to begin its telling with your friends: "After high school I got a job as a chicken catcher."

4 Describe a dream. Record the events as they happened in your dream, without explanation, fantastical, mysterious. After you are finished writing and have typed up your paper, observe how your words look side by side. Have you used words in combinations, or individually that you don't ordinarily write? Do your words contain the mysteriousness of your dream?

5 In a single typed page, describe *the bomb*. Choose from everything you've ever heard said about it, or read about it, or

☐

imagined about it yourself, a page of words that best evokes your ideas or feelings about the bomb. Imagine being asked these questions: When did you first hear about the bomb? How old were you? How large a part has the bomb played in your life? Is there life after the bomb?

You might share papers in your class. How many views of this modern "threat" of annihilation are there?

6 Write a portrait of a person from your past who "haunts" you. Mark Helprin's Johanna, in "Willis Avenue" (Chapter One), is just such a person. Think of someone you have known whose face or voice comes back to you while driving, or at an unexpected moment. What is it you remember when you do remember this person? In your portrait try to capture the *meaning* of this person to you, without directly writing about it. As in the portrait of yourself (#1), merely describe the memory, letting the reason for it arise naturally from your details.

7 Try a communal writing exercise as a warm-up akin to free writing. This is a form loosely termed a "renga" after an ancient Oriental communal poetry form of the same name. Divide into groups of four. Each participant should have a sheet of paper that will be, at the end, returned to him as his renga. The idea is to write a line or two on your own paper, and then pass to the person on your right who does the same to his neighbor. Write a line or two on the paper passed to you responding to the words found there. Pass again. Each pass is a turn, and each of the four rengas in your group should have its own subject and its own character. Write in sentence and paragraph form, this being a communal essay-renga, and enjoy the leaps and the surrealism of communal language. In the ancient form participants believed their written dialogue to be a communication of the soul. A renga has twelve turns, each person writing on it comprising a turn. You should write on your own renga a total of three times. Each renga will have a unique character. When your renga is completed and returned to you, you must give it a title.

8 Write a *risky piece*. Anything is risky that is something you don't ordinarily do. A skier on a mountain is no risk. If one doesn't know how to ski however, the first time can really get the adrenalin going. Get your adrenalin going with words. Try humor if you're always serious; try a serious topic if you're always clowning around. Take an opposing side of an issue you always support. How about this for risk, try for a perfect composition, one with no mechanical errors. Attempts at perfection can be very risky.

9 The linguist L. M. Myers writes in *The Roots of Modern English:* "It seldom occurs to most people that when writing and speech

□

differ, the simplest explanation is that writing is falling down on its job of reflecting speech."

How might your writing look if it actually reflected your way of speaking, your voice?

Attempt a *classification* of your own voice. Listen to yourself carefully, then find a way to record what you *hear* in written form.

What can you say about your "voice" now that you can see it in writing? How would you classify it: scholarly, casual, tough, sweet?

10 Who are you the most like, your mother or father? And why? Write an analysis of your own character, comparing and contrasting it to the person(s) who influenced you the most.

11 This is another good warm-up exercise using memory. Think of something outside the classroom, a place, an event, a memorable moment. Write every *word* that comes to your mind about this place and/or event. Do not write in sentences. What you want to end up with are strings of words that evoke the event.

Each word in a word string tends to be interesting since all helping words and connectors are left out.

12 Using your strings of words from #11 above, write a short paper on the place, moment or event you were remembering. Is your final paper more vivid than it might have been if you had not found so many interesting, concrete words and images on which to base it?

13 Spend ten minutes recording every thought that comes in your mind, every thought you can catch, that is. The rush of the mind is a very elusive thing to record. You may find yourself recording one thought only to have it interrupted by another. Go with the new thought. Fragments and run-ons are allowed in this exercise. Non-coherence can have value too. Don't worry if the hand feels tired and frustrated at its inadequacy. Record away.

With your completed sampling of your mind in front of you, write an analysis of your thoughts, of the way your mind works. What kind of thoughts do you have? Do you repeat yourself?

14 Reveal your own writing process. Write an essay on how *you* write an essay.

15 Describe a picture so that your reader can see it in his mind's eye. Bring the picture to class. Did others "see" it the way it actually is, from your description of it, your words? Why or why not?

16 Try writing to music. (See Jack Kerouac's "Frisco Jazz" in Chapter Eight.) How does the music you write to influence the rhythms and ideas of your writing?

Write one page with a slow or soothing background. Write

□

another with loud or prominent sounds. How do the two writings compare?

17 Find the voice closest to your own in *The Writer's Voice*. Define your voice by showing how it is similar to, or different from, another writer's. (Reading first paragraphs or browsing through *The Writer's Voice* should glean you somebody you can compare yourself to.)

18 What's the worst thing that ever happened to you in school? (See Dick Gregory's "Shame.") Recount the incident in such a way that your reader experiences it as you did.

19 Write a paper in which you argue that you are a good writer. Now try to believe you really are. List your strong points. Support them with examples, samples of your writing. What do you think a good writer is?

20 Make up the perfect ending to the story of life. Use your imagination to make real to the reader your vision. (Serious or comic versions are acceptable.) What is it going to be like?

☐

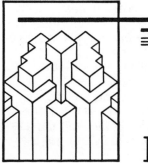

Index

☐

In preparing the next edition of THE WRITER'S VOICE, we would appreciate your evaluation of the present edition. Your suggestions will help us make the book better. Please return this questionnaire to the English Editor, College Department, Holt, Rinehart and Winston, 383 Madison Avenue, New York, New York 10017.

School _____   Course Title _____

Instructor _____

	Keep	Drop	Didn't Read
1. The Sources of Writing			
Mark Helprin, *Willis Avenue*	____	____	____
E. M. Forster, *My Wood*	____	____	____
Francis Bacon, *Of Suspicion*	____	____	____
Narcissus, or Self Love	____	____	____
Tythonus, or Satiety	____	____	____
Woody Allen, *The Early Essays*	____	____	____
William Saroyan, *Why I Write*	____	____	____
2. The Words Have to Do Everything			
Larry McMurtry, *Dalhart*	____	____	____
Bonnie Angelo, *Good Ole Boys*	____	____	____
Jack Smith, *Fox-Trot, Yes; Cat-Trot, No*	____	____	____
Edwin Newman, *Is Your Team Hungry Enough, Coach?*	____	____	____
William Saroyan, *Meditations on the Letter Z*	____	____	____
H. Allen Smith, *The Ugliest Word*	____	____	____
Dylan Thomas, *Notes on the Art of Poetry*	____	____	____
Gabriel G. Marquez, *The Insomnia Plague*	____	____	____
3. Description: The Language of the Senses			
Thomas Wolfe, *Tim Wagner*	____	____	____
F. Scott Fitzgerald, *The Buchanan's Mansion*	____	____	____
Peter Bogdanovich, *Bogie in Excelsis*	____	____	____
Langston Hughes, *Salvation*	____	____	____
Dick Gregory, *Shame*	____	____	____
4. Narration: To Tell What Happened			
The Spoken Voice			
Black Elk, *High Horse's Courting*	____	____	____

	Keep	Drop	Didn't Read
Maxine Hong Kingston, *The Woman Warrior*	_____	_____	_____
Bartolomeo Vanzetti, *Apology*	_____	_____	_____

The Written Voice

Colin Turnbull, *The Village Wife*	_____	_____	_____
Anaïs Nin, *A House in Acapulco*	_____	_____	_____
Michael Herr, *Breathing In*	_____	_____	_____

5. Exposition: To Present Ideas

By Process

Oliver La Farge, *The Eight-Oared Shell*	_____	_____	_____
Jessica Mitford, *To Bid the World Farewell*	_____	_____	_____
Yasunari Kawabata, *Chijimi Linen*	_____	_____	_____
Ernest Hemingway, *Killing a Bull*	_____	_____	_____

By Definition

Huston Smith, *The Story of Lao Tzu*	_____	_____	_____
Rachel Carson, *Waves*	_____	_____	_____
Dennis Farney, *The School of 'Messy Vitality'*	_____	_____	_____
Jack Kerouac, *The Origins of the Beat Generation*	_____	_____	_____

By Classification

Alex Petrunkevitch, *The Spider and the Wasp*	_____	_____	_____
Simone de Beauvoir, *The Discovery and Assumption of Old Age*	_____	_____	_____
Robert Sherrill, *The Saturday Night Special*	_____	_____	_____
Lewis Thomas, *Death in the Open*	_____	_____	_____

By Cause/Effect

Sir James Jeans, *Why the Sky Looks Blue*	_____	_____	_____
Virginia Woolf, *The Death of a Moth*	_____	_____	_____
Lincoln Steffens, *I Became a Student*	_____	_____	_____
Sylvia Plath, *Lenny's Place*	_____	_____	_____

By Comparison/Contrast

Russell Baker, *"Italian Realism and American Delusion*	_____	_____	_____

	Keep	Drop	Didn't Read
Donald Peattie, *Chlorophyll: The Sun Trap*	___	___	___
Annie Dillard, *Strangers to Darkness*	___	___	___
Richard Selzer, *Yeshi Dhonden*	___	___	___
By Analysis			
Tom Wolfe, *The First Tycoon of Teen*	___	___	___
X. J. Kennedy, *Who Killed King Kong?*	___	___	___
William Golding, *Thinking as a Hobby*	___	___	___
Clarence Darrow, *Why I am an Agnostic*	___	___	___
6. Argumentation: To Persuade			
By Emotion			
Cleveland Amory, *Little Brother of the Wolf*	___	___	___
Larry Woiwode, *Guns*	___	___	___
Lawrence L. Langer, *The Human Use of Language*	___	___	___
By Logic			
Anne Roiphe, *Confessions of a Female Chauvinist Sow*	___	___	___
Andy Rooney, *An Essay on War*	___	___	___
By Ethics			
Loren Eiseley, *The Last Magician*	___	___	___
Will and Ariel Durant, *Religion and History*	___	___	___
Clarence Darrow, *Crime and Criminals*	___	___	___
7. Humor and Irony			
Mark Twain, *Advice to Youth*	___	___	___
R. Emmett Tyrrell, *Robert Preston: Awash in History's Wake*	___	___	___
Woody Allen, *My Speech to the Graduates*	___	___	___
James Thurber, *The Ladies of Orlon*	___	___	___
8. A Study of Four Writers			
George Orwell, *Marrakech*	___	___	___
A Hanging	___	___	___

	Keep	Drop	Didn't Read
John McPhee, *The Pine Barrens*	_____	_____	_____
Curve of Binding Energy	_____	_____	_____
Joan Didion, *On Morality*	_____	_____	_____
Going Home	_____	_____	_____
Jack Kerouac, *The Bullfight*	_____	_____	_____
The Flop Hotel	_____	_____	_____
Frisco Jazz	_____	_____	_____